Wittgenstein on Ethics and Religious Belief

'*An honest religious thinker is like a tightrope walker. He almost looks as though he were walking on nothing but air. His support is the slenderest imaginable. And yet it is possible to walk on it.*'

Wittgenstein: Culture and Value, p. 73.

'*Et vae tacentibus de te quoniam loquaces muti sunt*':
'*And woe to those who are silent about You, since the talkative are dumb.*'

St Augustine: Confessions I, 4.

Wittgenstein on Ethics and Religious Belief

Cyril Barrett

BLACKWELL
Oxford UK & Cambridge USA

First published 1991

Basil Blackwell Ltd
108 Cowley Road, Oxford, OX4 1JF, UK

Basil Blackwell, Inc.
3 Cambridge Center
Cambridge, Massachusetts 02142, USA

Library of Congress Cataloging-in-Publication Data
Barrett, Cyril.
    Wittgenstein on ethics and religious belief/Cyril Barrett.
        p.   cm.
    Includes bibliographical references and index.
    ISBN 0-631-16815-X (alk. paper)
    1. Wittgenstein, Ludwig. 1889–1951—Ethics. 2. Wittgenstein, Ludwig, 1889–1951—Religion. 3. Ethics, Modern—20th century. 4. Belief and doubt.   I. Title.
    B3376.W564B36   1991
    170′.92—dc20   91-10148
                                                                                CIP

British Library Cataloguing in Publication Data

A CIP catalogue record for this book is available from the British Library.

Typeset in 10/12 pt Ehrhardt
by Acorn Bookwork, Salisbury, Wiltshire, England
Printed in Great Britain

This book is printed on acid-free paper.

Contents

Acknowledgements

I should like to thank Professors A. Phillips Griffiths and Terry Penner, and W. Mathews, S. J., for their assistance and encouragement in what proved to be a more arduous undertaking than I had anticipated. I should also like to thank those anonymous critics who helped to get the original text into better shape, Meg Davies who compiled the index, and the Basil Blackwell team, in particular Valerie Mendes.

Abbreviations

BB	The Blue and Brown Books	PR	Philosophical Remarks
CV	Culture and Value	PRv	Philosophical Review
LC	Lectures and Conversations	RF	Remarks on Frazer's 'Golden
NB	Notebooks, 1914–1916		Bough'
OC	On Certainty	TLP	Tractatus Logico-
PAS	Proceedings of the Aristotelian		Philosophicus
	Society	WWK	Wittgenstein and the Vienna
PG	Philosophical Grammar		Circle (Wiener Kreis)
PI	Philosophical Investigations	Z	Zettel

Note: In general I have quoted from published translations. Where, for one reason or another, I have seen fit to give my own version, this is indicated. In almost every case this is to bring the translation closer to the original. Where there is disagreement, this is discussed in a footnote.

Preface

The purpose of this book, as its title states, is to study Wittgenstein's thought on ethics and religious belief. This will take the form of a detailed commentary and criticism. I do not propose in this book to propound ideas of my own beyond what may emerge from my criticisms.

At the outset it should be said that, while differing from Wittgenstein on certain important points, I accept his basic approach to both ethics and religious belief. In doing so I may be at variance with some traditional forms of philosophy of religion, to say nothing of 'orthodoxies' in theology. It will be part of my task to show that in many cases it is these 'orthodoxies', not Wittgenstein, that are out of step, and that he had a sounder grasp of what ethics and religious belief are about than many of the so-called orthodox. What these orthodoxies are will emerge in the course of the book. However, I should like to say here that they are not exclusively religious or sectarian orthodoxies; there are atheistic and agnostic, as well as theological 'orthodoxies'. It will also be part of my task to show that, however unorthodox Wittgenstein's views may seem, they are firmly rooted in a traditional theology and philosophy of religion.

What I regard as my principal task is to show that these considerations, Wittgenstein's interest in values, whether ethical, religious or aesthetic, were not incidental to his thinking but central to it. Initially Wittgenstein was regarded, particularly by Russell and the Vienna Circle, and young English philosophers such as Ayer, as what came to be called a Logical Positivist, that is, an empiricist or positivist who had given empiricism and positivism a logical underpinning it had hitherto lacked, or, to be more precise, a seemingly more watertight underpinning, if that is not too harsh a verdict on Hume and Mill. By his theory of language, it was thought, he had nailed down once and for all the coffin of metaphysics, which Kant had built with his critical method. A great deal of what Wittgenstein said in the *Tractatus Logico-Philosophicus* lends support to this view, particularly the last entries (*TLP* 6.53–4;7): 'whenever someone else wanted to say something metaphysical, to demonstrate to him that he had failed to give a meaning to certain signs in his propositions ... what we cannot speak about we must pass over in silence.' The whole tenor of the book seems to lead in the direction of Logical Positivism, of what A. J. Ayer was to call the 'elimination of metaphysics'. Wittgenstein's distinction – once again in the penultimate entries of the *Tractatus* – between what can be said, which, from the philosophical point of view amounts to propositions of natural science, which has nothing to do with philosophy, and the unsayable, the nonsensical, that about which one must be silent, which includes the *Tractatus* itself, was taken as the definitive elimination of metaphysics, ethics, aesthetics and religious utterances from the realm of knowledge. Wittgenstein encouraged that view in his preface when he said he considered the truth of the thoughts imparted in his book unimpeachable and definitive.

Russell, to his credit, realized that the matter was not quite so straightforward. Indeed, he had a suspicion that to regard the *Tractatus* as the definitive elimination of metaphysics, despite the seemingly overwhelming evidence to the contrary, might be a misinterpretation, even a total misinterpretation of the book. At the end of his introduction he criticizes Wittgenstein's notion of the inexpressible, which is called 'the mystical', to which belong ethics, aesthetics, religious belief, metaphysics and philosophy that is not natural philosophy or science, including the philosophy of logic. He also offered Wittgenstein an alternative account which Wittgenstein vigorously rejected. This, Russell thought, would help Wittgenstein to answer his (Russell's) objections to the inexpressibility of language about language. But it would not help, as Russell himself realized, with other instances of the inexpressible, such as ethics and aesthetics. Russell is very humble about all this. He does not set great store by his alternative hypothesis. Nevertheless, he thought that, if tenable, it would deal the death blow to the mystical. All of this will be discussed later. The point I want to make here is that Russell thought his alternative hypothesis would leave untouched all but that on which Wittgenstein laid most stress. 'Even if this very difficult hypothesis should prove tenable, it would leave untouched a very large part of Mr Wittgenstein's theory, though possibly not the part upon which he himself would wish to lay most stress.' (*TLP* xxii)

Russell realized, if only through a glass dimly, as Waismann, Ramsey, Neurath and Ayer did not, that those last four or so pages of the *Tractatus* (*TLP* 6.4–7) were possibly the climax and culmination of the book, not a feeble appendage and an aberration, to be ignored or somehow explained away.

Ayer in his recent book on Wittgenstein has acknowledged that he, along with other young English philosophers, took the Vienna Circle's view of the *Tractatus*. He realized it was a misinterpretation of Wittgenstein but he still stuck to his view that ethical, aesthetical and religious utterances are not sources of knowledge. They are, in his view, a combination of statements of fact and expressions of emotion. He says that F. P. Ramsey's quip 'But what we can't say we can't say, and we can't whistle it either' was not directed specifically at Wittgenstein, but it was certainly accepted as in some way putting the final gloss on Wittgenstein's final sentence. Neurath was more explicit. His gloss on the final sentence was: 'One must indeed be silent, but not *about* anything.' Ayer is still happy with that interpretation.

Subsequent commentators, with some exceptions, notably Elizabeth Anscombe, have tended to follow the injunction of the final paragraphs and pass over the last pages of the *Tractatus* in silence. Either they do not understand them or they are embarrassed by them. Certainly they are not of universal interest to students – but students are free to take from an author what they will. Something more is expected of commentators, particularly since the publication in 1967 of Wittgenstein's letter to Ludwig von Ficker (printed in the editor's appendix to Wittgenstein's letters to Paul Engelmann) and Engelmann's own memoir. Of the *Tractatus* Wittgenstein says:

> The sense of the book is an ethical one. I once wanted to include in the preface a sentence which actually is not now in it but which I will write out for you here since it will perhaps be a key (to the book) for you. I wanted, then, to write: my work consists of two parts: of that which is under consideration here and of all that I have *not* written. And it is precisely this second part that is the important one . . . I would now recommend you to read the *preface* and the *conclusion*, since these carry the sense to its most immediate expression.[1]

Wittgenstein also remarked that, though the book says much that von Ficker himself wants to say, he might not see that it is said *in* it. Whatever Wittgenstein meant by saying that the most important part of the book is the part that is not written and that what is not written in the book is still said in it, it is clear what the *Tractatus* meant for Wittgenstein. For him, it is not primarily a work on logic and language. It is an ethical book.

With a growing recognition that this is how Wittgenstein would have us take the *Tractatus*, more commentators are concentrating on the ethical aspect of his work. The result has been that in some cases this aspect of Wittgenstein's thought, important and central though it is, has been carried to extremes. Difficult though it is to interpret his thought, some commentators have carried their interpretations far beyond anything Wittgenstein said or what can plausibly be regarded as what he meant but did not say.

The purpose of this book, therefore, is not only to attempt to interpret that part of Wittgenstein's thought that he regarded as central, and to explain why he should have thought that a book that to all appearances was about language and logic was in fact about ethics. It is also its purpose to lay down limits to the interpretation of this elusive, if central, area of his thought.

This enterprise is open to the objection that to attempt to interpret Wittgenstein's thought is to do something perverse and wrongheaded. The reason why Wittgenstein is silent about what is most important to him and most important in itself, is that it cannot be spoken about. If what he had to say could be said in any way other than the way he has said or did not say it, he would himself have said it in that other way. So it is futile, presumptuous and perverse to attempt to do what he himself did not attempt to do, and said could not be done.

This would be an insuperable objection if interpretation were taken to mean something like translating or paraphrasing Wittgenstein's thought or, worse still, offering a substitute for it. That would be like attempting to find a verbal substitute for a piece of music or a prose substitute for a poem. And yet we do offer *interpretations* of music and poetry. At least we can talk about such things in a way that may be illuminating to the listener. We can talk around the subject; suggest approaches; ward off misunderstandings; help the listener or reader to make connections that will lead to understanding. This is what I shall attempt to do. I shall approach Wittgenstein's early thought as a critic would a work of art or literature. I say his 'early thought' because there is a marked difference, not only between his thought prior to and immediately after the publication of the *Tractatus* and that which followed a decade later, but also in its presentation. Though his style in his later writings is rarely anything but oblique, leaving the reader to fill in the gaps and make the necessary connections, these gaps are not too wide nor the connections too difficult to make. It is possible, therefore, to discuss his thought as one would that of any other philosopher without leaving oneself open to the reproach of misinterpretation or, indeed, of having the audacity to attempt an interpretation in the first place.

Wittgenstein's later writings, however, present other problems, particularly for his account of ethics and religious belief. During the 1930s he abandoned some of what he had said about language in the *Tractatus*, in particular in relation to the so-called picture theory of language, and adopted new ideas and new terms: 'language-games', 'forms of life' and 'logical grammar'. As we shall see, the picture theory was used to distinguish between what can and cannot be said: that is, propositions of science (and common sense) on the one hand, and propositions or rather expressions of logic, theory of language, metaphysics and value on the other. Under value were included expressions of ethics, aesthetics and religious belief. The question then arises: when Wittgenstein abandoned the picture theory of language, did he also abandon the clear-cut distinction between propositions of science and expressions of value? If not, ought he to have done so? If he was not logically compelled to do so, on what did he or could he then base the distinction?

These are vital questions. Any account of Wittgenstein's thinking on ethics and religious belief depends on answers to these questions. One has to decide whether there was a radical change in the account of value given before and after the 1930s; if radical, how radical; if not radical, how can the earlier account be reconciled with the later? The trouble is that there is very little evidence one way or the other. Wittgenstein nowhere discusses the matter. This may be interpreted either way. Either he said nothing on the matter because there was nothing to say – his views were basically the same as they had been; or he did not think it worth his while to repudiate his earlier views explicitly since it should be obvious from what he said later that a fundamental change had taken place.

Matters are further complicated by an asymmetry between the attention given to ethics and religious belief in the earlier and later periods. The early period is dominated by ethics. Of the three sources for the period, the *Notebooks 1914–1916*, the *Tractatus* and a 'Lecture on Ethics' (*c*.1929), there are some scant references to religious belief in the *Notebooks*, some oblique references in the *Tractatus* and a mention in the lecture. Admittedly much of what is said about ethics can be applied to religious belief, but it is ethics that is formally discussed, particularly in the lecture – hence the title given to it by its editor. On the other hand, what information we have about Wittgenstein's later thinking on value is chiefly devoted to religious belief and aesthetics. What is said about ethics, apart from a discussion with Moritz Schlick, which can be taken as belonging to either period, is in the form of casual remarks, mostly concerned with practical ethics.

It is not surprising that commentators, in so far as they address themselves to the subject at all, are rather tentative about taking a stance. Janik and Toulmin, who were among the first, if not the first, to raise the question, are inclined to think that Wittgenstein's earlier views on ethics and religious belief were no longer tenable in the later period.[2] W. D. Hudson, on the other hand, is not sure of this.[3] He contents himself, however, with interpreting Wittgenstein's views as contained in his lectures on religious belief in the light of his philosophy in the later period. Other commentators, such as R. Rhees and D. Z. Phillips, seem scarcely aware of any change in Wittgenstein's views. They move freely from one period to the other.[4] While aware that there is no conclusive evidence either way and mindful of the damage done to the earlier account by the abandonment of the picture theory, I am prepared, none the less, to take a stance. I am prepared to go so far as to say that Wittgenstein did not abandon his earlier views on ethics and religious belief with their attendant notions of the mystical, transcendental, inexpressible, viewing *sub specie aeternitatis*. I wish to state that, on the one hand, there is no compelling reason to assume a radical change of view and, on the other hand, all the features of the earlier views can be fitted into the new conceptions of language-games and forms of life.

In taking this stance I am aware I am depriving myself of a possible polemical tool. It might be argued that a theist could claim Wittgenstein as an ally by holding that in his later period he abandoned the notions of ethics and religious belief as 'inexpressible' and 'nonsensical', terms that he had used to describe expressions of value in the earlier period and that the Logical Positivists and others had taken at their face value, the better to reject and dismiss as ridiculous all forms of ethical and religious discourse. With these notions rejected, and ethical and religious discourse set up as autonomous realms of discourse, that is, distinct language-games with their own independent rules and forms of life, ethics and religious belief would be expressible after a fashion, immune from the assaults of science and atheistic philosophy. Tempting though this line of interpretation might be to an apologist, I do not find it attractive. It seems contrary to Wittgenstein's thought. Moreover, if pragmatism were to be a factor in deciding what stance to take, it could be argued that the position I am adopting would be better for an apologist than the one suggested.

Someone may ask why I am treating ethics and religious belief together and on an equal footing, so to speak. I could reply that whatever the relationship between them, it is legitimate to compare them. It is true that in his early period Wittgenstein treats of ethics with hardly any reference to religious belief and in his later period he treats of religious belief with apparently no reference to ethics; yet, in the early period at least, the two are interrelated in such a fundamental way that it is impossible to treat of one without the other.

Moreover, even in his later writings Wittgenstein sometimes makes connections between ethics and religion. In an entry in his notebook for

1946 (*CV* p. 48) he discusses the difficulty of understanding oneself. The difficulty arises from the possibility of doing similar actions out of contrary motives. An action can be done out of good and generous motives or out of cowardice or indifference; out of genuine love or out of deceit and coldness of heart. He concludes: 'Only if I were able to submerge in religion could these doubts be silenced. For only religion could destroy vanity and penetrate all the crevices.'

But, it will be objected, if ethics is included in a book on Wittgenstein's views on religious belief, why not aesthetics as well? In one place in the *Tractatus* (*TLP* 6.421) Wittgenstein even says that ethics and aesthetics are one. Indeed, it is very difficult to understand some of what Wittgenstein has to say about ethics without referring to what he says about aesthetics. I am fully conscious of this and, where necessary, make references to aesthetics. But I do not discuss it on an equal footing with ethics and religious belief for a variety of reasons.

Though ethics and aesthetics are closely related in the earlier period, aesthetics is treated separately and at some length in the later writings and recorded utterances. It would, therefore, require separate treatment in a book on value. And, if the book is on value, why should metaphysics be excluded? Thus, apart from becoming vast, the book would become unwieldy. Ethics, aesthetics and religious belief would each have to be treated separately and then in relation to one another. If aesthetics were to be treated satisfactorily, it should be given pride of place, with ethics, religious belief and, possibly, metaphysics mentioned, only in relation to it. Provided aesthetics is brought in when needed, ethics and religious belief can be treated satisfactorily together.

Yet, it might be asked, is it necessary to deal fully with both ethics and religious belief when there are large areas where they do not relate to one another? It is true there are such areas, but where they are related it is not always easy to discuss the relationships without having dealt with each separately at some length. Besides, there are also doubtful areas where the relevance of each to the other is not immediately apparent. For instance, in discussing the apparent absence of any further account of ethics in the later period, it is necessary to be able to draw on the fullest possible account of it in the earlier period.

The programme, therefore, is to show that (a) what Wittgenstein had to say on ethics and religious belief was for him of the utmost importance, if not of sole importance; (b) his views on these subjects did not radically alter throughout his life, appearances to the contrary notwithstanding; and (c) what Wittgenstein said about ethics was intimately interwoven with what he said about religious belief.

PART I

The Earlier Wittgenstein

1

The Sayable and Unsayable

Wittgenstein tells us in the preface to the *Tractatus* that the purpose of that book is to draw a boundary to thought, 'or rather – not to thought, but to the expression of thoughts' (*TLP* p. 3). (To draw a boundary around thought, we would have to be able to think on both sides of the boundary, and hence, be able to think what cannot be thought, as well as what can be thought.) In other words, one could say that the *Tractatus* is about what can and what cannot be *said*.

It has been said that the *Tractatus* came into being as a result of Wittgenstein's attempt to find a satisfactory explanation of how elementary propositions signify, or the general concept of a proposition that accounts for both elementary and complex propositions. By 29 September 1914 he believed, as he records in his *Notebooks 1914–1916*, he had found the solution:

> The general concept of the proposition carries with it a quite general concept of the co-ordination of proposition and situation: the solution to all my questions must be *extremely* simple.
> In a proposition a world is put together experimentally. (*NB* p. 7)

The solution has come to be called the 'picture theory of the proposition'. There is a hint of it in an entry for 20 September: 'That a proposition is a logical depiction (*Abbild*) of its meaning is clear to an uncaptive eye' (*NB* p. 5), and also for 27 September: 'A proposition can express its sense only by being a logical depiction of it' (*NB* p. 6). But, to return to the entry of the 29th, the passage continues with a reference to the way in which toy models of vehicles and pedestrians are used in a Paris lawcourt to depict how a car accident occurred.[1] This, Wittgenstein asserts, should have given him the essence of the truth, if only he had not been blind. And then he goes on to explain how the pictorial analogy works. 'Let us think of hieroglyphic writing in which each word is a representation of what it stands for', says Wittgenstein (*NB* p. 7). He then gives the example of two pin-men with swords (e.g. rapiers), A and B, A on the right

and B on the left. He then goes on to say:

> the whole might assert, e.g. 'A is fencing with B'. The proposition in picture writing can be true or false. It has a sense independent of its truth or falsehood. It must be possible to determine everything essential by considering this case.

Here we have the essential ingredients of the picture theory of language:

a. The juxtaposition of the two hieroglyphs can in some way '*assert*' that A and B are fencing.
b. This assertion can be true or false – perhaps they are acting in a play or doing a dance or doing something else with swords that has nothing to do with fencing, yet, on the other hand, they could indeed be fencing.
c. Whether what is represented in the picture is true or false, the picture has what Wittgenstein calls *sense* (*Sinn*). Sense is independent of truth or falsity. It is the *possibility of truth or falsity*. This juxtaposition of hieroglyphs *can* represent an actual situation, i.e. two people fencing, just as toy vehicles and toy pedestrians can represent how an accident occurred. Whether fencing was going on or whether the accident occurred as represented by the toys does not affect the sense of the picture, the possibility of its being either true or false.
d. Finally, there is Wittgenstein's conviction that this analogy can determine everything that is essential in order to analyse the nature of the proposition, and hence of language and thought.

This preliminary account of the picture theory left many questions to be answered and much work to be done. How, for instance, does a picture picture? How does it engage with reality or actuality? In what way is it analogous to a proposition where, for example, the *sentence* 'A is fencing with B' does not *look* at all like a pair of pin-men in a certain and particular relationship.

In the *Tractatus* these questions are answered fully and elegantly, principally in sections 2 and 4. The gist of what is said goes as follows:

a.   Marks (shapes, colours, etc.) in a picture, or toys, represent objects. They are the elements of the picture (*TLP* 2.131).

b.   These elements, be they marks on paper or toys, are related to each other in a particular way; it is this relationship which, according to Wittgenstein, represents the way that things can be related to one another (*TLP* 2.15). He calls this relationship between the elements their structure; the possibility of such a structure he calls its pictorial form (*Form der Abbildung*).

c.   A picture can represent anything that has the same structure or pictorial form as *it* has (*TLP* 2.71). The pictorial form is the possibility that things can be related in the same way (*TLP* 2.151) – that people can fence or duel, that an accident can occur in a particular way.

d.   A picture must have something in common with what it purports to depict (whether it be a duel or a car accident) (*TLP* 2.16–161).

e.   But it may agree or fail to agree with reality (with the facts, with what is the case); it can be a true or a false picture, correct or incorrect (*TLP* 2.21).

f.   In itself a picture is indifferent to truth or falsity, correctness and incorrectness. (*TLP* 2.22: 'What a picture represents it represents independently of its truth or falsity, by means of its pictorial form.') It represents a possible state of affairs. (I'm not sure this is quite correct. The child's drawing of a dog that looks more like a sheep may represent a possible state of affairs but does not represent, either truly or falsely, correctly or incorrectly, the *intended* state of affairs the child had in mind.)

g.   'What a picture represents is its *sense* (*Sinn*)' (*TLP* 2.221. My italics). Sense is independent of truth or falsehood. It concerns the structure of the proposition.

So much for the nature of picturing and what it involves by way of conditions. The next and more important question is how it engages with reality. How can picture A be said to be a picture of an object or situation or event B? It has been established that there must be an identity of sorts, some kind of similarity and equivalence in structure and content. But is this sufficient?

At this point Wittgenstein becomes somewhat metaphorical. He says that by having pictorial form (the possibility that things are related to one another in the same way as the elements of the picture (*TLP* 2.151)) '*that is how a picture is attached to reality: it reaches out to it (es reicht bis zu ihr)*'

(*TLP* 2.1511. My italics). He then compares a picture to a measure or standard (*Massstab*) which is 'laid (*angelegt*) against reality' (*TLP* 2.1512). A measure, however, touches an object only at the limits of the measurement (*TLP* 2.15121). It is important that there is a correlation between the elements of the picture and reality: 'The pictorial relationship consists of the correlations of the picture's elements with things' (*TLP* 2.1514). 'These correlations,' says Wittgenstein, 'are, as it were feelers (*Fühler*) of the picture's elements, with which the picture *touches* reality' (*TLP* 2.1515. My italics). As he would say later, these contacts with reality are not made by the picture itself but by the person using it. For instance, it is not the colour or relative size and thinness of the pin-men that is being correlated, but their shape, posture, spatial relationship and, perhaps, some other qualities. It should also be said that reaching out, sending out feelers and being laid against reality touches only the *possibility* of there being an actual state of affairs corresponding to the picture, not that there is one.

Wittgenstein is fairly broadminded in his use of the notion of pictures. Apart from drawings, paintings and three-dimensional representative objects he includes diagrams and, surprisingly, musical scores and, more surprisingly still, the grooves of a gramophone record. Now while even a diagram or a map may be said to picture an electrical circuit or the layout of the streets, buildings, parks, rivers and canals of a city or the rooms, doors, windows or floors of a house, it is hard to see how musical notation, much less gramophone grooves, can *picture* anything. Leaving aside gramophone grooves, what Wittgenstein has to say about musical notation is important for the next step between pictures and propositions.

In *TLP* 4.014 Wittgenstein says:

> A gramophone record, the musical idea, the written notes, and the soundwaves, all stand to one another in the same internal relationship of depicting that holds between language and the world.
> They are all constructed according to a common logical pattern.

One thing all four (record, idea, score and soundwaves) have in common is that there is no question of they themselves being heard. (In the case of the musical idea and the soundwaves there is no question of their being *seen* either.) Perhaps the most significant of the four is the musical idea. This is a thought, a complex thought, with an internal relationship similar to that of the played sounds in music. In that way it 'depicts' the internal relationship of sounds – 'internal' meaning the relationship they have to one another and not to anything outside themselves (such as the sound of a cuckoo or a cannon). Both in the *Tractatus* (*TLP* 4.011) and later in *Philosophical Investigations* Wittgenstein compared the sense of a proposition to understanding a theme in music (*PI* 527).

There remains one more observation that Wittgenstein makes about picturing as such, as distinct from the pictorial aspect of language, that is vital to what will follow. A picture cannot depict its own pictorial form; yet it *shows* it (*TLP* 2.172). The reason is that 'a picture represents its subject (*Objekt*) from a position outside it' (*TLP* 2.173) and, therefore, it cannot place itself *outside its representational form (Form der Darstellung) so as to represent itself* (*TLP* 2.174). This is crucial to what is to follow. Just as a picture cannot picture its own form of representation, so a proposition cannot *say* what it is and does when it pictures reality. It can, however, *show* or display it (*aufweisen*); but only that. How a proposition can be said to picture reality is explained in section 4.

By way of a bridging operation, the following features of pictures, as Wittgenstein understood them, should be noted:

a. they picture *facts* (*Tatsachen*). (*TLP* 2.1)
b. they present a state of affairs (*Sachlage*) (translated by Pears and McGuinness as 'situation') in logical space, that is, the possibility of the existence or non-existence of a state of things (*Sachverhalten*) or situation ('state of affairs' – Pears and McGuinness). (*TLP* 2.11)
c. there are pictures whose pictorial form is a logical form. (*TLP* 2.181) These, I presume, are of the form 'exit →' or '*aRb*'.
d. but all pictures have a logico-pictorial form in common with what they depict. (*TLP* 2.2) 'Every picture is *at the same time* a logical one.' (*TLP* 2.182)

From this aspect of the logical form of pictures it is not a great step to the pictorial form of propositions. Wittgenstein, however, makes the transition via thoughts. (*TLP* 3ff.) TLP 3 states that a thought is 'a logical picture of facts'. This is elaborated (*TLP* 3.001) by saying that to call a state of affairs 'thinkable' means we can picture it to ourselves. Hence 'the totality of true thoughts is a picture of the world (*TLP* 3.01). The transition from thought to proposition is achieved by *TLP* 3.1: 'In a proposition a thought finds an expression that can be perceived by the senses'. This is elaborated by the following entries:

3.11 We use the perceptual sign of a proposition (spoken or written, etc.) as a projection of a possible situation.
    The method of projection is to *think* of the sense of the proposition. (My italics)

> 3.12 I call the sign with which we express a proposition a propositional
> sign. And a proposition is a propositional sign in its projective
> relation to the world.

This description of a proposition may give the impression that Wittgenstein is making a distinction and separation commonly made by philosophers between thought, proposition and sign, as though there are three entities: the proposition which has sense, the thinking which understands the sense and the sign which expresses it. On this interpretation there would be a thought that was the understanding of a proposition (its sense) expressed by various propositional signs – 'It is raining', '*Il pleut*', '*Es regnet*' – all expressing the same sense. Nothing could have been further from Wittgenstein's thinking. As we shall see, with the development of his notion of the relationship of language to its use, his repudiation of this suggestion became almost violent. A *distinction* can be made between proposition, thought and sign, but the idea they are *separate entities* was anathema to Wittgenstein.[2]

Much of the rest of *TLP* 3 is taken up with a discussion of signs and symbols. It is not immediately relevant to this book, but a brief summary might be in order. What Wittgenstein means by a sign (*Zeichen*) is a mark on paper, a sound or something perceptible (a touch or smell or taste, perhaps) which in itself has no significance. It is given significance (sense, meaning) by the way an intelligent being uses it. A sign so used he calls a 'symbol'. A sign is a symbol as perceptible (*TLP* 3.32). The same sign can be common to more than one symbol. The sign 'bank' (one of Wittgenstein's own examples) can signify the side of a river, a place for dealing in money, or a bench, and variations on these objects, such as a pile of earth for sitting on or a row of rowers. If, as in this case, the 'modes of signification' are different, the symbols are not related by any common characteristics, and different signs could be used. (German uses *Bank* and *Ufer*; Turkish: *banka, kenar, bayir* and *yigin*.)[3] In order to recognize a symbol by its sign,' Wittgenstein says, 'we must observe how it is *used* with a sense' (*TLP* 3.326. My italics). 'If a sign is *useless*, it is meaningless (*bedeutungslos*). That is the point of Occam's maxim' (*TLP* 3.328).

In section 4 (*TLP* 4.01) Wittgenstein finally reaches the core of the *Tractatus* with his bold assertion:

> 4.01 A proposition is a picture of reality.
> A proposition is a model of reality *as we imagine it*. (My italics)

There is a seeming weakness here. Why 'as I imagine it'? Why not 'as it is'? 'Imagine' (*sich verstellen*) does not mean what it *can* mean in English, namely, to fantasize, to suppose, guess or entertain in one's head. It is much more rigorous, and means 'to put before one's mind': in this case, an image or model of what one conceives reality *to be*. No wavering here. And the passage goes on:

4.011   At first sight a proposition – one set out on the printed page, for example – does not seem to be a picture of the reality with which it is concerned. But neither do written notes seem at first sight to be a picture of a piece of music, nor our phonetic notation (the alphabet) to be a picture of our speech.
   And yet those sign-languages prove to be a picture of what they represent even in the ordinary sense.

4.012   It is obvious that a picture of the form '*aRb*' strikes us as a picture. In this case the sign is obviously a likeness of what is signified.

'*aRb*' signifies that in certain propositions a subject (*a*) is in a particular relationship (*R*) to an object (*b*), and that in the written proposition the subject usually stands to the left of the expression of a relationship and the predicate on the right; or, in a spoken proposition, the subject comes before the expression of relationship and the predicate after it. Thus in the proposition 'Jack loves Jill' the subject ('Jack') comes before (to the left of) the expression of a qualitative identity ('loves') and the object ('Jill') comes after (to the right of) it.

Wittgenstein regarded this as hieroglyphic. He says:

In order to understand the essential nature of a proposition, we should consider hieroglyphic script, which depicts the facts that it describes.
   And alphabetic script developed out of it without losing what was essential to depiction. (*TLP* 4.016)

As a graphemical statement this is open to question.[4] But, given Wittgenstein's broad notion of depicting and picturing, it may be accepted. Whether alphabetic script developed out of the hieroglyphic script is immaterial. An alphabetic script depicts a sound at least in the sense that the letters in the combination 'bat' look different from those in the combination 'cat'. The point is that a proposition can be expressed or conveyed only by a perceptible sign, but that sign must bear some resemblance to the proposition and, ultimately, to the thought conveyed. In that sense it must be hieroglyphic. What is essential is that a proposition is expressed by something perceptible, a sign, which depicts what it signifies, in a broad sense of 'depict'.

In *TLP* 4.021 Wittgenstein makes another, more important, point. He says: 'A proposition is a picture of reality: for if I understand a proposition, I know the situation that it represents. And I understand the proposition *without having had its sense explained to me*' (my italics). This presupposes that one knows what a picture, a model, a diagram, an illustrative sign is, its mode of signification, conventions of representation. (A medieval picture of a city does not look anything like what a city would have looked like to a medieval person, yet he would easily and naturally see it as a city.) The same applies to a proposition. To understand it, one has to know the language in which it is expressed and the grammatical structure of the language. Once one knows these things, the *sense* of the proposition does not have to be explained. If the sense of a proposition has to be explained, one has not understood it. If one understands it, explanation is unnecessary. For someone who does not know Turkish the proposition, *Ariza var arabada*, would have to be explained; to a Turk who had never come across it before, a peasant, say, who had never seen a motor-car but was familiar with carts, its meaning ('There is something wrong with my car-conveyance') would be perfectly intelligible. Moreover, if there were no propositions that could be understood without being explained, explanation itself would be impossible. We would be involved in an infinite regress.

The reason why we do not have to have propositions (in languages with which we are familiar) explained is, as Wittgenstein says, because 'a proposition *shows* its sense', it '*shows* how things stand *if* it is true' (*TLP* 4.022). If it *can* be true, therefore, it has sense. If it has sense, it displays or shows (depicts) a possible situation or state of affairs in reality. This can, so to speak, be read off from the proposition just as one can recognize the subject of a picture or model from its elements and structure. This much is clear: a proposition shows its sense by showing what can be a situation or state of affairs in reality. But Wittgenstein goes on to say: 'And it *says that* they do so stand' (*TLP* 4.022). That a proposition shows something is plausible enough, but that it *says* (in the sense of asserts) anything is hardly correct as stated.[5] A proposition does not itself say anything. It is *used* to say something by affirmation (*Bejahung*), as Wittgenstein says in *TLP* 4.064 where he makes the point that the *sense* of a proposition cannot be given by affirmation: the sense of a proposition '*is just what is affirmed*' (my italics). Affirming merely *says* that the sense of the proposition *is* how things stand;[6] it does not say *how* they stand. That is the sense of the proposition, which cannot be either given by or affected by affirmation or denial. Saying is, thus, something that supervenes on sense. It, as it were, projects the proposition into the actuality of the real world and commits it to being either true or false. For an affirmation to 'say' what it is saying, i.e. its sense, would be like a picture picturing its own mode of picturing. It (the proposition) depicts its sense and what it depicts is *said* to be depicted correctly (or incorrectly); but within the proposition, nothing is said about what it depicts. That is *shown*.

Thus, the proposition 'It is raining' *shows* a possible situation or state of affairs (that is its *sense*) and (if it is affirmed, orally or in writing) *says* that this is so, that the situation or state of affairs obtains. If it is negated in the form 'It is not raining' the sense is altered. What is said is that the situation does not obtain.[7] And what is said is either true or false. As we have seen, its truth or falsity depends on whether the depicted situation obtains or not. (In the case of negation, the truth or falsity of the affirmation depends on whether or not the situation does *not* obtain.)

Here two distinctions must be made: on the one hand, between what can be said and uttered, and, on the other, between a genuine and a seeming or pseudo proposition. One can utter almost anything. Infants and lunatics do it all the time. Sometimes these utterances are in the form of a proposition ('Cows' green is sweeter than the square on the hypotenuse'). These utterances make no sense and, hence, though they are in common parlance 'said', nothing has actually been said, i.e. affirmed: words have merely been uttered. Utterances could make sense, however, and still not be said. One obvious example is the use of sentences in language classes. The teacher who says: 'How do you say "It will not rain this afternoon" in French?' is not giving a weather forecast, is not *saying* anything about the weather in his or her locality. However, the proposition could be true or false. It is a genuine proposition. But there are, according to Wittgenstein, pseudo propositions. They appear to say something but in fact say nothing, either because they cannot *say* anything but only show something or because they have nothing even to show. They picture nothing, although they give the appearance of picturing something, even something profound. Since they picture nothing, and, hence, lack sense, they cannot be affirmed (or negated). They cannot be said; they are unsayable.

Wittgenstein is quite specific on this (rather too specific and limiting in what he regards as sayable). 'The totality of true propositions is the whole of natural science' (*TLP* 4.11). It is clear that this conclusion was reached by the route we have just travelled: picturing – depicting possible states of affairs – having the possibility to be true or false, (*Sinn* or sense) in accord with or not in accord with what is the case – what is the case as facts about the world, what can be or cannot be the case (nothing *a priori*) in the world. This is reiterated in the last but two entries of the *Tractatus* (*TLP* 6.53): 'The correct method in philosophy would really be the following: to say nothing except what can be said, i.e. propositions of natural science . . . *this* method would be the only strictly correct one.'

So, then, the only true propositions, those that actually say something, or, more importantly, only those that *can say* something, be it true or false, are statements of empirical fact, of what is or is not the case. It is somewhat restrictive to limit these to the propositions of natural science as it is ordinarily understood. Surely such banal observations as: 'It is raining', to say nothing of historical reports and geographical, archaeological and biological records, which used to be described as 'natural history', are factual, i.e. capable of being strictly speaking either true or false and, hence, sayable. The word Wittgenstein uses is *Naturwissenschaft* where just *Wissenschaft* (learning, scholarship) or, better still, *Wissen* (knowledge) would have been closer to what he meant. However, *Wissenschaft* (whatever about *Naturwissenschaft*) has a broader extension than 'science' currently has in English: witness Wittgenstein's proposition: 'All roses are either red or yellow' which would hardly be uttered by a botanist (*TLP* 6.111).

However, the point is that 'All roses are either red or yellow' is a proper or *real* proposition because what it depicts can be true or false. It is sayable, even though, in this instance, it does not happen to be true. It differs from a tautology in that it cannot be self-evident, even if it is true. It would remain a picture of a *possible* state of affairs with its truth dependent on this being the case.

This is essentially what every *real* proposition is and does, to quote from notes dictated to G. E. Moore in Norway in 1914: 'Every *real* proposition *shows* something, besides what it says, about the Universe.' (*NB* p. 107) There are, however, in Wittgenstein's view other propositions, to which reference has already been made, pseudo propositions (*Scheinsätze*), that say nothing because they cannot.

Wittgenstein uses three different words to describe seeming propositions: *bedeutungslos* ('meaningless'), *sinnlos* ('lacking in sense') and *unsinnig* ('nonsensical'). The *bedeutungslos* propositions are hardly worthy of the name 'pseudo proposition'. In *TLP* 3.328 and 5.47321 Wittgenstein speaks of meaningless signs. If a sign is useless, it is meaningless. If it is unnecessary, serves no logical purpose, it is logically meaningless. This is an application of Occam's maxim that entities should not be multiplied unnecessarily. In *TLP* 5.4733 Wittgenstein gives the following example:

> Thus the reason why 'Socrates is identical' says nothing is that we have *not* given any *adjectival* meaning to the word 'identical'. For when it appears as a sign for identity, it symbolizes in an entirely different way.

Tautologies and contradictions say nothing; they are *sinnlos*. They have no truth conditions: a tautology is unconditionally true; a contradiction is not true under any conditions (*TLP* 4.461). They are not pictures of reality; they do not represent any possible situation. A tautology admits *all* possible situations. The tautology: 'it is either raining or not raining' tells us nothing about the weather. A contradiction admits no situation: it cannot be true under any circumstances. ('It is both raining and not raining simultaneously in the same place' might be an example.) (*TLP* 4.462) Tautologies and contradictions are not, however, nonsensical (*unsinnig*): they are part of the symbolism, just as '0' is part of the symbolism of arithmetic (*TLP* 4.4611).

There are many other kinds of proposition that are *sinnlos*. Towards the end of the *Tractatus* Wittgenstein lists some of them. First, there are propositions of logic. They are tautologies; they say nothing (*TLP* 6.1–6.11). Like all tautologies their truth can be recognized from the symbolism alone 'and this fact contains in itself the whole philosophy of logic' (*TLP* 6.113). As tautologies, propositions of logic *show* the formal, i.e. logical, properties of language and the world. They describe or rather represent the 'scaffolding' of the world. They *presuppose* that names have meaning and elementary propositions have sense. That is their connection with the world (*TLP* 6.124). Propositions of logic do not have to say anything since they *show* their sense – they are not nonsensical (*unsinnig*). And to try to say it for them by talking about such things as the 'laws of inference', as Frege and Russell do, is, in Wittgenstein's view, lacking in sense and superfluous. To represent how we can speak about the world, to be a mirror-image (*Spiegelbild*) of the world in a formal sense, is the domain of logic. In this sense, as Wittgenstein says, logic is transcendental (*TLP* 6.13). It applies to no particular fact about the world and yet can be applied to any:

The next set of propositions Wittgenstein refers to as pseudo propositions are mathematical. 'Mathematics is a logical method,' he says, but it shows the logic of the world not in tautologies but in *equations*. Like propositions of logic it says nothing about real life. 'Rather,' he says:

> we make use of mathematical propositions *only* in inferences from propositions that do not belong to mathematics to others that likewise do not belong to mathematics. (*TLP* 6.211)

Though *sinnlos* (unsayable) and, hence, saying nothing about the world, they help, by equating, and, hence, calculating (in the Wittgensteinian sense), to move counters around the logical mirror of the world.

With the next kind of pseudo propositions we move out of the tautological into a further realm of the unsayable. This, in the first instance, includes the *a priori* principles of science. These include the 'law of causality' in physics, which is not a law but the form of a law, just as in mechanics there are 'minimal principles' such as the law of least action (*TLP* 6.32–6.321). They differ from the so-called law of induction in so far as they are *a priori* and logical laws (laying down what *must* be), whereas the so-called laws of induction govern only what can or may be, the accidental (*TLP* 6.3–6.31). They are the presuppositions of science without which the natural sciences would not be possible.

After what has already been said about the propositions of the natural sciences being sayable, it might come as a surprise to learn that the most fundamental principles of the natural sciences are unsayable. But it should not be a great surprise. A moment's reflection should reassure us that Wittgenstein is being perfectly consistent. Though the propositions of the natural sciences are sayable, this does not mean that the principles, assumptions, presuppositions on which they are based are sayable. Wittgenstein would, and does, ask by what means of expression can they be said. The kernel of what he has to say is contained in *TLP* 6.3432–6.361:

> 6.3432   We ought not to forget that the description of the world by mechanics is always entirely general. In it there is e.g. no mention of *particular* material points, but (it is) always about *any whatsoever* only.
>
> 6.35   Laws, such as the principle of sufficient reason, etc., treat of the net, not of what the net describes.
>
> 6.36   If there were a law of causality, it could read thus: 'There are laws of Nature'.
>   But, of course, one cannot say that: it displays itself.

What is this net to which Wittgenstein refers? It is described in *TLP* 6.341. It is an analogue of science. What science does is to reduce the irregularities of nature to regularities sufficient for a particular purpose. So, if you have a surface covered with irregular black and white dots you can describe the precise position of each of these dots by imposing a net, a grid or a mesh on them as fine as is required and reading off their positions. While the net – be it the principle of sufficient reason or the law of causality, which, according to Wittgenstein, can be read as the laws of Nature – helps us to *describe* natural occurrences in an orderly and rational fashion, it *cannot itself be described*. Thus (a) the natural sciences have assumptions about the world which science cannot either justify or disprove by its own methods, for the simple reason that those methods depend upon them; (b) these presuppositions are not *part* of natural science, as the net, grid or mesh is not part of the picture it tries to formalize; and (c) even if they are not describable, their presence and operation, and their necessity, is *evident*: it manifests itself.

Like tautologies, contradictions and propositions of logic, the *a priori* principles of science are not nonsensical (*unsinnig*). They tell us nothing about the world, about how things stand. They say nothing. They may be expressed in a form that makes them look as though something is being said. But about what? The general principle that every event has a cause tells us nothing about events or causes, or even whether there are, or ever have been, any events or causes. They can be translated without remainder into the symbolism: 'if p then q' or '$p \rightarrow q$'. To that extent they have sense and picture reality, but only the formal structure of reality, not any particular fact, still less the totality of facts. Their sense resides in their symbolism. And they show it by their symbolism.

There are, however, other pseudo propositions that are both *sinnlos and unsinnig*. They both lack sense, can say nothing, are unsayable, and also they have no sense. They picture nothing. They represent nothing; they show nothing, not even a symbolism i.e. a significant sign. No significance can be given to their signs; hence their signs cannot be symbols (*TLP* 3.32, *passim*). They are 'nonsensical'. They are not, however, nonsensical, that is, absurd in the popular sense, as gibberish is or as meaningless (*bedeutungslos*) propositions are. They manifest themselves (*zeigt sich*) (*TLP* 6.522). What this means is none too clear. Perhaps it cannot be made clearer, and such is their nature. For the moment we have reached the position that the 'nonsensical' pseudo propositions do not picture anything, much less say anything about the world. But they manifest something, if only their inability to say anything.

The *unsinnig* that Wittgenstein deals with at any length (and that is not great) are propositions of philosophy and expressions of value, which are our main concern.

Of philosophy he says (*TLP* 4.003) that most of the propositions and questions to be found in philosophical material are not false but nonsensical. They arise from a failure to understand the logic of our language. Wittgenstein concedes that Russell did us a service: he showed that the apparent logical form of a proposition need not be its real one (*TLP* 4.0031). This may or may not be so. As Wittgenstein states it in *TLP* 4.003, it seems an empirical matter. Maybe some philosophical questions and propositions are of this kind; maybe most are; maybe none are. What Wittgenstein does not assert is that *all* are. And even if they were, they would, at worst, be meaningless (*bedeutungslos*) or lacking sense and purpose (*sinnlos*). (And this would not be exclusive to philosophy. Many questions and propositions in science and other forms of discourse arise from failure to understand the logic of our language.)

However, in the last entries in the *Tractatus* (*TLP* 6.53–6.54) Wittgenstein pronounces his final verdict on philosophy as such. He says that the right method in philosophy is to say nothing but what can be said. What can be said is the exclusive preserve of the natural sciences (however these are interpreted). What then of his own work, the *Tractatus Logico–Philosophicus*? Being philosophical, it says nothing either about the world or logic and language, its putative subject-matter. Wittgenstein agrees. He admits the work is nonsensical. Why then, we might well ask, did he bother to write it and devote between 75 and 95 pages (according to the edition one reads) to saying nothing? His answer in the penultimate entry of the book is elegant and somewhat mysterious (*TLP* 6.54):

> My propositions serve as elucidations in the following way; anyone who understands me eventually recognizes them as nonsensical, when he has used them – as steps – to climb up beyond them. (He must, so to speak, throw away the ladder after he has climbed up it.)
> He must transcend (*überwinden*) these propositions, and then he will see the world aright.

Here Wittgenstein makes two important points. The first is that philosophy (which he seems in the previous entry (*TLP* 6.34) to equate with metaphysics, and rightly so) shows that it is nonsensical, that it is attempting to say what cannot be said, to go beyond the boundaries of language. But, secondly, what it says can be a means of seeing the world, logic, and language correctly. It is not a scaffolding with which to build a picture of the world, as logic is. Nor is it a net, grid or mesh in which to capture reality, as are the principles of natural science. It is a ladder up which we climb in order to see the world (including logic and language) aright. Some commentators, Max Black, for instance, have objected to the notion of throwing away or kicking down the ladder, since the *Tractatus* contains much good philosophical material. This completely misses the points Wittgenstein is making. Black and fellow commentators of the same ilk want to cling to the rungs of the ladder, like the Israelites, who would have preferred to linger in the desert rather than reach the promised land. There is nothing wrong in that (Wittgenstein has many good things to say on language and logic, particularly his criticisms of Frege and Russell, to say nothing of lesser, anonymous, miscreants) but it misses the point of the *Tractatus* as a whole. The point is that metaphysics, philosophy of language, philosophy of logic *tell us nothing* about anything. At best they do two things: (a) they *show* us it is nonsensical to attempt to talk about them, that *talk* about such matters is nonsensical: they do not represent or picture what is in the real world; (b) in doing so they show (manifest) how seeming propositions of a philosophical kind should be taken, that is, as indicators, pointers, rungs of a ladder, steps leading upwards, pointing to an intuition of what cannot be stated, as one might say: 'Look, a tree!'

This could be regarded as a naïve view of philosophy. Few, if any, reputable philosophers believed they were describing the *facts* about the world, how things stand or stood. This may be so. But many, if not all, gave the impression that this was what they were doing. And they were interpreted in this light. Wittgenstein insisted that not only was this view of philosophy nonsense, but that philosophy of its very nature is nonsensical (*unsinnig*). It tells us nothing about the world, about how things are or about why they are as they are. What it does – indirectly, and as a result of much talk – is to *show* what kind of apparatus is necessary in order to understand the world and say something about it.

This, according to Wittgenstein, is also the function of expressions of value, primarily those of ethics, aesthetics and religious belief.

By expressions of value Wittgenstein means what is usually called cultural value: what is valued for its own sake, not for any utilitarian or pecuniary gain that may be derived from it.

Wittgenstein prefaces his remarks by saying that all propositions are of equal value (*TLP* 6.4). If they are true, they have the same value, that of being true rather than false. To say: 'Germany has just invaded Poland', said on the morning of 1 September 1939, would have been to state a fact. To say that on the same day Mrs Jones's linen was blown off the clothes-line in Bangor, North Wales, if true, has equal value *as a proposition*. It also states a fact. So, stating facts, which is the function of (real, proper, genuine) propositions as Wittgenstein understands them, has nothing to do with value, whether the importance of what is being talked about or the manner in which it is said is greater or less.

Propositions are about facts, what happens to be the case, the accidental. Value – and here Wittgenstein has in mind ethical value, though, as we shall see, what he says also applies to aesthetic and religious value – has nothing (directly) to do with facts, with what happens, with the accidental. 'Ethics is transcendental' (*TLP* 6.421). It is concerned with what Wittgenstein calls 'the sense of the world' (*der Sinn der Welt*). The *sense* of the world cannot be *within* the world, cannot be a *fact* among other facts making up the world, cannot be something accidental. The *sense of the world* must, as Wittgenstein says, *lie outside it* (*TLP* 6.41).

In the world everything is as it is, and everything happens as it does happen; *in* it no value exists.

Wittgenstein goes on to add, somewhat rhetorically (though effectively, perhaps): '*in* it no value exists – if it did exist, it would have no value. If there is any value that does have value . . .' However, he continues sensibly enough:

> it must lie outside the whole sphere of what happens and is the case. For all that happens and is the case is accidental.
> What makes it non-accidental cannot lie *within* the world, since, if it did it would itself be accidental.
> It must lie outside the world.

It is clear from what Wittgenstein means by lying 'outside the world' as stated elsewhere, that it means: coterminous with the world, lying its whole length and beyond it, so as to view its whole length from a viewpoint or vantage-point. But, above all, it means being necessary and absolute, not accidental or relative (as the accidental is). One may kill someone accidentally, but one cannot *murder* someone accidentally. Taking account of the connotations of murder – intention, deliberation, malice – it cannot be accidental. It cannot *happen* that somone *murdered* someone. Murder, like all things transcendental, belongs outside the world. That is, it is not a fact about the world nor a happening in it. It is something – a view, a judgement, an appraisal – that we place upon the world and its happenings.

Now it will be objected that murder *is* a fact of the world and a *happening* in the world. Like every other fact about the world it is accidental: it could and might not have happened. 'So many murders happen every day.' If a woman had not walked home alone late last night, she might not have been murdered? Killed, yes. But murdered? What if the killing was unintentional, truly an accident? If it was, it was not a murder. But even if it was an intentional, consciously willed act (and, hence, murder) was it not *a fact* that the assailant had the intention? The thought of killing was in his mind. At some point or other he took a decision to kill his victim. Are not all these facts, things that happened that might not have occurred, and, hence, accidental? Allowing that these are facts, there remains the element of malice that is essential to establishing that an act of killing is murder. Not all deliberate killings are murder, though it is popular in certain quarters to regard 'judicial killings' or executions, as 'murder'. Malice is neither a physical nor a mental act. It is not an act of any kind. It is not even a quality, though it may be a characteristic of certain people. But then it is an attitude of mind that pervades them totally, not an incidental *act* such as thinking of something or deciding to do something.

It may be objected that, though malice may not be an act, but something supervening on certain actions, it either is or is not a fact that certain people are malicious, just as they may be obstinate, irritable, avaricious or ambitious. Moreover, malice is not an habitual state. Someone might act maliciously only once or twice in his or her life; for the remainder of the time they lead a normal, if uneventful, life. Hence, if someone behaves maliciously or is just of a permanently malicious turn of mind, this is surely a fact about the person, and, hence, a fact like any other.

I shall return to this discussion later. At this point I can only say that this was not how Wittgenstein regarded matters concerning value, whether ethical, aesthetic or religious. Value was not a matter of fact; it was not something that happened (or happened to be); it was not accidental in that it could not be otherwise; it was *outside the world, not in it.*

The reason why expressions of value, in Wittgenstein's opinion, are not about facts, happenings and the accidental is that these are all (a) particulars (even the world itself *is* only the totality of *particulars* – 'The world is the totality of facts' (*TLP* 1.1) – though, as we shall see, it can be *regarded* as holistic, as a limited whole) and (b) they can happen to be or happen not to be. They can therefore be pictured in genuine propositions which can have truth value. What can be pictured in a proposition can be shown to be possible, and if the proposition is stated (said) and says what is the case, it is true; if it says what is not the case, it is false. According to Wittgenstein, since value of whatever kind is outside the world and not a fact in the world, like other facts, it cannot be pictured. So it cannot be expressed in a genuine proposition as something possible, nor stated (truly or falsely) as something that is the case.

From this it follows that statements or expressions of value say nothing, tell us nothing about the world or anything in it, about what happens, can happen or does not happen. They are nonsensical (*unsinnig*).

But surely, it will be objected, this itself is nonsensical, or, in Wittgensteinian terms, nonsense (*bedeutungslos*). Surely value judgements can be true or false, just like historical or scientific statements. It is surely false to say that murder is a good thing, Shakespeare was a mediocre poet, or idolatry should be practised more widely and more often, as should witchcraft. We have already discussed murder as a concept with evaluation of the act attached and have found it hard to pin it down to facts.

Now we are asked to attach a contrary evaluation – and one of a universal nature. The facts, the physical and mental facts, are the same, as are our observations of them and inferences from them. In what sense, therefore, is it true to say that the statement 'murder is good' is false? If you disagree with this moral view, you say it is wrong or evil or wicked. You may call it 'false', as one talks of false money or false bottoms on crates; but, at least according to Wittgenstein, this use of 'false' has nothing to do with truth value. It may have to do with agreement or disagreement, approval or disapproval, acceptance or rejection. That something is good or bad morally, aesthetically or religiously has nothing to do with *possibility* (or probability, for that matter), what can or cannot be the case, what *can or cannot happen*. Therefore, it cannot have any truth value in the logical sense. It is either totally and in all circumstances acceptable or in all circumstances it must be rejected. Its logical status is like that of tautologies and contradictions which must in all circumstances be true or false, and, therefore, play no part on a truth-function table.

So, in Wittgensteinian terms, if one says that it is false that murder is a good thing to commit, one is not using 'false' in the same sense as when one says that it is false to say that the Romans captured Hibernia. They could have done but they didn't. This cannot be said of murder, Shakespeare or idolatry. It cannot be said of them that they could have been good but weren't; or that they were once good but aren't any more; or that they may become good some day. Either they are good or not. If they are, then they are good eternally; they are not affected by the happenings of the world. Not even the changes of taste and fashion in the world (which must be taken as happenings) (a) change the world itself, except as historical events within it, or (b) affect the general moral, aesthetic and other principles on which they are ephemerally based. This will be taken up again in a later chapter.

To return to the nonsensicality of expressions of value. They are not nonsensical because they have nothing to say, as tautologies are; or because they cannot say anything, as contradictions cannot. Nor are they nonsensical as are the propositions of mathematics and logic, which show the possible structure of the world but say nothing whatsoever about it. They are like the propositions of philosophy. They do not picture or mirror the world and its facts in any way. Their signs – or some of them – lack meaning (*TLP* 6.53). They help us to 'see the world aright'. But, in endeavouring to do so, they attempt to go beyond the boundaries of language. It is in this that their nonsensicality lies.

Wittgenstein does not use the expression 'going beyond the boundaries of language' or 'attempting to say the unsayable' in the *Tractatus*, though the notion is implied in what he says there. The expression first appears in his 'Lecture on Ethics', given around 1929, a decade after the completion of the *Tractatus*. It appears towards the end of the lecture where he is speaking about the miraculous, the absolutely miraculous, the miraculous in itself, that is, not in relation to anything else, such as a 'miraculous' (i.e. lucky) escape or a 'miraculous' stroke of good fortune (*PRv* p. 11). According to Wittgenstein, one feature of the miraculous is that it is *inexpressible*. You cannot *say* what it is, why it occurs or anything else about it. In the *Tractatus* Wittgenstein had described the good or bad exercise of the will as being able to alter the world only at its limits, but not the facts, 'not what can be *expressed* by language' (*TLP* 6.43. My italics). In the lecture he elaborates on this notion. He says that a feature of the miraculous in the absolute sense is that it cannot be said or expressed in language: 'all I have said is again that we cannot express what we want to express and that all we *say* about the absolutely miraculous is nonsense' (ibid.).

Wittgenstein then poses an objection to what he has just said. Perhaps the reason why the absolutely miraculous is not expressible is because the correct mode of expression, the correct logical analysis for something of absolute value, has not yet been found. Thus expressions of absolute value might not be nonsense. An experience of absolute value might be '*just a fact like other facts*', if only we can find the correct mode of expression. To this Wittgenstein instantly and vehemently replied:

> Now when this is urged against me I at once see clearly, as it were in a flash of light, not only that no description that I can think of would do to describe what I mean by absolute value, but that I would reject every significant description that anybody could possibly suggest, *ab initio*, on the ground of its significance. That is to say: I see now that these nonsensical expressions, were not nonsensical because I had not yet found the correct expressions, but that their nonsensicality was their very essence. (*PRv* p. 11)

To try to say anything about absolute value or about reality or the world as a whole is to attempt to say the unsayable, to go beyond the boundary of language. The passage quoted above continues:

> For all I wanted to do with them (expressions of absolute value) was just *to go beyond* the world and that is to say beyond significant language. My whole tendency and I believe the tendency of all men who have ever tried to write or talk Ethics or Religion was to run against the boundaries of language. (*PRv* p. 11)

This attempt to say what cannot be said, to use language for purposes for

which it was not intended, to talk nonsensically in this special Wittgensteinian sense of 'nonsense', he also described as 'running against the
walls of our cage'.

Waismann recounts a conversation with Wittgenstein held in Moritz
Schlick's house in Vienna on 30 December 1929, when Wittgenstein
linked his own ideas with those of Heidegger and Kierkegaard.

> I can well understand what Heidegger means by Being and Angst. Human
> beings have a drive to run up against the boundaries of language. Think
> for example of the astonishment that anything exists. This astonishment
> cannot be expressed in the form of a question and also there is no answer
> at all. All we can say can *a priori* be only nonsensical. Nevertheless we dash
> ourselves against the boundaries of language. Kierkegaard also had seen
> this throwing of oneself and even described it in a very similar way (as
> throwing oneself against a paradox). (*WWV* p. 68)

This passage has long been a scandal to British Wittgensteinians.
When it first appeared in *The Philosophical Review* in 1965, the first
sentence referring to Heidegger was not included. It subsequently
appeared in Waismann's *Ludwig Wittgenstein and the Vienna Circle*. Since
then it has become widely accepted that not only was Wittgenstein
familiar with the writings of Phenomenologists, but that he regarded
himself as in some sense a Phenomenologist.[8]

This tells us something about what Wittgenstein meant by 'nonsense'
as he used it of expressions of value and philosophical utterances. Unlike
propositions of logic and mathematics which show their sense by their
abstract structure, metaphysical propositions and expressions of value
show their sense in attempting to go beyond the bounds of language, to
say what cannot be said, to express the inexpressible – which can
nevertheless be divined in the mode and nature of the expression. They
are nonsensical in a special sense. It was Frank Plumpton Ramsey, the
Cambridge mathematician and philosopher, who coined the phrase
'important nonsense' to describe this kind of nonsensicality. In this he
was ironical, if not hostile. It is to be found in his posthumously
published (he died at the age of twenty-seven in 1930) work, *Foundations
of Mathematics and other Logical Essays* (1931) in the essay 'Last Papers of
Philosophy'. The passage, directed chiefly at *TLP* 6.53, goes as follows:

> Philosophy must be of some use and we must take it seriously; it must clear
> our thoughts and so our actions. Or else it is a disposition we have to
> check, and an inquiry to see that this is so; i.e. the chief proposition of
> philosophy is that philosophy is nonsense. And again, we must then take
> seriously that it is nonsense and not pretend, as Wittgenstein does, that it
> is important nonsense. (p. 263)

Ramsey, alas, did not live to complete his inquiry. Perhaps if he had done so he might have come to see that Wittgenstein was not pretending that philosophy and value are important nonsense; that he was not, as the passage implies, deluding himself; and that the way in which he uses the terms 'nonsense' and 'nonsensical' cannot be reduced to the ordinary sense of the term, to which sentences such as 'Socrates is identical' or even 'Smith and Jones are identical' belong.

But at least Ramsey saw, as did Russell in his introduction to the *Tractatus*, that Wittgenstein was using, or attempting to use, these terms in a different sense from their ordinary usage. Others of a Logical Positivist tendency took Wittgenstein to mean that expressions of value and metaphysics are nonsensical in the ordinary sense of the term. It was for that reason they welcomed the *Tractatus* so warmly and took Wittgenstein to be one of their own. It came as a nasty shock to discover towards the end of the 1920s that he did not regard himself as anything of the kind. Since he had put into clear and dramatic expression what they were thinking, though he meant something quite different by the words he used – this is one of the delightful ironies of language and its ambiguity – they had somehow to explain his fall from grace. Ramsey suggests he was deluding himself; that, had he considered the matter more carefully, he would have seen that there is no room in the scheme of things for any other sense of 'nonsense' than the ordinary one. A. J. Ayer in his recent book on Wittgenstein accuses him, in a very gentle way, of trying to have it both ways. He says: 'It cannot be the case both that his assertions are true and that they are devoid of sense.'[9]

Taken at its face value, Ayer's statement cannot be refuted: it is patently true. Moreover, as a criticism of Wittgenstein, at least one half of it is irrefutable. In the preface Wittgenstein states: 'it seems to me the *truth* of the thoughts imparted here is unimpeachable and definitive' (*TLP* p. 4). However, in the passage Ayer quotes, Wittgenstein does not speak of truth but of the 'correct method of philosophy'. This may be a quibble, but my reply to the second half of Ayer's sentence is not. Nowhere does Wittgenstein say that expressions of value or metaphysical propositions are '*devoid* of sense'. Not only would it be false to say so, but it itself would be devoid of sense. To write and have printed over twenty-five thousand words and say at the end, quite seriously, that they are devoid of sense, would not only make the author a candidate for a mental home but the publisher as well, particularly as every sentence is well formed. No. There is no contradiction between what Wittgenstein says in *TLP* 6.53 and the rest of the book. I shall return to this in a moment, but first I should like to take the conflict into the opposite camp.

Assuming that expressions of value and propositions of metaphysics are nonsensical in the strict sense of being devoid of sense, what does this mean? Clearly it does not mean something like 'The cat is older than the square root of minus one's plus-fours', much less 'Qwertyuiop asdfghjkzxcvbnm?' So in what sense are they devoid of sense? The only sense of 'sense', in which they can be devoid of it, is that they do not state facts that are verifiable by observations of phenomena in the natural world: that is, the observations of the natural sciences. But by what feat of logic do these so-called natural sciences have the monopoly of sense? In the belief, perhaps, that those other disciplines – psychology, sociology, ethics, aesthetics and religion – can prove themselves as making sense only if it can be shown they are ultimately branches of the natural sciences? But, if this can be done, what sense is left in ethics, aesthetics, religious belief and metaphysics? In the case of metaphysics, none at all. It has no scientific basis whatsoever. As nonsense it is not quite as pure as the examples given in this paragraph, and certainly not so amusing. Though no doubt an unsympathetic reader could get some amusement out of reading Plato, Aristotle, Augustine, Aquinas, Descartes, Spinoza, Leibniz, Hegel and Bradley, these authors would have to be deemed to be at best playing elegantly with words and weaving elaborate fantasies of prose poetry, which is, some might say, precisely what Nietzsche does, and, to a much lesser extent, Schopenhauer.

But what of ethics, aesthetics and religion? Religion can be dumped on the scrapheap of pure nonsense beside metaphysics or treated more sympathetically, psychologically or sociologically, as though the result of some aberrant but prevalent disease of the human brain. Its sense can be attributed to the attempt of primitive, unenlightened people to come to terms with their environment before science came on the scene to explain everything. Its survival can be attributed to human stupidity, resistance to change of ideas, vested interest and other psychological and sociological factors. But in the end this means its 'sense' is nonsense in the ordinary sense.

Ethics and aesthetics are treated with somewhat more respect, but very little more. Their sense consists in (a) certain statements of non-ethical or non-aesthetic *facts*, such as that someone took money out of a till or that a canvas is covered with blue, red, yellow and white areas defined by black lines, and (b) that someone has certain feelings towards these facts or a group of people have. As an account of ethical or aesthetic statements these are pathetic, inadequate, just short of being irrelevant and miles away from the true meaning of statements in ethics and aesthetics. The statement: 'Pilfering is wrong' is not a statement of feeling: not even of a feeling of disapproval. We can have feelings of disapproval towards all manner of things that are in no way immoral, such as introducing the car registration prefix on 1 August, the Union

Flag or the size of the pound coin. On the other hand, if we disapprove of pilfering it is because we think it is wrong; we do not think it is wrong because, for some reason or another, we disapprove of it. Similarly with aesthetic judgements. At best they are negative expressions of feeling, and that by implication. To say of a painting by Mondrian that it was a beautifully balanced composition implies you approve of it; this in turn implies you are not utterly revolted by it. But this is not the meaning of your statement. If you were utterly revolted by it, as some people are by most of even the best Neo-Expressionist paintings, or just bored by it, you could still sincerely say it was a beautifully balanced composition.

What the moralist and the critic or art theorist is doing, on Wittgenstein's account of their use of language, is not primarily, much less exclusively, expressing his feeling towards a way of behaving or an object. He is trying to get the reader or listener to *see* the action or object in a certain way – as right, wrong, good, evil, beautiful, ugly, kitsch or sublime. This is not an identifiable feature of actions such as opening a till and taking out cash or of an object as are its colour, shape and markings. The sense of such terms as 'right', 'wrong', 'good', 'evil', 'beautiful' and 'ugly' cannot be explained solely by observable features of the action or object. Indeed these terms cannot be explained at all: they can only be exemplified. Ethical and aesthetic statements are not true statements in Wittgenstein's view: they do not *say* anything as do statements of fact; nor do they *show* their sense (or lack of it) by their symbolism as to propositions of logic (or illogical sentences) and equations of mathematics. It is by the way they are used to get the reader to see the world or an action or an object (including a piece of literature such as a poem) aright that its sense is conveyed. I shall have more to say about this in the next chapter.

This is all explained in *TLP* 6.54 quoted above in which Wittgenstein says that the propositions of the *Tractatus* are explanatory or elucidatory by being climbed up and over, like climbing a ladder that is kicked away when we get to the top and can see the world correctly. This again is something that cannot be explained. That is why Wittgenstein calls his propositions nonsensical. If he were to attempt to explain them, that would be nonsensical in the ordinary sense. But because of the way they work, they are not nonsensical in the ordinary sense. Sense is being conveyed, but it is not being conveyed in the ordinary way. Therefore the propositions are neither nonsensical in the ordinary sense nor conveyers of sense in the ordinary sense.

In what sense are they conveyers of sense and to whom? For an answer to these questions we shall have to wait until chapter four on Wittgenstein's notion of the mystical. Whatever way it is conveyed, it does not seem to be the way in which the sense of propositions of logic or of the *Tractatus* itself are conveyed. The expressions of value are not treated as dispensable ladders to be kicked aside after they have been mounted. Grasping their sense is more like reading between the lines of a poem. Through what is said, one grasps what has not been said. Any attempt to say it would destroy it. It is in this light that Wittgenstein's letter to von Ficker to which reference was made in the Preface should be read. It was stated there that the sense of the *Tractatus* is ethical. But, more importantly, Wittgenstein said that the second section of the book, the important section, had not been written. And yet it is there. This will explain the disproportion of the book and the brevity of the section on expressions of value. After all, what cannot be said cannot be said at any great length.

Perhaps Wittgenstein was unwise to use the term 'nonsensical'. He could hardly have foreseen that the Vienna Circle and the Logical Positivists would have misunderstood it in the way they did, though he must also have realized it was open to misinterpretation – otherwise why did he write in the preface: 'This book will perhaps only be understood by someone who has himself already had the thoughts expressed herein or perhaps similar thoughts' (*TLP* p. 3)? But if we look for an alternative term that is not misleading it is hard to find. Perhaps the best would be 'inexpressible'. Wittgenstein uses it several times. For instance in *TLP* 6.42 he says: 'Propositions cannot express anything higher' and in the next entry he says: 'It is clear that ethics cannot be put into words.' But the notion of the inexpressible presents as many difficulties as it solves. How can you express the inexpressible? Philosophy of both the East and West is long accustomed to the notion of expressing the inexpressible and knows what is meant by such a paradoxical expression. (I shall have more to say about the inexpressible in a later chapter.)

The use of the term 'unsayable' is open to a similar objection. How can one say something that is unsayable? If you attempt to say something that is unsayable you are talking nonsense, so you might as well come clean and speak about the nonsensical as Wittgenstein does. I nevertheless find 'unsayable', though odd, less open to misinterpretation and less shocking than 'nonsensical', and, because less traditional, more challenging than 'inexpressible'. However, all three terms are necessary in order to convey Wittgenstein's thought, as are others such as 'transcendent', 'absolute' and the expression 'attempting to go beyond the boundary of language'. We must now see how they were applied to ethics.

2

Ethics

Engelmann, as we have seen, reports that Wittgenstein regarded the *Tractatus* as a whole as ethical. It is to be hoped that in what follows it will become apparent why. Perhaps the suggestion of an analogy with Spinoza's *Ethics* might suffice for the present. Both books give the appearance of being about logic and metaphysics, though Spinoza's is more obviously ethical in its later sections. (It has been alleged that the title of Wittgenstein's book was suggested by Spinoza's *Tractatus Theologico-Politicus*.) However, Wittgenstein confines himself to a mere handful of remarks explicitly on ethics at the end of his work.[1]

These are prefaced by some remarks on value in general (*TLP* 6.4–41) discussed in the previous chapter (pp. 17–18). There Wittgenstein says that all propositions are of equal value, that value must lie outside the world, outside the accidental ('all happening and being the case'). Then, abruptly, in *TLP* 6.42 he says: 'And so it is impossible for there to be propositions of ethics.' However abrupt this statement is, the logical nexus is clear. If propositions picture facts, and if facts are about what is *in* the world, what makes up its composition? If, on the other hand, expressions of value do not picture what is in the world, it follows that there can be no propositions of ethics (as Wittgenstein uses that term 'proposition'). In the same entry (though it seems to belong to the next) he says: 'Propositions can express nothing that is higher.' In the next entry (*TLP* 6.421) he says:

> It is clear that ethics cannot be put into words.
> Ethics is transcendental.

We have here three features of what Wittgenstein understood ethics to be: (1) there are no propositions of ethics; (2) ethics is inexpressible; and (3) the ethical is transcendental.

The first of these follows logically from Wittgenstein's notion of a proposition. For him, not only can a proposition be true or false, but *only* a proposition can be true or false, and only what can be true or false is a proposition. Moreover, truth and falsity depend on conformity with the facts, with what is the case. 'A proposition is an expression of agreement and disagreement with truth-possibilities of elementary propositions' (*TLP* 4.4). Ethics is not about facts. Hence, there are no propositions of ethics. Hence, ethical pronouncements cannot be true or false. But, in saying this, is not Wittgenstein flying in the face of common sense and ordinary usage?

From the beginning of recorded time – Egyptian, Babylonian, Hebrew, Hittite – Oriental writings are full of propositions of ethics: 'It is wrong to steal your neighbour's ass'; 'Blessed is he who forgives'; 'The righteous are at peace'. Admittedly more often than not ethics takes the form of commands, prohibitions, exhortations and admonitions; but there are a sufficient number of categorical, apodictic and assertorial propositions to make the notion that there can be no propositions of ethics sound questionable. Those propositions I have mentioned – and there are hundreds more – are either true or false like any other. Either it is or is not wrong to take one's neighbour's ass unlawfully; either it is true or false that he who forgives is blessed or that the righteous are at peace. This is obviously correct. Everyone would agree it is false to say that to rape a child, to kill a harmless old lady, to take what money you can from whatever source is perfectly permissible and to be applauded if you can get away with it. Everyone would accept these unquestionable facts. From this the obvious conclusion is that for Wittgenstein to say there can be no propositions of ethics, that ethical statements are neither true nor false but nonsensical, seems itself nonsensical (in the ordinary sense of the word).

I agree with this view of propositions of ethics i.e. I believe they can be true or false, and, moreover, that for ethics and morality it is most important to know which they are. Anyone who doubts the falsity of the proposition that the Aryans are a superior race and that Jews, Negroes, gypsies and other inferior races must be exterminated is, to say the least, mistaken. Still, I think that Wittgenstein's philosophical analysis has something in its favour, apart from being consonant with his own theory of ethics and of propositions. For one thing – though he is often ambiguous about this and shifts back and forth – what he has in mind in his statement about propositions is an *ethical theory*. In Wittgenstein's view there can be no ethical theory. He would also exclude general principles such as those I have instanced above. Even if they can be called true or false in some sense, they are not true or false statements of *fact* because they are not statements about how the world happens to be. At best, they are statements about how it ought or ought not to be; but as such they are not statements of how it *is*, that is, statements of fact.

This is clear from the examples I have given. An elaborate description such as we get in courts of law may establish that someone took from another person something that did not belong to him. This may be regarded as a fact. But that it was *wrong* is not a fact of the same order. It is a judgement placed on the action. Similarly it may be possible to establish that someone forgave someone else, but to say that he is blessed on that account is not to state a fact of the same order. Being 'wrong' or 'blessed' are not facts in the way that being a dirty grey or a brilliant white are facts about the world. We have techniques for establishing whether these are facts that we do not have for establishing that deeds are wrong or blessed. As for the statement 'The righteous are at peace', it is hard to see how either of the terms of this equation can be facts. Admittedly, it may be a fact that England is currently at peace with Germany, but this is not what is meant. No doubt factual criteria could be found to establish *whether* someone was righteous and at peace, but not that he is 'righteous' and 'at peace' in the moral, as opposed to the psychological or social sense. So, whatever meaning one gives to the term 'proposition' and whatever one's view of the possible truth or falsity of expressions of ethical value, it must be conceded that Wittgenstein has a point when he says dramatically there can be no propositions of ethics. He draws attention in his own fashion to the peculiarity of ethical utterances.

When Wittgenstein goes on to say that ethics cannot be spoken about (*aussprechen*) because propositions cannot express (*ausdrücken*) what is higher than facts, he is again consistent with his own theory of language. But does what he says make sense? Surely, even if they may not be factual, ethical expressions are expressions and ethics can be spoken about. Even if the expression 'It is a morally good thing to be kind' may not be either true or false in the way the proposition 'The plank is five feet long' is true or false, surely it can at least be expressed and spoken about. Indeed, Wittgenstein himself constantly speaks about ethical matters and expresses ethical ideas. He could reply that the moral expression quoted above says absolutely nothing; it does not refer to anything. Kindness is not a thing nor a quality of things in the world that can be pointed out, demonstrated or described. What kindness is can be conveyed obliquely only, by means of examples, and also by contrasting examples: i.e. by showing what it is not to be kind or to be positively unkind. Often, many examples are needed, since the same action may be kind in one context and unkind in another. It may be kind to give a child a bag of sweets and unkind to take sweets from a child in one set of circumstances, and yet unkind not to take them away if he is gorging himself and making himself ill. In that case kindness would consist in gently taking them away with reassurances that they will be returned later. If this is an acceptable interpretation of what Wittgenstein is saying, seen from outside, as it were, it is one to which we could subscribe. But once again I would try to find a less dramatic and paradoxical term than 'inexpressible'. However, the term has shock value, be it a trifle unintelligible on first encounter.

Finally, there is ethics as transcendental. 'Transcend' means to 'surmount, pass or lie beyond a limit, exceed'. Its use in philosophy has been various. It usually means going beyond either perceptual or conceptual boundaries. Traditionally the so-called transcendentals were those concepts or ideas that belong to no particular category but that can be applied to all categories: concepts such as 'being', 'something', 'unity'.

In the context of *TLP* 6.41 it is clear that in calling ethics 'transcendental' Wittgenstein is doing no more than reiterating the contents of that entry. What is outside the world, as value, and, hence, ethics is, transcends the world and, hence, is transcendental. Earlier (*TLP* 6.13) he says: 'Logic is transcendental'. By this he clearly means that logic is concerned with the structure of the world as a whole; not with facts but with the totality of facts. The transcendentality of ethical, aesthetic and religious expression is not identical with that of logic and mathematics. They do not mirror the structure of the world. They treat the world as a whole: they transcend the facts of the world. They are, like the medieval transcendentals, applicable to everything and so to nothing in particular. They do not refer to classes, categories, genera or species that comprise the world of things. Like Kant's transcendentals that not only transcend experience as the necessary conditions *a priori* of its possibility, but also attempt to transcend both space and time and the categories that make the world intelligible, Wittgenstein's transcendentals are an attempt to go beyond the bounds of language and say what cannot be said. Like Kant, who said of thoughts without content that they are empty, but unlike the Transcendentalists who believed we can have knowledge of what is beyond possible experience, Wittgenstein regarded these attempts to go beyond the bounds of sense as nonsensical. And yet, like Kant, who found it necessary to postulate Ideas of Reason, Wittgenstein found it necessary to regard ethics as transcendental.

An entry (*TLP* 6.422), which will hardly detain us, makes Wittgenstein's conception of ethics clearer. Ethics, he says, has nothing to do with rewards and punishments. The consequences of actions are not necessarily relevant to their morality. However, he is prepared to concede there may be 'consequences', 'rewards' and 'punishments', in a sense, but 'at least these consequences should not be events'. He concedes this because he thinks there must be something in the response to the imperative 'thou shalt . . .': 'And what then, if I don't do it?' In his opinion this 'reward' or 'punishment' lies in the action itself; it is not consequential on it. He adds that the reward must be agreeable and the punishment disagreeable. (This latter is in parenthesis, so it may be taken as no more than the meaning Wittgenstein gives to reward and punishment in this context.)[2]

This excludes the more crassly pragmatic forms of so-called Christian ethics beloved of certain elements of nonconformity and certain strains in Catholicism and Protestantism. If the *only* reason why someone behaves in a certain way is because he knows if he does not he is liable to be punished, either here on earth, by the civil (or perhaps military) authority or power, or in another place, his behaviour, though wise – and to that extent moral – is pragmatic rather than moral. No doubt rewards and, particularly, punishments have their uses in helping to inculcate a moral sense, but in this respect they are in themselves no more moral than beating a dog if it misbehaves, and giving it food if it behaves as we wish.

But what of consequentialism in its most common and widespread version, Utilitarianism? This question is more difficult to answer than might at first appear. Wittgenstein was no Utilitarian. But the question here is whether he excludes all consequences of actions from ethical consideration. He certainly excludes such consequences as being hanged or going to Hell or being given a peerage or going to Heaven. But what of the consequences of one's actions, such as not hurting someone's feelings if at all possible, as opposed to riding roughshod over everybody's feelings if they get in your way? I believe that personally Wittgenstein would have abhorred the latter. Theoretically he seems neutral. In other words, he seems not to have given the matter much thought either way. What he is sure about – and in this he was right – is that consequences such as reward and punishment have nothing to do with morality as such. I shall have more to say later on the question of Utilitarianism.

Lastly a word on the parenthesis. It has been variously translated: 'acceptable' and 'unacceptable' (Ogden), 'pleasant' and 'unpleasant' (Pears and McGuinness) and 'agreeable' and 'disagreeable' (me). There may not be much between us. But I should like to give my preference. If I were prepared to be killed rather than betray a principle or a colleague, I should find it neither acceptable nor pleasant, though it would be agreeable to find that for once in my life I had done something worthwhile. Not until after the last moment could I be pleased with myself and then it would be too late.

Consistent with saying that no value exists in the world, that value is outside the whole sphere of what happens and is the case, outside what is accidental (*TLP* 6.41), Wittgenstein in *TLP* 6.43 goes on to say:

> If the good or bad exercise of the will does alter the world, it can alter it only at the limits of the world, not the facts – not what can be expressed in language.
> In short the effect must be that it becomes an altogether different world. It must, so to speak, wax and wane as a whole.
> The world of the happy man is a different one from that of the unhappy man.[3]

Here we have five new ideas: (1) the good and bad exercise of the will; (2) good and bad will altering the world; (3) not, however, altering the facts in the world but altering it at its limits; (4) these alterations waxing and waning (in the German text it is the converse); and (5) the notions of the happy and the unhappy man corresponding to the man of good and bad will respectively. In effect only two new ideas have been introduced: those of the good and bad will, or, more precisely, that of the part the will plays in ethics; and the notion of happiness as a criterion (or symptom) of a good or bad will. The other ideas follow from the fact that ethics is a value and from what Wittgenstein has already said about values: that it is outside the world and cannot be expressed.

The most puzzling of these ideas, perhaps, is the notion of the good or bad will altering the world at its limit and as a whole, but not altering the facts of the world. The ordinary view is that ethical decisions do just that. Empirical decisions, it is true, change the world by changing certain facts. These can be as portentous as Caesar's decision to cross the Rubicon or as trivial as a decision to have one's hair cut. But the decision of the mobsters to gun down their rivals in a Chicago garage on St Valentine's Day 1929, though an empirical decision leading to an historical fact – the St Valentine's Day massacre – was also a moral decision to do evil. Yet, according to Wittgenstein, the morality of that decision, its bad will, is not a fact along with the fact of the massacre and its attendant circumstances. Nor can it be expressed through propositions.

But surely, it will be objected, this is not so? First, the bad will shown by the mobsters of the St Valentine's Day massacre is evident: they had decided and intended to commit a mass murder. Secondly, we can express this through language, as I have just done. Wittgenstein, however, would say: no. It is not evident that what the mobsters did was evil. It might equally well have been good. But, more importantly, their decision to do it may have been morally good; misguided, perhaps, but still good in the sense they thought this was the morally right thing to do under the circumstances. The Maquis in France might have done something similar in 1944. The goodness or badness of the action lies *outside* the action. No action is in itself either good or evil, not torture or lingering death by burning or starvation, nor betrayal or exploitation or discrimination or vilification; nor any of the other actions taken to be intrinsically evil. It is not that in certain circumstances they might be good actions if they resulted from a good will: it is simply that the will, good or bad, is not a part of the event. There are no events that are *in themselves* good or bad. They are merely occurrences, happenings, events in the world. Their goodness or badness depends on the good or bad will of the person deciding to bring about the event; this, according to Wittgenstein, is not a fact along with other facts.

But, it will be objected, surely it is a fact like other facts in being *a decision*. The mobsters' decision, if it was evil, was an evil decision; that surely is a fact. In being a decision, Wittgenstein would agree, it is a fact, but a psychological fact. The mobsters decided to kill their rivals. But *that it was evil is not a fact*. It is a *judgement placed upon a fact*. There are no factual criteria to move us to a moral judgement. All the facts are there: the mobsters gunned down their victims who had been lured into the garage. But that what they did was an evil deed, if it was, is not a fact among other facts, otherwise the work of courts would be relatively easy. It is a judgement *on* the facts, and, to that extent is *outside* the facts.

However, it has to be admitted that Wittgenstein is pretty isolated in his view. He is poles apart from the naturalistic ethics of the Aristotelian, Hedonist or Utilitarian varieties, which hold that ethics can be explained in terms of a tendency towards ultimate happiness (*summum bonum*) or the highest degree of pleasure or the correct balance of pleasure over pain, either for oneself or others. Though Wittgenstein would be ranked as an ethical subjectivist, he is certainly not an Emotivist of the Humean persuasion, nor, at that time at least, an Ethical Relativist. He obviously has affinities with Moore and Kant. With the former he eschews reductionism: the good cannot, for him any more than for Moore, be reduced to non-ethical properties of actions. But with Moore, goodness seems to be a property of an action, albeit unanalysable, and thus a fact, something in the world, which it is not for Wittgenstein. His view seems closer to Kant's, in so far as Kant sees moral imperatives as *a priori*, independent of the determination of nature and nothing to do with reward or punishment. Possibly his closest ally is William of Occam.[4]

Now we come to the more obscure part of the passage quoted above (*TLP* 6.43). This deals with the good or bad will changing the boundaries of the world, and the world, as a result, becoming entirely different, or, so to speak, shrinking and growing, or, like the moon, waning and waxing. I can only speculate as to what this means. The *Notebooks* (*NB* p. 73) contain some of this material, but throw little light on it apart from one most useful addition to the last sentence about waning and waxing.

The phrase is: 'as if through accretion or falling off of a meaning'.[5] This phrase gives us a clue but leaves one question unanswered. The way in which ethics changes the world and makes it entirely different is not by changing any facts in it but by changing our attitude to it. An event that in one context may be viewed as innocent, harmless, even good, if not exactly laudatory, may, in another context or brought about by a different person, be regarded as evil, vile and intolerable. The action as a *fact* has not changed; its *significance* has. But in what sense has the world changed, albeit at its boundaries? In what sense is it entirely different? Surely this is not too difficult to understand. The eating of an apple can change in a twinkling of an eye from being an innocent, even praiseworthy pursuit into an evil act, the eating of forbidden fruit. Its significance (*Sinn*) has changed. The key might be that it is not that the *whole world* changes – which clearly it does not: it doesn't change one bit – but that the world changes *as a whole*. I understand this to mean that someone with a bad will takes an entirely different view of the world from someone with a good will.

This can be illustrated by what happens when civil strife suddenly erupts into violence and murder, as we have seen happen recently in the Lebanon and Northern Ireland. In the initial stages there is rioting, fisticuffs and destruction of property but nobody gets killed. Killing is regarded as beyond the limit of the permissible. Then one day someone is killed deliberately, in cold blood. The spell is broken. Into a world where killing was wrong is injected the evil thought that murder is permissible or at least is going to be done regardlessly. As with communities, so with individuals. For years a person will pass through life committing petty misdemeanours – cheating, lying, pilfering, over-indulging – but the thought of murder is firmly excluded from his thoughts. Then, one day, the occasion and the opportunity arise. It may be jealousy, greed, a thirst for revenge. He commits the deed. The spell is broken. His world is changed: he is a murderer. He may repent and his world will change back again. He may accept his new status and go on to kill and kill again; or he may just remain unrepentant. Of course he may, and usually does, try to justify his attitude, at least to himself, particularly if he is a terrorist, who declares that all Muslims, Christians, Catholics, Protestants and Marxists or just innocent people going peaceably about their lawful business are enemies and legitimate targets. Here madness lies. But it remains that, at least in one respect, his world, and, for him, the whole world, has changed as a whole. Yet, in a sense, nothing *in* the world has changed. There has been a killing. That it was legitimate or deemed legitimate or illegitimate is not a fact about the world.

The question that is left unanswered is whether the waning and waxing, the shrinking and growing, the accretion and falling off of meaning may be taken to refer to good will (waxing, growing, accretion of meaning), on the one hand, and bad will (waning, shrinking and falling off of meaning) on the other. If so, what does this mean? Is it a description or merely a value judgement? I can only speculate. The reason for my hesitancy is that to equate the waxing, etc. with the good will makes sense, but to equate the waning and a falling off of meaning with the bad will seems to make the effect of the bad will too negative. However, if Wittgenstein is saying that the world whose bearer is a bad will is a diminished, narrow, miserable world, whereas the world whose bearer is a good will is expansive, broad and happy – and I think this is what he means – it makes sense. It also fits in nicely with the next entry. But before coming to that I should like to make a suggestion for which I can offer no independent support. It is this. By waxing and waning Wittgenstein may also have meant what I have been talking about, namely, about evil-doing and repentance, about the world being changed one way and then being changed back again. To do evil – real evil, not just something morally weak – one has to reject an attitude to the world, an understanding of it, a meaning, a way of viewing the value of human action. To repent is to return to one's former view of the world and acknowledge that one was wrong in rejecting it.

But why should doing evil be a shrinking of my world and a falling off of its meaning (*abnehmen oder zunehmen, Dazukommen oder Wegfallen eines Sinnes*)? Again I can only conjecture, but it seems to me that Wittgenstein is here making a traditional remark. He is saying that evil (bad will) is negative, a deprivation of being, and, hence, of meaning. Good, on the other hand, is positive, an increase in being, and, hence, an accretion of meaning. Evil is meaningless in every sense of the word. It is negative, pointless, unproductive spiritually or materially. Goodness, on the other hand, is not only positive but also meaningful, and productive, spiritually, and, possibly, materially too.

This fits in with the next remark of the entry (*TLP* 6.43): 'The world of the happy (fortunate, lucky) is a different one from that of the unhappy (unfortunate, unlucky).' It is clear from the *Notebooks* (*NB* particularly pp. 73–5, 77–8 and 81, 2.8.16, 13.8.16) that being happy is connected in Wittgenstein's mind consistently with a good will and being unhappy with a bad will. It might seem both obvious and banal to say that the person of good will is fortunate, lucky or happy (*glücklich*) or content, but it is not at all obvious that the person of bad will is unhappy, discontented and unfortunate, or, if he is, he usually does a good job at disguising it. Fortunately the *Notebooks* can help us out.

The reader must be reminded, however, that in resorting to ideas in the *Notebooks* not included in the *Tractatus* I may not be faithfully presenting Wittgenstein's thought at the time of the latter, so the interpretation is tentative, but, I think, tenable.

I shall take the remarks roughly as they are entered in the *Notebooks* and under the following headings: (1) happiness and the purpose of existence; (2) happiness in relation to the world; (3) happiness in relation to death; (4) happiness in relation to eternity; (5) conscience; and (6) happiness in relation to knowledge.

I shall have more to say about Wittgenstein's views on the purpose and problem of life later. Here I shall merely quote from some entries for 6.7.16 (*NB* p. 73):

> And Dostoevsky is indeed right in so far as he says that whoever is happy fulfils the purpose of existence.
> Or one could say also that he fulfils the purpose of existence who needs no purpose any more besides life (itself). That is to say, namely, (one) who is content.

But what is the source of that contentment? This is the next point. It consists in being in agreement with the world, which in turn consists in being in agreement with an alien will, which turns out to be the will of God. More of God and the alien will later. Here I shall merely quote one sentence: 'In order to live happily I must be in harmony with the world, and that indeed *is called* "to be happy".' But in what does this harmony and agreement consist? Wittgenstein cannot say because there is nothing to say. Here entries for 30.7.16 (*NB* pp. 78–9) should be quoted at length:

> I always come back again to this: that the happy life simply is good, and the unhappy is bad. And if I *now* ask: but *why* exactly should I have to live happily, then it seems to me that this itself is like a tautological form of question; it seems that the happy life is self-justifying, that it *is* the only right life.
> All this is in a certain sense, truly, deeply mysterious! *It is clear* that ethics does not *allow* itself to be expressed.
> But one could speak thus; the happy life seems in some sense to be more *harmonious* than the unhappy. But in what sense?
> What is the objective feature of the happy, harmonious life? It is again clear that there can be no such feature that can be *described*.
> This feature cannot be a physical, but only a metaphysical, a transcendental one.
> Ethics is transcendental.

This appears to be some kind of intuitionism, which is hard to doubt. And it is a very rarefied intuitionism that cannot even be spoken about. But, then, as Wittgenstein says about that which cannot be spoken about in 6.522 of the *Tractatus*: 'There are, of course, those things that cannot be spoken about. These *show* (*manifest*) themselves.'

One of the signs that Wittgenstein singles out as a manifestation of the happy or unhappy life is our attitude to death. In entries for 8.7.16 we find the following: 'Whoever is happy must have no fear. Not even of death . . . Fear of death is the best sign of a false, i.e. bad life' (*NB* pp. 74–5). This is most important for an understanding of what Wittgenstein meant by being happy and unhappy. As we know, he had an obsession with death, particularly with suicide. But this criterion of happiness and unhappiness was not a personal matter. Nor, indeed, was it an original idea. It has a reasonably good pedigree in devotional literature, to say nothing of evangelical and missionary preaching. And it has biblical foundations: witness the rich man who fills his barn lest he go short of grain, only to find that death of another kind is upon him. It might be an exaggeration to say that Wittgenstein's insight – bad will=unhappiness =fear of death; good will=happiness=no fear of death – is profound, but it is an insight for all that. However, even if the equation is correct, there are different reasons for fearing death and different senses of 'afraid of death'. Take the latter first: one may fear the fact of death as something that brings an untimely end to one's life and one's annihilation; or as something that brings one face to face with one's maker, with possible unpleasant consequencs. On the other hand, one may have no fear of the aftermath of death but fear the manner of dying. The latter is compatible with being happy, i.e. being good, in Wittgenstein's sense, as we shall see. But as to the former – which, incidentally, provide some of the reasons for fearing death – it does not seem they are necessarily connected with a bad will. It is true that certain kinds of evil-doing such as robbery, fraud, murder for gain, murder for power or lying to escape ignominy would be pointless if one did not hope to survive. But it is not clear that killing for revenge or lying out of spite imply a fear of death. However, to be fair to Wittgenstein, what he said was that fear *in the face of death* is the best *sign* of a false, i.e. bad life; not that it is an infallible sign or symptom in all circumstances.

Yet we are entitled to ask the converse question: is the absence of the fear of death the best sign of a true, i.e. a good, life? Once more I have to admit that my interpretation is speculative. But I think the absence of fear of death is a sign of a good life in Wittgenstein's mind. And this verdict will be supported by what is to follow. Against it one can only argue that there are certain fanatics, hoodlums, suicidal maniacs and world-weary Sybarites, who have no fear of death but positively welcome it as furthering a cause, or because they don't care about anything, or because they want relief from life one way or another. Are these, then, good people, with good wills, leading good lives? And, moreover, are they happy? I very much doubt that Wittgenstein would have thought so. So the absence of a fear of death, though it may be a necessary, is not a sufficient condition for the happy, true, good life.

Another necessary condition, however, may also be sufficient. It is certainly beyond the reach of fanatics, hoodlums, suicidal maniacs and the world-weary. It is that one should not live *in* time or *for* time, but in the eternal present. Its connection with the foregoing condition is obvious. The person who lives in the eternal present need have no fear of death; in St Paul's words: 'Death has no dominion over him.' In the entry for 8.7.16 Wittgenstein says: 'Only he who lives, not in time, but in the present, is happy. For life in the present there is no death. Death is not an event in life. It is not a fact of the world' (*NB* pp. 74–5). What death is in Wittgenstein's view will be discussed later. Here we are concerned with living in the present and its connection with eternity and with ethics. At this point the *Tractatus* and the *Notebooks* coincide. The *Tractatus* entry goes: 'If one understands by eternity not unending temporal duration, but timelessness, then he lives in eternity who lives in the present' (*TLP* 6.4311). This is not an original thought of Wittgenstein's. It goes back in tradition to Augustine, Boëthius, Aquinas and the Scholastics. It is also to be found in Oriental spiritual and mystical writing.

Now, you may ask: how can someone living in time also live in eternity and, moreover, in the eternal present? In one sense it cannot be done. Today becomes yesterday, tomorrow becomes today and then yesterday and so on. But certain values survive the passage of time. One of these is a good will; another is a promise to be kept; another a debt that can never be fully repaid. There are many more. These are timeless and, consequently, spaceless. The ethically good person views the world *sub specie aeternitatis*. This means two things. First, it means that an action is not judged solely on its temporal value and the temporal advantage or gain it may bring. Robbing a bank may be good because of the easy money it brings and all that it can buy. But it may also be bad because of the risk involved, particularly if it is armed robbery, and the possibility of a long jail sentence. Neither of these considerations, however, are moral. Nor are they, in themselves, immoral, any more than it is either moral or immoral in itself to draw money out of our deposit account in order to buy a car or go on holiday. When we view these actions morally, we do not take into account the temporal circumstances but judge them to be good or bad irrespective of these circumstances. What makes an action morally bad, an action such as committing armed robbery, is not the risks involved and the possible unpleasant consequences. There are other considerations. What these are, as Wittgenstein and Kant before him, have said, is difficult, if not impossible, to describe in general terms. But they are certainly not pragmatic, not concerned with the here-and-now practical advantages or disadvantages. And if I understand Wittgenstein correctly, the person of bad will does not live in the eternal present. He or she is concerned with the future, with temporal gain and advantage. This is the second meaning of viewing actions *sub specie aeternitatis*. Moral action is, in the words of the Gospel, to take no thought for the morrow, for impending disaster nor solely for what advantage can come from a present action.

Thus we are back again with the notion of being in harmony with the world, with the alien will, and with having no fear of death. 'For life in the present there is no death' (*NB* p. 75). This is not rhetoric on Wittgenstein's part. He is obviously not saying that good people do not die. He is saying they are not preoccupied with death. They live for the day; when they come to die, they die, and that's that. Here we can return to the *Tractatus* (6.4311): 'Death is not an event of life. One does not live to experience death.' Ogden translates this as: 'Death is not lived through'; Pears and McGuinness translate it as: 'we do not live to experience death'. Both are perfectly good translations. Ogden's caused a bit of bother (and a piece of music by Elizabeth Lutyens). All Wittgenstein is saying is that one does not experience death any more than one *experiences* going to sleep. Incidentally, this sentence does not appear in the *Proto-Tractatus*. It appears in embryo in the *Notebooks* (*NB* p. 75) as: 'It is not a fact of the world'. It is interesting that Wittgenstein might first have thought of it as not being a fact of *my* world, which, of course, it is not; but he then realized that it is, after all, a fact of the world, even if I come to be buried anonymously in a communal grave. So eventually for '*ist keine Tatsache der Welt*' he substitued '*erlebt man nicht*'. But the point is still clear. Death *comes* to the person of good will, the happy, contented person: he neither fears nor courts it.

A few matters need to be cleared up before we move on. First, it is hardly necessary to say that Wittgenstein's notion of living in the present has little, if anything, to do with the hedonist notion 'eat, drink and be merry for tomorrow we die', *carpe diem* ('grab what you can today'), even in its most subtle and seductive version in Herrick's 'To Virgins, to Make Much of Time' – 'Gather ye rosebuds while ye may ...'. Indeed, it is diametrically opposed to such a view. The hedonistic notion of living for the day is immersed in the temporal – 'Old Time is still aflying' – and the fear of old age and death, which are rapidly catching up, is quite the opposite of what Wittgenstein meant by living in the eternal present. In his eternal present there is no need to grab at anything passing: all that is of value is permanently present. But it may be objected that the next meal, the mortgage or the rent, the children's education have all to be taken care of and are not, one hopes, in the permanent present. This is the other side of the coin: how to live in the eternal present and still *provide* for the future. I do not know how Wittgenstein would have coped with this question, but it should not have caused him much difficulty. Morally speaking, living in the present and providing for the future do not pose a problem. It is part of living *in* the present – as opposed to living *for* the present in a hedonistic way – that one should provide for one's dependants and generally fulfil one's obligations.

Granted this, it can still be asked how a good person can be *happy, in harmony with an alien will* and *live in the present* with no money to buy food for his or her family, with, in famine areas, no food to buy, or money to pay the rent or buy clothes, when one is suffering from an incurable disease, estranged from a spouse, or on the run from the police as a subversive. Psychologically it would border on the heroic. It would certainly be exceptional, though such people can be found. Yet Wittgenstein is unperturbed. I shall return to this in the next chapter, when dealing with the ethical will. But first a word must be said about conscience.

Conscience appears in the entries for 8.7.16 (*NB* p. 75). Some of these will be discussed in a later chapter. The ones that are relevant here are:

> It is certainly right to say: Conscience is the voice of God.
> For example: it makes me unhappy to think that I have offended this or that person. Is this my conscience?
> Can one say: 'Act according to your conscience, whatever it may be'?

To these should be added part of another entry, which begins: 'When my conscience throws me off balance'. The idea, if I understand it correctly, is that (a) there are those who perform morally bad acts but are not conscious of or do not reflect on the fact, or do not care that they do so. These people are unhappy but they are unaware of their unhappiness. Then (b) there are those who are conscious that they are behaving in an off-balance way; it is not as it should be. In that case their unhappy state reaches consciousness and they feel unhappy. Their consciences nag them. Wittgenstein gives the relatively mild, but not trivial, example of feeling bad about having offended or insulted someone, presumably knowingly and willingly.

All these entries are tentative, in the form of questions, apart from the surprisingly apodictic remark that conscience is the voice of God. This may not be a bad place to discuss something that must have been lurking somewhere, if not in the forefront, of many readers' minds: namely, the different attitudes to death of a believer and an unbeliever. A believer, particularly a Christian – but it goes for members of other faiths as well – has greater reason to fear death than an unbeliever, or so it would seem. While the unbeliever may be unhappy because he has acted contrary to his own standards of behaviour or those of the society that he accepts, and he may fear death as an end to his worldly desires and ambitions, morally he is ultimately answerable only to himself; his fear of death is fear of annihilation, of his life coming to an end. But that is in a way consoling compared with the unhappiness of the believer whose conscience is truly the voice of God telling him that he has offended not only a fellow human but God himself and that unless he repents divine retribution awaits him after death. This again raises the point about rewards and punishments. If the sinner repents solely in order to avoid damnation, that may be a religious act, but is it a moral or ethical act? I think Wittgenstein would say it is not. Conversely, is a person who does good acts and avoids bad ones solely to avoid damnation acting ethically and so is he happy in the Wittgensteinian sense? I think not: he is acting out of a fear of death and its aftermath.

If this is a correct interpretation, we have an asymmetry here. The person of bad will, the unhappy person, who is a believer, may have different or additional reasons for remorse from those of the unbeliever. But when it comes to the person of good will, the happy person, there is no difference between them. From the ethical point of view, it does not matter how he identifies the alien will, the world with which he is in harmony, nor how he regards death, whether as total annihilation or something he will survive. The simple fact is that he is in harmony with the world and with the alien will (whether they are identical or not); he has no fear of death and is not acting out of a desire for reward or fear of punishment, whether in this life or another.

Here it might be in order to make a further digression to discuss Wittgenstein's views on immortality. There is one longish entry in the *Tractatus* that should be quoted in full:

> The temporal immortality of the human soul, that is so to say, its everlasting survival after death, is not only in no way guaranteed; but, above all, this assumption not at all performs (the task) that one always wishes to accomplish with it. For will any riddle be solved through (the fact) that I survive perpetually? For is this everlasting life not just as puzzling as the present one? The solution of the riddle of life in space and time lies *outside* space and time. (*TLP* 6.4312)[6]

First, it must be said that this entry disposes of the notion that immortality solves any ethical problems. Wittgenstein raises a number of them. (1) Temporal immortality is by no means guaranteed. This is certainly true philosophically. Even Aquinas agrees about that. Whether its theological guarantees are watertight is open to question, though the overwhelming weight of current opinion seems to be that they are. (2) Even if it were true both philosophically and theologically, it would solve no problems of ethics or of the meaning of life. In fact, it would raise more problems than it would solve. What would it be for a temporal being to live endlessly? Theologians may say post-mortal existence would be different from mortal existence. It would have to be if it was to be endurably *for ever*. But that is not a solution to any ethical problem, though many people think it is. Some think that, if there is no afterlife, there are no moral restraints in this life. Adultery, fornication, robbery, torture, murder, exploitation, cheating, lying, deception, breach of promise: all would be permissible if one could get away with them. I presume that is why certain political regimes are hostile to religion. They think the threat of retribution in an afterlife puts moral restraints on one's activities in this. Restraints it may put. People may be inhibited from fear of divine retribution. But they are not *moral* restraints, as Wittgenstein understands morality. They are to do with rewards and punishments. (3) Ethics lies outside time and space, and therefore has nothing to do with immortality as continuing temporal existence.

We touched on this last point when discussing the eternal present, but the context of immortality adds something to it by way of consequences. First, if one lives in the eternal present, it does not matter whether one lives for ever or only for a day: the future as such is unimportant. Perhaps that is the bliss of everlasting life: we do not have to take thought for the morrow. But the point is that not taking thought for the morrow operates in the here-and-now, though presumably with greater difficulty. In other words, to be moral one has to be outside space and time both in this life and the next. Thus the notion of immortality does not solve any moral problem. Much less is immortality relevant to a theological view prevalent among Catholic theologians that one's moral status, and, hence, one's everlasting destiny, is, as it were, frozen at the moment of death. If one were not living in the eternal present at the moment of death, one could never live in it; and if one were living in it, one would live in it for ever. This view makes the notion of immortality totally irrelevant to ethics even if it remains relevant to religious belief.

A decade after finishing the *Tractatus*, and after he had returned to Cambridge, Wittgenstein delivered a lecture on ethics to a society known as The Heretics. In this he elaborated his ideas on ethics and religious belief as presented in the *Tractatus* and entered in the *Notebooks 1914–1916*.

The main theme of the lecture is a discussion of absolute value, but it begins with some attempts to define ethics. Wittgenstein initially adopts G. E. Moore's definition of ethics as 'the general inquiry into what is good'. But he wants to use 'ethics' in a wider sense than Moore's; as he says: 'in a sense in fact which includes what I believe to be the essential part of what is generally called aesthetics' (*PRv* p. 4). (This reminds us of *TLP* 6.421 and *NB* p. 77.) In fact, his definition is not one as ordinarily understood. In one way it looks forward to his method as described in *Investigations* and backwards to such medieval Conceptualists as Abelard and Occam.[7] It also resembles Sir Francis Galton's method of constructing a typical face by superimposing numerous photographs of people of a particular race. In the case of ethics what are superimposed are various synonymous descriptions such as: an inquiry into what is valuable, what is really important, the meaning of life, what makes life worth living and the right way of living. 'I believe,' Wittgenstein concludes, 'if you look at all these phrases you will get a rough idea as to what Ethics is concerned with' (*PRv* p. 5). This is a broad definition of ethics. It amounts to the whole of one's way of living and is not confined to deontological ethics, the ethics of duty, or to a narrowly teleological and eudemonic or goal-seeking ethics where the goal is some supreme good (*summum bonum*) one has to attain in order to achieve happiness. Happiness is intrinsic to the way of living. For Wittgenstein the ethical way of life is the one worth living, the right way to live. It informs everything one does: a view with which Aquinas would have concurred, since for him there are no morally neutral acts. Every action is either good or evil, and an act however trivial (brushing one's teeth or playing Pooh-sticks), which is untainted with evil, is morally good.

(Though Wittgenstein does not say so in his lecture, it is to be assumed that by being valuable, important, meaningful and right, Wittgenstein means, as he says elsewhere, that an action should be done for its own sake and not to gain reward or avoid punishment. This is not to say that acts performed for gain or to avoid unpleasant consequences are immoral but merely that their morality resides in the action done and not in consequences beneficial to the agent.)

Having established his definition or description of what he considers ethics to be, Wittgenstein goes on to discuss one of its chief characteristics: namely, that it is an expression of absolute value. He distinguishes between the 'absolute good' and 'good' in the trivial or relative sense. In the trivial or relative sense we talk of means to ends, of something being good *for* something. Thus, a good chair is one which 'serves a predetermined purpose'. 'In fact the word good in the relative sense simply means coming up to a predetermined standard' (*PRv* p. 5). To say that someone is a good pianist is to say that 'he can play pieces of a certain degree of difficulty with a certain degree of dexterity'. Similarly if it is important not to catch a cold, what is not to happen is a 'certain disturbance in my life', and if a road is the right road, it is 'the right road relative to a certain goal'. A characteristic of these kinds of judgement is that they can be rephrased as statements of fact. Thus, 'This is the right road to Granchester' can be rephrased as 'This road will get you to Granchester in the shortest time'. Moreover, in the case of relative judgements it makes sense to say, if one is bad at some activity, such as playing tennis, that one does not want to be any better. But this according to Wittgenstein does not hold where ethics is concerned:

> suppose I had told one of you a preposterous lie and he came up to me and said 'You're behaving like a beast' and then I were to say 'I know I behave badly, but I don't want to behave any better', could he then say 'Ah then that's all right'? Certainly not; he would say 'Well you *ought* to want to behave better.' (*PRv* p. 5)

In other words, an ethical judgement is not relative to some goal: it is absolute. It cannot be translated into a statement of fact plus a conditional: 'You ought not to tell a preposterous lie if . . .' There can be no content for the conditional clause. Wittgenstein does not say this, but it is obvious that he would not regard a statement with a content such as 'if you want to be trusted' or 'if you want to be respected in society' as part of an ethical judgement.

Wittgenstein thus presents the moral imperative in a novel way and draws some far-reaching conclusions. He says first that if someone were to write a book describing everything that ever happened or will happen in the world, it would not contain a single ethical proposition. A description of a murder in that book would be on the same level as the description of the falling of a stone. It would have no value-content whatsoever. The description might cause pain and rage (as did descriptions of the massacres in Beirut in 1982) but all you have are 'facts, facts and facts but no Ethics'. A book on ethics, if such a book were possible, would, in Wittgenstein's opinion, cause an explosion. Perhaps before attempting to expound his thoughts on this matter, it might be as well to quote him extensively:

> And now I must say that if I contemplate what Ethics would have to be if there were such a science, the result seems to me quite obvious. It seems

to me obvious that nothing we could think or say should be *the* thing . . . I can only describe my feelings by the metaphor, that, if a man could write a book on Ethics which really was a book on Ethics, this book would, with an explosion, destroy all other books in the world. (*PRv* p. 7)

This is potent stuff. Wittgenstein's reason for such a dramatic (or should we say melodramatic?) suggestion is as follows:

Our use of words in science and ordinary discourse is confined to natural meanings and to expressing facts. That is all they are capable of containing. To attempt to use them to express ethical thoughts is like trying to pour a gallon of water into a teacup. Our words only express facts. 'Ethics, if it is anything, is supernatural', that is, it does not have to do with *natural* meaning and sense. To talk ethically is like saying that there is 'the absolutely right road', down which '*everybody* on seeing it would, *with logical necessity* have to go, or be shamed for not going'.

Stating the notion of 'absolute good' or 'absolute value' more fully, Wittgenstein then continues:

And similarly the *absolute good*, if it is a describable state of affairs, would be one which everybody, independent of his tastes and inclinations, would *necessarily* bring about or feel guilty for not bringing about. (*PRv* p. 7)

He concludes:

And I want to say that such a state of affairs is a chimera. No state of affairs has, in itself, what I would like to call the coercive power of an absolute judge. (*PRv* ibid.)

If the notion of absolute good and absolute value is a chimera, what, Wittgenstein asks, do we all (including himself) have in mind, and what are we trying to express when we use the expressions 'absolute good' and 'absolute value'? He replies that it would be natural for him to recall cases in which he would certainly use these expressions. Doing this, he says, is like inviting an audience, as a self-chosen illustration to a lecture on the psychology of pleasure, to recall a typical situation in which they always felt pleasure. Someone might take as his stock example the sensation of walking on a fine summer's day. So when Wittgenstein wants to fix his mind on what he means by absolute or ethical value, one particular example always happens to present itself to him. It is his first and foremost example, his 'experience' *par excellence*, which is: wonder at the existence of the world. This is also mentioned in the *Notebooks* and the *Tractatus*. 'I will describe this experience in order, if possible, to make you recall the same or similar experiences, so that we may have common ground for our investigation (*PRv* p. 8).

In a later chapter I shall discuss the nature of this and other such experiences in greater detail in the context of the mystical. Here I shall confine my attention to their relationship with absolute value, absolute good and ethics. For reasons to be given later, they cannot be described. All Wittgenstein can do is to refer to them in such a way that those who have also had them would recognize what he was describing.

Besides wonder that anything exists, Wittgenstein cites two other experiences: that of feeling absolutely safe and that of feeling absolutely guilty; not just relatively safe or relatively guilty, but *absolutely* safe or guilty. How can these be instances of an 'experience' of absolute value and absolute good? And in what sense are they experiences? Wonder, feeling safe and feeling guilty are experiences. But how does one experience absolute good and absolute value? Let us say that 'absolute' is something like a feature or an attribute that accrues to these experiences. It is *how* they are experiences.

Thus, to wonder that *anything* exists is absolute in the sense that it is not like wondering that the sky is blue when it might be overcast. That would be relative. What would make it absolute is wondering that there is a sky, be it blue, overcast or whatever. Likewise to feel safe from anything whatsoever and not just from fire or earthquake, famine or public disorder, is to feel absolutely safe. And to feel guilty, not about this or that, but to be basically a wretch and someone who is ashamed of his very existence, is to feel guilty absolutely.

What has this to do with ethics? Ethics for Wittgenstein, as we have seen, is action viewed *sub specie aeternitatis*, outside the world and its happening: it is seeing the world as a whole. In a conversation in Moritz Schlick's house in 1930, Wittgenstein repeated the ideas expressed in his lecture. 'The facts of the matter,' he said, 'are of no importance for me. But what men mean when they say that "*the world is there*" is something I have at heart.' Friedrich Waismann asked him whether the existence of the world was connected with what is ethical. Wittgenstein replied:

> Men have felt there is a connection and they have expressed it thus: God the Father created the world; the Son of God (or the Word that comes from God) is that which is ethical. That the Godhead is thought of as divided and, again, as one being, indicates that there is a connection here. (*WWK* p. 118)

We are not told how Waismann, Schlick and the others at the conversation took this answer. That people should be able to make a connection between wonder that there is a world, with God the Father who created it, is straightforward enough. That they should connect this with God the Son, the Word who proceeds from God the Father, is also straightforward, and straightforwardly Johannine: 'In the beginning was the Word, and the Word was with God, and the Word was God . . . All things were made by him and without him nothing was made that was made' (John 1.1 and 3). But what is the connection between the Word and the ethical? A number of connections suggest themselves. The most obvious is the Word Incarnate, Jesus Christ, the supreme revelation of God's will and, hence, of the ethical. In creating the world through his Son, the Word, God the Father revealed his will, not in the world, but by and through and outside the world. After all, for Wittgenstein, the ethical, the happy life, is being in harmony with the world as a whole and with its happenings, and thus with the will of God. Hence, there is an ascent towards God from the ethical, through the world, to the Son and the Father.

But this still leaves the final sentence. That the distinction between the Father and the Son divides the Godhead, in some sense, is clear enough. But what of this thinking of it 'again as one'? And how does this indicate there is a connection between the existence of the world and the ethical? Thinking again of the Godhead as one could be nothing more than thinking of the one God of whom the Father and Son are two persons. But I feel that in Wittgenstein's mind there is more to it than that. It is this something more that indicates the connection between the existence of the world and the ethical. This something more might be no more than that, just as Father and Son are one Godhead (that is, the ethical (Son) and creator of the world (Father) are one and the same God), so the world and the ethical are one, and mutually interdependent in this sense. To marvel at the existence of the world is to take an ethical attitude towards it, and to take an ethical attitude towards the world involves wondering that there is one.

Whatever about this piece of exegesis, it is clear from the passage that wonder at the existence of the world was not an example of absolute value of which ethical value was another and different example. Wonder at the existence of the world must, if this passage is to make sense, be an example of absolute *or ethical* value, just as much as a sense of being invulnerable to the miseries of the world or feeling inadequate in the eyes of God. This brings Wittgenstein's ethics so close to religion as to be almost indistinguishable from it. As we shall see in chapter five on God, that seems to be the case.

At the end of his 'Lecture on Ethics' Wittgenstein says:

My whole tendency...was to run against the boundaries of language.
This running against the walls of our cage is perfectly, absolutely hopeless... Ethics... does not add to our knowledge in any sense. But it is a
document of a tendency in the human mind which I *personally* cannot help
respecting deeply and I would not for my life ridicule it. (*PRv* pp. 11–12.
My italics)

At that meeting in Schlick's house on 17 December 1930, Wittgenstein
is reported to have said:

> At the end of my lecture on ethics I spoke in the first person. I think that
> this is something very essential. Here there is nothing to be stated any
> more; all I can do is to step forth as an individual and speak in the first
> person... Running against the limits of language? Language is, after all,
> not a cage.
>
> All I can say is this: I do not scoff at this tendency in man; I hold it in
> reverence. And here it is essential that this is not a description of sociology
> but that I am speaking *about myself*. (*WWK* 117–18)

From these quotations it is clear that Wittgenstein (a) shared the
common tendency to run against the boundaries of language; (b) makes a
personal avowal that he does so; and (c) regards this as the essential way
of talking about ethics, since expressions of absolute value in general,
and of ethics in particular, are not statements of fact, not sociological
observations. One may ask why Wittgenstein did not treat absolute value
sociologically, i.e. why he did not simply report a tendency he found in
his fellow men. Whatever about religious values, he unquestionably
shared ethical and aesthetic values with them. But the reason seems to lie
deeper than that. For him, sociological and anthropological observations
can be superficial, limited merely to recording behaviour and attempting
some explanation, as often as not in quite inappropriate and insensitive
conceptual terms. To speak about absolute value one must have experienced it and understood it from within; otherwise the proper course is
silence. (In a later chapter the possibility of a lack of a moral sense or
'moral blindness' will be discussed.)

Although what is said about absolute value and the absolute good does
not (and cannot) have the objectivity of a statement of fact, neither is it
subjective in the sense of being idiosyncratic or eccentric. Though
Wittgenstein cannot describe his experiences of what he regards as
absolute value, he can appeal to others who have had the same or similar
experiences. To that extent his personal avowals are objective (or inter-
subjective, if that term is preferred).

It has been a source of surprise and wonder in certain quarters that

Wittgenstein deeply respected, held in reverence, did not scoff at or ridicule the tendency in human beings to run against the boundaries of language in talking about the absolute values of ethics, or even religious belief. This attitude is expressed with considerable vehemence by Kai Nielsen:

If he really believes ... that such talk is unintelligible, why should he have such a respect for those who ... give in to this tendency of the human mind? ... Why encourage a kind of ideology that rests on something that is incoherent ('beyond significant language')? Why, it might be thought, encourage man in his infantilism?[8]

The short answer to these questions is that Wittgenstein confessedly shared these 'infantile' views, at least where ethics is concerned. Moreover, as we saw in the previous chapter, ethical expressions are not unintelligible or incoherent on Wittgenstein's account. To be sure, they are not about facts. They lack truth value in the strict sense, i.e. they cannot be verified by empirical tests, and, in that sense of unintelligible, are unintelligible. To understand them one has to share a personal experience that cannot be described as one describes the size and qualities of a piece of timber.

It will be noted that at the end of his lecture Wittgenstein speaks of 'running against the walls of our cage', the cage being the boundaries of language. In the conversation reported by Waismann, however, Wittgenstein says that language is, after all, not a cage. What weight are we to give this discrepancy? Apart from the unlikely possibility that Waismann's notes were faulty, one can say (a) that Wittgenstein contradicted himself, (b) that he changed his mind in a remarkably short time, or (c) that he made a mistake. My preference is to reject all these suggestions and to rest my case on that short German word *ja* ('after all', 'indeed', and, of course, 'yes' – *Die Sprache ist ja kein Käfig*). As Wittgenstein himself might have said: language is in one sense a cage and in another sense not a cage. As a cage it sets limits and establishes boundaries to what can be said. We run up against these boundaries when we try to say what cannot be said in the manner in which we try to say it. But in another sense it is not a cage: by using it obliquely or by just running up against it, we can transcend it and make ourselves understood. We are still not 'saying' anything but we are communicating with one another and can, therefore, be understood.

At that same meeting in Schlick's house in 1930 Wittgenstein discussed Schlick's book on ethics which had recently been published. This discussion could be said to sum up Wittgenstein's views on value and ethics.

In his book Schlick distinguishes between two theological interpretations of moral goodness. One he calls in the German edition the 'shallower' (*flachere*) according to which an action is good if it is what God wills. The other interpretation, which he calls the 'deeper', is that the good is good in itself and, if God wills it, it is because it is good, not vice versa. Wittgenstein took exactly the opposite view:

> I think that the first interpretation is the profounder one: what God commands, that is good. For it cuts off any explanation 'why' it is good, while the second interpretation is the shallow, rationalist one, which proceeds 'as if' you could give reasons for what is good.
>
> The first conception says clearly that the essence of the good has nothing to do with facts and hence cannot be explained by any propositon. If there is any proposition expressing precisely what I think, it is the proposition 'What God commands, that is good.' (*WWK* p. 115)[9]

This is a long-standing debate in moral theology. Schlick states the stark antitheses of the two views, but there is much subtle argument surrounding both of them. The trend of modern opinion favours Schlick's naturalistic view, though not, perhaps, the view to which Wittgenstein objected. But there are moral theologians who hold this view and yet realize that, if there is to be a moral imperative and if it is not to stand alone and unjustified, as does Kant's categorical imperative, there must be a command of some kind; a divine ordinance seems as good a candidate as any.

Such a view goes some way towards mollifying the seeming arbitrariness of Wittgenstein's view. He is not committed to saying that anything that God arbitrarily decides is good is *eo ipso* good, as though actions that we consider evil could become good if he commanded them. On the other hand, there is the case of God's injunction to Abraham to sacrifice Isaac which was later rescinded. This, to say the least, smacks of arbitrariness in moral matters.

Fortunately, it is not necessary to decide this matter in order to grasp the point Wittgenstein is trying to make. Whether or not God could or would command only what we ourselves would regard as good and right, there is still an important difference between deriving one's notions of good and evil from the commands and prohibitions of God and deriving them by some other means. Schlick's second position is shallower than the first, according to Wittgenstein, because it implies we can give an explanation why an action is morally good, an explanation in terms of facts and expressed in propositions. The only proposition that Wittgenstein will allow – 'the good is what God commands' – cuts off the road to an explanation of why an action is good. The whole burden of the 'Lecture on Ethics' is that ethical or absolute value has nothing to do with facts, and is inexpressible and nonsensical, unlike relative, practical value and trivial good, which concern facts and can be expressed in propositions. But surely not all our ethical beliefs and principles are derived from God's commands and prohibitions? Wittgenstein is not committed to saying they are. All he is saying is that if one had to choose between saying that an action is good because God commands it and saying that one can explain why certain actions are good in some other way, the only position to choose would be the first. It will be noted that he is tentative when he says: '*If* there is a proposition that exactly expresses what I mean, that proposition is: good is what God commands' (my italics).

Wittgenstein has a few interesting remarks about value which in part follow from what we have been discussing, as, indeed, from much of what has been said in the previous chapter. They are concerned with theory and explanation. Is value, Wittgenstein asks, a particular state of mind or a form inhering in certain data of consciousness? He replies that he would reject any answer, any explanation of what value is, 'and that not because the explanation was false but because it was an *explanation*'. Likewise with theory.

> If I were told anything that was a *theory*, I would say, No, no! That does not interest me. Even if this theory were true, this would not interest me.
>
> *For me* a theory is without value. A theory gives me nothing. (*WWK* pp. 116–17)

Wittgenstein sums up his attitude to ethical theory by saying: 'If I could explain the ethical only by means of a theory, then what is ethical would be of no value whatsoever.'

In later chapters I shall discuss Wittgenstein's views both on the teaching of ethics and his personalist approach to talking about it. Suffice to say here that both eke out his account of it as inexpressible. They follow logically from that notion. What is inexpressible (i.e. unstatable) cannot be taught as we teach carpentry or grammar or even logic. They can be inculcated only by examples. These examples will inevitably be personal, but not necessarily subjective in an idiosyncratic sense. Anyone giving a personal view on what is good and evil, right and wrong, will hope and indeed expect that these views will be shared by others, that they will find a common ground in spite of the fact that this common ground is not factual, and, hence, not scientific, as Schlick would have wished.

The discussion of Schlick's ethics is most useful in focusing Wittgenstein's ethical views. Pre-eminently, in his view, ethics *as such* had nothing to do with facts, with what happens to be, with events in the world *as such*. It transcends the world of facts and happenings, of what is or is not the case. It is outside the world of events and happenings. It cannot, therefore, be expressed in propositions, since they are concerned with what *can be* and with what *is or is not*, whereas ethics is concerned with what *must be*. To that extent it is inexpressible. In making ethical judgements one is not stating what *is* the case in the world but rather what *ought to be* or *ought not to be* the case. This 'ought' is not relative and conditional. Ethics does not say that if you want to achieve Z you must do X or Y. It is an absolute imperative. It shows (but does not state), by means of examples, how a human being should behave in certain circumstances. Its views, like those of an art critic giving his verdict on a work of art, are presented for *general* agreement by way of these examples; yet they are expressed as personal but *not individual* or subjective opinions. They are such as can and, in the opinion of the moralist, should be generally accepted. Acceptance of moral principles is not a matter of proof in any strict sense, but of agreement, of persuasion, of getting people to see things a certain way.

This is how I understand Wittgenstein's ethics, and I shall discuss them further in the final chapter. But first I shall continue the exposition with a presentation of what is as important to his notion of ethics as anything in this chapter: his notion of the ethical will.

3

The Ethical Will

In the previous chapter the question of being happy (the morally good state) while living in misery was raised and postponed. It was postponed so that it could be put into the context of Wittgenstein's treatment of the ethical will, or, to be more accurate, the part played by the will in ethical matters and what will is at play. Wittgenstein distinguishes between the psychological will of which we are conscious in desiring, deciding, refusing to act and such like, and the metaphysical will (though he does not call it that), the Will, of which we are not directly conscious: 'It is impossible to speak about the will in so far as it is the subject of ethical attributes. And the will as a phenomenon is of interest only to psychology' (*TLP* 6.423).

But, first, to return to the question of being happy while living in physical or psychological misery.

The following entry was made by Wittgenstein in his *Notebooks* on 13 August 1916 (when he was serving in Galicia and winning decorations for bravery in an artillery regiment):

> Suppose that man could not exercise his will, but had to suffer all the misery of this world, then what would make him happy?
>
> How can man be happy at all, since he cannot ward off the misery of this world?
>
> Through the life of knowledge.
>
> The good conscience is the happiness that the life of knowledge preserves.
>
> The life of knowledge is the life that is happy in spite of the misery of the world.
>
> The only life that is happy is the life that can renounce the amenities of the world.
>
> To it the amenities of the world are so many graces of fate. (*NB* p. 81)

These remarks echo ideas found in Oriental philosophies and in Western philosophy since Plato. They reiterate the ascetic notion that one can overcome adversity by knowledge. Wittgenstein, in his usual way, does not quote his sources, but here his ethics is closest to that of Schopenhauer and, indirectly, Spinoza. Schopenhauer wrote, in *The World as Will and Representation*, of the moral, the happy, man:

> Nothing can alarm him any more, nothing can excite him; for he has cut all the thousand threads of will that bind us to the world, and which in the form of appetite – fear, envy, rage – drag us this way and that in constant pain.

Spinoza devotes most of Part V of his *Ethics* to the same theme. His aim, as he tells us in *De intellectus emendatione* (*The Emendation of the Understanding*) was to find out whether there was anything that could communicate itself to him in such a way as to enjoy 'continuous, supreme and unending happiness'. He found it in what he called the third kind of knowledge (the 'intellectual love of God') by which we come to understand that whatever happens had to happen 'determined by an infinite chain of causes to existence and action' (*Prop*. vi). For Spinoza, once we realize that the vicissitudes of life occur of necessity, that we cannot influence them, we cease to fear them, rage at them or grieve over them; so we are happy and at peace. This is, ultimately, a version of Stoicism; but it is not necessary to go back so far in time.

There is, however, an important difference between Spinoza and Schopenhauer. Spinoza claims to know what kind of knowledge will make someone happy. It is knowledge of the chain – the *infinite* chain – of causes leading to actions and states of affairs. What Schopenhauer has in mind is not so much knowledge as an attitude of mind towards the vicissitudes of life. It could, but need not, include a belief that everything that happens had to happen anyway. For Schopenhauer, and certainly, in my opinion, for Wittgenstein, the 'life of knowledge' is not knowledge that what happens had to happen, and for that reason one should not be disturbed about what happens, and so remain happy and content. It is an attitude of detachment, renunciation and defiance towards both life's miseries and its amenities or comforts. Just as the miseries are unavoidable, so the amenities and comforts of life must be regarded as pieces of good luck, as graces or favours granted to us by fate. This repeats an earlier entry, of 11 June 1916 (*NB* p. 73):

> I cannot direct the happenings of the world according to my will, but am completely powerless.
>
> I can only make myself independent of the world – and so in a certain sense dominate it – in so far as I renounce any influence on the happenings.

Now, apart from the difficulty of acting as Wittgenstein describes, is he not exaggerating, or advocating some form of fatalism? It simply is not true that we cannot ward off the misery of the world, cannot direct the happenings of the world and are completely powerless. Not only can we, but we do it all the time. We plant crops to avoid starvation, wear protective clothing to avoid getting wet, build houses for shelter and warmth. Of course we are hardly ever in complete control of the happenings in the world. Excessive rain or frost or drought may ruin the crops; an earthquake may destroy our homes; we may get caught up in wars and civil strife and be subject to all the ills that flesh is heir to. But even if we do not have complete control over our destiny, we are not completely powerless either. If one were to take Wittgenstein literally, the human race should never have survived. I do not think for a moment that Wittgenstein is advocating pessimism – though his view of the world is tinged with Schopenhauerian pessimism – or fatalism leading to indolence and despair. Rather, he is cautioning against a foolish, egoistical and egotistical, attitude towards the world, and doing so in a somewhat dramatic and rhetorical manner. He is proposing the correct attitude as he sees it, the ethically good way, the way of the happy person.

In view of Wittgenstein's analysis of our attitudes to the miseries of the world and its happenings, the bad, the unhappy, will could manifest itself in two opposing ways. On the one hand, there is the person who lives only for the comforts and amenities of life, who dreads its miseries, particularly the ultimate misfortune of death, and strives by fair means or foul to avoid them. Since he can never avoid them, he is perpetually unhappy and frustrated. At the other extreme, there is the person who is overwhelmed by the miseries of the world, whether actual or imaginary, foreseeable or unforeseeable – it is hard to say which are worse – and in consequence is unhappy, metaphysically if not psychologically. The two kinds of person are different sides of the same coin. Both are locked into temporalities, into the happenings in the world and their consequences on themselves. The one kind resents the miseries of life and regards its comforts and amenities as theirs by right and not as good fortune; the other kind are so preoccupied with what may and does befall them that their hold on the graces of fortune is tenuous and treated with suspicion. But the person who regards the comforts and amenities as graces and favours of fortune, and takes up an attitude of detachment, renunciation and even defiance towards both the miseries and the comforts and amenities of the world, and is prepared, at least in his mind, to forgo the latter if necessary, would undoubtedly be a happy man, happy metaphysically, that is, in his deep heart's core. He would have prised himself free of temporalities, of happenings. He would be living in the eternal

eternal present, without fear of adversity, death, disappointment or anything else. Whether it is possible to live in this way is an empirical question. It is more to the point to ask whether, in order to live morally, this degree of asceticism, verging on the monastic, and, some might say, the heroically ascetic, is not fanatical. Indeed, one may ask whether this is ethics as commonly and traditionally understood.

Before coming to these questions, I should like to take up two more particular points. The first has to do with what Wittgenstein calls the 'grace of fate'. It crops up in the *Tractatus* 6.374 in a slightly different form, but one not unconnected with its use in the *Notebooks*. The passage goes:

> Even if everything we wish for were to happen, yet it would then be only, so to speak, a grace of fate, since there is no *logical* connection between will and world which would guarantee it, and again the assumed physical connection itself we ourselves surely could not will. (*TLP* 6.374)

This gives an underpinning to what was said in the *Notebooks* about the comforts and amenities of the world being graces and favours of fate. We can want them to happen, wish them to happen, and, in the popular sense, 'will' them to happen, but there is no logical connection between our willing and their happening. One can work to bring them about by hard work or devious and opportune practices. But – and Wittgenstein knew this better than most – a vast amount of good fortune is clearly outside the scope of our will: being born into a wealthy or aristocratic family, having the advantage of a good, socially promising education, having gifted parents, growing up in an advantageous environment. But it does not stop there. These are superficial advantages. There is also moral good fortune, recognized by Aristotle and Augustine, who realized that the good person is one who has the good fortune not to find himself in morally unfavourable circumstances – 'But for the grace of God, there goes John Bradford.' For Wittgenstein, the man of good will, the happy man, is the one who recognizes how fortunate he is to have any comforts in life.

The second point is more sombre, but it follows from what we are discussing. It is to do with one of Wittgenstein's obsessions: suicide. The *Notebooks* end dramatically with the startling assertions (*NB* p. 91):

> If suicide is allowed then everything is allowed.
> If anything is not allowed then suicide is not allowed.
> This throws a light on the nature of ethics. For then suicide is, so to speak, the elementary sin.

And when one investigates it, it is like investigating mercury vapour in order to comprehend the nature of vapours.

How can this be so? In Wittgenstein's view of ethics it is perfectly obvious and logical. But, you might say, surely someone who takes his own life shows not only courage, but a contempt, not a fear, of death. Leaving aside those who kill themselves so as not to betray a vital secret, or to put an end to hopeless and useless suffering, or as a result of mental derangement, suicide, though it may call for courage, is not contempt for death, but just the opposite. It is an extreme form of the fear of death: the attempt to anticipate and hasten it. It is the starkest example of the frustration at not being able to control the happenings in the world, of not being able to come to terms with the miseries of the world, of living in time and not in the eternal present. Indeed, to add a variant to Wittgenstein's chemical analogy, it is the litmus test of his ethics. In his view, the person of good will, the happy person, is the one who is not defiant in the face of the miseries of the world and is prepared to forgo the comforts of the world, who can renounce the world, and, thus, make himself independent of it. The suicide is the opposite of such a person. He has withdrawn from the ethical situation as Wittgenstein understands it.[1]

But to return to the question from which I digressed: is this ethics as is commonly and traditionally understood? Wittgenstein himself was not sure. Let us start where we left off, with suicide. He asks: 'Or is even suicide neither good nor evil?' (*NB* p. 91). In the entry for 8 July 1916 (*NB* p. 74) he writes: 'I am either happy or unhappy, that is all. One can say: there is no good or evil.' Later that month he is asking all kinds of questions. First, he asks if one can will good, will evil and not will at all. Then he asks if it might not be that the happy person is one who does *not* will. He further complicates matters by asking about wishing good or evil on others or not wishing anything at all. He concludes that it seems to depend on *how* one wishes. In the middle of all this speculation Wittgenstein remarks: 'Here I am still making gross errors. No doubt about it!' (*NB* p. 78). It is somewhat surprising, therefore, that there is no reference to all this in the *Tractatus*. Good and evil willing is referred to only once (*TLP* 6.43). It should also be noted that in the passages just quoted from the *Tractatus*, Wittgenstein is talking about *willing* good or evil rather *having* a good or evil will. This may seem a rather fine distinction, but it is not. If the good thing to do is to wish nothing on your neighbour, neither good nor bad, which Wittgenstein surprisingly says is 'according to the general notion', to wish your neighbour well might be a case of an evil will! Then, having conceded that it is generally assumed it is evil to wish someone else unhappiness, he immediately asks whether this is correct, whether it is worse than wishing him happiness. This, in Wittgenstein's terms, is not quite so eccentric as it may appear. He is not suggesting it is *better* to wish evil and unhappiness on your neighbour than to wish him good. What seems to worry Wittgenstein is that in wishing him anything, whether good or ill, one is trying to influence the happenings in the world. He makes this explicit when he asks a little earlier: 'But can one wish and yet not be unhappy, if the wish is not fulfilled? (And this possibility is there always.)' (*NB* p. 77).[2] He is, thus, consistent in his ethical views.

It is not surprising, therefore, that Wittgenstein should ask whether there is any moral good or evil, whether even suicide is good or evil. For Wittgenstein the ethical is concerned with one's attitude to the world or to life. One is either happy or unhappy, in agreement with the world or fruitlessly at variance with it; either defiant of it, detached from it, spurning its comforts and spiritually unaffected by its miseries or pursuing its comforts fruitlessly, hopelessly attempting to bend it to one's will in order to avert its miseries, immersed in temporality or living in the detachment of the eternal present.[3]

Unquestionably Wittgenstein's account of ethics is a minority view; his philosophical companions were possibly the Pythagoreans, certainly the Neo-Platonists, the Cynics and Schopenhauer. What he is proposing is not so much a theory of ethics as ordinarily understood, but an analysis of a certain way of life which he chooses to call ethical. In fact it is an analysis of the ascetic life. By this I do not mean a life of penury, of penitential exercises such as fasting and other forms of mortification, or of segregation from the world, hidden in a monastery or a hermit's cell. Rather it is an attitude towards the world one might describe as a *prerequisite for any form of morality*. What Wittgenstein is talking about – though he might not have agreed – are the necessary conditions, not for something being ethical, but for anyone *behaving* ethically.

What is the difference between the two? One difference is that you may think you know the correct way to behave in a given circumstance but, because you have a wrong attitude to the world and its happenings, you will not do the right thing when it comes to the test. Thus you may know it is wrong to lie and cheat or that you have an obligation to come to the aid of someone in distress, but you do the one either from moral cowardice or a desire for the amenities of life (hoping that you will get away with it), or fail to do the other because it might inconvenience you.

Whether one wants to call this ethics or not is perhaps a matter of choice. What, after all, is ethics? In a broad understanding of ethics Wittgenstein's analysis falls under that concept. His considerations are, by any criterion, ethical considerations. What is perplexing is that, after the doubts in the *Notebooks*, he comes down on the side of talking about good and evil in the *Tractatus*. One hesitates to call it meta-ethics. Neither at this stage, nor even in his later period, is Wittgenstein greatly interested in what the common man or other philosophers take ethics to be. He is not much concerned with questions of obligation, freedom, or any of the other concepts that occupy the minds of most ethical philosophers. His notion of ethics is neither the blessedness of Spinoza, based on an adequate understanding of the nature of things, nor the authenticity of Sartre and others who insist on our acting freely, provided we act in good faith. But Wittgenstein's ethics partakes of the defects of both these ethical doctrines. Like them – and the same could be said of Kierkegaard – it assumes ethics is always a matter of choice, of the either/or: either you are happy or unhappy, blessed or a slave to passion; either you are free and authentic, or in bad faith. If that is how Wittgenstein and the others see it, so be it. They might say in reply: this is what it means to behave morally. What happens in practice is an empirical matter. But that is not good enough. It is an empirical matter whether someone does good or evil acts, but, as Wittgenstein himself says, whether they are good or evil is not an empirical matter. It is not sufficient – at least not sufficient as a description of ethics as normally understood – to say that the acts of the happy man are good and those of the unhappy man bad. Is there not something other than the attitude to the world that makes them good or bad?

In fairness to Wittgenstein, he does talk about ethics in more traditional terms when speaking of rewards and punishments. In *TLP* 6.422 he talks about setting up an ethical law of the form 'thou shalt...' It is not that he ignores traditional ethics, but that he is not interested in it, since in his view it is a bad attempt to say the unsayable. He did not believe it was possible to theorize about ethics (any more than it is to theorize about religion or aesthetics or logic), nor to explain any ethical proposition. At best ethics can only be *shown* by examples. If the other person does not grasp the meaning of the example, too bad. There is nothing more to be done. Talking will not help.

So far we have been discussing the attitude of our wills to the vicissitudes of life, how we can overcome or succumb to its miseries, and, on the other hand, take its favours as graces of fate and not as the result of our willing them.

We must now consider, more generally, Wittgenstein's account of the will in relation to ethics. In *TLP* 6.423 he speaks of the will as the 'bearer of the ethical' and says: 'Of the will as bearer of the ethical nothing can be said.' Both Ogden, and Pears and McGuinness translate '*Träger*' as 'subject'. I accept that and will refer henceforth to the will as the ethical subject, understood as the will as the bearer of the ethical. As has just been said, according to Wittgenstein, this subject cannot be known: it can only be postulated. However, it fares better than the thinking (or, in Schopenhauerian terms, the representing subject, beloved of Descartes) which, Wittgenstein says, is non-existent: 'There is no thinking, representing (*vorstellende*) subject' (*TLP* 5.631). This echoes a remark in the *Notebooks* (p. 80, 5.8.16) that the representing or thinking subject is a mere delusion or illusion (*Wahn*).[4] Interesting though this idea is, it does not concern us. We are concerned with the ethical subject, the will, the bearer of ethics.

In the *Notebooks* (p. 80), continuing the remarks just quoted, Wittgenstein says:

> If the will did not exist, neither would there be that centre of the world, which I call the I, and which is the bearer of ethics.
> What is good and evil is essentially the I, not the world.
> The I, the I is what is deeply mysterious!

The I is indeed deeply mysterious, whether it be the metaphysical I, the ethical I or even the empirical I. But what is clear is that only the will, the ethical subject, can be the source of good or evil. The world is morally neutral. It is strange that this did not find its way into the *Tractatus*. It would have made *TLP* 5.621–6332 and 6.423 more intelligible.

A few days before, Wittgenstein had marked some more remarkable entries. He says religion, science and art arise 'only from the consciousness of the uniqueness of my life' (p. 79, 1.8.16). He continues (2.8.16):

> And this consciousness is life itself.
> Can there be any ethics if there is no living being but myself?
> If ethics is supposed to be something fundamental, there can.
> If I am right, then it is not sufficient for the ethical judgement that a world is given.
> Then the world in itself is neither good nor evil.

Leaving aside the first statement, which says little more than that the only form of life worthy of the name is a conscious life that can generate religion, science and art, the rest draws the consequences of the moral neutrality of the world. It is not sufficient to ground ethics; ethics is more fundamental. The only controversial assertion is that ethics does not require any other living being but myself. This is not a view shared by many philosophers. Most regard ethics a relation of rational beings towards one another and, possibly, towards other living beings. For them, the notion of a one-man morality would be incomprehensible. Yet, given his particular view of ethics, for Wittgenstein it is perfectly consistent and logical. Provided there is a world of some sort to have an attitude towards, that is sufficient. But to return to the moral neutrality of the world. This notion is elaborated in the next entry.

> For it must be all one, as far as concerns the existence of ethics, whether there is living matter in the world or not. And it is clear that a world in which there is only dead matter is in itself neither good nor evil, so even the world of living things can in itself be neither good nor evil.

That inanimate nature cannot be good or evil, despite animistic notions that survive in such metaphors as 'cruel sea', 'treacherous mountains', 'hospitable shores', is a proposition easy to accept. Again, any moral virtues or vices attributed to vegetation – 'encroaching forests', 'stubborn weeds', 'innocent lilies' – can be dismissed as animism or metaphor. With animals things are not so clear, but clear enough. Animals go about their affairs – hunting for food, protecting themselves and their young, often coming to each other's assistance – by natural impulse. Though this behaviour may be described as virtuous or vicious, these terms are being used metaphorically. Sometimes it is hard not to describe the action of animals, such as the 'wanton' destruction of chickens by foxes, the 'fidelity' of dogs, or the 'sadistic' treatment of mice by cats, but no sane person would say these are strictly good or evil acts.

The world of inanimate and even animate beings up to the highest of the animal kingdom is neither good nor evil. But what of that other animal species, man? He is a living being, and, if good and evil can be attributed at all, it can be attributed to this kind of being. Is one to say that what Francis of Assisi, Peter Claver, Mother Theresa, Joseph Stalin, Adolf Hitler or Idi Amin did in the world was neither good nor evil?

Wittgenstein would say that what they did *in* the world was neither good nor evil. It was what they did *outside*, or, as he calls it at the 'boundaries of the world', that made their actions good or evil. By this I understand him to mean that *in itself* – and he stresses this – distributing goods to the poor, looking after slaves in Carthagena, rescuing the destitute in Calcutta are merely events, neither morally good nor evil; just as shooting people or letting them starve or sending them to die in Siberia or in gas-chambers, or torturing and massacring one's own people is *in itself* neither good nor evil. In a properly run society the poor and destitute would be looked after; there would be no slaves to take care of; and there might be no saints. Some people *happen* to be shot, exiled, allowed to starve, forced into starvation, or executed or tortured. *In themselves* these events are neither good nor bad: they are merely facts, happenings. What, then, makes them good or evil? According to Wittgenstein it is the attitude of the subject of these actions.

'Good and evil,' he says, 'enter only through the *subject*. And the subject does not belong to the world, but is a boundary of the world' (*NB* p. 79). This is an interesting remark. It throws light not only on what Wittgenstein means by good and evil not being part of the world, but also on that rather obscure notion of outside and at the boundary of the world, and also good or evil willing altering only the boundaries of the world, not the facts (*TLP* 6.43). The subject, as Wittgenstein envisages it, is rather like a director who supervises everything that is done but does nothing himself, beyond supervising. Everything can be attributed to him, yet nothing that happens, be it in a factory, a retail business, a theatre, a film studio or an orchestra need have been *done* by him. He has not personally and physically changed or brought about anything. He is outside the action, as it is called colloquially, beyond its boundary; and yet, from his vantage point, he can alter it totally, adopt a different policy, a different conception. The analogy is not perfect, because, although a director can by his very directing bring it about that things are altered, Wittgenstein's subject cannot. All I wish to illustrate here is the detachment of the subject from what is happening, and why Wittgenstein should wish to detach it. One other point. He speaks of the subject as *a* boundary of the world (*eine Grenze*) which suggests there are other boundaries, other subjects.

After this, in attempting to designate the ethical subject, Wittgenstein becomes a little disconcerting. Having said in a Schopenhauerian way that the world of representation (ideas) is neither good nor evil, it is the willing subject that is good or evil, he then says he is conscious of the complete unclarity of these propositions. Finally he says that the essence of the subject is completely veiled, yet he goes on talking about it almost to the end of the *Notebooks*. All these remarks, however *distrait* they may appear and however seemingly tentative, are in fact both firm and consistent, as we shall see. However he soon comes up with a mildly perplexing entry:

> As the subject is not a part of the world but a presupposition of its existence, so good and evil are predicates of the subject, and not properties in the world. (*NB* p. 79)

That good and evil are not properties (*Eigenschaften*) of the world is clear enough in Wittgenstein's ethical philosophy, but what is one to make of the subject as a presupposition of the world's existence? That can be easily taken care of in Wittgensteinian terms. Since a condition for the existence of the world as Wittgenstein understands it is the presence of a conscious being such as a human being, a conscious subject is a presupposition of the existence of the world. 'I am my world' (*TLP* 5.63; *cf.* *TLP* 5.641). Conversely, 'The I makes its appearance in the world through the world being my world' (*NB* p. 80, 12.8.16).

All this is confirmed in the entries for 7, 11 and 12 August 1916 (*NB* p. 80). This explains the unclarity of his propositions about the subject that wills and why it is essentially completely veiled. Dramatic as ever, he has only one entry for 7.8.16: 'The I is no object.' This is elaborated somewhat in the entries that follow:

> I objectively confront every object. But not the I.
> So there really is a way in which there can and must be mention of the I in a *non-psychological sense* in philosophy.
> The I makes its appearance in philosophy through the world's being *my* world.

This is not so fully stated in the *Tractatus* (5.641). The stark statements that the I is no object, that I stand objectively facing every object except the I itself, are missing. But there is a useful addition:

> The philosophical I is not the human being, not the human body nor the human soul with which psychology deals, but the metaphysical subject, the boundary of – not a part of – the world.[5]

The message, however, is the same: the philosophical, metaphysical subject is not to be observed like other facts of the world. It is like the eye in the visual field that is not itself visible and whose existence cannot be inferred from anything in the visual field, which includes, presumably, mirrors, camera lenses and one's own spectacles (*TLP* 5.633–6331, *cf.* *NB* p. 80, 12.8.16). If the analogy is not perfect, it is adequate for its purpose. The metaphysical and ethical I is not a part of the world any more than the eye is a part of its visual field. (A better analogy might have been the ear. Whoever, in hearing, has heard his ear hearing?) But, though this analogy helps to clarify what Wittgenstein is saying, it leaves some problems to be solved.

If (a) there is no evidence in the world for the existence of a metaphysical I, any more than there is evidence in the visual field for the existence of an eye, and (b) if the subject that wills cannot affect anything that happens in the world, what reason is there for believing that there is such a thing as a metaphysical subject to which ethical predicates can be attributed? Wittgenstein's answer, already given, is simple and straightforward, if not immediately comprehensible. It is that 'the world is *my* world' (*TLP* 5.641 and *NB* p. 80, 12.8.16. Italics only in the latter). This says that as far as I am concerned there is only the world of which I am conscious; whether I can influence it or not, whether things just happen in it or follow a rigid pattern that is not mine, it is still *my* world and there is no other. But I, as the metaphysical, philosophical, ethical subject, am not a part of it. I am in a sense an observer of a passing show.

The force of Wittgenstein's argument is this. We have evidence of a psychological I, whether it be just human or the human body or the human soul (*TLP* 5.641); this in a limited way can influence the happenings in the world. Wittgenstein dreams up a book called *The World as I Found It* (*TLP* 5.631); in it there is a report on which parts of my body obey my will and which do not. This is the psychological will. But the parts over which the psychological will has no influence are still parts of my world and I am the subject of them, though *as subject* I do not get a mention in the book. The book is 'a method to isolate the subject, or, much more, to show that, in an important sense there is no subject: namely, of it alone, in this book, there could *not* be a mention'. Nevertheless it is *my* world. Therefore there must be some subject, some I other than the psychological I, that is somehow connected with the world, whose world it is.

This, however, raises as many problems as it solves. First, it seems to be a form of solipsism. Second, it seems a very poor, if not totally ineffectual, way of explaining ethical concepts. Third, it verges on the incomprehensible when it says in *TLP* 5.631 'in an important sense there is no subject', while in *TLP* 5.641 it says there is a real sense in which there can be a non-psychological I.

First, solipsism. Wittgenstein is prepared to agree that to a certain extent my world is solipsistic. In *TLP* 5.62, just before the passages we have been discussing, he says:

> This remark provides the key to the problem, how much truth there is in solipsism.
>
> For what the solipsist *means* is quite correct; only it cannot be *said*, but makes itself manifest.
>
> The world is *my* world: this is manifested by the fact that the limits of *language* (of that language which I alone understand) means the limits of *my* world.

This cannot be right. It cannot be that solipsism is 'completely correct' (*ganz richtig*) and that all that is wrong with it is that it cannot be put into propositional language, into a statement or statements of fact. What is right with it is merely that *for me* (a) the only world that exists is what I know or know I do not know, but possibly could; and (b) that I can never fully know (hardly even in imagination) other people's worlds, whether they be living or dead. But perhaps this is all Wittgenstein means to say. This is what it shows: and that I have been crass in trying to state it. Nevertheless, however one takes it, this is not solipsism as properly understood: i.e. a belief that not only is there no *evidence* that anything else besides oneself exists, but that *this is the case*. Berkeley and Leibniz escaped solipsism by a whisker. They had to admit there were areas of their world, the world of individual spirits and monads, over which they had no control, and areas over which they did have control. They rightly concluded that though their world was theirs, it was not theirs alone, to do with as they liked. But, better, they were not alone in their own world, even though it was their own world. Wittgenstein reached the same conclusion by a slightly different route. He distinguished between the metaphysical, philosophical (ethical, aesthetic, religious) subject and the subject that acts in the world or fails to influence it but would like to, the empirical subject, the subject that controls some of my bodily movements, that is part of the world, an object of psychological study. He concludes:

> Here it can be seen that solipsism, when its implications are followed out strictly, coincides with pure realism. The self of solipsism shrinks to a point without extension, and there remains the reality co-ordinated with it.

If I follow Wittgenstein correctly, the argument goes as follows. If you follow through the notion of solipsism rigorously, you must come to the conclusion that you are not part of *your* world. *You* are not observable, except as an empirical agent in a tiny section of the world that you observe. But that is not the philosophical, metaphysical you. That is not part of your world at all. Therefore the solipsistic 'you' vanishes, as it were, and all that is left is *the* world. In other words, pure realism. Of course, you have a limited view of it and in that sense it is yours.

Wittgenstein developed this idea in the *Notebooks* (*NB* p. 82, 2.9.16):

> What has history to do with me? My world is the first and the only one.
> I want to report how *I* found the world.
> What others in the world have told me about the world, is a very small and almost negligible part of my experience of the world.
> *I* have to judge the world, to measure things.

This is not solipsism, it is realism. Realism on two fronts, so to speak.

First, it acknowledges the existence of other beings, whether they be conscious or not. Secondly, it acknowledges the indubitable fact that most of our world is made up of our own experiences and not what we are told (truthfully or falsely), though that too forms part of our world. Someone born into an African tribe will see the world very differently from that of someone born and growing up in the Bronx; both will see it differently from someone born into an aristocratic family in Italy. It is not just that their direct and immediate experiences will be different: all they know about the world, past and present, will be different, will be broader or narrower. All this goes to make up their world. They might even feature in each other's world, though this is hardly likely. If they do, they might appear so different from the way they see themselves as to be unrecognizable, just as the way in which Blacks appear in the world of an Afrikaner might be unrecognizable to a Black. Yet they each have a place in the other's world. And the world of each is continually changing with new experiences, new knowledge, new attitudes.

Wittgenstein adds some other remarks that deserve to be noted. He says that his body and all other human bodies are part of the world along with other bodies: animals, plants and stones. Echoes resound of Wordsworth's: 'A slumber did my spirit seal':/'Rolled round in earth's diurnal course,/with rocks, and stones, and trees'. Not only that. Neither my body nor any other human body has a preferential place in the world. Anyone who realizes this will view human beings as 'quite naïvely' similar and belonging to one another. Charming though this conception is, in this context Wittgenstein is talking of the human body, not the I, whether empirical or metaphysical. It is an important distinction. As a body I shall be either burned or buried, just as one disposes of any waste material; even in life I take up space, exert pressure, cause an obstruction like any other body. Neither the empirical self, much less the philosophical and metaphysical self, do any of these things.

Wittgenstein continues his reflections on the relationship between human beings and other members of the animate and inanimate kingdoms (*NB* pp. 84–5). Enchanting though it would be to follow him through these green mansions, I shall quote only his concluding entry, which sums up all we have been discussing:

> This is the way I have travelled: Idealism singles men out from the world as unique, solipsism singles me alone out, and at last I see that I too belong with the rest of the world, and so on *the* one side *nothing* is left over, and on the other side, as unique, the *world*. In this way idealism leads to realism if it is strictly thought out. (*NB* p. 85)

It is obvious that a good deal of rigorous thinking is called for to make the journey from Idealism via solipsism to realism, pure or tarnished. In the first place, it looks as though in Idealism the human being is unique but separate from the world. But what kind of Idealism is this? Berkeleyan, Kantian, Fichtean, Hegelian, Bradleyan? And how are we to understand 'unique' – as one of a kind, or one kind among others, or a class with only one member? And what is this 'world' from which the human being is separated? Presumably it is the phenomenal world that confronts us all, whether or not it has any substance behind it. Mercifully, Wittgenstein dropped Idealism from his philosophical itinerary in the *Tractatus* (5.64). The route is now directly from solipsism to pure realism. But it would be crass not to remark on the elegant balance between the human being as unique in Idealism and the world as unique in realism, with solipsism holding the balance, as it were. Moreover, some explanation of '*nothing* remains left over' and 'the world is unique' is called for. The explanation I would give is as follows. If one were to take Idealism, and, in particular solipsism, seriously, there would be little or nothing left over to form the world. The world would be I, the self. But if there is something else, not only beyond myself, but also beyond other human beings – if there is 'a world beyond'; and if the I shrinks to an extensionless point, then all you are left with is the world – hence realism – and the world is unique in the sense of being all there is.

Having cleared the hurdle of solipsism, we now approach another, namely, whether Wittgenstein it talking about ethics as generally understood. The general understanding is that: (a) there are certain actions or forms of behaviour that are good or evil; (b) *as good and evil* actions they are events in the world; that is, *facts*: that is, their being good or evil is a fact; (c) these good or evil actions are *willed*. Wittgenstein seems to deny all three. So either what he is saying is wrong, or he is not talking about ethics as ordinarily understood – in which case he may be right or wrong. One person who thinks he is 'obviously wrong' is his literary executor, Elizabeth Anscombe. Her reason is that 'what happens' includes actions to which the predicates 'good' and 'bad' can be applied. But in the *Tractatus* Wittgenstein says there is only 'the chimerical "will" which effects nothing in the world, but only alters the "limits" of the world'.[6] Anscombe concedes that in the *Notebooks* Wittgenstein 'entertained some more reasonable considerations', though he made a mess of things, in her opinion, at the end of the entry (perhaps the most sustained) of 4 November 1916 (*NB* pp. 86–8). In her view he righted the boat in the *Philosophical Investigations*, e.g. *PI* 644, p. 165: 'Did not your intention lie in that which I did? What justifies the shame? The whole story of the incident.'

I take issue with Anscombe on two counts. First, that Wittgenstein was obviously wrong. Secondly, that he rejected his reasonable considerations. The question whether his views in *Investigations* are radically different from those in the *Tractatus* and the *Notebooks* is something I shall discuss later. First let us examine those 'reasonable considerations' in the *Notebooks*. I shall not discuss them all. Some are traditional, such as that the will must have an object and an idea to guide it. One cannot will in general. The question is how the will works – another traditional problem much beloved of the Occasionalists. That is: (a) how do I know that *I* waved my arm when *I* decided to wave it? Was it not just coincidental with my deciding to wave it? and (b) can a decision on my part to wave my arm *necessarily* result in its waving or even *accidentally* (like bashing a machine to make it work)? That is, can a decision of mine affect the movement of my arm at all? Fascinating though these questions are, they must remain suspended. I suspect that Anscombe was referring to the, to my mind, more tractable entries that begin (*NB* p. 87):

> The act of the will is not the cause of the action, but the action itself.
> One cannot will without acting.
> If the will must have an object in the world, the object can be the intended action itself.

Wittgenstein goes on to say that the will must have an object in order to get a hold on the world. This is the difference between willing and wishing. A wish latches on to nothing. Willing an occurrence means bringing it about; waving my arm when I want to. But I cannot will everything. What is it, he asks, to say: 'I cannot will this'? Can I then try to will something?

> For the consideration of willing makes it look as if one part of the world were closer to me than another (which would be intolerable).
> But, of course, it is undeniable that in a popular sense there are things that I do, and other things not done by me.
> In this way the will would not confront the world as its equivalent, which must be impossible.

There is no denying this is a puzzling passage. Some parts are clear. It is clear that we do certain things and don't do others that either we might or could not have done. It is also clear what Wittgenstein means by saying that the things we do in the world seem nearer to us than ones we do not do, that are out of our control, and hence in a sense more remote. But why should this be intolerable? It is intolerable because the ethical will is not concerned with this or that part of the world, but with the world as a whole: it is outside the world. It must stand over against the world as a whole, as its equivalent. Therefore, if it is an ethical, metaphysical, philosophical, transcendental will, it is impossible it should merely will this and not that.

Here a distinction, traditional in moral theology, not only between wishing and willing, but also between willing and acting, may be useful. As Wittgenstein says, 'The wish precedes the event, the will accompanies it'. If the wish is fulfilled, this is accidental. It does not accompany the event in the way the will accompanies it. The punter who puts a bet on a horse *wishes* it to win; the jockey who guides it to the head of the field in the last furlong *wills* it to win. But he could have willed it to lose and was not strong or clever enough to stop it. Assuming morality in horse-racing, and that it is immoral to try to make a horse lose, traditional moral philosophy would say the jockey who won the race, in spite of willing/intending his horse to lose, was *acting* immorally. There was certainly action in the physical sense on his part: he was trying as inconspicuously as possible to hold it back. What, however, of the person who wants and intends to shoot someone dead, but fails because at the last minute a van stops between them; when it moves on, the intended victim is no longer there? No event has occurred, but the would-be assassin is as guilty of murder as he would have been had he killed or only wounded his intended victim.

This may help to illustrate what Wittgenstein is saying. He admits that moral actions take place in the world: jockeys try to, and often succeed in pulling horses; assassins shoot people dead. However, the *goodness or badness* of their actions is not an event *in* the world. Unless you hold that it is impossible to intend to do good or evil without performing some action or bringing about some event or occurrence, then it must be conceded that the good or evil is not in the event, but in the mind and intention of the person acting. At least some event that can be described, such as killing, must be intended; but it need not have been carried out or even attempted (e.g. no shot fired) for it to be an evil intention. Moreover, though some actions, such as drawing and aiming a gun, may be necessary to establish a prima-facie case for an evil intention, it is not necessary subjectively. The mere carrying of the gun with the intent to use it is sufficient. However, even if the ultimate action does not take place, some action is necessary. Walking out with the intention of shooting someone in the street, but without any weapon, would suggest either carelessness or lack of genuine intent.

The problem, however, is that, granted that the ethical value of an action is not a part of the event itself, which is neutral, neither good nor evil, but still willed by me, how can it receive its ethical value by being *outside* the world, regarding the world as a whole, and changing the world at its boundary? In something resembling Anscombe's objection, one may ask: how can an individual act of will – which it has to be in order to be a moral act – be, at the same time, equivalent to the world as a whole and change it as a whole for better or worse, from being meaningful to being meaningless, or from being good into being evil? Wittgenstein's answer is that the action is not seen as one action among others in a world of events, but *alone, sub specie aeternitatis*. This will be considered at length in the next chapter.

Finally, there is the question of the status of the subject. Wittgenstein has said that the thinking, representing, idea-producing subject does not exist (*TLP* 5.631). Yet what brings the I into philosophy is that the world is *my* world (*TLP* 5.641). The I also appears to operate in parts of the world where I seem to act. Indeed, even the representational world is under my control. I can close my eyes or turn my head or plug my ears or hold my nose. I am conscious that I can do this. When I do it, surely I am conscious of myself? But what is that self of which I am conscious? It is nothing, in so far as it cannot be described except in terms of what it does or observes. But how can nothing be the subject to which good and evil are attributable? It is precisely because it is nothing in the sense of *no thing in the world* that it can. It is because it is *no thing* that it can be both outside the world and yet related to it. But it is related variously: (a) as the observing subject; (b) as the subject that affects the world; and (c) as the subject that wills about the world as a whole. Of all this, more in the next chapter on Wittgenstein's notion of the mystical.

4

The Mystical

Wittgenstein used the term 'mystical' only four times in his published writings: three times in the *Tractatus* and once in the *Notebooks*. The following appear in the *Tractatus*:

> It is not *how* things are in the world that is mystical, but *that* it exists. (*TLP* 6.44)
> Feeling the world as a limited whole – it is this that is mystical. (*TLP* 6.45)
> There are, indeed, things that cannot be put into words. They *make themselves manifest* (*zeigtsich*). They are what is mystical. (*TLP* 6.522)

The term appears in the *Tractatus* without preparation, as though it were a household word, as if everyone was expected to know what it meant. In fact it is extremely difficult to understand what it means or why Wittgenstein decided to use it. Linguistically it presents no problem. *Das Mystische* means no more nor less than 'the mystical'. But what is mystical about the fact that there is a world, that it is, or that it is a limited whole? In what sense here is the word being used?

It is hardly being used in the traditional sense, that is, esoteric knowledge of and union with God or Being, Ultimate Reality or the Ground of Being. Yet this usage cannot be ruled out. The notion of the mystical is intimately bound up with the Wittgensteinian notion of God, which, if neither traditional nor orthodox, has, as we shall see in the next chapter, certain elements of the traditional notion, both philosophical and theological.

The OED gives two principal meanings of 'mystic'. One is the narrower, traditional, theological meaning. The other is wider and more easily intelligible: 'Spiritually allegorical; occult, esoteric; of hidden meaning; mysterious; mysterious and awe-inspiring'. Leaving aside the spiritually allegorical, which refers to one of the ways of interpreting Scripture in Christian hermeneutics, and also the occult, esoteric and hidden meaning, a useful beginning might be made with the mysterious and awe-inspiring. That this is a promising approach is confirmed by the *Notebooks* (*NB* p. 86, 20.10.16) where Wittgenstein says: 'The artistic marvel (*Wunder*) is that there is a world. That there is what there is.' Anscombe translates this passage: 'Aesthetically, the miracle is that the world exists.' Doubtless this is what Wittgenstein meant, but it is not precisely what he said. Why he did not use *ästhetische* rather than *künstlerische* I cannot say, but it was the latter word that he used. As for *Wunder*, it can mean miracle, but that seems too dramatic. It need mean nothing more than 'astounding', 'amazing', 'something to ponder on and wonder at'. What it holds in all its senses is that core of wonder at something that cannot be fully understood.

The importance of this passage for an exegesis of *TLP* 6.44 should be obvious by now. In both passages Wittgenstein is referring to the same thing: *that* the world is, that there is a world, that there is what there is. In the *Tractatus* the experience of this is called the mystical; in the *Notebooks* the identical experience is called a marvel, a miracle, an astonishing thing, albeit it is connected with art and aesthetics. But the interconnection between all these strands should have been established by now.

I would, therefore, suggest that, in the first instance, the mystical be interpreted as the marvellous, remarkable, inexplicable; and that no greater strain be put upon it.

What makes the world remarkable and mysterious, and, hence, gives rise to a mystical feeling about it, is, in the first place, a certain suspicion that when all scientific questions have been answered, there remains unanswered the question: why it is at all? Physical theories, such as the 'Big Bang', the Quantum Theory; biological theories, such as the DNA helix and the Darwinian survival of the fittest; psychological theories such as those of Freud, Jung and Piaget, may go some way towards explaining why the world is as it is, or, in Wittgenstein's terms, *how* the world is, *how* it comes to be as it is. But they will not explain *why* it is, *why* there is this world or any other kind. This is not a question that science can answer and, therefore, for Wittgenstein, it cannot be asked either. This is stated in various ways:

> The solution of the riddle of life in space and time lies *outside* space and time.
> (And it is certainly not the solution of any problems of natural science that is required.) (*TLP* 6.4312)
> How things are in the world is a matter of complete indifference for what is higher. (*TLP* 6.432)
> The facts all contribute only to setting the problem, not to its solution. (*TLP* 6.4321)[1]

When the answer cannot be put into words, neither can the question be put into words.

The *riddle* does not exist.

If a question can be framed at all, it is *possible* to answer it. (*TLP* 6.5)

We feel that when *all possible* scientific questions have been answered, the problems of life remain completely untouched. Of course there are then no questions left, and this itself is the answer. (*TLP* 6.52)

The solution of the problem of life is seen in the vanishing of the problem.

(Is not this the reason why those who have found after a long period of doubt that the sense of life became clear to them have been unable to say what constituted that sense. (*TLP* 6.521)

These quotations can be reinforced by some from the *Notebooks*:

The solution of the problem of life is to be seen in the disappearance of this problem. (*NB* p. 74)

And, above all, the fourth use of the word 'mystical':

The urge towards the mystical comes of the non-satisfaction of our wishes by science. We *feel* that even if all *possible* scientific questions are answered *our problem is not touched at all*. Of course in that case there are no questions any more; and that is the answer. (*NB* p. 51)

Although this entry is not reproduced in its entirety in the *Tractatus* (6.52), it clinches the matter.

The following points emerge from all this:

1　The mystical, unlike the scientific, has nothing to do with questions and answers, with textbook exercises. 'Why is there a world?' 'What is the meaning of life?' may look like textbook questions, but they are not. And they are not questions because they do not have answers in the way that such textbook questions as 'how do organisms propagate their kind?' 'why does the planet Mars move in an ellipse?' have answers.

2　Yet these pseudo questions are problematical in the sense that we have a feeling that when all scientific problems have been answered the most important question (or pseudo question) will not have been answered: namely, 'Why is there anything – a galaxy, a DNA helix, an animal kingdom, a human race?' 'What sense does it make?' to say nothing of 'What purpose do they serve?'

3　What is problematical in this way cannot be solved as a puzzle is

solved or a question answered. One must see that things must be so; that the problem is a pseudo problem; that its 'solution' is to see this.
4   This is not a matter of reasoning but of feeling. Feeling here has little to do with emotion. It has to do with insight or intuition.
5   The 'solution' to this pseudo problem is its dissolution, its disappearance, to see it as a pseudo problem.
6   This is the marvel, the miracle, the wonder (*das Wunder*), the mystical experience, as Wittgenstein understands it.

The mystical is inexpressible: it cannot be said: but it can be shown. There are, indeed, things that cannot be put into words. They *make themselves manifest*. They are what is mystical (*TLP* 6.522).[2] This is nothing more than the reverse of the coin. If the mystical is not an answer to a scientific question, then it cannot be expressed in language. Only statements of fact, according to Wittgenstein, can be expressed in language, and statements about the mystical are not statements of fact, if they can properly be called statements at all.

What Wittgenstein is saying may be paradoxical, but it is not contradictory. This is made clear in *TLP* 6.54. In *TLP* 6.53 Wittgenstein is trying to correct a misunderstanding about philosophy in general and metaphysics in particular. The general, or a general and traditional, belief is that philosophy and/or metaphysics is a kind of super-science, a generalized science that is not about physical, organic, physiological, psychological or social phenomena, but about Being, about what is, what can be, what must be and what cannot be. Wittgenstein says, as Kant said before him, that there cannot be such a science. Science is about empirical, contingent and verifiable matters. Metaphysics is not about contingent, empirical or verifiable matters. It is about what is absolute and necessary. But language is not geared to coping with the absolute and the necessary. As Wittgenstein puts it, certain signs in a metaphysical proposition lack meaning. As will be seen in the next chapter, this came as something of a revelation to Wittgenstein. But he did not conclude, as did Ramsey, that this rendered metaphysics inarticulate. It is just that the articulation is somewhat different from the statement of scientic and common-sense facts.

But if mystical language is not being used to make statements of fact, to what use is it being put? How does it show what it cannot state or express? It does so in this way, as has been described in chapter one. Its propositions, or, rather, sentences, act as rungs of a ladder that lead the reader to 'see the world aright'. In order to understand these sentences he must have or have had the experiences described. In doing so he both apprehends what the speaker or writer means and, at the same time, realizes how inadequate language is to express it.

The further question can be asked: is everything that cannot be expressed but can be shown mystical? The answer seems to me that it is.

To answer this question in detail would be unnecessarily tedious. All that need be said is that there is a network of concepts linking the inexpressible that shows itself in the ethical, religious, aesthetic and metaphysical. The wonder that there is anything, the prime and explicit example of the mystical, is directly linked to ethics and aesthetics; and by implication to the religious experience. They all belong to the 'higher', they all involve seeing the world as a limited whole and *sub specie aeternitatis*.

Metaphysics is mystical by the contiguity of *TLP* 6.522 and *TLP* 6.53, and for other fairly obvious reasons. The only other candidate for the status of mystical by way of being inexpressible but showing itself is the structure or form of propositions in a language: that is to say, logic. It may seem to be going too far to call the understanding of the logic of language a mystical experience. Perhaps it is. It is certainly not very like the traditional notion of the mystical. Yet, if Zemach were right, and God was the general form of the proposition, it would be entirely in line with the traditional notion: it would be an experence of God.[3] McGuinness has argued ably that the understanding of logical structure, which represents the structure of reality, its possibilities, what can, cannot or must be the case, is a mystical experience. He says that 'there is no difference between "that something is", which is the experience presupposed by logic, and "that there is a world" which is what is mystical'. He is referring to *TLP* 5.552 where Wittgenstein says:

> The 'experience' that we need in order to understand logic is not that something or other is the state of things, but that something *is*; that, however, is *not* an experience.
>
> Logic is *prior* to experience – that something *is so*.
>
> It is prior to the question 'How?', not prior to the question 'What?'

But for this interpretation to be valid Wittgenstein would have to have meant something different by mystical experience than by any other kind of experience. This is precisely what he does by saying this is no experience in the ordinary sense, no experience of something (like travelling at 150 mph in a train or falling in love): it is the prerequisite for any ordinary experience. Hence the inverted commas: 'experience'.

But if our understanding of logic is a mystical 'experience', and, moreover, is common to everyone who has experiences and uses language and its propositions even in 'their unanalysed form', in what sense is it mystical? I shall return to this question in a later section. Here I must content myself with saying that it is mystical to the extent that (a) it is inexpressible but shows itself; and (b) it is concerned with the 'thatness' and not the 'howness' of the facts that constitute the world. To demonstrate what I think Wittgenstein means, let us take two or three basic logical expressions: $p{\sim}p$, $p{\supset}q$, and $p{\supset}p$. We say of the first that it is impossible; of the second that, if it is true, then given p there must be q; of the third that it is self-evident, tautologous and redundant. How do we know this? And how could we prove to people who doubt these assertions that they are true? We cannot. It is not like demonstrating to a child or a cat that if it puts its hand or paw on a red-hot cooking ring, it will get burnt. Logical expressions of this kind are the conditions for demonstration. They themselves cannot be demonstrated. You have to grasp that they are true by seeing them at work; and see, however obscurely, that, if they are not true, nothing is true. This, as I have said, may not sound mystical; but it should sound metaphysical.

But, even if it, and all those other experiences, can be described as 'mystical' what is mystical about being inexpressible? There are many cases where we are left speechless. For instance, one cannot express one's rage, disgust, passionate love, profound hatred or utter dedication, but one can show it. Are these mystical experiences? If not, why not? They are not, and this can be explained by the fact that the mystical has to do with the higher, with seeing the world as a limited whole and *sub specie aeterni*. The other inexpressible experiences mentioned above are not inexpressible for that reason, nor do they necessarily show themselves in verbal utterances.

The notion that the mystical involves seeing the world as a limited whole and *sub specie aeterni* are best taken together since they complement each other, as is clear from *TLP* 6.45:

> The view of the world *sub specie aeterni* is its perception as a – bounded – whole.
> The feeling of the world as a bounded whole is the mystical.[4]

We have already discussed Wittgenstein's notion of the world as a bounded or limited whole – more simply as 'a whole'. Here we must ask what is mystical about it. To regard the world as a whole, the totality of facts, of what can be the case, is to transcend individual facts. It is mystical at least in the sense that to experience the world in this way, if it is a real experience, fits into no other category. It certainly cannot be expressed in propositions, since they picture facts, and the totality of facts or the world (or reality – *cf. TLP* 2.063) is not a fact about the world any more than space is an object, much less an object in space, or our visual field an object in it. To experience the world in this way is, in a sense, to transcend space, though Wittgenstein has not been explicit on this point.

He is much more explicit about time. To contemplate something *sub specie aeterni* is to contemplate the world outside its temporal context. It is to regard it in the eternal 'now', not as part of a sequence of past and future events as has already been discussed in relation to ethics and aesthetics (*TLP 6.4311; TLP* 4.312; *NB* pp. 74–5, 8.7.16; *NB* p. 83, 7 and 8.10.16). Now since what we perceive are the objects of propositions that exist in time, that belong in a temporal sequence, we can only make temporal statements about them. We cannot make eternal statements. Though there is a sense in which a statement such as 'Julius Caesar crossed the Rubicon in 49 BC' is eternal: that is, it has always been and will always be true ever since the event occurred, given that it did occur. But this is a loose use of 'eternal'. The event occurred in time: it was an event: it was temporal. The mystical is not concerned with the 'eternal' in this sense. Expressions such as 'was', 'will be' or 'is currently' are not applicable to it. What one says about ethics, aesthetics, metaphysics, God and logic are in no way temporarily determined. In so far as these utterances are intelligible, they must be what Wittgenstein calls 'mystical': they must show themselves.

An interesting connection can be made between the world as a bounded whole and contemplation *sub specie aeterni*. They are mutually dependent. It is impossible to contemplate the world *sub specie aeterni* unless one views it as a bounded whole; one cannot view it as a bounded whole unless one contemplates it *sub specie aeterni*. To take events as a whole is to view them outside time i.e. *sub specie aeterni*; to view them *sub specie aeterni* one cannot regard them as part of a temporal sequence (*cf. Notebooks* p. 83, 7.10.16) but together with space and time.

Finally, 'mystical', as Wittgenstein uses the term, describes a feeling or experience (*das Gefühl, die Erfahrung*), albeit in *TLP* 5.552 Wittgenstein calls it '*no* experience' and puts experience in inverted commas. McGuinness refers to it as a quasi-experience.[5] Yet, in spite of *TLP* 5.552, Wittgenstein, in the 'Lecture on Ethics' refers throughout to experience – 'one particular experience', 'my experience *par excellence*', 'the same or similar experiences', 'another experience' (all on page 8), and so on. This does not necessarily contradict what was said in *TLP* 5.552. After all, he was giving a public lecture where refinements such as quasi-experience, or 'experience' (waggling one's fingers in the air), or, even worse, 'experience that is *no* experience' would have baffled his audience and distracted it from the points he was making.

I hardly think that anyone who had a Wittgensteinian mystical experience, as described above, would be said to have been idiosyncratically subjective. He does not fail to see what is before him. He does not 'see' what is not there. Nor does he interpret what is there in a manner that cannot be either understood or accepted by reasonable people, however prejudiced in other respects he may be. Not everyone may share his 'experience'. But even if someone does not share his experience, and to that extent may not fully understand what he is talking about, that person cannot say that he contradicts any piece of sensory evidence or that what he says is manifestly contrary to available evidence of whatever kind. To that extent, though personal, it is not subjective in the sense in which I have used the term in the last paragraph.

Is it then an objective experience? To ask this question is to presuppose there is a perfect dichotomy between what is subjective and what objective. It is like saying that what is not black must be white. The mystical experience as Wittgenstein understands it cannot be described as either objective or subjective. It is not subjective for the reasons already given. It is not objective in the sense that (a) with the possible exceptions of the experience of the fundamental principles of logic and metaphysics, it is not (may not be, need not be) a universal experience, though this is debatable; and (b) there are no independent checks by which to validate it. If someone says he does or does not find the world problematical, that he does or does not find the existence of something a matter of wonder, something miraculous, marvellous, mystical, there is no independent criterion by which he can be proved right or wrong. In that sense the mystical experience as Wittgenstein describes it is not an experience of an objective reality as the term is popularly understood. Nor is it inter-subjective in the strictest sense.

An inter-subjective experience, of which the most typical are ethical and aesthetic, has an element of universality, but it is without independent criteria that have to be accepted on pain of some form of logical or semantic incoherence. Thus, although there is nothing logically incoherent in saying that mugging old-age pensioners is a respectable occupation or that Michelangelo is a rather indifferent artist, it is not to be expected that anyone who seriously examines the arguments and evidence in favour of these propositions (if such there be) should take them seriously. In the strict sense of proof, there is no way of proving him wrong – he has committed no logical or scientific howler – but by accepted criteria, that are not easily definable, what he says makes no sense. It is not unreasonable to think that any right-thinking person should reject both propositions. There is a certain objectivity in this, a consensus working towards a truth. But one cannot claim even this degree of objectivity for Wittgenstein's mystical experience. One can pity someone who does not have it, but one cannot say that his view of the world is wrong even in the sense in which one can say that to view Michelangelo's work as indifferent is wrong.

What is 'objective' about saying there is something problematic about the world or that it is a limited whole? If one must use this misleading word, then two things can be said. First, the mystical experience is outgoing: it looks to the world outside, albeit *my* world, not inwardly towards myself. Second, it is an experience that can be shared: other people can see the world as a limited whole and wonder that anything at all exists. But, it may be objected, one may share experiences of incomprehension and paranoia. Incomprehension, perhaps. Whatever about simple arithmetic, most people are baffled by higher mathematics and the latest in quantum physics and field theory. This is a shared negative experience; it has no content. Paranoia, on the other hand, has a content but that content is not shared. If you think there is a vast world conspiracy against you and I think there is a world conspiracy against me, there is an important difference in the two experiences. You are one of those who are conspiring against me. Since I know I am not conspiring against you, I have reason to doubt your sincerity. Perhaps you are just pretending to be paranoic all the better to disarm me. You can feel the same about me, and, in that sense, share my experience of doubt. But the important difference remains. While we both suspect the whole human race, I suspect you but not myself, whereas you suspect me but not, presumably, yourself. To that extent our experiences are not shared, whereas the experiences of wondering that anything exists can be shared absolutely.

In the *Tractatus* and the *Notebooks* Wittgenstein confines himself to one explicit example of the mystical: seeing the world as a bounded whole and marvelling that anything at all exists. I say one explicit example since it would seem that the apprehension of the logical structure of propositions and, hence, of reality, i.e. metaphysics, is also a mystical experience.

In his 'Lecture on Ethics' Wittgenstein gives two new experiences and elaborates on the example '*par excellence*', i.e. that anything exists. It should be emphasized that, for Wittgenstein, these are *examples*. This leaves open the question whether there might not be other examples, and the further and more vexatious question of determining whether they are mystical experiences in the sense in which Wittgenstein uses the term.

The two additional experiences are: the experience of 'feeling *absolutely* safe', and 'that of feeling guilty'. I shall return to these. But first a word has to be said about the context in which they appear and also about Wittgenstein's additional material on the example '*par excellence*'.

As to the context, this has been discussed fully in chapter two. Briefly, what Wittgenstein is saying is that ethics is concerned with absolute good, not with relative good. But absolute good makes no sense – everything that is good must be good for something, i.e. relatively good. Hence ethics is nonsense. However, what does not make ordinary sense may make extraordinary sense; what cannot be said can, perhaps, be shown: it can manifest itself. These manifestations can be called the 'mystical', following the terminology of the *Tractatus* and the *Notebooks*, though Wittgenstein does not use the term 'mystical' in his lecture.

To begin with the experience of absolute value '*par excellence*', the 'first and foremost example' (*PRv* p. 8), Wittgenstein is at pains to show that statements of absolute value are nonsense, because they involve a misuse of language. They are an attempt to say what cannot be said in language. It makes sense to wonder that something is other than it might have been – a dog larger than ordinary dogs, a house still standing, the sky being blue rather than overcast. But it makes no sense to wonder at 'the sky being *whatever* it is', i.e. whether blue or overcast. That amounts to wondering at a tautology: that the sky is blue or not blue. This, says Wittgenstein, is nonsense: 'it's just nonsense to say one is wondering at a tautology' (*PRv* p. 9). According to Wittgenstein, to wonder at something in the ordinary sense one must be able to conceive it as being other than it is: 'To say "I wonder at such and such being the case" only has sense if I can imagine it not to be the case.' But to wonder at a tautology is to wonder that something is whatever it is: that it is or is not what it is, like wondering whether it is going to rain or not going to rain.

It is easy to see that it would be odd to wonder at every size of dog, at a building that had been demolished as at one that is still standing, at a clouded sky equally with a blue sky. But why can one not wonder at the very existence of dogs, large and small, houses, whether past or present, the sky, whether blue or not? It might have been the case that not only no dogs, houses or sky, but that nothing whatsoever exists or existed. Of course, there would be, or there would have been no one around to wonder. But that is not the point. The point is that by Wittgenstein's own criterion of ordinary usage, I can only wonder at something *being* the case if I can imagine it *not* being the case. My question is: can I not imagine nothing being the case, and if not, why not?

If nothing ever existed, that, in a curious way, would be the case, though it could never be stated. But I am not sure this is the sense in which Wittgenstein intends the phrase 'is the case'. To be the case for him seems to mean to be a such and such, not just anything. Thus one can wonder at the sky being blue rather than its usual overcast grey; or at herds of elephants roaming Hyde Park, but not roaming the forests and scrubland of Africa or India. Presumably, one can wonder at the reappearance of the dodo but not at the appearance of baby elephants in Africa. On this interpretation, for something to be the case or not the case has nothing to do with with *that* it exists or does not exist, but with *how* it exists: is it big or small, standing or demolished, clear or overcast? On this interpretation, therefore, for something to be the case or not to be the case, *something* must exist. If nothing existed it would make no sense to talk of 'something' either being or not being the case. This interpretation has the advantage of being conditional. It does not commit Wittgenstein to the view that something *must* exist, that non-existence is unimaginable, either in particular or in general. Hence, *a fortiori*, it does not commit him to the view that *what is must be*. What is might have been otherwise. What it does commit him to – and this is why I think it is the correct interpretation – is the view that, when we talk of the possibility of there being nothing at all, we are speaking a different language from the one we speak when talking about the possibility of there being no elephants in twenty years' time.

Thus, in Wittgenstein's view, the use of 'wondering' and 'existence', when we speak of wondering that anything exists, is a misuse of language, and hence nonsense.

The same may be said of the use of the word 'safe' to express an experience of being absolutely safe. Normally, if we are safe, nothing can happen to us – indoors we cannot usually be hit by a bus. If we have had whooping cough, it is not unlikely to recur. On the other hand, while being absolutely safe, all manner of things might happen to us. But the point is that they have no effect on our equilibrium. We are beyond, above, and outside the vicissitudes of life. We may be run over by a bus or have a recurrence of whooping cough, but this has no effect on our mind and soul. Once we have accepted the fact that we are prone to these vicissitudes, we are safe from them. In a sense they affect us; but in another sense they do not and cannot. We have accepted them as the accidents of life, so they can neither surprise nor hurt us. This is an Oriental notion that Wittgenstein must have embibed through Schopenhauer. But it ties in with the wonder that what is, is. It is merely a step further: from wonder to acceptance or renunciation of personal interest.

About what he calls 'a third experience', that of feeling guilty, of being disapproved of by God, Wittgenstein says nothing more than that it is an experience 'of the same kind' as the other two experiences. By that I presume he means it is a mystical experience and inexpressible; any attempt to express it is nonsense. This seems obvious enough. Anyone who says he is absolutely guilty is certainly using 'guilty' in a strange way. Most of us have been guilty of sins of commission or omission of varying degrees of gravity. But to say we are in a permanent state of guilt without being guilty of anything in particular does not make sense. Yet mystics, religious people of all kinds, even philosophers such as Augustine, Aquinas, Pascal, Kierkegaard and Schopenhauer say this kind of thing and mean it. In one sense it is as basic to ethical and religious belief as wondering that anything exists or feeling absolutely safe. Since Wittgenstein did not even suggest how this experience might be explicated, it would be idle to speculate on what he might have said. But he did say it was the same kind of experience as the other two, so it might not be idle to speculate on what else they might have in common besides being mystical experiences. I would suggest that the feeling of absolute guilt is the reverse of the feeling of wonder. It is the realization that, in so far as we are facts, things, states of affairs that make up the world and have a psychological 'I' we are inadequate: that is our status. We realize our place in the scheme of things. This is more shame than guilt. But it is not entirely shame either. No one should feel ashamed of being born poor, crippled, mentally disabled, a Catholic, a Negro, a Puerto Rican or a Jew, much less should he feel guilty – what has he done wrong? Nor should anyone feel guilty or ashamed of being a healthy, intelligent, well-balanced, rich, Protestant Anglo-Saxon (though some do). But if the feeling of guilt (I would prefer 'humility', but 'guilt' is stronger) as I think Wittgenstein is using the term, is experienced, if someone realizes that he or she is insignificant, without having an inferiority complex, then he or she is having a mystical experience in Wittgenstein's sense.[6]

The next point may throw some light on what Wittgenstein means by saying that the mystical can be shown, not stated in a proposition. He says rather pompously:

> I want to impress on you that a certain characteristic misuse of our language runs through *all* ethical and religious expressions. All these expressions *seem*, prima facie, to be just *similes*. (PRv p. 9)[7]

Thus we think that words such as 'right', 'good', 'safe', 'existence', 'value', 'wonder', 'guilty' are being used in a similar way to their ordinary use, in what Wittgenstein calls the relative or trivial sense. The right way to behave may seem similar to the right way to Granchester; a good fellow similar to a good footballer. A man's life being valuable may not be the same as jewellery being valuable, but there seems to be some sort of analogy between the two senses of 'valuable'. All religious terms according to Wittgenstein seem to be used as similes or allegorically.

> For when we speak of God and that he sees everything and when we kneel and pray to him all our terms and actions seem to be part of a great and

elaborate allegory which represents him as a human being of great power whose grace we try to win. (*PRv* p. 9)

The three experiences Wittgenstein has described are also treated allegorically. The first, he believes, is exactly what 'people were (sic) referring to when they said that God created the world'. The feeling of absolute safety has been described as feeling safe in the 'hands of God'. And the feeling of guilt 'was (sic) described by the phrase that God disapproves of our conduct'. 'Thus,' he concludes, 'in ethical and religious language we seem constantly to be using similes' (*PRv* p. 10).

But are we? he asks. He goes on:

a simile must be a simile of *something*. And if I can describe a fact by means of a simile I must also be able to drop the simile and describe the facts without it. (*PRv* p. 10)

In the case of ethical and religious language there are no facts behind the similes. 'And so what at first appeared to be a simile now seems to be mere nonsense' (*PRv* p. 10).

I am not sure I correctly understand what Wittgenstein means by a simile. Does the term also cover metaphors? It is an important distinction. Most metaphors are merely similes with 'like' or 'as', and possibly something more, left unexpressed. Thus Captain 'Tiger' Saunders, is equivalent to the more long-winded: 'In battle Saunders is as ferocious as a tiger'. He could as well be called Saunders the Ferocious. Then why do we use the metaphor? Presumably to emphasize the form Saunders' ferocity takes and his mode of attack, or to make his image more vivid. As Wittgenstein says, in this case we can drop the metaphor or simile and describe the fact – Saunders' ferocity in battle – straightforwardly. But not all metaphors (or similes, if you prefer) are like this. As Aristotle pointed out, there are some metaphors where the fourth term of the proportionality can be known only by means of the metaphor. That is the reason for using it. It is not A : B (ferocity is to Saunders): : C : D (as ferocity is to a tiger), but rather A : B : : C : X or even A : B : : Y : X, where X and Y are subjects and attributes that cannot be known directly.

I take it that what Wittgenstein means by 'a simile of *something*' that can be described without using the simile is that A, B, C and D can be known directly. The simile, then, is nothing more than a rhetorical device, another way of saying what can be said in a more sober, less imaginative way; as, for instance, 'lift attendant' rather than 'bell hop'.

Value terms look like similes for something, but what that something is cannot be described in any other terms. To be morally good is not like being gastronomically good (a good meal) or good for a purpose (a sharp knife) or good at something (tennis, cooking, administration). A good man is not necessarily good for or at anything. So why use the term 'good'? We use the word because it has, in common with other uses of 'good', the implication of approval. We approve certain actions, attitudes and modes of behaviour for their own sake. Why we should do so can never be stated with any precision, as we can with utilitarian goods, goodness in achievement and even goodness of gratification. Morality can be given a utilitarian interpretation; in this way being morally good may appear like being good at tennis, or a good action like having a beneficial effect, and that it is in this that its goodness lies. But Wittgenstein will have none of that, no more than Kant or Schopenhauer before him.

Likewise of the other ethical and religious expressions. We can say of someone that he is a father to us, and other people will know what is meant. Kamil Ataturk was the father of the Turkish people; George Washington was the father of the American people; Faraday might be described as the father of the electric motor and Fielding of the novel. They not only brought into being a state, an invention, a literary form, but also sustained and nurtured it in its early years, as a father does his children. Similarly, we can understand such expressions as 'father-figure', 'sugar-daddy', or 'paternal' because of the similarity between the behaviour of those to whom these epithets are applied and the behaviour, or assumed behaviour, of fathers. But when we talk of God as a Father we are not likening him to an earthly father. Rather the reverse; St Paul says that all paternity descends from God. Therefore God should not be compared with fathers, but fathers with God. And this is the difficulty, not to say absurdity, to which Wittgenstein refers. In saying that Ataturk or Washington was the father of his people, you have some idea of what it is to be a father and in what respects these gentlemen may be regarded as fathers. But since we do not know God and have no direct acquaintance with him, we cannot know what divine paternity is like. If it is like human paternity in any recognizable way, that would be a bonus.

But it goes further than that. We can be confident that the paternity of God, whatever it is, is so different from human paternity as to render the term 'God the Father' almost meaningless. It might be described as an inverted simile. It is not: 'God is like a father' but rather 'a father is like God', except that, since we do not know God directly, we do not know in what respects a father is like God. In other words, to put it bluntly, we do not know what we are talking about. Hence, as Wittgenstein says, our ethical, theological and pious utterances lack sense; what seemed to be a simile turns out not to be one after all, since one term of comparison is unknown.

But, then, in his discussion of metaphor Aristotle suggests that we do get some knowledge, if only by analogy. If someone asks me what lychees taste like, I could tell him they taste the way roses smell only sweeter. I already know what they taste like, but he does not and he has to take my word for it. Yet he knows something about the taste, even if it is largely negative. Similarly, when we speak of God as a creator, or speak of being absolutely safe in the hands of God, or of incurring his wrath though not conscious of any misdemeanour, there is some meaning to what we say. But it is not what the words would ordinarily mean. A creator does not make things as do a carpenter or shoemaker; being absolutely safe in the hands of God does not mean that nothing can harm us; nor does incurring the wrath of God necessarily mean we have done anything wrong. Yet the analogy may hold in each case, even though it may be impossible to say wherein the likeness lies.

Wittgenstein next turns his argument on its head. The three experiences just described, he argues, must be facts since they take place at some time and in some place, and last a certain length of time, and are describable. But if they are facts, they cannot, on Wittgenstein's account, have absolute, intrinsic value, and it is nonsense to say that they have. Here Wittgenstein is using 'nonsense' in its ordinary sense, and not in his special, dare we say, mystical sense. To make the point of the paradox more acute, Wittgenstein says of it, 'It is the paradox that an experience, a fact, should seem to have supernatural value' (*PRv* p. 10).

Wittgenstein then proceeds to expound a way in which he 'would be tempted to meet this paradox'. At first sight, it may seem circuitous, but in fact it is not. It involves the notion of the miraculous. Wittgenstein defines a miracle as 'an event the like of which we have never yet seen'. This is how we ordinarily understand it. He gives as an example someone in the audience suddenly growing a lion's head and beginning to roar. What would we do in such circumstances? We would have the matter scientifically investigated. But 'when we look at it in this way everything miraculous has disappeared', unless by 'miracle' we mean what has not yet been explained by science. 'The truth is that the scientific way of looking at a fact is not the way to look at it as a miracle.' Wittgenstein goes on to say: 'For imagine whatever fact you may, it is not in itself miraculous in the absolute sense of the term' (*PRv* p. 11). So we have an absolute and a relative sense of 'miracle', just as we had an absolute and a relative sense of 'good'.

If I understand Wittgenstein correctly, for him, a miracle in itself, in the absolute sense, is not a fact. Nor is it something weird and inexplicable. It is not a natural wonder, like a two-headed man or a woman who could live without food, as, it is alleged, Catherine Emmerich could, or a blind man given sight. These are, in the words of Jesus, merely 'signs and wonders'. They may involve – must involve – facts; but the factuality of these facts has nothing to do with their being miracles. Thus the fact that water is turned into wine does not make it a miracle in the absolute sense, any more than it is a miracle to turn blue litmus red. At most they are relative miracles: marvels to be wondered at by schoolchildren or to be investigated by scientists. It is the way the facts are viewed that makes them miraculous. One can describe the experience (a fact) of wonder at the existence of the world (another fact) by saying 'it is the experience of seeing the world as a miracle'. But seeing the world as a miracle is not a fact either in or about the world. To someone who does not see it that way, there is no point in saying: 'But look here. Can't you see it is a miracle?' It is not like saying: 'Look here, it is dark green, not black.'

Though Wittgenstein says little about miracles beyond using the word *Wunder* in connection with aesthetics and in this passage in the lecture, it is clear that for him the miraculous and the mystical enjoyed the same logical or grammatical status.[8] It is not clear whether, for him, they were synonymous. It is hard to see how the experience of feeling guilty in the eyes of God, while not being conscious of having committed, or even contemplated, any heinous deed can be a miracle in any ordinary sense of the word. Yet there are the notorious, in the sense of well-known, cases of 'deathbed conversion', when someone approaching death sees his or her life in an entirely different way; sees acts of commission and omission or just a style of living that were, hitherto, merely facts of life, in a new light: as sinful. I am not saying that was what Wittgenstein meant. He meant something more profound, less intelligible and closer to what theologians, mystics and saintly people have said on the matter. But it could, at a stretch, be called, in ordinary parlance, miraculous.

Before leaving this matter of miracles a few further observations seem in order. Wittgenstein seems to have reached the heart of the notion of the miraculous. His account is invulnerable to Hume's gibes against miracles. Hume assumed that according to popular and theological belief, what makes something a miracle is that it is against the laws of nature. This, according to Hume, is absurd. His belief in the laws of nature led him to consider it more probable that the so-called miraculous event had not occurred, or had been wrongly described, or, if it had occurred and had been accurately described, awaited natural, i.e. scientific, not supernatural explanations. Wittgenstein simply bypasses this. For him the miraculous may in itself be perfectly ordinary, everyday and natural. What makes it miraculous has nothing to do with how it is in itself but with the way in which we look on it. He has more to say on this in his lectures on religious belief and in later remarks which will be considered in chapters nine and ten.

Wittgenstein suggests a possible solution to the paradox of miracles and mystical experiences. He suggests the problem may be met by saying that we do not express the miraculous or mystical *in* or *by means of* language, but *by the existence of* language itself. But he sees this will not do. Even if the miraculous and mystical were expressed by the existence of language itself (whatever that means), it is just another way of saying that the miraculous and the mystical are inexpressible: 'all we *say* about the absolute miraculous remains nonsense' (*PRv* p. 11). Wittgenstein also proposes the objection that this solution does not account for our awareness of 'this miracle at some times and not at others'. I presume he means that if language as such were an expression of the miraculous and mystical, we should be aware of the miracle of the existence of the world at all times, during all our waking and thinking hours.

Since this is a Wittgensteinian solution that he himself rejects, and rightly to my mind, it is hardly necessary to dwell on it. What is of greater interest is the way he deals with a possible reply to objections to his own suggestions. It deserves to be quoted in full:

> Now the answer to all this will seem perfectly clear to many of you. You will say: Well, if certain experiences constantly tempt us to attribute . . . to them . . . absolute or ethical value and importance, this simply shows that by these words we *don't* mean nonsense, that after all what we mean by saying that an experience has absolute value *is just a fact like other facts* and that all it comes to is that we have not yet succeeded in finding the correct logical analysis of what we mean by our ethical and religious expressions. (*PRv* p. 11)

In chapter one we discussed Wittgenstein's answer to this objection: namely that expressions of absolute value, of the miraculous and the mystical, are not nonsensical because a means of expressing them satisfactorily has not yet been found. No expression can express them, since to say of an experience that it is mystical or a miracle is to attempt to go beyond the boundary of language, to say the unsayable. Of its essence, such language is nonsensical in the Wittgensteinian sense.

Finally, we move to the application of the notion of the mystical to ethics and religious belief. Religious belief gets only a brief mention in the 'Lecture on Ethics', and none at all in either the *Tractatus* or the *Notebooks*, apart from what is said about God, which will be dealt with in the next chapter. But one can safely take it that what is said in the *Tractatus*, and, by implication, in the *Notebooks*, refers to religious belief as well as to ethics, since clearly they are coupled in the final paragraph of the lecture: 'I believe the tendency of all men who have ever tried to write or talk Ethics or Religion was to run against the boundaries of language' (*PRv* p. 12).

Ethics is not specifically mentioned in connection with the mystical in the *Tractatus*. But there are bridges. Ethics has to do with value; propositions of ethics are not possible, since propositions express nothing 'higher' (*TLP* 6.42); the higher is not concerned with *how* things are in world (*TLP* 6.432); value lies outside the world (*TLP* 6.41); it is not how things are that is mystical, but *that* the world exists (*TLP* 6.44). Hence: ethics=value=the higher=outside the world=not *how* but *that* the world is=the mystical. All this is made explicit in the *Notebooks* and in the lecture. So why did Wittgenstein not make it more explicit in the *Tractatus*? Perhaps he thought that anyone who shared his thoughts could make the connections for himself and it would be an insult to make them for him. The rest could fend for themselves. Mercifully, we have the *Notebooks* and lecture to guide us in our wanderings.

In the *Notebooks*, though, there is no mention of the mystical as such, but there is mention of seeing *sub specie aeternitatis* (*NB* p. 83, 7.10.16). These entries are mainly concerned with art and aesthetics, but there is an entry connecting art and ethics:

> The work of art is the object seen *sub specie aeternitatis*; and the good life is the world seen *sub specie aeternitatis*. This is the connection between art and ethics.

We can reasonably assume that what follows applies both to ethics and aesthetics.

> The usual way of considering (things) sees objects from within their midst; the consideration *sub specie aeternitatis* is from outside.
> Thus it is that they have the whole world as background.
> Is it something like this, that the object is seen *with* space and time instead of *in* space and time? (My translation)

Wittgenstein goes on in the next entry (*NB* p. 83, 8.10.16) to compare contemplating a stove among other objects in a room with contemplating it *as* a stove. In the latter case it becomes *my* world and everything else momentarily pales into insignificance. He concludes:

> For one can comprehend the mere present perception just as an insignificant momentary picture in the whole temporal world, but also as the true world beneath shadows.

To take it out of its insignificance, its meaninglessness, its temporality, its momentarity and give it significance, is to see it aesthetically as an object in its own right, outside space and time, with the whole of space and time as a mere background, a mere shadow. (This is the *Ode on a Grecian Urn* syndrome – 'She cannot fade, though thou hast not thy bliss/For ever wilt thou love, and she be fair!')

But what has this to do with ethics? Everything. You can give someone some money to get rid of him, to win his vote, to bribe him to do something for you, to reward him for having done something for you, because you feel sorry for him, or for him to buy you a packet of cigarettes. None of these are necessarily bad motives. But are they morally good? And, if they are, why? As actions they are like any others, facts about the world; physical facts – the handing over of money; and psychological facts – irritation, ambition, cunning, generosity, sympathy or pragmatism. As such they have no significance, no meaning, as Wittgenstein understands it. Indeed, if he is correct, they are just that: facts about the world. So where does ethics break in? It breaks in where it always breaks in. Aquinas believed that all acts that are not evil are, however trivial, morally good acts. Scotus and his followers held that there were good, evil and morally neutral acts. Cleaning one's spectacles seems to be pretty neutral morally, especially if performed in the privacy of one's study, though it could have mildly moral implications of conscientiousness, discipline and seriousness of purpose, as opposed to slackness, laziness, slovenliness, lack of personal discipline and neglect of personal hygiene. But what makes it moral, either way? Utilitarians would say the consequences of the action are the morally determining factor. In many instances they may be right. If I do not take care to keep my spectacles clean when marking examination papers, I may be doing the candidates an injustice. But is that all there is to it? Why should I have to clean my spectacles or even use a magnifying glass to read obscure handwriting and thus be fair to a student who does not think it his duty to be fair to me and write a fair hand – and I am not talking of students under pressure of a three-hour examination, but students with months at their disposal? If I take a moral stance on the matter and decide to do the decent thing and either clean my spectacles or use a magnifying glass or both, it is to be fair to the student who should have written in legible handwriting. Viewed *sub specie aeternitatis* it is the right thing to do, the morally right thing. Pragmatically it might not have been in the candidate's long-term best interests. This is where morality can be a nuisance.

So trivial though it may be to clean one's spectacles, it may take on ethical, even transcendental, significance if viewed not just as an action done in the privacy of one's study (as a fact, like other facts such as shifting the chair or scratching one's cheek) but from outside the world, in the eternal present, *sub specie aeternitatis*, with the whole world as its background.

Though Wittgenstein tells us what it means to see an object *sub specie aeternitatis*, he gives no example in the *Notebooks* of what it is to see life or an action in it *sub specie aeternitatis*. However, since both in the *Tractatus* and in the *Notebooks* he says that 'Ethics and aesthetics are one' (*TLP* 6.421) and more explicitly in the *Notebooks* (*NB* p. 83, 7.10.16) that this, namely, seeing *sub specie aeternitatis* 'is the connection between art and ethics', it seems safe to extrapolate from what he says about aesthetics to ethics.

Before leaving the mystical, there is a remark about the mystical and God that Wittgenstein did not make but could have made. Whether he would have made it is another matter. It is this. Could it not be said that what differentiates someone who believes in God from one who does not is that the first marvels at the existence of the world, the miracle that anything exists, that things exist as they do, whereas someone who does not believe in God does not share this experience? The non-believer may accept that things could have been other than they are and that there might well have not been anything. But *that* anything, rather than nothing, exists is not, for him, mysterious, miraculous, marvellous, a matter for wonder. It is just how things are. If he has any problem, it is about how they got to be there, how things came about. Hence, for the non-believer the world is not seen as a limited or a bounded whole but as a conglomerate of things and events. These can be either explained by science; or they must be left as inexplicable facts; or they are simply meaningless in themselves: there is no God and no teleology to explain them.

Let us follow this through a little further. If there is any truth in this, two questions arise: (1) is it a *necessary* condition for belief in God that someone should marvel that anything exists? and (2) is it a *sufficient* condition? It might be argued that it is a sufficient condition, provided a certain latitude can be given to the notion of God. It could be said that someone who had Wittgenstein's mystical experience of existence *eo ipso* qualified to be at least a pantheist of sorts. But he could also be a believer in a transcendent God, a God outside the world. Indeed, if I read Wittgenstein aright, any pantheism would need to have an element of transcendence. It cannot be the mere pantheism, belief in the divinity of the things in the world, of rocks and stones and trees. An experience of the marvel of existence, however, would seem to be a normal *consequence* of belief in God. It would be hard to prove that it is a necessary *condition for* such a belief.

5

God

God is mentioned four times in the *Tractatus*. Each reference is incidental to the philosophy of religion, except, perhaps for *TLP* 6.432: 'God does not reveal himself *in* the world.' I shall return to this.

However, these passages give us some insight into Wittgenstein's thinking about God at the time. They refer to (a) the limitations of God's power in creating; (b) the logical implications of the act (or acts) of creation; and (c) God and Fate in relation to the laws of nature.

As to the first (*TLP* 3.031) he says:

> It used to be said that God could create everything except what would be contrary to the laws of logic. The reason being that we could not *say* what an 'illogical' world would look like.

I do not think much should be made of the phrase 'It used to be said' (*Man sagte einmal*). What, if anything, one may ask, are they saying now? But I do not think Wittgenstein is quoting this view as out-dated. I interpret it as: 'I do not know whether this view is still held. It was once. Whether it is still held is irrelevant to what I have to say. I am using it to make a philosophico-logical point.' That point was that nothing illogical can be said or thought, which has nothing directly to do with creation. What is clear is that Wittgenstein is not making a theological commitment. Why should he? He is not concerned with theology in this or any other part of the *Tractatus*, so he is entitled not to reveal his views on divine creation. Perhaps he wished to distance himself, not committing himself either way, lest his philosophico-logical point be obscured by theology.

Back to creation again in the second passage (*TLP* 5.123). Here we may have made a slight advance on *TLP* 3.031 to the extent that it looks, after all, as if Wittgenstein may have believed that God could not create anything contrary to the laws of logic.

If a god creates a world in which certain propositions are true, he thereby also creates a world in which all their consequences hold. And similarly he could not create a world in which the proposition 'p' is true without creating its collection of objects.

Once again we have an entry that is reinforcing a logical point. This point concerns truth-grounds (*Wahrheitsgründe*) and the relationship between propositions that follow from or contradict one another. In this context the appearance of God is curious. Strictly speaking he adds nothing to the argument. Quite the contrary. What is said of him is a consequence of the argument, almost an aside; at least as stated. The insertion of an 'even' would have given the entry more obvious relevance. The argument would then run: even God is governed by these logical laws; that is, he could not create a world in which the proposition 'p' is true and its consequences, together with their objects, are not.

Given this, together with what Wittgenstein says about contradictory propositions in *TLP* 5.1241, one would be led to conclude that in his view God could not create what is contrary to the laws of logic. *TLP* 5.1241 asserts: 'Every proposition that contradicts another is a negation of it.' Now if God creates a world in which proposition 'p' is true and similarly all its consequences and their objects, and if a proposition that contradicts another proposition negates (*verneint*) it, it follows that God cannot create a world in which both propositions are true. Hence even he is subject to the laws of logic. He has to choose between a world in which either 'that p' or 'that not-p' is true; he cannot create a world in which both are true.

The third reference to God is in *TLP* 6.372. Once more God is introduced within the context of a philosophico-logical discussion. This time it is about causality and the laws of nature. Wittgenstein maintains, after the Occamites, the Occasionalists, Hume and others, that there is no logical foundation for the process of induction and the natural laws resulting from it, since there is no logical foundation for causal necessity on which those laws depend.

> A necessity (*Zwang*) by which one thing must happen because another has happened does not exist. There is only a *logical* necessity. (*TLP* 6.37)[1]

But, according to Wittgenstein:

> The whole modern world-view (*Weltanschauung*) is based on the illusion that the so-called laws of nature are the explanations of natural phenomena. (*TLP* 6.371)

At this point enter God, or rather believers in God, who attributed every occurrence in the world to his will rather than to natural laws.

> Thus they halt at the natural laws as at something untouchable, as the ancients (stopped) at God or Fate.
>
> And, indeed, both are right and wrong. The ancients are certainly clearer in so far as they accept a clear end to the matter (*Anschluss*), while the new system would have it appear as if *everything* were explained. (*TLP* 6.372)[2]

It is not clear who 'the ancients' are. They may be pre-Christian and pre-Muslim, and probably were. This is immaterial. What is important is to understand what these passages mean.

The point Wittgenstein is making is that, whereas those who believed in Fate (whether abstract or personified) and in the Will of God had a cutting-off point in any explanation of natural phenomena, however inadequate it may have been, those who believe that natural laws can explain everything have no cutting-off point and, hence, explain nothing.

If you say that event B occurred because God willed it or Fate ordained it, whether or not event A that preceded it caused it to occur, you have offered an explanation for the occurrence of event B. God could will or Fate ordain that A should cause B to happen, but it would still remain that the occurrence of B was due either to an ordinance of God or a disposition of Fate. This may or may not be complete or adequate as an explanation, but at least it has a 'terminus' (the term used by the translators). Further questions may be asked such as: why did God will all bodies magnetically charged to attract bodies that have the opposite charge and repel those that have a charge (negative or positive) similar to their own? It may not be possible for mere humans to answer this question, but this would not detract from the explanatory force of the theological explanation, any more than the explanation of a defenestration would lose its explanatory force if someone could not explain why bodies thrown out of windows fall to the ground: the explanation as it stands is complete enough.

But, according to Wittgenstein, this is not true of scientific explanations. In his opinion, even if they explain something, they do not *and cannot* explain *everything*. Yet that science does or can explain everything is, according to Wittgenstein, part of the communal belief of the modern, the new system. (It is unclear where the ancient ended and the new or modern began chronologically.) The reason is they believe that when a causal explanation has been given, that is the end of the matter. But it is not. To explain the falling of a body from a window as due to a law of nature does not fully explain the phenomenon since there is no logical necessity compelling bodies to fall rather than rise or maintain their position and direction, as they would, presumably, if thrown out of a spacecraft. To say that God has decreed that all bodies attract one another, if correct, does explain why a body falls out of a window rather than rises or continues in a straight line. It does not, however, explain why God made such a decree; but that is another matter.[3]

A few further comments on this entry are called for. The first is the juxtaposition of God and Fate. At times it almost seems that Wittgenstein identifies the two. This will be more fully discussed in chapter eleven on predestination. Secondly, God is, so to speak, reinstated. It is no longer *a* god that is being discussed. The reason is obvious. If there were a plurality of gods, all doing their own creating and willing, the situation as Wittgenstein envisages it would be impossible. To attempt to explain a natural phenomenon by recourse to the Will of God would make no sense. One can ask: which god? 'Some god' would be less than satisfactory. Either each god had his or her specific area of creating and willing, as they had in the pantheons of Mesopotamia, Greece and Rome (Egypt is somewhat different), or they could poach on each other's territory. If the latter, then there would be no way of knowing whether, from the fact that the sun has always risen in the morning, that it will rise tomorrow morning. Perhaps a god who, for some reason, is against the sun rising will decree there will be no more sunrises or sunsets. The world will henceforth be in perpetual darkness or perpetual light. In such a situation our predictions would be just as hypothetical as Wittgenstein believed the moderns' to be: we should have no more grounds for believing the sun will rise or that the sun will not rise than those who believe in natural laws. For this reason it was wise of Wittgenstein to talk of God rather than a god.

Thirdly, and most importantly, this entry throws light on Wittgenstein's thinking about the Will of God. As is evident from what he says about God and ethics (chapter two) he seems to regard God's Will as all-powerful. He is prepared to admit that whatever God wills to be right is right. But here he seems to admit that even the laws of nature could be subject to God's Will. If one accepts the Humean analysis of the laws of nature, then recourse to the Will of God is very tempting.

Finally there is *TLP* 6.432. Here at last Wittgenstein makes a direct contribution to philosophical theology within his system of thought, albeit a negative one.

> *How* the world is, is, for the higher, perfectly indifferent. God does not reveal himself *in* the world. (*TLP* 6.432)

Here God is being brought in to reinforce a philosophico-logical point about what Wittgenstein calls the 'higher' to which ethical, aesthetic and religious values belong. But this time a substantive point about God is made: namely, that he is not *in* the world. In Wittgenstein's thought this means that God is not a fact like other facts, much less a thing among other things. Like everything 'higher' God is transcendent. It is worth noting (though, perhaps, not too much significance should be attached to this) that the tentative, hypothetical, distanced approach to God – 'it used to be said', 'if a god . . .', 'the ancients held . . .' – is absent. Here we have a straightforward statement about God. This does not imply that Wittgenstein believed in God. The sentence could be phrased without change of meaning: 'If there were a god, he would not reveal himself *in* the world.'

However, no matter which way the sentence is put, it seems to run counter to the teaching of almost every religion. For the Pantheist, God is the world or Nature. For the Hebrew, God revealed himself in historical events. For the Christian, God reveals himself not only in historical events in general but particularly in the life of Jesus Christ. For the Muslim, God reveals himself in the world as Kismet or Fate.

Wittgenstein does not contradict any of this. He is not saying God does not reveal himself, but that he does not reveal himself as a fact or event or state of affairs that form part of the world. God, therefore, like value, is 'outside the world', not part of it. God, like value, belongs to what is higher. So, in so far as he reveals himself, it is not as part of the world, the world of historical facts or scientific data. Even a Pantheist such as Spinoza could accept this. Even if the world (*Natura Naturata*) is God (*Natura Naturans*), God is still in some way distinct from and 'outside' the world in so far as it evolves from his nature or essence.⁴

I shall discuss later how this can be reconciled with Christian doctrine. I should also like to make an observation that has a bearing on proofs for the existence of God. There are two kinds of proof: *a priori* derived from the concept of God, and *a posteriori* based on facts about the world and the principle of causality. It is usually said – Aquinas and the Thomists said it; Kant said it; countless others are still saying it – that you cannot argue from a concept to the existence of anything. So if there is to be a proof for the *existence* of God, it must be *a posteriori*. In the light of what Wittgenstein said this would make God a fact in the world – a prime mover, a first uncaused cause, that on which everything depends but which depends on nothing, an exemplar cause or a governing intelligence, or a combination of all five. Though in a vastly more exalted way and of a very different kind, God would be no more than a part of the world's machinery, just as an autocratic ruler is part of the state he governs and the executive of a great industrial firm is part of the firm he runs. But this is not quite how everyone conceives of God.

I am not suggesting that the *a priori* proof is superior, as a proof, to the *a posteriori*. The lesson may be that the notion of proving the existence of God is a delusion, as Wittgenstein later demonstrated (*cf.* chapter eight). But the *a priori* approach has one thing to recommend it: it does not make God part of a causal chain. Indeed, as the Necessary Being, as opposed to contingent beings, he is an admirable candidate for the post of Wittgensteinian God. Whatever may be said about the Necessary Being as revealed in the concept of 'god', he is not revealed in the world, in the sense of being a *fact* in it. And, moreover, being a non-contingent being, he transcends the world as is proper for 'the higher'.

But it is doubtful whether Wittgenstein would recognize him as his God. Following the logical sceptical line, Wittgenstein says there is only logical necessity. This statement certainly applies to causality. Does it also apply to the notion of a being whose non-existence is unthinkable, inconceivable and, hence, impossible? It is not clear. One can see why a logician might be reluctant to say that one event necessarily followed from another if there was no entailment, even though there was no known case of the sequence of events not occurring. The possibility of there being a rogue case is, to say the least, a logical possibility. But none of this applies to a Necessary Being, if the necessity of its existence follows from its nature. It looks as though its necessity is a logical necessity: if there is even the hint of its possible non-existence, it simply is not God.

When we turn to the *Notebooks*, God features quite prominently. This must be treated with caution. It is said that Wittgenstein had given instructions that the *Notebooks* were to be destroyed; it is certain that he incorporated very little of this material into the *Tractatus*. What is beyond dispute is that, if he later repudiated these ideas, he had once held them. It is, therefore, perfectly proper to discuss them as his ideas. It is no less proper to ask why they were not incorporated into the *Tractatus*, and I shall offer an answer to this question later.

The entries concerning God were made on 11 June 1916 and 8 July 1916 (*NB* pp. 72–3 and 74–5). The significance of these dates may be of interest, but it is not relevant to what Wittgenstein recorded in his *Notebooks*.[5]

In the first entry he gives a list – what I am inclined to call a 'litany' – of the things he claims to know about God and the purpose of life. There are thirteen propositions in all. Only the last five deal directly with God. I shall consider them first. They are:

The meaning (*Sinn*) of life, i.e. the meaning of the world, we can call God.
And tie this in with (*daran knüpfen*) the simile of God as a father.
Prayer is thought about the meaning of life.
I cannot steer the happenings of the world according to my will: am entirely powerless.
I can only make myself independent of the world – and thus, in a certain sense, master it – only in so far as I renounce any influence over its happenings.[6]

On the face of it this, theologically speaking, seems a mess: it includes God, the meaning or purpose of life, prayer, my control (or lack of it) over the world, and, for good measure, God as father. But in Wittgensteinian terms it makes sense, though what that sense is may be hard to determine.

Let us begin with the suggestion that the meaning of life, the sense of the world, is God.

We shall have to take this by stealth. It falls into three parts. First, what does Wittgenstein mean by 'the meaning of life'? Secondly what does he mean by the 'sense of the world', and why should the two be regarded as synonymous? Thirdly – and oddest of all – why should we call either 'God'?

I take it that Wittgenstein does not understand 'the meaning of life' in a purposive sense. I do not think for him the life of a human being, much less a barn-cat, had a meaning in the sense of performing a function. 'Why are we here and what are we supposed to be doing?' does not seem to be the question he is asking. Nor would he pose it in the form in which it is usually posed: 'What is our destiny? Where do we go from here and how should we go?' Nor has 'the meaning of life' anything to do with scientific explanation, whether physical, chemical, biological, historical, psychological or sociological. 'The meaning of life' is simply what Wittgenstein says it is: the sense of the world. Life and the world are one and the same.[7] The sense or meaning of the world is that which makes it intelligible. Now the facts that constitute the world are not intelligible in themselves: they simply are or happen to be. They are not self-explanatory nor explicable by science or history, or they are only partially so. The sense of the world, if it has any, cannot lie within the world; it must lie outside it.

But many things lie outside the world: ethics, aesthetics, metaphysics, logic and language itself. Why cannot one of these be the sense of the world? I think that they are, in Wittgenstein's view, in their different ways. They make sense of the world. How they do so I have attempted to explain elsewhere. But, if I understand Wittgenstein correctly, their explanatory value is not exhaustive or complete. Something else is needed for a full explanation of the world. And that we call God. So God gives sense to the world or, in Wittgenstein's own terms, *is* the sense of the world, the meaning of life.

But what does that mean? It could mean that God is not a being, but the name we give to explanations of facts at a higher level. 'God' is a composite or portmanteau word for ethical, aesthetic and other values with which we grace the world.

The other entries on that fateful 11 June 1916 seem to confirm this view. But first we have to deal with God as a father, and with prayer.

It is hardly an exaggeration to say that it comes as a surprise when Wittgenstein tells us that the meaning of life and the sense of the world are closely associated with the simile that God is a father, and that prayer is thought about the meaning of life.

As regards God as a father, Wittgenstein could mean something quite interesting. The most obvious sense of 'God the Father' is that he created us, directly or indirectly, in creating the world; that we depend on him as we depend on a natural father; that he is concerned for our welfare and well-being. There is no reason for believing that Wittgenstein would either deny or support any or all these interpretations. What he actually says is that the notion of God as a father is connected with the notion of God as the meaning of life and of the world. My explanation of this cannot be more than speculative, since there is no direct supporting evidence. It goes as follows. One thing a father can give is a sense of reassurance and stability. He may be a tyrant; but, even if he is, and, perhaps because of his tyranny, he gives a sense of stability and, in a curious, arbitrary way, a feeling that there is, after all, meaning, sense, rationality even (if of a somewhat irrational kind) in this paternal activity.

This may not be consoling. Wittgenstein, if I understand him correctly, would be the last person to say it should be. For him, God was not the Christian Heavenly Father or even the Hebrew God of compassion. The Muslim God, Allah, not as the all-merciful but as Fate, the reason for everything that happens, would, of all deities, come closest to Wittgenstein's God. But perhaps it would be simpler and more accurate to say that his God is a philosopher's and, in Pascal's phrase, has nothing to do with the God of Abraham, Isaac and Jacob. That, however, will not quite do. It does not explain the 'simile of God as a father'. Wittgenstein's God is a religious God in the sense that he fits into a religious context in a way that Spinoza's does not.

This is confirmed by the next entry where Wittgenstein says that prayer is 'thought about the meaning of life'. This is not prayer as ordinarily understood – prayer of petition. But prayer, whatever form it takes, is a religious act. Moreover, prayer of petition or supplication, though the root sense of prayer, whether religious or secular (e.g. in a legislature), is not by any means regarded as the highest form of prayer. Indeed, in some circles it is regarded as superstitious. It is noteworthy that in the paradigm of prayers, the Lord's Prayer, half the invocations are not petitions in any ordinary sense and would make nonsense if taken literally. If God's name is not already hallowed, then he is not God, unless, as is dubious, 'hallow' is taken in the sense of 'reverence'. But even then, to petition God that his name be reverenced, that his Will be done and that his kingdom should come is something different from asking for daily bread. Experts on prayer regard mystical contemplation as the highest form of prayer, and there need not be the remotest element of petition in it. It consists in contemplating the nature of God and being in union with him. Now, if God is the meaning of life and the sense of the world, why should thought about the meaning of life not be prayer?

In an entry made almost a month after the litany of 11.6.16 came another, on 8.7.16 (*NB* pp. 74–5). This one lists the consequences of believing in God.

Much of the list repeats what was said in the earlier entry, but says it more fully; and there is additional material. It repeats what Wittgenstein said about the connection between God and the meaning of life: 'To believe in a god means to understand the question of the meaning of life' and 'To believe in God means seeing that life has a meaning'. Here Wittgenstein uses 'a god' and 'God' indiscriminately. But that is of no consequence since he is talking about *belief*, about what it means to believe in a deity, so there is no commitment on his part to believe, disbelieve, be agnostic or sceptical on the subject. He is not saying what he believes, but what he considers to be implied by a belief in God or a god.

Next there is the question of our relationship to God as an 'alien will'. This was broached in an earlier entry where Wittgenstein says:

> I cannot steer the happenings of the world according to my will, but am entirely powerless.
> I can make myself independent of the world – and thus, in a certain sense, master it – only in so far as I renounce any influence on its happenings. (*NB* p. 73)

To this the later entry adds:

> The world is *given* to me, i.e. my will enters the world entirely from the outside as into something already there . . .

Hence we have the feeling that we are dependent on an alien will.

Be that as it may, we *are* at any rate in a certain sense dependent, and that on which we depend we can call God.

God, in this sense, would be simply Fate, or, what comes to the same thing, the world independent of our will.

This is a development of 'I cannot steer the happenings of the world according to my will, but am entirely powerless' in the earlier entry, and it contains the following elements:

1   *The 'givenness' of the world.* I am, so to speak, pitched into it. It is there independent of me, and has been for some time. (One could elaborate this with reference to parents, relatives, various institutions, one's tribe, class or country, social institutions or historical background.) I did not even choose it, any more than I chose my name.

But this is somewhat psychological, or at best metaphorical. I did not enter the world entirely from outside. I was begotten *within* the world. I had no previous existence. And yet this description of how a child feels as it grows up is accurate. Entering the world is like going to school for the first time: one is entering a world already there, and the others make it their business to impress on the newcomers the fact that they are new.

2   *One's feeling of powerlessness in the world.* This is an undoubted fact. Even the most powerful dictator on whose *dictat* the fate of millions may depend, is powerless to control the forces of nature or even ensure that his minions will operate as he wishes; much less can he control the activities of his opponents. Every dictator or dictatorial person should have before him or her Wittgenstein's dictum: 'I cannot steer the happenings of the world according to my will.'

But what of 'I am entirely powerless'? Surely this is an exaggeration. If I were entirely powerless, I could not be writing this book. Or is it being written by some higher power, to which I am in a relationship similar to my own relationship with my typewriter, as some have conceived the relationship between the writers of Scripture and the Holy Spirit? I do not think this is what Wittgenstein meant. So we can dismiss *'vollkommen machtlos'* ('perfectly/completely/entirely powerless') as rhetoric and exaggeration. Yet it expresses a feeling: the feeling that most of the things I have power to do are relatively trivial. Over the important things that affect my life, I have no power at all.

3   *Dependence on an alien will.* This must be taken in two parts: (a) dependence on something; and (b) an alien will.

I take it that what Wittgenstein says about dependence on God in the 8

July entry follows from what he said about the feeling of powerlessness in the world written on 11 June, and is an elaboration of it. He says four things about dependence: (i) we have a feeling (*Gefühl*) of being dependent; (ii) we *are* (and he underlined '*are*') dependent in a certain sense; (iii) that on which we are dependent can be called 'God'; and (iv) in this sense God would be Fate or the world which is independent of our will.

That we have a feeling of being dependent is incontrovertible to all but a psychotic megalomaniac. But dependent on what? We know we are dependent on our parents, friends, employers, the air, and thousands of other things. What is bothering is the statement that we *are* (underlined) dependent 'in a certain sense'. What is this 'certain sense'? Does this mean that we are independent in a certain sense? I think that this is, indeed, what Wittgenstein means. And this is confirmed by what comes later.

That what we are dependent on is God, is traditional theology, though it does not follow immediately from the fact that we are dependent. We might call our parents or the weather or the community 'that on which we depend'. We might widen the scope of dependence to include the State (particularly those who depend on social security) or Society or Nature or even such things as the Economic Infrastructure or History. Abstract though these entities are, we can be said to depend on them in their concrete manifestations. We are certainly not masters of our own destiny, or if we are it is only to a very limited extent. We are victims of the caprices of Nature (droughts, earthquakes, floods), of politicians and civil servants, of our inheritance (riches or poverty, language, culture) and so on. But how do we get from these dependences to dependence on what we call 'God'?

We could say that all those things upon which we are obviously dependent are in their turn dependent. They cannot shape their own destiny any more than we can. A Five Year Plan for agriculture can be thwarted by drought or excessive rain; the 'course of history' does not determine itself, any more than Nature does. This leads us to think of something on which everything depends. One can call this Fate. But that does not say very much more than that whatever will happen, will happen. Wittgenstein is careful not to say this. Instead he says that 'God, *in this sense*, would be simply Fate', where 'this sense' is that on which we depend and is independent of our wills. To a certain extent this is traditional theological thinking: the theology of the 'will of God'. This is more than Fate understood as what will inevitably happen: it is the result of will, or even wilfulness. Of course the result is the same whether it was willed or merely happened: it is what happens, where we can do nothing to alter it.

The second part of (3) concerns the notion of an 'alien will'. It is not absolutely clear in what sense the will is alien. It could mean hostile. But the German *fremde* ('foreign') carries no such sinister connotations. 'Foreign' would come closer to Wittgenstein's meaning, but I admit that 'foreign will' sounds odd in English. Perhaps 'will of a stranger' might be better. But 'alien will' has by now passed into the language of English-speaking philosophy and, provided it is taken with the connotations of foreigner or stranger, and not in the sense of alienation or hostility, no harm is done.

More difficult to interpret is the italicized phrase that follows: *'Be that as it may'* (*Wie dem auch sei*). Be what as it may? The adjective 'alien', the noun 'will' or both? I take it to mean that to regard as alien something that is a will is what is questionable. The next entry can be interpreted as saying that, at any rate, there is something on which we depend that is independent of our will. We can call it Fate or God or the world.

Wittgenstein returns to this theme in later entries on the same day. They refer to the happy life and to conscience. To live happily, he says, is (a) to be 'in accord with the world'; (b) 'I am then, so to speak, in accord with that alien will on which I appear to depend'; and (c) 'That is to say: "I am doing the will of God".' So we have here the three elements we have already encountered: (1) the world, (2) the alien will, and (3) dependence on something. To these are added the will of God. (There is also the notion of being in accord (*Übereinstimmung*) with all four.) Fate is not mentioned. Is it fanciful, therefore, to conclude that Fate is to be understood more in the sense of Kismet than of the blind forces of Nature or 'what will happen will happen'? No, it is not. We are being invited to conceive of God as a will, whether benign or hostile, a will independent of our will that, in some sense, we cannot influence or deflect from its purposes and to that extent a will alien to our own.

The brief discussion of a troubled conscience, which Wittgenstein describes as not being 'in accord with something' (or, in Anscombe's translation, 'Something') leads him to ask what this something or Something is. 'But what is that? Is it *the* world?' And he gives a partial answer: 'Certainly it is correct to say: conscience is the voice of God.' So now we have a further element (the *voice* of God), to be added to the *Will* of God.

It seems that Wittgenstein, in time of war, is desperately trying to make sense of traditional religious expressions. (We must never forget that these notes were not intended for publication and, moreover, ordered to be destroyed, or so it is alleged.) So he translates 'doing the Will of God' into being in accord with the world, and the 'voice of God' as the voice that tells us that we are not in accord with something, i.e. the world. Wittgenstein is obviously talking here about a bad conscience. A good conscience implies doing the will of God, being in accord with the world. The voice of God, in that case, is heard only when we go off-course. Scripturally this makes sense. The voice of God is seldom heard in praise of what we do but invariably in condemnation of our misdeeds.

4 *The independence of my will.* Though the world is independent of my will I can in a sense make myself independent of it and so master it. This, however, is only by renouncing any influence on its happenings. It may seem a strange thing for Wittgenstein to say, since, according to him, we cannot influence them anyway. We have discussed *TLP* 6.37 in connection with *TLP* 6.372 where Wittgenstein talks about God and Fate in relation to natural laws. It is made explicit in *TLP* 6.374 (which, except for one word – 'itself' – is identical with an entry of 5.7.16 in the *Notebooks*):

> Even if everything that we wish for were to happen, this would be only, so to speak, a grace of fate, since there is no *logical* connection between the will and the world that would guarantee this, and the supposed physical connection itself, in turn, is surely something we could not will. (*NB* p. 73)[8]

So what, then, are we to renounce? It seems clear we are to renounce any attempt or desire to influence what is independent of our will. As long as we think we can influence the world and try to master its happenings, we are doomed to failure. We are banging our heads against a brick wall and thus hurting ourselves, without achieving independence. But how does renunciation give us independence?

Renunciation is one side of the coin, of which accord with the world and the alien will is the other. That is to say, renunciation is the negative condition for accord. It is a prerequisite for being in accord with the world, doing the will of God, answering the voice of God. You cannot renounce any desire or attempt to influence the world (the alien will) without *eo ipso* being in accord with it: one entails the other.

We master the world and become independent of it by rising above its vicissitudes or happenings. In one sense, they affect us – we are caught up in a war that is not of our making; we are, perhaps, menaced by incompetent, officious, malicious officials; or perhaps our wife leaves us for another man; or our firm goes bankrupt and we are unemployed; or we contract a terminal illness. Now we can either fight ineffectually against all this, accept it passively, or accept it actively: that is, recognize that we are a victim of Fate, or forces over which we have no control, and recognize that that is how matters are. Taken in the latter sense, these vicissitudes do not affect us at all. We rise above them, rather as a martyr or a political prisoner or prisoner-of-war can rise above torture and cruel death. He accepts it and, therefore, thwarts it, robbing it of its purpose, which is to bring him to heel, to subdue him and force him to repent, confess, conform or yield information. On a more mundane level, there are those who accept the fact that they cannot influence the rain, the snow or extreme heat; though affected by these vicissitudes of weather, they do not allow them to affect them spiritually. To that extent they become independent of the elements; they master them, though not in the sense of stopping the rain, the snow or the extreme heat. In mastering them, and becoming independent of them they are, in a sense, in accord with them.

This is nothing more than what spiritual writers and mystics from both the East and the West have been saying for centuries. Think, for example, of St Francis addressing 'Brother Fire' when his eye was about to be cauterized.

According to Wittgenstein, this can be only achieved at the boundaries of the world. Willing, good or bad, cannot change the facts of the world. I interpret this as meaning that it is the construction we put on the facts – in this case rising above them rather than trying to react against them or succumbing to them. In neither case are we independent of them.

Thus, according to Wittgenstein there is a certain connection between God, the world, Fate, meaning or purpose of life, and an alien will, something on which we all depend. Whether they are synonymous or aspects of the same entity is not of immediate concern. They are intimately connected. What is of immediate interest, arising from (4) is the independent 'I', my will as independent of the world, and its relationship to God.

If I can, in any sense, be independent of the world or of Fate, then I am a force to be reckoned with. This leads Wittgenstein to the remarkable statement: 'There are two deities: the world and my independent "I" '. (Anscombe translates *Gottheit* as 'Godhead' and *Ich* as 'I'. While 'Godhead' will serve for 'deity', it usually refers to the divine nature, and is, in any case, an odd word to use here. Its oddity makes it sound like a technical term, whereas in German it is no more odd than 'deity'. I presume Wittgenstein used this word in preference to *Gott* so as not to put the independent 'I' fully on a par with God.)

Strange though Wittgenstein's statement may seem, it is echoed by something that Cardinal Newman said. Ultimately there are only two beings that matter in the world: God and myself.[9] Everyone and everything else are relevant only in so far as they relate to these two beings. We must work out our *own* salvation; no one, not even God, can do it for us. Sartre has expressed this same idea dramatically in *Les Mouches* (*The Flies*) where Orestes confronts Zeus and taunts him for having made him free, and, therefore, to that extent independent. As long as his will is free he is impervious to the forces, even divine, arraigned against him. This is echoed in the thoughts of other Existentialists and Phenomenologists, and also in Nietzsche and Schopenhauer. This does not mean that Wittgenstein's thought is identical with theirs, simply that it is not as unusual as his terse statement would suggest.

So in what sense are we to take this statement? What has my independent 'I' in common with the world that warrants it being called a deity or a godhead? They have in common that both are:

a. *wills*: the *alien will* and my *independent will*;
b. they *transcend the world*; they are not facts in the world; they are outside the world;
c. they *give meaning to the world*.

That the 'I' is a will is clear from 5.8.16 ('If there were no will, then neither would there be that centre of the world that we call "I" ') (*NB* p. 80). Or rather it is the subject that wills. In so far as my will is independent of the alien will, it stands over against it, and so is, in a sense, one divinity or godhead face to face with another.

The world is clearly not a fact in the world. But neither is the independent 'I' that wills, since according to 4.11.16 (*NB* p. 87) the will is an attitude or position taken towards the world. To take up an attitude towards something, one cannot be part of that thing. One is taking up an attitude *towards* it. One must be able to detach oneself in some way from it.

I have already demonstrated that the world or God gives meaning to itself or is the meaning of itself. But the 'I' also gives meaning to the world in so far as it gives values to it and the objects in it: ethical, aesthetic and religious values. This is clear from the entry for 15.10.16: 'Things acquire significance only (*erst*) through their relation to my will' (*NB* p. 84). But it is stated specifically with reference to value in the entry for 5.8.16, quoted in part above, where Wittgenstein describes the 'I' as 'the bearer of ethics'.

Finally that both are 'outside the world' is evident from their not being facts in the world. But there is a particular reason for this in the case of the 'independent I' as bearer of ethics, since ethics, like all other values, lies outside the world.

Whether or not this was what Wittgenstein had in mind when he wrote that sentence is a matter for speculation. But at least it is consistent with his thought and should offer a framework for its interpretation. It is possible that Wittgenstein is not being as assertive as I have assumed. It may have been a merely speculative remark on his part. It certainly never reappears, though it would have fitted in easily and mysteriously to the *Tractatus*. Perhaps it was meant metaphorically, with, as it were, a suppressed 'like': 'in so far as I am independent of Fate I am like God.' If this is so, then it must be a very strong metaphor indeed, because, as we have seen, Wittgenstein toys with the Schopenhauerian idea that his will is the world will (*NB* p. 85). In that case he would indeed be God. That would leave no room for the *alien* will. So 'godlike' might be the best rendering of the sentence, though it might not suit Wittgenstein's style.

However this may be, the suggestion that the 'independent I' is a godhead or is godlike rounds off Wittgenstein's account of our relationship to God. God is the world, the alien will, the meaning of life. As the meaning of life, he is something to be contemplated (an object of prayer, God as a father). As the alien will he is something with which we can be in accord. Being in accord with it, we paradoxically become independent of it. In becoming independent of it, we confront it face to face, our wills in agreement with its will or not, as the case may be. This does not put us exactly on a par with the alien will, since we have no control over it. It largely controls us but only up to the point where we exercise our metaphysical will. Thus it does not exercise complete control over us. To that extent we are independent and godlike.

That single, brief statement – in the light of many others – encapsulates ideas about our relationship with God that have been expressed by various religions and philosophies throughout the ages. Initially in this section I referred to a few. What is basic to all of them is that, if we have a will, we are free, we can decide our destinies for better or ill. We are godlike. But, as Wittgenstein emphasizes, we can only affect the better or ill aspect of the world.

Finally, we may ask how Wittgenstein's God fits into the pantheon of philosophical gods. Rather well, I should say. He has all the essential attributes of a monotheistic God. He is transcendent. He is that on which everything depends, and in that sense is the creator. He is the arbiter of good and evil, right and wrong. He is the alien will with which we have to conform in order to be happy and at peace. After a fashion, he is, in these capacities, a father to whom we can pray, though prayer is to be understood as contemplation rather than petition; it is this contemplation that gives meaning to life in so far as life has meaning.

It cannot be too strongly emphasized that this compilation of Wittgenstein's ideas on God has been taken out of context. The items are largely taken from the *Notebooks*: the references to God in the *Tractatus* are, with one exception, incidental. More importantly, they are, for the most part, metaphysical rather than descriptive. But not entirely so. Our principal sources are the *Notebook* entries for 11 June and 8 July 1916. There Wittgenstein is not asking *what God is*, but either asking 'What do I know about God . . .?' (*NB* p. 72) or saying that 'To believe in God means . . .' (*NB* p. 74). So, to that extent, what he says is descriptive. The remarks in these entries tell us how Wittgenstein thought of God and for that reason alone deserve to be recounted. Moreover, if we take the 'Lecture on Ethics' into account, what is said about ethics applies to his Godtalk: 'I believe the tendency of all men who ever tried to write or talk Ethics or Religion was to run against the boundaries of language' (*PRv* pp. 11–12). In a few words, this chapter has attempted to express the inexpressible, say the unsayable, and, hence, to run against the boundaries of language. In subsequent chapters in Part II we shall consider Wittgenstein's later thinking on the language of religious belief.

PART II

The Later Wittgenstein

6

Language-games and Forms of Life

Reading the 'Lecture on Ethics' (*c.* 1930) one could hardly believe that Wittgenstein had altered his position on ethics and religious belief as expressed in the *Notebooks* and the *Tractatus*. If anything, the lecture expressed more forcefully and explicitly the views expressed in the earlier writings, particularly the view that ethical and religious expressions are nonsensical. We are told that it is of their essence to be nonsensical. Admittedly the term 'mystical' is not used. It has been translated into 'experience of absolute value'. But all the rest is there and elaborated.

If we reflect on this, it should seem strange. Whenever the lecture was delivered, it must have been some time after Wittgenstein had returned to Cambridge. As I understand it, his return to Cambridge and to philosophy was prompted in part by the fact that he no longer believed that the last word had been said on language and philosophy in the *Tractatus*. This, one would have thought, must mean he already had other ideas on these matters. Indeed, there are hints of these new ideas in the lecture. That makes it all the more surprising that the earlier ideas should reappear, reinforced, added to and further developed.

One of three conclusions can be drawn. Either the lecture was, as it were, a sort of backwater of earlier thought that had not yet been blocked off and dredged. Or, by the late 1920s or early 1930s, Wittgenstein had not yet hit on the account of language in terms of language-games. Or, even if he had, he still retained his views on the logical status of expressions of value. Even if a philosopher is dissatisifed with his earlier ideas, this does not mean he should abandon them before a new set of ideas is forthcoming.

It seems to me that at that time, around 1930, the ideas that were later to be expressed in *Philosophical Investigations* had reached no further than an embryonic stage. So there was no question at that stage of abandoning the previous theory of value. On the other hand, from the fact that the earlier ideas on value were being vigorously advanced in the late 1920s or early 1930s, it does not follow that these ideas persisted in Wittgenstein's thought to the end. The question is: did they? and, if so, how? and, if not, what consequences does this have for Wittgenstein's ideas on ethics and religious belief? I shall address myself to these questions in general here and deal with them more specifically in subsequent chapters.

Here we run up against a number of problems.

Of these the most serious from the point of view of Wittgenstein's previous distinction between fact and value is the abandonment of the picture theory of language and the adoption of the theory of 'language-games'.

The second, consequential on that, is Wittgenstein's relativism or apparent relativism.

Both undermine the distinction between fact and value by destroying, or seeming to destroy, the distinction between the sayable and the unsayable, sense and nonsense. Later in this chapter I shall discuss the seeming destruction of that distinction. For the moment I shall presume it to be so and discuss its consequences for Wittgenstein's views on ethics and religious belief.

It is popularly believed that Wittgenstein abandoned the notion of language as a picture or model of reality after the Italian economist, Piero Sraffa, making a gesture of disgust typical of Neopolitans, by flipping the back of his hand under his chin and asking what it pictured. I don't doubt that this incident occurred, but I doubt whether it had the effect on Wittgenstein attributed to it. Be that as it may, by the 1930s – when precisely is hard to say – Wittgenstein had become aware, not so much of the inadequacies of the picture theory of language, as of the absurdity of a *single* theory of language. He realized there can be no uniform theory of language: language itself is not uniform.

He also realized that logicians and philosophers talking about language were talking about an abstraction. There is nothing wrong with that. To talk about anything we have to abstract. But in abstracting we have to be careful not to lose sight of what we have abstracted from. This, Wittgenstein came to see, was precisely what philosophers of language, including himself, fail to do. They treat language as though it has an existence of its own and is greater than all of us. It certainly has an existence that is, to a great extent, independent of individuals. But it is not independent of mankind nor of the society of its users. It is basically a tool of communication, though it may be encouraged to take off from there into flights of imagination.

In the period between the late 1920s and the 1940s Wittgenstein came to see language as a tool, or rather a set of tools, as something which people *use* in order to do a variety of things. As we have seen in a previous chapter, the notion of the *use* of signs as determining their meaning is to be found in the *Tractatus* (*TLP* 3.326: 'In order to recognize a symbol by its sign, we must observe how it is used with a sense'; or *TLP* 6.211: ' "what do we actually use this word or this proposition for?" repeatedly leads to valuable insights'). The notion of language as a tool or set of tools seems to have occurred to Wittgenstein on his return to Cambridge in 1929. In *Philosophical Remarks*, thoughts jotted down during that period, there appears the remark: 'A word only has meaning in the context of a proposition: that is like saying only in use is a rod a lever. Only the *application* makes it into a lever' (*PR* 14, p. 59. My italics). In the previous entry (*PR* 13, pp. 58–9) he compares language to handles in a control room. Superficially they all look alike, and they have something in common in their application – they are worked by hand, they are handled. But their function and mode of handling is different. The crank is adjusted continuously; switches may have two or more positions; the pump has to be moved up and down. The moral of this analogy is that we should not treat similar words and sentences as if they have the same function, but we should look to the way they are applied, to the context in which they are being applied and the function they perform.

The analogy of the lever reappears in *Philosophical Investigations* (*PI* 12, p. 7) in a somewhat more elaborated way. It is joined with an equally elaborate analogy of the tool-box (*PI* 11–12, pp. 6–7):

> Think of the tools in a tool-box: there is a hammer, pliers, a saw, a screwdriver, a ruler, a glue-pot, glue, nails and screws. The functions of words are as diverse as the functions of these objects . . .
>
> Of course, what confuses us is the uniform appearance of words when we hear them spoken or meet them in script or print. For their *application* is not presented to us so clearly. Especially when we are doing philosophy!
>
> It is like looking into the cabin of a locomotive. We see handles all looking more or less alike. (Naturally, since they are all supposed to be handled.)

The message is the same: don't be deceived into thinking that words and sentences that look or sound alike mean the same thing. Look to the use they are being put to; look to their function.

Granted that words and sentences get their meaning from their use, whether in the language as practised by users of it or in eccentric uses of it (*cf. PI* 43, p. 21), it must, in Wittgenstein's view, be governed by rules and order. It is no good to anyone if a sign means one thing to one person and something else to someone else, or one thing at one time and something else at another, *without rationale*. Nevertheless, language is not so homogeneous as to provide a single set of rules. So how do we provide rules while still preserving the heterogeneity of language? Wittgenstein came up with a brilliant solution: the notion of the 'language-game'.

The notion of language as a game can be traced to an entry in the *Notebooks 1914–1916* (p. 37):

> The following question might also be asked: If I were to try to invent *language* for the purpose of making myself understood to someone else, what sort of *rules* should I have to agree on with him about our expression? (My italics)

The comparison of syntax to the game of chess is recorded in Friedrich Waismann's account of a discussion held in Vienna in 1930 on the nature of mathematics.[1] Wittgenstein is reported to have said that chess does not consist in the physical movement of wooden figures. It consists in the movement of certain pieces, some designated (king, queen, bishop, knight, castle), some variable (pawns) 'like the "x" in logic', *according to rules*, to a grammar, a syntax: the bishop can only move diagonally, the castle only straight; 'the word "can" means grammatically possible. What is against the rules is a violation of syntax.' At this stage Wittgenstein regarded games as on an analogy with mathematics as much as he regarded mathematics as on an analogy with games such as chess. Both involved rules: but more importantly, rules that were susceptible to a calculus – 'If there were men on Mars who made war like the chess pieces, then the generals would use the rules of chess for prediction.'

In his next set of philosophical remarks, *Philosophical Grammar*, covering the period 1932–3 or thereabouts, Wittgenstein has a section on chess and language (*PG* pp. 49ff.).[2] In the course of it he uses (apparently for the first time) the term *Sprachspiel*, which might more obviously (and less confusingly) be translated as 'word-play' or, if you must, 'language-play', but, in the received translation, it is 'language-game'. This appears in *PG* on page 62. On page 67 is a suggestion that there are other games than chess, games that are not 'calculus games'. These two movements in Wittgenstein's thought are most important for what is to follow.

Let us take *Sprachspiel* first. This arises, appropriately enough, in the context of teaching a child a language by so-called 'ostensive definitions' ('so-called' because Wittgenstein is not clear in what sense they can be called 'definitions'). Pointing to an object and naming it is, for a child, a form of play, a game in the broader sense. But while for the child this may be a form of play, for Wittgenstein it is play, or a game, in another sense. It is using language according to a set of rules, in this case the rules of naming objects, a rather primitive game.

The language-game is still very simple and the ostensive definition has not the same role in this language-game as in more developed ones. (For instance, the child cannot yet ask 'What is it called?') But there is no sharp boundary between primitive forms and more complicated ones.

In this passage Wittgenstein still talks of language as a calculus, an application of strict rules, as in chess. But he is hesitant.

I can only *describe* language-games or calculi; whether we still want to call them calculi or not doesn't matter as long as we don't let the use of the general term divert us from examining each particular case we wish to decide.

The reason for his hesitancy becomes apparent a little later (*PG* p. 67). He begins: 'I said that the meaning of a word is its role in the calculus of language. (I compared it to a piece of chess.)' He then goes on to show how an unpromising word, such as a word for a colour ('red') could be part of a calculus. But what of 'oh!', 'hurrah' and 'hm'? 'Oh!' he says, could be described as a sigh, as in 'Oh, it is raining again already'. That would describe its use. 'But what corresponds to the calculus, the complicated game that we play . . .?' These expressions may be symptoms (e.g. 'hm' may be a symptom of dubiousness), but they are not signs ('hm' is not the name for dubiousness).

By the time he had come to write *Philosophical Investigations* (the two sets of dictated notes of 1933–4 and 1934–5, published subsequently as *The Blue Book* and *The Brown Book*, intervening) these ideas had matured. The notion of language as a calculus on the analogy with such games as chess had yielded to a broader notion based on a wider analogy. So wide has it become – including ring-a-ring-a-roses, throwing a ball about or against a wall – that it is closer to free play than to rule-governed play such as 'game' implies. Wittgenstein never defines what he means by a 'language-game'. Indeed, we are pitched into the notion unceremoniously at the beginning of *Philosophical Investigations* (*PI* I, 7, p. 5) at the point where we first encountered it in *Philosophical Grammar*, in connection with children learning a language.[3] But an important addition towards the elaboration of the concept is made by the sentence: 'I shall also call the whole, consisting of language and *the actions into which it is woven*, the "language-game" ' (*PI* I, 7, p. 5: My italics). The actions into which language is woven are the key to Wittgenstein's mature account of language. It is described as a 'form of life' (*ein Lebensform*).[4]

Before coming to that, there are other matters to clarify. Apart from the fact that the concept 'game' is used by Wittgenstein as (a) an analogue of language itself, and (b) the prime example of what he himself regarded as a concept in normal usage (as against one with a specific or even unique purpose), what he chose to call 'family resemblance' (of which little, if anything, need be said in the present context), it is not immediately clear what counts as a language-game. Wittgenstein has not helped us by purloining the terms 'grammar' and 'grammatical' to speak of the use of language (i.e. the rules, whether conscious or unconscious, for its use in a given context) as opposed to the linguistic usage of the terms applied to grammar as traditionally understood. But, of course, he is right. The distinction is artificial. However, I am going to resuscitate the original usage to this extent: that I want to make a distinction between what I shall call 'syntactical language-games', that is, language-games within the structure of a language, and games that are played by the way in which language is used. This is not a rigid distinction but is one made by Wittgenstein himself.

In the *Tractatus* Wittgenstein confined himself to assertions, to statements of fact, and to what purported to be statements of fact, to expressions of value, but which, in his opinion, were not statements of fact. Through the 1930s he turned his attention to other uses of language such as instructions (*Philosophical Remarks* 10, p. 57) and exclamations, such as 'oh!', 'hurrah', and 'hm' (*Philosophical Grammar* 32, p. 67). In *Philosophical Investigations* he gives a fuller list and this time these grammatical differences are described as language-games.

> Here the term 'language-*game*' is meant to bring into prominence the fact that the *speaking* of language is part of an activity, or a form of life.
> Review the multiplicity of language-games in the following examples, and in others:
> Giving orders and obeying them
> Describing the appearance of an object, or giving its measurements
> Constructing an object from a description (a drawing)
> Reporting an event
> Speculating about an event
> Making up a story; and reading it
> Making a joke; telling it
> Translating from one language into another
> Asking, thanking, cursing, greeting, praying. (*PI* 23, pp. 11–12)

It is interesting to note that the analogy of games is combined here with the analogy of language as a tool-box. He goes on (*PI* 27, p. 13) to draw attention to the peculiarity of our use of exclamations such as:

Water!
Away!

Ouch!
Help!
Lovely!
No!

Apart from 'water' none of these name objects; even it, in the context of an exclamation, does so incidentally. What it and the other words or sounds are meant to signify can be understood only in the context of their use. 'Water!' may be a cry for that precious liquid in the desert, an exclamation of horror at its being added to malt whisky, or a cry of joy on reaching a lake on a hot day. The other expressions are not the names of anything (though they might be given as proper names to horses or pets, and 'help' can be both noun and verb). 'Ouch!' is the only pure exclamation, and joins 'oh!', 'hurrah' and 'hm' in the list of words that do not belong to a strictly rule-bound linguistic calculus.

This leads us smoothly into the second kind of language-game where the syntactical language-games play their part, but they play it within what I shall now call a 'cultural language-game'. Wittgenstein, as a matter of principle, has not given us a taxonomy of language-games or even a clear enough principle on which to base one.[5] But he has indicated what he had in mind. The key to a cultural language-game is to be found in the context of the form of life in which it is played. The form of life determines the rules; it also determines how rigorous or flexible these rules are, how closely they approximate to or depart from a calculus. This is their 'grammar'. What I call a cultural language-game is one invented for a purpose. Its rules are not autonomous (or 'arbitrary' (*willkürlich*) the word Wittgenstein used to express this notion, somewhat misleadingly in my opinion), as are those of chess and syntactical language-games.[6] Grammar, as ordinarily understood:

> does not tell us how language must be construed in order to fulfil its purpose, in order to have such-and-such an effect on human beings . . .
> The rules of grammar may be called 'arbitrary', if that is to mean that the *aim* of grammar is nothing but that of language. (*PI* 496–7, p. 138)

Cultural language-games, on the other hand, have an aim and purpose other than that of language as such. When someone buying a loaf of bread says: 'How much?', he is asking a question, and in that sense, playing a syntactical language-game; but he is also playing a cultural language-game, that of negotiating. Whether this activity is common to all cultures (it is certainly not common to all in the same form), it is a form of life and a cultural activity, and, as such, gives meaning to the words uttered.

This is a comparatively simple language-game, as is choosing the colour of a fabric or a paint from a sample-book or a colour-chart. More complex language-games involve such operations as doing the exact or physical sciences, doing psychology or anthropology, or making moral, aesthetic or religious judgements, conducting political or diplomatic discussions, discussing politics, ethics, aesthetics or theology, engaging in medical, architectural, technological, legal and economic discussions – the list is endless.[7] As Wittgenstein says (*PI* II, p. 224): 'We remain unconscious of the prodigious diversity of all everyday language-games because the clothing of our language makes everything alike.' But we can also remain unconscious of the diversity of more articulate and academic language-games which play no less an important part in the conduct of our lives.

The examples so far given involve talking about something. Language also has roles that are more integral to everyday life, whether mundane or exalted. Clear examples of these are the use of spoken or written words in making promises or contracts. When the bride and groom say 'I do' it is not as though they are answering a question of fact. Those words bind them together in wedlock. When someone takes an oath to tell the truth, the whole truth and nothing but the truth, he commits himself by his words, and, if he is of a religious disposition, calls on the Almighty to be his witness. Words are woven into ritual, particularly sacramental ritual. In *Philosophical Investigations* (*PI* 23, p. 12) Wittgenstein lists other examples: making a joke, making up a story (neither of which are strictly informative), thanking, cursing, greeting, praying, and what Anscombe translates as 'play-acting' which is an odd way to render *Theater spielen*. (Play-acting, in the sense of frivolous pretence or even inept acting, need not involve words at all.)

Though Wittgenstein does not say so explicitly, it seems reasonable to suppose that he would admit a diversity of language-games belonging to a wider language-game that embraced them all. Just as there is a diversity of games, all of which come under the term 'game', so there can be a diversity of scientific language-games – physics, chemistry, biology, geology, meteorology – and even within these games themselves – e.g. in physics: mechanics, thermodynamics, hydrodynamics, optics, crystallography – there can be a diversity of language-games. (The difference between scientific language-games is determined by the difference of the activity in which scientists are engaged, the methods they employ and the goals at which they aim, whether as scientists or as scientists working in a particular field.) Each scientist, while engaging in a common activity – scientific investigation – is engaging in it by acting according to the rules of his own particular branch of science. Language-games are not so dissimilar that they cannot share activities and certain rules. Just as there is no game that does not have some rules in common with other games – some require a ball to be hit, others for it to be kicked, thrown, rolled or spun – so there is no language-game that does not have some activities and rules in common with other language-games.

Yet a language-game, to be distinct from other language-games, must be characterized by a distinctive set of activities (with their attendant beliefs and assumptions) and a distinctive set of rules. However much it may resemble other language-games, it must be unique in its combination of activities and their purposes, as well as in its set of rules. Thus not only are, say, the various scientific disciplines distinct language-games because of their distinctive activities and rules, but science itself is a language-game as distinct from law, politics, commerce, or farming, as practices, as they are from one another and from their theoretical counterparts (jurisprudence, political economy, economics, agriculture) which, in turn, are distinct from one another. One of the greatest mistakes that can be made in philosophy and everyday life, according to Wittgenstein, is to mistake one language-game for another and try to apply the rules of the one to the other. Its equivalent in sport would be to whistle up someone in basketball or ice hockey for being 'off side', or to penalize a rugby player for handling the ball and running with it. In subsequent chapters we shall see how attempts are made to play the religious language-game according to the rules of scientific investigation. (This is not a one-way traffic. We need only recall the Galilean incident. And, more recently, the narrowly averted condemnation of the theory of polygenism.)[8] In his lectures on aesthetics Wittgenstein exposes the tendency in his time to attempt to reduce aesthetic judgements to the status of psychological reactions, and subject them to either statistical or in-depth analysis.

Thus religious belief, aesthetics, and, presumably, ethics and other expressions of value, such as metaphysics, appear to be in watertight compartments, impregnable to outside attack. This does not mean that value language-games are immune from internal, internecine attacks and controversy. But it does mean that anyone who attempts to refute a statement or expression belonging to one language-game according to the rules of another, entirely different one, is making a mistake. If he thinks he has succeeded, the mistake is compounded, for he has deceived himself. On the face of it this should give comfort to astrologers, parapsychologists, palmists and phrenologists, as well as to religious believers. However absurd their beliefs and practices may seem to those who do not share them, their positions seem unassailable, at least in terms of other language-games such as science (including the human sciences such as anthropology, psychology, sociology), history and archaeology or ethics. We shall be considering the relationship of science to religious belief at some length in later chapters, so it might be opportune at this point to illustrate what has just been said in relation to ethics and religious belief.

At first sight it might seem that religion and morality are so intricately interwoven that they cannot be distinguished, or, at least, not as clearly as both can be distinguished from the sciences. There is a belief in certain Churches, notably the Roman Catholic Church, that religion has the decisive say in moral matters. On this view there can be no conflict or attempted conflict between religion and morality. They are not two separate language-games. What others call morality is, in effect, merely a part of the religious language-game, alongside ritual, worship, the administration of the sacraments, devotion and aesceticism. It differs from such Church laws and injunctions as those governing attendance at worship, the reception of the sacraments and fasting and abstinence, in that it is claimed to reside in human nature where it was implanted by God. The Church cannot *legislate* on questions of morality; it can only *declare*, in the name of God, what is and is not moral. Clearly, on this view, there is no problem of a clash of language-games, since there is only one language-game.

At the other extreme there is the view that morality has nothing whatever to do with religion. This is the view of most modern Humanists and, indeed, most modern philosophers. Sartre is particularly eloquent on the subject. Indeed, in *Existentialism and Humanism* he even regrets the fact that this is so.[9] Some holders of this view also hold that religion is a chimera, a meaningless mumbo-jumbo incapable of sustaining or underpinning moral principles. It may be a language-game, they would say, but, as such, it is as truly a game as is charades or some other form of pretence. Others, not content with this attitude, attempt to refute it on moral grounds.

This latter seems to be a promising move. After all, a form of behaviour that offends against moral principles cannot be good and holy. Moreover, we accept or reject a religious system as much on the morality of the practices it prescribes as on its doctrine. Before embracing a faith we must ask ourselves if it is morally right to do so, if we are morally justified, whether in doing so we are infringing a moral law or not. This seems a sound way to proceed. Few people today would embrace a religion that prescribed human sacrifice, head-hunting or ritual murder. Many would reject a religion that required a widow to burn herself on her late husband's pyre, prescribed stoning as a punishment for adultery, sanctioned polygamy or ritual prostitution, or prohibited remarriage after a divorce. But to an adherent of a religion to which these rules apply, moral considerations to the contrary cut no ice at all. The law of God transcends moral codes when necessary. What is prescribed, prohibited or permitted by God cannot be immoral. Nor can God himself be immoral even when he permits the innocent to suffer or predestines certain souls to salvation and others to eternal damnation. To expect God to follow the rules of human morality is to misunderstand the language-game of divine activity and to try to apply to it the wrong set of rules.

Thus the distinction between the language of value and every other form of language is maintained, and, if anything, reinforced. Being a language-game along with other language-games it has its own internal meaning. The fact that within the scope of this language-game there are other distinct language-games – ethics, aesthetics, religious belief – does not alter this. The ethical, aesthetic and religious language-games belong to the wider language-game of 'expression of value', just as physics, chemistry and biology belong to the language-game of science. More accurately, they are manifestations or realizations of the language-games of the expression of value and of science respectively.

This may give a more respectable status to expressions of value, but perhaps at a price. The distinctions within expressions of value are to be found in the earlier works. Although religious belief is not mentioned explicitly in terms of value, except at the end of the 'Lecture on Ethics', much is said about it in the *Notebooks*, in which a clear distinction between ethics and aesthetics is made (*NB* p. 83: 'The work of art is the object seen *sub specie aeternitatis*; the good life is the world seen *sub specie aeternitatis* . . .'). But, it would seem, the clear-cut distinction between statements of fact – what is sayable, the expressible, what can be pictured as a possible state of affairs – and expressions of value – the unsayable, inexpressible, what is not a possible state of affairs, and, hence, cannot be pictured – is lost. All manner of other modes of expression have crowded in; expressions of value are on a par with them, and even with statements of fact, in so far as *they are all language-games*.

Worse still, with the disappearance of the picture theory of language, that special status of nonsensicality which expressions of value formerly enjoyed seems also to have disappeared. It would seem that they had ceased to be nonsensical, that they had become modes of discourse like any other, with their own rules of conduct, unlike, and independent of, all other rules of conduct. Within these rules what they say is sayable, at least for anyone who is prepared to accept the rules.

To draw this conclusion would be over-hasty. It puts a wrong emphasis on the autonomy of the language-game and on its status as a means of communication. It also misrepresents the change that had taken place in Wittgenstein's thinking about language. In place of a static view of language he had introduced a dynamic view. He had not gone back on his view on what is sayable and unsayable. There is no reason to believe that, as a language-game or set of language-games, expressions of value become any more sayable in later Wittgensteinian thought than they were earlier. They become more animated, that is all.

The notion of language in the *Tractatus* is static, because the picture theory suggests a picture hanging on the wall, enjoying an autonomous existence, but lifeless and immobile. It is nothing more than a mirror reflecting the world about it, or, rather, reflecting possible states of affairs – how something would look if it were to exist. Such pictures can range from an accurate portrait or landscape to a scale model or diagram. Understood in this way it is confined to facts and states of affairs. But it is a way of looking at them as though they and the mode of representation were frozen and still. The fact that expressions of value cannot be described in this way, since they do not picture or mirror anything – there is nothing to picture or mirror – does not enter into the static/dynamic account of language.

The account of language in *Philosophical Investigations* is dynamic, related as it is to activities and uses. Moreover, these uses are ordinary, everyday uses (*PI* 97–8, pp. 44–5). 'Proposition', 'language', 'thought', 'world' do not have any higher status than 'table', 'lamp' or 'door'. This reiterates what is said in *TLP* 5.5563: 'all propositions of our everyday language, just as they stand, are in perfect logical order'. The tendency to 'sublime' the proposition leads to treating it as an intermediary between the propositional signs and the facts (*PI* 94, p. 44).[10] This leads to another illusion: 'Thought, language, now appear to us as the unique correlate, picture, of the world' (*PI* 96, p. 44). But what, asks Wittgenstein, are these words to be used for? A language-game in which to apply them is lacking. We might have thought they could be applied in the language-game he played in the *Tractatus*. Not so Wittgenstein. Such a language-game is illusory.

The mistake Wittgenstein made was to treat these concepts as 'super-concepts' in trying to 'grasp the incomparable essence of language' (*PI* 97, p. 44). Though what he says here does not rule out the picture theory entirely, it curtails it. Not all meaningful uses of language are pictorial. It is no longer the sole account of language. The dichotomy between what can be pictured and, hence, said, i.e. the expressible, and what cannot be pictured and, hence, cannot be said, i.e. the inexpressible, no longer applies – or, at least, can no longer be applied usefully to the variety of language-games. And, while the concepts of the sayable and unsayable, the expressible and inexpressible, may still have a limited application, it can no longer serve uniquely to distinguish expressions of value, propositions of logic and mathematics, tautologies and contradictions, from other forms of expression. Not all expressions that do not picture the world, and, hence, in the Tractarian sense, are not propositions, are expressions of value.

Not only do expressions of value no longer enjoy their former status of being exclusively unsayable in *Philosophical Investigations*, but they also appear to have lost the exclusive status of being an attempt to run one's head against the boundaries of language. Replying to the objection that in bringing back such words as 'being', 'object', 'I', and 'proposition' from their metaphysical to their everyday use we seem to be destroying everything that is interesting, great and important (*PI* 116–18, p. 48), Wittgenstein says:

> The results of philosophy are the uncovering of one or another piece of plain nonsense and of bumps that the understanding has got by running its head up against the limits of language (*PI* 119, p. 48).

In other words, we are not destroying buildings but houses of cards, and we are clearing the ground of language on which they stood. Thus, not only are expressions of value attempts to run against the boundaries of language, but a large variety of other expressions that have no immediate relation to value are attempting to do the same.

In what Wittgenstein says about propositions picturing facts in *Philosophical Investigations*, it is clear he has restricted their range within language, or, rather, that he has widened his view of language to include, besides propositions of fact and pseudo propositions of various kinds, all manner of other language-games that have little or nothing to do with facts and yet are not necessarily nonsense or nonsensical. Nonsensicality arises when words are used, not just contrary to the rules (the grammar, in Wittgenstein's sense, not merely the syntax) but, in fact, have no rules, and, consequently, no home, no language-game in which to dwell. This is the force of the remark in *PI* 96, p. 44, where Wittgenstein talks of such concepts as thought, language, proposition, world: ('But what are these words to be used for now? The language-game in which they are to be applied is missing').

Before pursuing this further, I must first discuss the account Wittgenstein gives of picturing in *Philosophical Investigations*. So far is Wittgenstein from abandoning the picture theory (except in its universal form) that he actually develops it (*PI* 518–26, pp. 141–3). He distinguishes between portraits, genre paintings and senseless drawings, on the one hand; and propositions referring to actual states of affairs or merely to possible states of affairs, fairy tales, nonsense verse and senseless propositions, on the other. In *PI* 518, Wittgenstein quotes two questions Socrates put to Theaetetus: 'If someone thinks, mustn't he think *something*?' and 'And if he thinks something, mustn't it be something real?' (p. 141). He continues:

> And mustn't someone who is painting be painting something – and someone who is painting something be painting something real! – Well, tell me what the object of painting is: the picture of a man (e.g.), or the man that the picture portrays? (*PI* ibid.)

Applying this to language, we could say that an order that has been carried out is a picture of the action performed; but we could also say that 'it is a picture of the order which *is to be* carried out on the order' (*PI* 519, p. 141). Wittgenstein is stressing here that a proposition, or any other expression, has sense if it depicts a possible state of affairs. The object of a proposition need not be a real, existing thing. This is straightforward *Tractatus*, and *PI* 520, p. 141, echoes *TLP* 2.1–301, especially 2.151–2.171, in its very expression:

> If a proposition too is conceived as a possible state of affairs and is said to show the possibility of the state of affairs, still the most that the proposition can do is what a painting or relief or film does . . . (*PI* 520, p. 141).

But here Wittgenstein adds something to the original notion of a proposition as picturing. First he points out that logical possibility depends entirely on what our grammar will permit. We cannot do something with every sentence-like formation nor does every technique have an application in our life. By not considering the application sufficiently, philosophers are tempted to count something quite useless as a proposition; *cf. TLP* 6.53: 'someone . . . had failed to give meaning to certain signs in his propositions.'

Secondly, he says that we can compare a proposition either to an historical representation or to a genre painting. An historical representation purports to depict someone or some event that existed or occurred. Even if we do not believe that people depicted in a genre picture ever existed or that people had really been in the situation depicted, yet it 'tells' us something (*PI* 522, p. 142). What it tells is itself. 'That is, its telling me something consists in its own structure, in its own lines and colours' (*PI* 523, p. 141). (Here and in *PI* 527, p. 143, Wittgenstein compares propositions and sentences to a musical theme that also 'tells itself' by the pattern of its sound.)

All this lay fallow in the *Tractatus*. But the ingredients were there. Propositions had sense if they pictured a possible state of affairs and they retained it even if, on being asserted, they were proved to be false. This gave scope for fiction which Wittgenstein did not then investigate. Fantasy, in so far as it deals with situations that, for one reason or another, could never be realized, would probably have been dismissed (after Plato) as false, or nonsense. But in *Philosophical Investigations* not only were paintings of fictitious subjects (genre painting) and fictitious narratives regarded as having an internal sense which justified their existence, but also fantasies in the form of fairy tales, such as the pot that sees, hears and talks. To the suggestion that a fairy tale only invents what is not the case but does not talk nonsense, Wittgenstein reacts guardedly. He asks what the circumstances are in which we would say that the pot spoke (*PI* 282, p. 97). They must surely, one would have thought, be those in which humans would talk; for, to be intelligible, they must conform to the primary uses of such concepts as seeing, hearing, talking, and, in the case of dolls, being in pain.[11] Even a nonsense poem, Wittgenstein concedes, is not nonsense in the same way as is the babbling of a child.

Thus, the picture theory of propositions is preserved in *Philosophical Investigations* and its implications developed, but within the new context of logical grammar.[12] True propositions are still true by virtue of picturing what is the case; all propositions have sense if, and only if, they picture a possible state of affairs.

In a previous chapter we identified in the *Tractatus* various kinds of nonsense. Apart from useless, and, hence, *meaningless (bedeutungslos)* combinations of signs (hieroglyphs, pictograms, grouped letters), there were senseless (*sinnlos*) propositions that lacked sense because they can be applied to everything (tautologies) or nothing (contradictions) or they are superfluous (e.g. the 'Laws of Inference' of Frege and Russell); and nonsensical (*unsinnig*) pseudo propositions that have the appearance of propositions but no semantic content (logic and mathematics) or are meaningless combinations of words (most propositions in philosophy) or are an attempt to go beyond the boundaries of language. As we have just seen, all these kinds of nonsense occur in *Philosophical Investigations*. To them are added fantastic propositions, such as those in fairy tales, fictitious propositions that picture possible but not actual or real states of affairs, and the babbling of infants, which I take to include sentence-like utterances.

Expressions of value would still come under the heading of pseudo propositions and would still differ from propositions lacking sense, i.e. pseudo propositions that do not and cannot say anything (tautologies and contradictions) and nonsensical propositions that have no semantical content and are, therefore, without sense and, hence, incapable of saying anything about the world (propositions of logic and mathematics). But, whereas in the earlier Wittgenstein, propositions of philosophy were nonsensical because no meaning could be given to the signs they used, expressions of value were nonsensical because they were an attempt to go beyond the boundaries of language, to say the unsayable, to express the inexpressible. It would seem from *PI* 116 and 119, p. 48, that this is not a real distinction, since seeming propositions in philosophy which use concepts such as 'knowledge', 'being', 'object', 'I', 'proposition' and 'name' are similarly the bumps that result from the understanding running against the boundary of language. This was hinted at in *TLP* 4.1272 and more than hinted at in *TLP* 6.53 in the clause 'he failed to give meaning to certain signs in his propositions'. But if philosophical nonsense and expressions of value have in common that they attempt to go beyond the boundaries of language, they do so for very different reasons and with very different results. Philosophical nonsense – as Wittgenstein understands it – is an attempt to say what cannot be said in the mistaken belief that it can; that to say 'There are objects' is the same as saying 'There are books' (*TLP* 4.1272). Philosophical nonsense is a conceptual error. The concepts employed are pseudo concepts.

The concepts used in ethics and religious belief – absolute good, God, absolute safety, that the world is, absolute sinfulness in the eyes of God – are also pseudo concepts but of a different kind from those used in philosophical nonsense and they are used in different ways. For one thing, they are not used *mistakenly*. Doubtless many people have mistaken notions of how they are used and should be used (they erroneously regard them as statements of empirical fact), but the expressions themselves are not due to conceptual (much less factual) error. As Wittgenstein says, for errors they are too enormous (*cf. LC* p. 62). While expressions of value run against the boundaries of language this does not cause bumps (*Beulen*) to the understanding as philosophical language does. Their discovery does not lead to their disappearance as it does with philosophical nonsense. Nor can expressions of value be brought back from their metaphysical to their everyday use, as pseudo propositions of philosophical nonsense can (*PI* 116, p. 48). 'Their nonsensicality (is) of their very essence'; they are not nonsensical 'because I have not found the correct expressions' (*PRv* p. 11). This is what Wittgenstein said about them in his 'Lecture on Ethics' and there is no evidence that he later changed his views. There is no 'language-game which is their *original* home.' Words such as 'God', and 'absolute good' do not have an *everyday* use to which they can be brought back from their metaphysical one (*PI* 116, p. 48. My italics).

Another difference between philosophical nonsense and the nonsensicality of expressions of value is that the former do not belong to any language-game and the latter do. 'The language-game in which they are to be applied is missing' (*PI* 96, p. 44). One remark in *Philosophical Investigations* makes it clear that Wittgenstein regarded ethics as a language-game. He is talking about the difficulty we encounter in trying to draw a sharply defined picture 'corresponding' to a blurred one, say, a rectangle. It is a hopeless task. If the blurred one shades into the surrounding colours, one might as well draw a circle or a heart as a rectangle. He concludes: 'And this is the position you are in if you look for definitions corresponding to our concepts in aesthetics and ethics'. He continues:

> In such a difficulty always ask yourself: How did we *learn* the meaning ('good' for instance)? From what sort of examples? In what language-games? Then it will be easier for you to see that the word must have a family of meanings. (*PI* 77, p. 36)

Aesthetics and expressions of religious belief are referred to as language-games in *Lectures and Conversations* (which occurred in the late 1930s and early 1940s, while *Philosophical Investigations* was being written): e.g. 'An entirely different game is played in different ages' (p. 8) referring to aesthetics. Thus, unlike philosophical nonsense, which is nonsensical because the words expressed lack use and application, and because they do not belong to a language-game, expressions of value, on the other hand, though nonsensical in so far as they are attempts to say what cannot be said, nevertheless belong to a language-game with its own particular rules.

An awkward objection to this might be raised. In the account of meaning and language in his later works Wittgenstein says that the meaning of a word is to be found by looking at the use to which it is put in the language-game to which it belongs (*PG* p. 67; *PI* 43, p. 20). If this is so, and if expressions of value belong to language-games, they must have meaning which can be discovered by observing how the words and sentences are used in the language-game to which they belong. In that case, they cannot be nonsensical. Some commentators of a religious disposition have welcomed this development in Wittgenstein's thought. They believe that in *Philosophical Investigations* he repaired the damage done to religious discourse in his earlier writings, particularly in the

'Lecture on Ethics'. This interpretation is mistaken and to be resisted if the earlier, substantially accurate, account of ethics and religious belief is to be preserved. But how is this to be done? Moreover, how can expressions of value that have meaning be distinguished from other meaningful expressions?

One way of answering this objection (for those who find it an objection and yet are not prepared lightly to abandon Wittgenstein's earlier account of ethics and religious belief), perhaps the only way or, at least, a way adequate in itself, is to distinguish between levels and senses of meaning. At the verbal level (the level of combinations of words, and even, exceptionally, of the use of single words) all propositions and pseudo, propositions, except meaningless combinations of signs, signs that serve no purpose ('Socrates is identical') have meaning: one can understand what the other person is saying. Of an unbeliever in conversation with someone who believes in a Judgement Day, Wittgenstein says: 'In one sense, I understand all he says – "God", "separate", etc. I understand. I could say: "I don't believe in this," and this would be true, meaning I haven't got these thoughts or anything that hangs together with them' (*LC* p. 55). He could understand the words but not make sense of what was meant by believing in a Judgement Day. It would not be something like an eclipse, which could be predicted, nor some sort of galactic explosion. Even more puzzling was belief in the existence of a god or God. Though he is a person because he sees, rewards and so on, he is not like any other person. We are shown pictures of him, but, unlike pictures of aunts, one was never shown what the pictures of God picture. Yet not to believe in his existence was something bad, although there was nothing wrong with not believing in the existence of something else (*LC* p. 59). Thus 'person', 'exists', and even 'sees', 'rewards', and 'judgement', are not used as we ordinarily use them. Someone attempting to interpret them in their ordinary sense misinterprets them. To such an interpreter they are nonsensical. But they are not mistakes or a misuse of language. For a believer they have a meaning that transcends the ordinary employment of language and cannot be translated into its ordinary use. The same is true of the fundamental beliefs and experiences of ethics. They, too, defy translation into ordinary use. In ordinary use, if something is good, it is good because it is *for* something (relatively good). In ethics, if something is good, it is because it is good in itself, an action worth doing for its own sake alone and not for any other reason (it is absolutely good). One may add, with Moore, that ethical good cannot be translated into constituent empirical qualities. (The aesthetically good is also good in itself, something worth admiring for its own sake, and not for any purpose it may serve or function it may perform, however well it does it.) But, as Wittgenstein pointed out in the 'Lecture on Ethics', to talk of absolute value (whether explicitly or implicitly) is to use words in a way other than that in which they are used in their original language-game. Hence it is an attempt to extend the boundaries of language and say what cannnot be said. Thus, from the point of view of someone who confines himself to the ordinary use of language, this use of language is nonsensical.

If this is so, how, then, can expressions of value, as part of a language-game, have meaning? Either, as nonsensical, they do not have meaning, or, as used in a language-game, they have meaning within that game. As we have just seen, they at least have verbal meaning. But that is not enough. 'Socrates is identical' and 'This is a square circle' have enough verbal meaning to enable us to declare them absurd or contradictory and know what utterance we are talking about. The expressions of value, however, have meaning, as we saw in Part I chapters one and two, only it is not stated or said, since there are no words with which to express it. It is silent meaning, meaning, so to speak, read between the lines, and, in the case of non-verbal communication, between the sounds and images. Wittgenstein in his early writings, including his letters, gave some indication of how this meaning is conveyed in poems, parables, narratives, prophetic utterances and metaphors (*cf.* chapter one). The meaning of these utterances cannot be translated or put into other words, much less explained. Attempts to do so by interpreters, commentators and other rhapsodes can be successful only to the extent that they convey by similar indirect uses of language something of the meaning of the original. But they cannot *say* (express or state) what that meaning is. Of that they must be silent and let the words (and, in the case of music and the visual arts, the sounds, rhythms, pauses, shapes and colours) speak for themselves. Theories based on such sources – theologies and ethical theories such as treatises on justice – never, in Wittgenstein's opinion, capture the meaning of an original source of expression of value. They belong to a different language-game where words are given more or less definite senses and meanings are based on ordinary use.

Understood in this way, the language-game or games of expression of values, conform to the account given in Wittgenstein's earlier writings. And the distinctions between what can be said and what cannot, and between the various forms of nonsense, remain intact despite the curtailment of and modifications to the picture theory of meaning. However, the later writings introduce a new use of the picture analogy. It is highly relevant to what will be said in the remainder of the book.

The notion of a proposition as a picture of a state of affairs, has something static about it, or, as Wittgenstein says, idle:

> a word picture of the facts has something misleading about it: one tends to think only of such pictures as hang on our walls: which seems simply to portray how a thing looks, what it is like. (These pictures are as it were idle.) (*PI* 291, p. 99)

But the other roles of pictures in our lives and language described in *Philosophical Remarks, Philosophical Grammar, The Blue and Brown Books* and *Philosophical Investigations* are dynamic. They are concerned with action. We have already encountered one instance of this in *PI* 519, p. 141 where Wittgenstein describes an order as 'a picture of the action which *is to be* carried out on the order' (*cf. PG* p. 212). Here there is a fairly close connection between the action to be carried out and the picture of it. A less specific picture of an action is described in *PI* 490, p. 137:

> How do I know that *this line of thought* has led me to this action? – Well, it is a particular picture: for example, of a calculation leading to a further experiment in an experimental investigation. It looks like *this* – and now I could describe an example.

Here the calculation suggests the kind of experiment to be carried out, and the example is a picture of that kind of experiment. These are examples of *what* is to be done. Wittgenstein also offers examples of pictures of *how* things are to be done. One is answering someone puzzled about how to put a particular mechanism into a particular box. A drawing may serve. Someone may say: 'See how it goes in here.' Wittgenstein adds: 'Of course the latter does not explain anything more (than the picture): it simply invites me to apply the picture I am given' (*PI* 425, p. 127). Another, not-so-specific example is that of various stances in boxing:

> Imagine a picture representing a boxer in a particular stance. Now this picture can be used to tell someone how he should stand, should hold himself; or how he should not hold himself; (*PI* addendum at the foot of p. 11)

Needless to say the boxer will not keep to these precise stances throughout a bout. Indeed, he may never take up any of them exactly as they are depicted. (For one thing, he may not have the build of the boxer in the picture.) All this is summed up in *Philosophical Grammar*, p. 163:

In what sense can I say that a proposition is a picture? When I think about it, I want to say: it must be a picture if it is to show me what I am to do, if I am able to act in accordance with it. But in that case all you want to say is that you act in accordance with a proposition in the same sense as you act in accordance with a picture.

In *Lectures and Conversations* Wittgenstein suggests some of the uses to which pictures could be put in aesthetics and religious belief. From other writings and Wittgenstein's *dicta* it is clear how they are applied to ethics. It should be noted, first, that the notion of picture is used broadly and variously. Broadly, since anything that could act as an exemplar, for instance, whether it be a piece of music, a poem, a play or a narrative, a dance movement or a gesture, can be said to be used as a picture. Variously, since pictures can range from paintings representing something ('picture' literally understood) to mental images to ideas with no pictorial content but thought-up and imagined ('Imagine yourself in an embarrassing situation' does not require a pictorial content to be complied with). Variously also because, besides picturing an action or a set of actions (a way of living), pictures can be used to envisage beliefs and ideas.

In aesthetics, pictures are used as exemplars, paradigms and ideals in order to establish critical judgements and analyses by way of comparison (*LC* pp. 13–14, 20–1, *passim*). In ethics, pictures to live and act by take the form of parables, allegories, moral tales and other narratives, plays, and, of course, edifying paintings and other illustrations. In religion there are pictures to live by and also pictures used as metaphors, symbols and analogies.

We know that Wittgenstein drew ethical pictures from Biblical stories, from Tolstoy's moral tales and other stories, from Bunyan, Gottfried Keller and other writers. These describe particular characters and fictitious events, yet they picture (represent by exemplifying) a way of behaviour and can thus act as models for the way to behave in similar circumstances. The parable of the Good Samaritan is an obvious example. It exemplifies both the way to behave and not to behave in a particular situation. *Master and Servant* by Tolstoy (one of Wittgenstein's favourites) is another good example. Caught in a blizzard, the master rides away leaving his servant to his fate only to find himself back where he started. But as the night wears on the servant protects the master with his body, thereby saving his life but losing his own. Though the stories are specific, the pictures are general, with a wide range of application. They also require a method of interpretation of what Wittgenstein calls the use to which the picture is put. We do not have to wait for a distressed member of an alien community to come along in order to practise altruistic charity; anyone to whom we have no personal obligations would do. Similarly, we do not have to confine heroic kindness to those to whom we have obligations and who behave badly towards us. This behaviour could also be pictured as turning the other cheek, though clearly a literal cheek need not necessarily be involved.

In Wittgenstein's opinion, this way of presenting ethical principles is not only a more enlightening way of inculcating them than formulating abstract and general propositions ('Help your neighbour in distress' – but who is my neighbour? – 'Return good for evil'), but is also vastly more effective. Not only do we have an injunction to behave in a certain way, but also a concrete model of how to do it.

Religious belief and practice not only calls for pictures to live by but also pictures by which to interpret religious teaching. Wittgenstein discussed both uses of pictures in *Lectures and Conversations* and in a few remarks published in *Culture and Value*.

In his first lecture on religious belief Wittgenstein speaks of someone believing in the Last Judgement and making 'this guidance for life' (*LC* p. 53). Whenever he does anything, this picture, the picture of a Judgement Day, when he will have to give an account of himself, is in his mind. He may say he has proof of his belief or has unshakeable faith in it. But his belief shows itself, not by reasoning or by any ordinary grounds of belief, but rather by his way of regulating his whole life. The strength and firmness of his belief lies in the fact that he is prepared to forgo pleasures in his life, 'always appealing to this picture' (*LC* p. 54). He risks things because of the picture that he would not risk on things far better established for him. The choice of the Last Judgement as an example of living a religious life according to a picture is particularly apt. The intention behind the Gospel description is not primarily to give information about future events or to terrify the listener or reader. It, along with such parables as that of the faithful and unfaithful servants or the foolish virgins, is an exhortation to constant vigilance, since we know not the day nor the hour when the Lord will come to claim our souls and bring us before his judgement seat. But the description of the Last Judgement, unlike the parables, clearly states the kinds of actions on which all humankind is to be judged and the consequences of an unfavourable judgement. So someone living by this picture will live in such a way as 'not to be dragged into the fire' (*LC* p. 56). Whether this is the noblest of motives for action or one of which Wittgenstein himself approved does not affect this example as an illustration of living according to a picture. (Incidentally, in medieval churches this picture was kept before the eyes and minds of the faithful by carvings of the scene in the tympanum of the main portal, and sometimes on the west wall, to be seen on entering and leaving the church.)

In a remark jotted down towards the end of his life in 1947, Wittgenstein expressed the view that religious belief, 'although it's *belief*, is really a way of living, or a way of assessing life' within a system of reference (*CV* p. 64). It is like a passionate commitment to a system of reference. This draws belief, picturing and a way of life, close together. The way of life and the belief are inseparable. The way of life confirms the genuineness of the belief because, unlike other kinds of belief, religious belief would not be what it is unless the particular way of life it sustains were lived. Nor would the way of living be religious without the belief.

Ten years earlier in 1937, before the lectures on religious belief, Wittgenstein made an important entry about picturing a religious way of life in his *Notebook* that was concerned more with adopting an attitude than performing an action. Having quoted the injunction to thank God for what we receive, and that we should not complain as we would if a human being were to do us good and evil by turns, he continues:

> Rules of life are dressed up in pictures. And these pictures can only serve to *describe* what we are to do, not *justify* it. Because they could be a justification only if they held good in other respects as well. (*CV* p. 29)

For instance, it makes sense to regard bees *as though* they were kind people who prepared honey for us, but not *as* kind people, since the next minute they might sting us.

As for the way pictures help us to envisage religious beliefs, Wittgenstein gives three examples. The first has to do with pictures proper – with paintings. He cites Michelangelo's *The Creation of Adam*. 'In general,' he says, 'there is nothing that explains the meanings of words as a picture' (*LC* p. 63). This sort of picture is used in quite a different way from a picture of a Biblical subject. It makes sense to ask if Noah looked as Michelangelo painted him but not to ask this of his 'God'. 'The picture has to be used in an entirely different way if we are to call the man in that queer blanket "God", and so on' (*LC* p. 63). One has to learn the technique of using a religious picture. Its meaning is not on its surface, on what it looks like or means literally. In that respect it is a simile.

A second example is concerned with the expression: 'God's eye sees everything.' Here Wittgenstein is dealing more precisely with the technique of using a religious picture. This is governed by the conclusions that are going to be drawn from the picture/simile. These determine which elements in the picture are relevant and which are not. 'Are eyebrows going to be talked of, in connection with the Eye of God?' (*LC* p. 71).

A third example concerns the expression 'we might see one another after death', spoken by someone embarking on a journey to a far-off country from which he may never return. In saying this, according to Wittgenstein, he is using a picture, which is not the same as expressing a certain attitude such as 'I am very fond of you' or anything else that might be substituted for it. Everything depends on what conclusions he draws from this picture. (Whatever they are, they will hardly resemble the sort of encounter that takes place in life when, say, two friends meet on a jetty after a long separation.) Wittgenstein adds: 'When I say he's using a picture I'm merely making a grammatical remark: (What I say) can only be verified by the consequences he does or does not draw' (*LC* p. 72). (More on this in a later chapter.)

Wittgenstein distinguishes this use of a picture where no other picture, no other form of expression would serve, from others which might just as well be replaced by something else. For instance, under certain circumstances, one projection of an ellipse could be drawn instead of another. In this case one picture would have the same effect as the other, just as the exact shape of chessmen does not have a role in chess. On the other hand, 'the whole *weight* may be in the picture' (*LC* p. 72). It may be that the conclusions a person wishes to draw in using a picture can be drawn from one picture only and no other.

Connected with this notion of using a picture is another relevant to our subject, the notion of 'seeing as'. The fullest, most explicit discussion of this notion is to be found in *Philosophical Investigations* II, pp. 193–214. Wittgenstein first distinguishes between the two uses of the word 'see'. The first might be called seeing what is there, seeing this and then giving a description of it or drawing it. The other is seeing a likeness between two (or more) 'objects' of sight, which someone else may miss or we may have missed hitherto. Coming to see a likeness Wittgenstein calls 'noticing an aspect' (*PI* p. 193). This may be 'continuous seeing' as with all pictures which one continuously sees as, say, a likeness to a rabbit, a *rabbit*-picture. Or one can suddenly see another likeness, another aspect, say, the likeness of a duck as in Jastow's famous 'duck–rabbit' figure.[13] This Wittgenstein calls the 'dawning' of an aspect (*PI* p. 94). There can also be the passing of an aspect. It may pass of itself with time or we can make it pass at will (*PI* pp. 212–13). (And it can pass never to return, where we have misinterpreted a visual object – seen bedclothes thrown back as a polar bear, for instance.)

'Seeing as', therefore, presupposes that there is 'just seeing', seeing an object for what it is (Wittgenstein's first sense of 'see'). It would be absurd to 'take' cutlery at a meal *for* knives and forks (*PI* p. 195) or see a green leaf *as* green (*PI* p. 213). The cases of 'seeing as' which immediately derive from this are cases of mis-seeing, taking something for what it is not on the basis of its appearance. For instance, on a dark night one may see a bush as a crouching assailant. The other examples Wittgenstein discusses are contrived examples. One category includes ambiguous figures, such as the 'duck–rabbit', which can be seen now this way, now that, but must be seen one way or the other. For someone to say that he saw neither a duck nor a rabbit but a horse would be puzzling. Then there are illustrative diagrams which can be seen in a variety of different ways, but in a given context must be seen in one particular way. Wittgenstein gives the example of a solid rectangle. In different places in a textbook it can be seen variously as a glass cube, an inverted open box, a wire frame or three boards forming a solid angle (*PI* p. 193). Finally, there are figures and objects that can be seen as many different things and in many different ways, undetermined by context. Wittgenstein gives the example of a right-angled triangle with its hypotenuse as base (*PI* p. 200–1). It can be seen as a triangular hole, as a solid, as a geometrical drawing, as standing on its base or hanging from its apex, as a mountain,

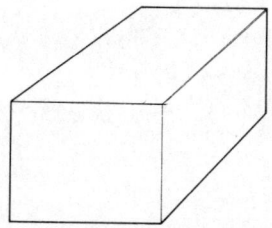

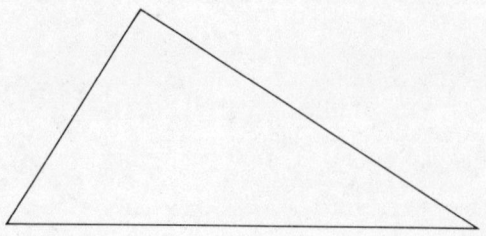

a wedge, a pointer, an overturned object, a half-parallelogram, and various other things. Wittgenstein sums up by suggesting a criterion for 'seeing as':

> How would the following account do: 'What I can see something *as*, is what it can be a picture of'?
> What this means is: the aspects in a change of aspects are those ones which the figure might sometimes have *permanently* in a picture. (*PI* p. 201)

Besides pictures Wittgenstein also spoke about seeing aspects of things, particularly faces: not just passing facial expressions, but physiognomies. In *PI* 536–7, pp. 144–5 he speaks of a face that gives the impression of timidity and yet one that can also be seen as courageous; and in *PI* 539, p. 145 of a smiling face as now kindly, now malicious. These kinds of face can also appear in pictures. (One is reminded of Pudovkin's experiment with the juxtaposing of a film clip of an expressionless face with those of a small child, a coffin and a naked woman, and getting a kindly, sad and lecherous expression respectively from the 'expressionless' face.)

The tantalizing thing about 'seeing as' and seeing now this aspect, now that, is that what it is we see seems to change and yet the object or picture itself does not. Is it my perception that changes? Then how was it that I did not see the aspect earlier? 'I describe the alteration like a perception; quite as if the object had altered before my eyes' (*PI* p. 195). We speak of the perception as though it were a new perception and at the same time of its being unchanged (*PI* p. 196). The truth is that 'seeing as' is not part of a perception; it is both like seeing and not like it (*PI* p. 197). It is both perception and thought. We look at an object without thinking about it, but if something arouses our attention (a rabbit running across a landscape) 'you are also thinking of what you see'. 'The flashing of an

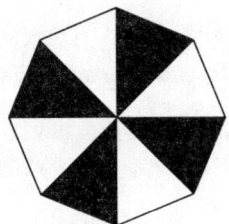

aspect on us seems half visual experience, half thought' (*PI* p. 197). But, however puzzling 'seeing something as . . .' or seeing an aspect that one had not noticed before may be, it is not nearly as puzzling as being incapable of seeing an aspect that others have no difficulty in seeing. Wittgenstein calls this 'aspect-blindness'.

He poses the question whether anyone could lack the capacity to see something *as* something. He does not know whether this would be a general incapacity or one confined to specific areas of seeing. If such a thing were possible, what would it be like and what consequences would follow from this incapacity? Would it, he asks, be like colour-blindness or not having absolute pitch? He had effectively ruled these out when (*PI* p. 210) he said that being blind to the expression on a face was not simply a question of physiology, of something like defective eyesight. Here we are dealing with something psychological, which in this case he calls a 'symbol of the logical' (*PI* p. 210). He is prepared to concede that, when asked to pick out black crosses, he could include the double cross (which can be seen either as a black cross on a white ground or a white cross on a black ground) as containing a black cross, but, on his own, he could not also see it as a white cross. The nearest Wittgenstein will go towards characterising aspect-blindness is to say it is akin to the lack of a 'musical ear' (which is quite different from a lack of absolute pitch) or the incapacity to experience (as opposed just to understand) the meaning of a word (*PI* p. 214). (There follows a discussion on experiencing the meaning of words – intonation, feeling, figurative use, which, though most interesting and important in itself, does not greatly add to what is meant by the concept of 'seeing (or not seeing) as', 'seeing (or not seeing) an aspect'.)

Though primarily psychological (albeit a 'symbol of the logical'), the concept of 'seeing as' or 'seeing an aspect' throws valuable light, not only on Wittgenstein's later remarks on value, but also on what he said in his earlier writings on value.

In *TLP* 6.45 we find:

> To view the world *sub specie aeterni* is to view it *as* a whole – a limited whole.
> Feeling the world *as* a limited whole – it is this that is the mystical. (My italics) (*Cf. NB* p. 83)

The world can be viewed as a collection of disparate facts, one fact alongside another and equal in value to any other. It can be viewed as 'the totality of facts', of whatever is the case and is not the case (*TLP* 1.1 and 1.12). On the other hand, it can be viewed as a single, limited whole. To view it as a collection of facts is to see it as it is, in Wittgenstein's first sense of 'see', seeing cutlery on the dinner table or a green leaf. To see this totality of facts *as* a self-contained or limited whole is to exercise one's imagination (as distinct from fantasy) and see an aspect of that totality that is not immediately apparent. The emergence of monotheism illustrates this. As long as the world was regarded as divided into facts ('The world divides into facts', *TLP* 1.2) it was natural, if not inevitable, that religion should be polytheistic, with a pantheon of gods of fertility, rain, thunder, war and so on. To limit the gods to one God entailed regarding the world as a single, limited whole, related as a whole to God. This whole, however, consists of many elements. Where the analogy breaks down where polytheists, and most monotheists, other than pantheists, regard the world as the totality of *things*, Wittgenstein regarded it as the totality of facts, not things (*TLP* 1.1).

Connected with this is Wittgenstein's prime experience of absolute value, the sense or feeling of the *existence* of the world. In the *Tractatus*, as we have seen, this is described as mystical: 'It is not *how* things are in the world that is mystical, but *that* it exists' (*TLP* 6.44). Combine this with the next entry ('Feeling the world as a limited whole – it is this that is mystical') and it would appear that marvelling that the world, that anything, exists (*cf. PRv* pp. 8–9) involves seeing an aspect of it that might otherwise have escaped us. But, it will be objected, it is as absurd to talk of seeing the world as existing as to talk of seeing a knife on the table as a knife. The world exists and we cannot help noticing that. Things and states of affairs exist, certainly, but we take their existence for granted. We are concerned with *what* they are, not with their existence. To wonder at existence, at their being anything at all, it is necessary to transcend the particularities of the world, the this and that, and regard it as a whole. This is an aspect of the world to which many people do not or possibly cannot (a form of aspect-blindness?) turn their attention.

In chapter four we discussed the following passage:

The work of art is the object seen *sub specie aeternitatis*; and the good life is the world seen *sub specie aeternitatis* . . .
The usual way of looking at things sees objects as it were from the midst of them, the view *sub specie aeternitatis* from outside . . .
Is this it perhaps – in this view the object is seen *together with* space and time instead of *in* space and time? (*NB* p. 83)

It is, in fact, an example of 'seeing as'. Objects and events can be seen either *as* having a definite place *in* space and time along with other objects and events, or they can be seen for their own sake, not divorced from their spacio-temporal context, but together with the whole of space and time and everything else in it colourless by contrast, not a 'worthless momentary picture', but '*as* the true world (my world) among shadows' (my italics).

On the subject of ethics, there is a passage in the *Tractatus* that may be connected with the notion of 'seeing as'. Wittgenstein is talking about the good and bad exercise of the will altering or affecting the world (*cf.* chapter three). He says that it cannot alter the facts: it can only alter the boundaries of the world (something that cannot be expressed in language). It must change as a whole, and, when it does, 'it becomes an altogether different world' (*TLP* 6.43). Wittgenstein then adds: 'The world of the happy man is a different one from that of the unhappy man.' The happy man is the man of good will; the unhappy man, the man of bad will. The altering of the world is here an act of will, not of perception. But must it not also involve a change of perception either prior to or subsequent on the act of will? The person of bad will views the world differently from the way the person of good will sees it. And the world can be seen in these two ways. It can be viewed, for instance, as something to master and turn to one's advantage, avoiding its vicissitudes as far as possible; or it can be viewed as a place where the interests of others must be respected and served, and its vicissitudes (when they cannot be overcome) accepted with resignation. To change one's attitude to the world is to see it differently, either as something hostile to be overcome and conquered or as something to be endured and, perhaps, made a better place (though whether this is achieved or not is irrelevant to goodness of will).

What of those other experiences described in the 'Lecture on Ethics', the feeling of being absolutely safe and of feeling guilty, of being disapproved of by God (*PRv* p. 10). Are these instances of 'seeing as'?

Whereas it is indubitable that the world exists and that existence is an aspect of it, if a strange one, it is not clear that either absolute safety or absolute guilt are obvious aspects of life or of the world. Yet it is a fact that we can detach ourselves from the world and, to that extent, be safe from its vicissitudes. Humankind, taken as a whole, is a pretty weak, hopeless and malicious race, prone to evil for which there is reason for shame. These are, indubitably, aspects of the world and of human life.

Not surprisingly the lectures on religious belief provide some interesting examples of 'seeing as'. Some concern Biblical narrative and its mode of depiction; others, our way of conceiving God; still others, a religious attitude towards life and death. Generally speaking we are dealing here with symbolism of one kind or another, which Wittgenstein tends to call 'simile'.

We have already seen how the creation story as depicted by Michelangelo is to be used. It is not to be seen as simply representing an energetic, bearded old man sailing through the air in a whirl of robes, but *as* a symbol of divine creative energy. Biblical stories are not to be read merely as historical narratives but *as* manifestations of mysteries (*LC* p. 57). In Christian tradition (going back to the Gospels), Old Testament stories were read *as* 'types' or prefigurations of the life of the Messiah. And the Gospel stories themselves (and depictions of them) are not read (seen) merely as stories (or illustrations of stories) but *as* having a spiritual and supernatural significance. Thus, the story of the Nativity is not just an account of an unusual family event: it is to be seen *as* a representation (in so far as that is possible) of the mystery of the Incarnation. The appearance of Jesus to Mary Magdalene after the Resurrection works on two levels: the man standing in a garden is to be seen *as* an apparition of the risen Jesus and, as such, *as* representing the mystery of the Resurrection. As for our ways of conceiving the nature of God, we have already discussed the picture of God's omniscience *as* 'seeing' everything (*LC* p. 71). The man leaving for a far country and speculating about meeting his friend after death sees the afterlife *as* a sort of inn where travellers meet after the journey of life (*LC* pp. 70–1). Then there is the case of the person who sees everything that happens to him *as* retribution, reward or punishment, where someone else would see the same events as simply fortunate or unfortunate accidents or happenings (*LC* pp. 54–5).

It might be said that in these last examples we have come a long way from the duck–rabbit. And indeed we have. There the aspects were limited to two, and clear for all (not suffering from aspect-blindness) to see, if need be with a little help. Wittgenstein also mentions hidden pictures, such as

faces hidden in the branches of trees (*PI* p. 196) or the girl and the old woman. These differ from the duck–rabbit only in being more difficult to see, since the image of branches is intended to disguise them. But the faces are there to be seen. The geometrical diagrams, whether shown in a context or freely interpreted, can be seen directly – a wire frame, a mountain. It may not be easy to see at will a bush as a crouching man or bedclothes as a polar bear, but we can understand what it would be for someone to do so, and we have ways of knowing what a crouching man or a polar bear looks like. Here we are dealing with visual perception. And even if we bring in audile perception – hearing a musical phrase as the song of a lark or an air-raid siren – we have the possibility of hearing the sound presented by other means.

When we come to value, matters become more difficult. There is no independent way of comprehending what it is we must see (hear) something as. 'Seeing as' has almost taken on a new meaning. It no longer sounds right to speak of seeing a likeness to something. Likeness to what? One might say that in calling a piece of music 'poignant' or 'plaintive', or a picture 'sombre', or a building 'overbearing', or a poem 'light-hearted' we are seeing in it a likeness to, say, a poignant situation, a plaintive cry, a sombre tomb, a happy, carefree child. There is an element of likeness there; because otherwise why use these words? But the use these words are put to in aesthetics is not the same as seeing the likeness to a duck in the duck–rabbit picture. Once the duck is recognized, that is an end of the matter. To call a song 'plaintive' is not to invite you to recognize its likeness to a plaintive cry – as it might be in describing the cry of a curlew. 'The epithet "sad", as applied to the outline face, characterizes the group of lines in a circle . . . (But this does *not* mean that a sad expression is *like* the feeling of sadness)' (*PI* p. 209). By calling the music 'plaintive', we are drawing attention to certain characteristics of the sounds that give the music its particular quality. The 'plaintiveness' of the music resides in the music itself.

When we come to strictly aesthetic terms such as 'beautiful', 'ugly', 'garish' or 'elegant', likeness becomes incestuous. To see something as beautiful is to see it as like other beautiful things. So someone who does not understand what is meant by 'beautiful' in the first place, cannot see the likeness. Until he breaks through this barrier, he may be said to suffer from aesthetic aspect-blindness, a common ailment it would seem (if not a generalized complaint, at least a particularized one). An instance of this kind of aspect-blindness once came my way in Venice. We were passing St Mark's Square in a vaporetto when a man turned excitedly to his teenage son and said: 'Look, son, look! See how it's opening out!' To which he received the rather anguished reply: 'I can't see anything opening out, Dad.' The person with an aesthetic sense can see the mundane and quotidian aspect and the aesthetic aspect of things, see objects *as* beautiful, garish or elegant, or just as objects, things among other things.

It makes even less sense to talk of 'seeing a likeness' where ethical epithets are used. In so far as there is a likeness, it is incestuous and empty but not entirely useless. To someone who understands what it is to perform a good or a bad action, it might be useful to point out that an action that he regarded as morally neutral or even good is bad because it is so like (almost indistinguishable from) actions that he himself regards as bad. This might bring him to see it *as* bad. There are well-meaning people ready to see and admit that it is wicked to be cruel to animals and children, but they are blind to the immorality of being harsh or even downright cruel to their servants and employees. This is a case of particularized aspect-blindness. It would appear that there are cases of total moral aspect-blindness. Psychopaths seem to fall into this category; but it would also seem it can be self-induced. Terrorists, violent criminals, and other amoral and anti-social individuals and groups often appear to have lost or rejected all moral values.

When we come to religious beliefs, talk of *seeing* a likeness in any literal sense is meaningless. Theologians talk of the use of analogies in speaking of religious matters, but these analogies are of a very peculiar kind. The usual analogy is between known objects, events and experiences. 'Like as the waves make towards the pebbled shore, So do our minutes hasten to their end' (Shakespeare: *Sonnets*, 60). It is because we know about the behaviour of waves and the ticking away of our lives that we can judge the aptness or otherwise of Shakespeare's simile. We can also learn about things we do not know or have not experienced at first hand by means of analogies. But we can only discover (a) in what respects the analogue resembles the *analogatum* and (b) whether it is an apt analogy after we have encountered the *analogatum*, be it a lychee said to taste as roses smell but more delicately, or the exhilaration of skiing or tobogganing in comparison with roller-coasting. However, the person using the analogy must know both the analogue and the *analogatum* at first hand. In the case of religious analogies, however, neither the recipient of the analogy nor the user of it knows in what respects it resembles the *analogatum*, nor whether or not it is apt. The most either can know are the respects in which the analogy does not apply to God (the Eye of God does not imply either an eyebrow or even an organ). In creating the world, God did not have to work. Something may be inferred from the effects of God's action with regard to the world. For instance, to create a world such as ours calls for intelligence, but we do not know what form that intelligence takes. Not knowing what God is like makes it absurd to speak of seeing a likeness to the divine and supernatural in the natural – hence a case for iconoclasm. We are told in Genesis that God created the human race in his image and likeness, as, indeed, the whole of creation. But we cannot tell in what respects creation is like God, since we do not know what God is like.

It would seem to follow that we cannot see a picture or story as having an aspect that is divine and supernatural. Yet someone who has a religious belief sees things differently from someone who has no such belief. The world *looks* different to him. He sees religious and moral significance in the very existence of the world, in its miseries and vicissitudes and in the fundamental, though redeemable, baseness of human nature. He also sees the Biblical stories not just as stories but as bearers of such mysteries as the Incarnation, the Redemption and the Resurrection. He will also see the accidents of life and death itself in a different, a religious light. The world has not changed. It appears to him as it does to a non-believer. Nor are the stories of Creation, the birth and death of Jesus or even the apparitions after his death altered in the perception of the believer in point of narrative. It is just that they are seen differently. Christ's birth and death are not seen as any ordinary birth or death, nor his apparitions as ordinary ghost stories. But what most clearly demonstrates the particular kind of 'seeing as' that is religious belief, is seeing the accidents of life *as* retribution, *as* either rewards or punishments. (It might be remarked that not all religious believers share this belief.) The non-believer does not see it in that way at all.

Can the non-believer, therefore, be said to suffer from aspect-blindness? In a sense, yes, and in a sense, no. He fails to see what the believer sees, and he may, for a variety of reasons – upbringing, deliberate choice, temperament – be incapable of seeing what the believer sees. As Jesus said to his disciples, those who have eyes to see, let them see; and 'their eyes they have closed: lest at any time they should see with their eyes ... and be converted, and I should heal them' (Matthew 13, 15). Yet what they fail to see is not strictly speaking an aspect, certainly not in the sense in which the likeness to a rabbit is an aspect of the duck–rabbit picture or even the appearance of a crouching figure an aspect of a bush seen in the dark. There is some justification for seeing a phenomenon, an event, a state of affairs, a narrative or a picture as the believer does. But the way he views these things comes for the most part from within himself. This partly explains the disagreements and misunderstandings that occur between believers and non-believers, which will be discussed in a later chapter.

By now it should be evident that far from altering his views on value propounded in his early writings, such notions as those of language-games and 'seeing as' help to elaborate Wittgenstein's thought on ethics and religious belief. We must now address ourselves to that other challenge to the earlier account, Wittgenstein's so-called relativism.

7

Relativism

Relativism comes in a wide variety of forms. Before discussing Wittgenstein's variety of relativism, or, indeed, one might say his alleged relativism, we must discuss some of the main types of relativism. But first a word about the context into which relativism is said to fit in Wittgenstein's later writings.

Given the variety of language-games based on a corresponding variety of forms of life, and given also that these language-games and forms of life appear to be mutually exclusive (even though in some cases they may overlap and, in any case, an individual may be involved in many different forms of life, and play many different language-games), it would not be surprising for someone to conclude that Wittgenstein was committed to some kind of relativism. Indeed, Wittgenstein's own utterances and remarks lend credence to this view. The question is: what form of relativism, if any, is he committed to by his notions of language-games and forms of life?

There are popular and trivial forms of relativism that allow everyone his or her own opinion, whether on matters of fact or general belief or value. This is given a spurious philosophical respectability by saying that people's views are conditioned by their temperament, upbringing and social and cultural environment. This is made somewhat more interesting and respectable when it is claimed that people of one culture or upbringing are so conditioned that they cannot understand the views of people of other cultures and upbringing. Such a claim is made by B. Whorf in *Language, Thought and Reality*.[1] In general, Whorf holds that language organizes our experience as well as expressing it.

> We are thus introduced to a new principle of relativity, which holds that all observers are not led by the same physical evidence to the same picture of the universe, unless their linguistic backgrounds are similar, or can in some way be calibrated. (p. 55)

Davidson sums up the objection to this line of reasoning in *Truth and Interpretation* when he points out that Whorf finds the metaphysics of the Hopi Indian language so alien to that of the English language that they cannot be calibrated, but 'uses English to convey the content of sample Hopi sentences'.[2]

This notion of the absence of calibration or, as it is more commonly called, 'incommensurability' takes various forms, some more extreme than others. Kuhn, for instance, in *The Structure of Scientific Revolutions* holds that 'after a revolution scientists work in a *different* world' (my italics) and even the data themselves change.[3] He illustrates this with reference to Dalton's law whereby atoms are said to combine in simple ratios, such as 1 : 1, 2 : 1, etc. Dalton 'beat nature into line'. 'As a result, chemists came to live in a world where reactions behaved *quite differently* from the way they had before' (my italics). Even the percentage composition of well-known compounds became different: 'the very numerical data of chemistry began to shift' (p. 134). Yet, as Davidson points out, Kuhn uses post-revolutionary language to describe what things were like before the revolution (*op. cit.* p. 184).[4] Feyerabend in *Scientific Explanation* holds that obsolete theories and points of view that are incompatible with new ones are eliminated. 'This will also,' he adds, 'lead to the elimination of the old meanings' (p. 82). But in *Beyond the Edge* he expresses the belief that contrasting schemes can be compared from a point of view outside the system or language (p. 214).

Against this form of conceptual relativism Davidson argues in *Actions and Events* 'on the very idea' that the very notion of more than one conceptual scheme, or of 'seriously different conceptual schemes or frames of reference', or of Whorf's 'radically incommensurate' languages is incoherent. If the conceptual schemes are as radically different as Whorf, and even Kuhn and Feyerabend, say they are, then we could never know that they existed, since they would be unintelligible. To be intelligible they would have to form some part of our own conceptual scheme. 'We can never intelligibly compare or contrast divergent schemes,' says Davidson (p. 243), nor even speak of one, since we cannot understand more than one. A conceptual scheme belongs to a whole language. This is not to say that there are not, or cannot be, conflicting and irreducible concepts or sets of concepts within the language 'and yet they may be essential to making sense of some, or all, of the rest'.[5]

But this calls for a distinction between what forms part of my conceptual baggage, so to speak, and that part of it that I am prepared to accept and to believe. Another distinction is useful: that between first- and third-person statements about conceptual schemes. There is an ambiguity about the notion of a conceptual scheme. It suggests homogeneity and multiplicity. If, as Davidson says, my conceptual scheme is co-extensive with all that I can say (and think, presumably), as a conceptual scheme it cannot be homogeneous, and if it is heterogeneous, this can only make sense if there are conflicting concepts or sets of concepts within the single scheme. This might be expressed by saying that these sets of concepts might form part of someone else's conceptual scheme, where they would not be in conflict. Whereas it does not make sense (according to Davidson) to talk of conceptual schemes that do not in some way form part of one's own, since otherwise they could not be known or understood, it makes sense to talk of a multiplicity of conceptual schemes, meaning those of others that are not identical with one's own.

Implicit in all this is the notion of reflective consciousness or self-consciousness or the growth of awareness, a notion that has its roots in Hegel's *The Phenomenology of Spirit*. The central idea is that as human beings, collectively or individually, progress (in the sense of moving from one stage of physical, experiential, intellectual development to another, though not necessarily for the better), they become aware of features of the universe and all that dwell within it (including themselves) of which either they or their predecessors had not been self-consciously aware hitherto. This does not necessarily give them a moral superiority over their former selves or over those that went before them, but it gives them an advantaged viewpoint, like someone standing on higher ground. There is no reason to believe they should lose the awareness that 'traditional societies' (once called 'primitive peoples') were limited to, as Kuhn and Feyerabend seem to imply. But one consequence of a developed, reflective consciousness or self-awareness is that it cannot be blotted out. There is no return to the age of innocence, ignorance and a more limited self-awareness. It is possible that some primitive awareness may be lost for ever (particularly where no written or oral records survive); but that all is inevitably lost is empirically false. What Quine calls the 'bulk term', 'a relic, half-vestigial and half-adapted', 'gives us a feel for the pre-individuative phase in the evolution of our conceptual scheme' (*Ontological Relativity*, p. 24).

Feyerabend suggests that contrasting conceptual schemes can be compared from a point of view outside the system and language. This, as Davidson points out, is paradoxical. 'Differing points of view,' he says, 'make sense, but only if there is a common co-ordinate system on which to plot them; yet the existence of a common system belies the claim of dramatic incompatibility.'[6]

But the crucial test of conceptual relativism is the possibility or otherwise of translation. For, if conceptual schemes and languages are incommensurable, translation should be impossible; if translation succeeds, and is, therefore, possible, in what and where does incommensurability lie? (What is said here applies equally to translation within a natural language and translations between languages.) It is not surprising, then, that relativists of all persuasions question the possibility of translation of any but a crude kind. Some assume that, if translation of any precision is to be achieved, it must be via something neutral and common that lies outside, and is common to, all schemes. Since no such thing exists, so it is concluded, precise translation is impossible. Davidson concedes this and says that even if it did exist, it could not be the subject-matter of contrasting languages (*Truth and Interpretation*, p. 190).

Another assumption is that theories can be compared by means of a vocabulary that attaches to nature in an unproblematic way, independent of theory. Kuhn tells us that he and Feyerabend have argued that there is no such vocabulary, since words change their meanings or conditions of application in subtle ways in translation from one theory to another. Though the same signs – e.g. 'force', 'mass', 'element', 'compound', 'cell' – may be used after a scientific revolution, the ways in which they attach to nature have somehow changed. 'Successive theories are thus, we say, incommensurable' (*Criticism and Growth of Knowledge*, p. 267).

This might be called a 'partial failure' of translation. A total failure of translation is something, according to Davidson, upon which we cannot pronounce. To do so we should have to have a common ontology ('concepts that individuate the same objects' (p. 192)). Then we could say that language X has no predicate (a). But if translation is totally impossible either because there is no common ontology or because we do not know whether there is or not, then talk about failure of translation is impossible, as is knowledge of whether we are dealing with another language. As for partial failure of translation, even here we have no general principle to tell us whether we are dealing with a difference in our concepts or our beliefs. Nor can an appeal to evidence decide the matter. To quote Davidson's example, if two people disagree as to whether a boat which they see is a yawl or a ketch, this may be a conceptual difference – we may regard all two-masted small sailing boats as ketches – or it may be that we did not think of the difference in the size of the masts or that the after-mast was sufficiently far aft to warrant calling it a 'yawl'. However, Davidson warns us that we have not shown how communication between people with different conceptual schemes is possible without a neutral ground or a common co-ordinate system. Similarly we should be mistaken in claiming that all mankind shares a common scheme and ontology. 'For if we cannot intelligibly say that schemes are different, neither can we intelligibly say that they are one' (*Truth and Interpretation*, p. 198).

Davidson, Kuhn and Feyerabend are primarily concerned with scientific conceptual schemes. Nearer to our subject is the recent work in anthropology and ethics, where there has been a resurgence in relativism. In anthropology a very radical form of relativism (the so-called 'strong programme') has been propounded by B. Barnes and D. Bloor.[7] ing separately or in tandem, Barnes and Bloor assert the social nature of all knowledge, including the principle of contradiction. Incommensurability can go no further. They also deny the possibility of successful translation, admitting only the roughest type used for crude purposes.

Bloor attempts to find support in alternative mathematical systems, instances of solutions arrived at by methods different from ours (the algebraic solutions of Diophantus), or conclusions regarded as true that in our system would be regarded as false (on the oddness or evenness of numbers in Greek number theory where 1 is not treated as a number).[8] But, in the first case, there is a difference of method but no contradiction is involved. In the second case, there is merely a difference of definition. It does not support the validity of bivalent deductive logic. In their attempt to illustrate the relativism of the principle of contradiction within logic itself, Barnes and Bloor looked to homely examples of what they took to be alternative systems of logic: 'yes and no' in answer to specific questions, and such variants as 'It was and it wasn't' or the use of the phrase 'some truth in that'; the seemingly contradictory statement 'The whole is greater than its parts.' But if these assertions are treated as abbreviations for fuller statements such as: ' "yes" under certain circumstances (stating the circumstances) but "no" under others (stating those circumstances)' no contradiction is involved. Barnes and Bloor might be better served by turning to Reichenbach and his 'infinite-valued logic' in which, between true and false, there is an infinite range of probabilities on a scale between 0 and 1. But, though multi-valent logic may undermine the clear-cut distinction between p and not p by allowing for an intermediary state of 'might be p' and 'might not be p', it does not allow '*both* p and not p'. Moreover, (a) multi-valent logic is artificial and does not have homely roots in society, and (b) it is subject to the principle of contradiction. A statement cannot both have a certain 'weight' of probability and at the same time not have that weight. What Barnes and Bloor, and like-minded people, fail to realize is that, though the trappings of logic may be conventional and arbitrary (not abstracted from experience), logic proceeds according to inexorable and inviolable laws, of which the principle of contradiction is the chief.[9]

The strong programme of relativism fares little better in its attack on the possibility of successful translation, which is the crucial test of extreme relativism. According to rationalist tradition, successful translation is possible if we start with a bridgehead of anchors: that is, assumed common perceptions and empirical judgements in simple (culturally uncomplicated) situations.[10] Barnes and Bloor deny that such perceptions and situations exist. They are affected by the specific conventions of the people whose language one wants to translate. They say that to learn

> even the most elementary of terms is a slow process that involves acquisition from the culture of specific *conventions*. This makes apparently simple empirical words no different from others that are perhaps more obviously culturally influenced. There are no 'simple perceptual situations' which provide the researcher with 'standard meanings' uncomplicated by cultural variables. ('Relativism, Rationalism and the Sociology of Knowledge' p. 38)

They cite Bulmer's discovery that the Karam of New Guinea use the word '*yakt*' for birds and for bats, but not for the cassowary. This discovery was made, they say, not by learning to translate the word '*yakt*' but by learning the conventions of the Karam.

But how, asks Margaret Archer in *Culture and Agency* (pp. 122–3), could Bulmer have discovered the *convention* of applying '*yakt*' to bats but not to cassowaries, other than by using his own language to get a rough correspondence between 'bird' and '*yakt*'? Even if it is a convention among the Karem not to apply '*yakt*' to cassowaries and yet apply it to bats (not unreasonably, since birds and bats fly but cassowaries do not), that convention could only be learned by ostentation and correction in perceptual situations. The relativist would have no other way of learning it.

Barnes and Bloor reply that it can be learned in the way the children of native speakers learn it. They do not learn it by translation, nor could they have done. Hence translation cannot be 'a necessary ingredient for subsequent learning' (*op. cit.* p. 37). Plausible though this may sound, it does not square with the facts. If we come to a new language already equipped with one of our own, we cannot shed it and start again from scratch. With our language, we have a conceptual scheme that we cannot shake off in order to be as concept-free as an infant. If such conceptual undressing ('linguistic strip-tease', as Archer calls it) were possible, then we should have no means of communicating alien beliefs or concepts later acquired (they would be our own) any more than the natives have until they encounter an alien language and learn it by means of translation.

Ethical relativism is less a conceptual matter and more a matter of judgement or appraisal as to whether an action or course of actions is good, evil, right, wrong, permissible or obligatory. It is also more deeply embedded in a culture or form of life than are scientific theories. An extreme form of ethical relativism, such as Edward Westermack propounded, maintains that: (a) the criteria with which ethical judgements operate in a particular society originate within that society or culture; (b) different cultures employ different criteria; (c) there is no set of absolute criteria by which one can adjudicate between incompatible criteria; and (d) there is, therefore, no reason why the holders of one set of criteria should reject or exclude those of another culture. Implicit in this position are two further elements: (e) a culture acquires its moral criteria by some deterministic process; and, most extreme of all is (f) that, consequently, it is impossible for someone brought up in one culture to acquire the criteria of another.[11] This latter is similar to Whorf's contention concerning our ability to understand the Hopi Indians, but it is not confined to remote tribes. In a popular view there is a culturally conditioned moral barrier between different social classes to the extent that those of one class cannot even understand, much less embrace, the ethics of another. This may or may not lead to what Bernard Williams calls 'vulgar relativism'; what amounts to a non-relativistic universal tolerance which involves being 'equally well disposed to everyone else's ethical beliefs' (*Ethics and the Limits of Philosophy*, p. 159).

However, just as conceptual relativism cannot dispense with the principle of contradiction, so ethical relativism cannot reduce the basic moral principle of good and evil, or right and wrong, to social convention so that the terms themselves can take on a different meaning from one culture to another. As Williams says: 'it is implausible to suppose that ethical conceptions of right and wrong have a logically inherent relativity to a given society' (p. 158). A culture may determine to what kind of behaviour these terms should be applied. In this it may differ from other cultures. And there may be no way of resolving this disagreement. But this does mean that the cultures differ as to whether calling an action 'good' or 'right' implies approval and calling it 'evil' or 'wrong' implies disapproval (where 'approval' and 'disapproval' can be shown to be meant in the same way within the cultures in question). There is an ambiguity in saying that what is good and right in one culture may be evil and wrong in another. If in one culture there is a belief that offering human sacrifice is a good, praiseworthy action, while in another culture the taking of an innocent human life is believed to be wrong and evil, this does not imply any conceptual difference as to what a good and right action is or what is an evil or wrong action. The difference lies in what actions each culture judges good and right, and what it judges evil and wrong. It may be added that the reasons for these differing judgements are irrelevant. Someone who believes that taking an innocent human life is wrong in every circumstance may concede that someone else within his frame of reference might justify human sacrifice to his satisfaction. Yet the first would have to say that what the other is doing is wrong. It is not all right *for him*. Even *for him* it is wrong, just as a false statement 'cannot be true for the Nuer and not true for us' (Archer, p. 244).

Williams argues that to talk of relativism at all there must be a real confrontation between two divergent outlooks such that at a given time both the outlooks present real options to a group of people. These people can either retain their own outlook or extend it to take account of the other option. Or they can go over to the other option, adapt to it and judge it to be right. The abandonment of slavery is a case in point. This rules out relativity, since one or other of the options is no longer treated as a real option. It recedes into the area of what Williams calls 'notional confrontation'. Notional confrontation occurs 'when some people know about two divergent outlooks, but at least one of these outlooks does not present a real option' (*op. cit.* p. 160). Here relativism can operate, but it is no longer judgemental. Judgement is suspended. There is no longer any question of one set of ethical beliefs being an alternative to any other. It is what Williams calls 'the relativism of distance' in contemporary space, in time past and in time future. This is a relativism without conflict, except, perhaps, for some surviving traditional societies. It is relational in the way that perceptual differences are relational. Given a certain culture, it is not surprising, though neither is it inevitable, that certain ethical beliefs – polygamy or monogamy, no quarter or inviolability of prisoners, respect or disregard for the rights of property – should prevail, just as it is most likely that water at room temperature will feel warm to a chilly hand and cold to a warm one. There is nothing dramatic in this. That there is no absolute criterion by which to decide these matters does not mean that firm stances cannot be taken and maintained in the face of conflicting beliefs. As Williams puts it:

> Even if there is no way in which divergent ethical beliefs can be brought to converge by independent inquiry or rational argument, this fact will not imply relativism. Each outlook may still be making claims it intends to apply to the whole world, not just to that part of it which is its 'own' world. (p. 159)

Finally, religious relativism. Religious relativism proceeds along much the same lines as ethical relativism. There is vulgar religious relativism which is equally well-disposed to everyone else's religious beliefs, a non-relativist universal tolerance. Then there is the extreme form of social relativism extended to religious belief. According to this view the form that a set of religious beliefs takes is determined by the social milieu it reflects (a fragmented society will be polytheistic and so on). Its function, according to Durkheim, is to help hold a society (at least a primitive or traditional society) together. According to some relativists, religious beliefs change with changing social conditions. This kind of relativism, as well as relational relativism of both the more robust and the modified ('relativism of distance') sort, are open to the same strictures as were levelled against ethical relativism. There are, however, a number of differences between religious and ethical relativism.

First, unlike ethics, no one is under any compulsion to adhere to a set of religious beliefs, least of all to a specific set of beliefs. Certain religious bodies insist that everyone has an obligation to seek God, but this obligation cannot be enjoined on those who do not share their beliefs. Of course, presented with a religious belief, one has to take some attitude towards it, but that can be one of indifference or agnosticism, which are not religious beliefs. Whether atheism may be regarded as a religious belief or merely a philosophical (or theological) position or not, it is not one branch of a dichotomy as are true or false, right or wrong. If someone claims to have an irrefutable argument to show that a divine being, such as more sophisticated people believe in, is an impossibility, we might say he was taking a stance on the question of religious belief. But the reason why he does not believe in God or any god is because he finds the term vacuous, and, hence, meaningless. It is hard to see how he could be said to take any kind of stance on religious matters whatsoever. He has opted out of the language-game of religious belief.

Secondly, as with ethics, there are no absolute criteria by which to decide between differing sets of religious beliefs; nor are there any absolute criteria to decide between the reasons for believing and not believing. Moreover, it is hard to see what form such criteria could take or how they could be applied. If we exclude Deism, no religion has claimed to ground itself on the principles of reason. Whether religion should be deemed irrational on that account is something that will be discussed in a later chapter. But, what with beliefs in miracles, revelation and mysteries, it so far transcends (or strives to transcend) reason and experience that it is impossible to envisage any kind of rational criteria that could ground a particular creed, much less adjudicate between different beliefs. As for criteria that could adjudicate between belief and universal disbelief in the divine and supernatural, the very suggestion is absurd. It would be like trying to prove that something was absolutely unthinkable.

But, it might be said – and this is the third difference between ethics and religious belief – ethical criteria might be used to adjudicate between various religious beliefs and even to eliminate them all. There is no denying that religion might be seen as encroaching on the territory of ethics in so far as its beliefs imply, or at least include, a way of life. Some of these practices – perhaps most – will be straightforward moral practices, such as caring for the needy or marital fidelity, done for some religious motive, however. Others will be compatible with secular ethics, if unlikely to be enjoined or even suggested – forgiving one's enemies, helping social aliens, suffering injuries and insults without seeking revenge. But there will usually be others that offend against secular ethics to a greater or lesser degree – human sacrifice, flagellation, suttee, head-hunting, ritual prostitution and similar practices. These may offend against the ethical beliefs and values of both secular and religious people alike (people who do not share the beliefs from which these practices derive). Indeed, a negative criterion, a reason for rejecting a set of religious beliefs, might be the rejection of these practices on moral grounds. But this in itself would not prove that the religious practices were wrong or the beliefs that supported them false. People who accepted these beliefs along with the practices they enjoined could say that ethical considerations have to yield to the higher considerations of religion; that the will of God overrides the conclusions of human reason. Conversely, ethical considerations in themselves can never be sufficient to justify embracing any religious faith, however laudable the ethical practices it inculcates. If it is to be a truly supernatural and transcendental religion, some of its doctrines must be such as to strain mere human credulity and rationality to the point where we are hard put to give a moral justification for embracing them. (More of this in a later chapter.)

Finally, there is something personal (subjective if you will) about religious belief that differentiates it from ethical beliefs and evaluations. This follows from its transcendental and supra-rational nature. It makes sense to expect others to subscribe to the same moral principles we adhere to. Indeed, it would be odd if it were otherwise. If someone believes that a certain course of action is the morally correct one and that moral action is rational action, it would be distinctly odd for him to agree that an opposite course of action, which he regarded as irrational, was equally correct. But it is different with religious belief. Precisely because religion (apart from Deism) is not entirely, or even importantly rational, a believer cannot say that everyone must accept the religious beliefs he has accepted. This is not to say he should not try to bring others round to his way of believing. But this is best done by personal example. In the last resort, accepting a faith is something that each must do for him or her self. As Kierkegaard says, faith is a leap in the dark; when one leaps in the dark, one leaps alone.

In view of what has been said, we are now in a position to ask where Wittgenstein stands. Is he a relativist or not? If he is a relativist, what kind of relativist is he? Extreme or moderate, that is, no more than anyone but an extreme and intransigent absolutist (a Platonist, for example) might be? Do language-games, forms of life, depth grammar, the rejection of the Platonic and Aristotelian essentialist accounts of general terms and other later ideas imply a relativist position?

The strongest claim that he was an extreme ('strong programme') relativist must surely be based on the notion of language-games and forms of life. They seem to imply that meaning determines reference. In itself this proposal is innocent enough; and, in most cases, correct. Everything depends on how we understand 'meaning' and 'determine'. To know what someone is referring to, the listener or reader *must* know the meaning of the words used and the sense in which they are being used. If we are not familiar with City of London slang, it will be impossible to know what someone is referring to if he uses such expressions as 'little fish', 'dawn raid', 'Chinese wall', 'dink' or 'yid'. In that sense the meaning determines the reference. But Wittgenstein's language-games and forms of life go much further than that in a deterministic direction.

First, the extension of the use of a word (its possible referents) is determined by the language-games that can be played with a particular term. Thus in Wittgenstein's list of games, children's games along with Olympic games are included because the same term is used with the same meaning. But the use of 'game' in this way blurs the difference between competitive games and mere play. This is harmless enough. We can substitute the word 'play' to cover all Wittgenstein's instances. But this may not be universally possible, and this is the second point.

According to Wittgenstein, the language-game in which 'game' is used is determined by more primitive language-games, the language-games we learn in childhood when we first learn language. We build on these primitive language-games. They become increasingly complex and sophisticated, yielding poetry, mystical writing, prophecy and all manner of esoteric forms of speech. But surely whatever the primitive origins of a developed and sophisticated language-game may be, it should be capable of accommodating itself to other sophisticated language-games from different primitive origins, and its user capable of understanding it. Common sense and experience would suggest that this is so. But this may seem to be blocked by the restraint of forms of life.

The meanings of words are determined by the form of life within which a language-game is played. This is particularly true of the primitive language-games on which subsequent language-games are based. Forms of life will differ from culture to culture and from age to age; they will give rise to and be the basis of more elaborate and sophisticated language-games with their corresponding forms of life. Now, if the forms of life that determine the primitive and basic language-games are such that they render it impossible to think otherwise or give alien meanings in other language-games a meaning in one's own, then Wittgenstein is an extreme relativist.

The question is: is Wittgenstein committed to taking this stance? Is he committed by his notions of language-games and forms of life to extreme relativism? What it comes down to in the end is, paradoxically for a relativist, how absolute is the primitive and basic language-game? This is the crucial issue; to deal with it some distinctions have to be made. First, we must distinguish between the basic language-game as (a) a necessary condition for speaking any language whatsoever and (b) the inviolable and incorrigible basis of what the speaker of that language can say thereafter. The former is obviously true. The second is far more problematical. If, as Wittgenstein seems to say, it is impossible to doubt our external or internal sensations (that we see a red colour, smell the scent of musk or feel a stabbing pain) then, in the face of such opponents as Goodman ('Sense and Coherence'), Wittgenstein ends up as a relativist. But this assumes that matters concerning sensation are not incorrigible, that, for instance, as Goodman claims, it is possible to doubt that one is seeing a red colour or smelling the scent of musk or feeling a stabbing pain. (Here we are talking about a first, not a third, party, who can clearly doubt whether claims made about sensations are correct. This doubt would be based on the behaviour of the claimant (in the case of pain) or some objective criterion (in the case of colour).)[12]

If Wittgenstein is to be called an extreme relativist on these grounds, then he belongs to a fairly wide group of philosophers and an even wider group of non-philosophers. The examples given seem so basic and universal in human nature that this kind of relativism can hardly be called cultural relativism. Moreover, as Goodman and others say, even if it is possible for someone to claim that he is not having a certain sensation when most people in a similar situation would say that they were having one, that is, using 'pain', say, or 'red' or 'the smell of musk' in a most peculiar way, this should not immediately brand (if that is the right word) the person who says it as a relativist. Wittgenstein, as we shall see, discusses the religious notion of life after death. He finds the notion unintelligible as stated and suggests that another word or phrase should be used. But he has no difficulty in discussing the matter and exploring ways of using the expression, even though he would not use it himself, since he did not believe in an afterlife. Similarly, Whorf happily discusses the language of the Hopi Indians, even though he does not share their primitive language-game and would not adapt English to it. Nor would Wittgenstein, any more than Whorf, say that the language-game that he does not play is necessarily incorrect. But Wittgenstein, at least on occasion, feels free to do so. And, in *On Certainty*, he admits the possibility of conversion, which could amount to admitting that one's primitive language-game was in some respect incorrect. This does not look like extreme relativism.

As for other later notions, depth grammar and the rejection of the Platonic notion of essence, these, though having a relativistic flavour, no more imply relativism than do the notions of language-games and forms of life. Depth grammar is so closely related to forms of life as not to need detailed discussion. The rejection of the Platonic notion of essence is somewhat more difficult to assess. What Wittgenstein is rejecting is not just Platonic realism, the notion that there are eternal, absolute and unchanging forms of classes of things, such as human beings, animals or beds, to which general terms correspond and refer. With his theory of 'family resemblance' Wittgenstein suggests that most general terms merely corral, as it were, certain groups of persons, objects, activities or organisms on the basis of certain similarities, and give the group a name. Each culture and sub-culture can corral the members of the group as it thinks appropriate and exclude from membership whatever it thinks does not fit, however much it may resemble the members of the group (the 'family'). Thus, the Karem excluded cassowaries from the category of birds (*yakt*) on the grounds that they never fly, yet they included bats, which are not birds (as ornithologists understand the species), because they have wings and *fly*. Other peoples cast the term 'bird' even wider to include not only bats but also insects and even, in some instances, aeroplanes. They are all flying things.

This may imply a certain arbitrariness in the choice of what similarities to classify under a general term. But it is not completely arbitrary. There must be objective similarities, over which the classifier has no control. Thus, though there may be a certain element of relativity in the choice of similarities, there is no incommensurability. Anyone can understand what the Karem mean by '*yakt*' and the others mean by their all-embracing concept of flying creatures as birds. We can even condone Wittgenstein's own inclusion of patience and the round-dance, round-elay or ring-a-ring-a-roses (*Reigenspiele*) into the category of 'games', since in German they would come under *spiel* (play or amusement, but not necessarily game).

There is, therefore, no implication of the extreme relativity that implies incommensurability in understanding between cultures or even individuals in any of Wittgenstein's later writings. In speaking about value, however, he does give a (false) impression of relativism. In his lectures on aesthetics he speaks very much like an extreme relativist. Of contemporary distant cultures, he says that the sculptor, Frank Dobson's, appreciation of Negro sculpture was '*entirely* different from an educated Negro's ... The Negro's and Frank Dobson's are *different* appreciations *altogether*' (*LC* 28, p. 9. (My italics). And of cultures distant in time he says:

> You talk in *entirely* different terms of the Coronation robe of Edward II and of a dress suit ... You appreciate it in an *entirely* different way; your attitude to it is *entirely* different to that of a person living at the time it was designed. (*LC* 31, p. 10. My italics)

He seems also to believe that the taste of a period is culturally determined. To describe what you mean by a cultivated taste, you have to describe a whole culture. 'An entirely different game is played in different ages' (*LC* 25, p. 8). It belongs to the language-game of a whole culture. Thus aristocratic musical taste in eighteenth century Vienna is described in terms of the way people lived at the time; when it came into bourgeois circles it changed: women sang in choirs. In a culture like our own, more active and less flamboyant than that of the eighteenth century, we get simpler dress, hairstyle and architecture (*LC* 34, p. 10). For this reason Wittgenstein thinks it is often more profitable to compare contemporary artists practising different arts than artists of different ages practising the same art (*LC* p. 32).[13]

If we take Wittgenstein quite literally when he says that, for a twentieth century European to appreciate a piece of Negro sculpture or the Coronation robe of a medieval monarch, is to do something entirely different from what an educated Negro would do or a medieval courtier would have done then he would be open to the objection that Davidson levelled at Whorf. He would be unable to say this; he could not know that the acts were different. But knowing Wittgenstein's use of the expression 'entirely different', it is more reasonable to suppose that, as so often happens, he is doing no more than warning his audience not to assume that people of widely different cultures who appear to be doing exactly the same thing are actually doing so.

Yet what Wittgenstein says about period taste and its relationship to the whole culture to which it belongs, smacks of cultural relativism. It looks as though he is saying that cultural conditions determine aesthetic values and that aesthetic values change with changing cultural conditions. In fact, he is saying nothing more than what has to be said: namely, that to understand the tastes of a particular culture we must look at the culture as a whole. This is not to say that aesthetic value itself is determined by the culture, any more than ethical value is. Nor is it to deny that someone living in that culture can reject its taste, in part at least. Wittgenstein explicitly says that a composer can change the rules, though not all of them at once (*LC* 16, p. 6). What kinds of works and objects are regarded as aesthetically good, beautiful, exciting, pretty and charming, or repulsive, vulgar and hideous may vary from culture to culture but what is *meant* by these terms need not, since this is not determined by the culture.

Though Wittgenstein has little to say on ethics in his later writings compared with what he said earlier, there is one passage recorded by Rush Rhees that has a relativistic ring to it. I shall discuss this passage later at greater length. Briefly, the matter arises in a discussion of a difficult case, that of a man who must either leave his wife or abandon his work on cancer research. If he adheres to a Christian ethic the solution might be clear to him: he should stay with his wife come what may. On the other hand, if he accepted a different ethic – Nietzsche's perhaps – the solution might not be so clear. To someone who says that one of these solutions must be the right one, Wittgenstein would reply by asking how the matter could be resolved, what sort of criteria would be used. Some years later he returned to the question. This time he said:

> suppose I say Christian ethics is the right one. Then I am making a judgement of value. It amounts to adopting Christian ethics. It is *not* like saying that one of these physical theories must be the right one. (*PRv* p. 24)

This may sound like honey to the ear of an extreme relativist, but it is nothing of the kind. Wittgenstein is merely demonstrating the difference between ethics and physical theory. As he says: 'The way in which some reality corresponds – or conflicts – with a physical theory has no counterpart here.' And he concludes:

> If you say there are various systems of ethics you are not saying that they are all equally right. That means nothing. Just as it would have no meaning to say that each was right from his own standpoint. That could only mean that each judges as he does. (*PRv* p. 24)

If proof were needed that Wittgenstein was not a hardline relativist, it is here.

But he was a relativist of sorts, as all philosophers who deal with value must be. Value is a matter of judgement, not of calculation, experiment or testable hypothesis. There are no ways of settling differences of opinion on matters of aesthetics, ethics and religious belief by measurement or by statistics, by crucial experiments or acid tests. Such devices belong to a different language-game. But this does not mean that within the language-game of value or the language-game of ethics and religious belief there cannot be ways of adjudicating between rival systems of ethics and rival creeds to the satisfaction of the adherents of these systems and creeds or, at worst, to the satisfaction of their rivals. Some ethical systems and some religious creeds and practices are regarded as preferable to others. An ethical system that does not condone slavery may be preferred to one that does; a religious system that does not include animal, much less human, sacrifice may be preferred to one that does. There may be various reasons for such preferences, but the important point is that there is a possibility of choice. While everyone is to some extent locked into a conceptual system, the key has not been thrown away. It is always possible, if sometimes difficult, to adopt a new ethical or religious system. That was Wittgenstein's view.

Wittgenstein concedes that there are differences of views on what constitutes acceptability and excellence in aesthetics (*LC* pp. 1–11). As we have just seen, he concedes the same for ethics. Though he is not explicit and has not discussed the question of religious belief directly, there is every reason to believe that had he done so he would have come to the same conclusion. As we shall see in later chapters, he was open to understanding (if not accepting, and, to that extent, to not understanding) religious beliefs of both primitive peoples and Christians. Nowhere does Wittgenstein suggest that differences of views on value are so deterministically ingrained that the holder of one set of views cannot understand the holders of other sets or alter his own views and accept a set of alternatives.

Thus Wittgenstein's abandonment of the picture theory of language and his adoption of the notion of language-games and forms of life did not lead to cultural relativism of the extreme, deterministic, Whorfian kind. Nor did it (nor need it have) lead to any radical alteration in his views on ethics and religious belief.

The one aspect of his earlier account open to question is the matter of absolute value. How can Wittgenstein's mild and moderate relativism be reconciled with the notion of absolute value? Is it, for all its relativism, completely compatible with a notion of absolute value? The fact that people hold different views on ethics and religious belief does not mean they do not hold them absolutely. What may lead someone to think that absolute value is incompatible with the relativity of value judgements is the presupposition that it must be possible to arbitrate definitively between the various judgements and decide which is the absolutely correct. But this is fallacious. To hold a view absolutely it is not necessary to believe that an absolute, supervening, arbitrating power would prove one's judgement right. It is sufficient that one holds it is right and cannot see how it could possibly be otherwise.

Moreover even where there are different customs, as among primitive tribes or ancient civilizations, there is good reason to believe that, despite the differences of practice, there is a belief in absolute value. It may be courage or fidelity or honesty or loyalty or devotion to duty. Whatever the manifestation, one or other of these values shines through. Otherwise it would be hard to recognize these beliefs as ethical or religious values at all.

This, however, is not exactly what Wittgenstein meant by absolute value. He was distinguishing absolute from relative value. That is, he was saying that it makes sense to talk of value as a relation and only as a relation. The relation may be one of use and efficiency or of market price or of performance or of what one would be prepared to sacrifice to keep or obtain it. Absolute value, on the other hand, purports to be non-relational. It is not good in relation to some purpose, goal or end. It is simply good (or bad) in itself. Wittgenstein's earlier writings present the view that judgements of value are absolute. This view is not altered by his later admission that we do not all, nor can we all, agree on what it is that absolute value consists. There is nothing to suggest that his earlier distinction between absolute and relative value has altered. It is true that he does not talk in these terms. But this in itself is not evidence of a change of view. Indeed, as I hope to show, in the later writings this distinction between absolute and relative value is stronger than ever.

However, we must distinguish between the attitude of the ethical, religious or aesthetic person (that is, the person making an ethical, religious or aesthetic judgement) and someone (a philosopher) commenting on what that person is doing. Someone who wishes to affirm a truth, that is, make a committed statement or assertion, as opposed to offering an opinion or just entertaining a thought about what could or might be, must be absolutely committed. This is not to say that such a person could not admit that he or she could possibly be wrong, but that under the circumstance this is not conceivable. The person in question can see no evidence to contradict the statement. Similarly with aesthetic, ethical and religious judgements. It makes no sense to say that Donne *might* be a great *poet, if that* is what you honestly and fervently believe. This does not mean that we have to have a definite opinion on everything. We can decide that Auden and Spender are good poets or Britten and Tippett are good composers without being able to decide which is better. The judgement that they are good at their art is absolute; that one may be better than the other is an opinion, and subject to revision. But, then, even the judgement that Donne is a great poet is open to revision, should the right evidence be produced.

The same is true of ethical and religious judgements. To be ethically or religiously committed we must say something like: suicide, voluntary euthanasia and genetic engineering on human embryos are morally permissible; or that they are not. And we must say this absolutely. One can hedge one's judgement with reference to particular situations and circumstances, but even this must be stated absolutely. It makes no moral sense to say of a particular case: 'Maybe it is all right or maybe it isn't.' This is not an ethical judgement at all. Similarly with judgements of religious belief. Either we believe or we do not. There is no room for 'maybe', 'perhaps', 'probably', 'possibly' or 'it is very likely' if we are talking about the Incarnation, the Resurrection and redemptive power of Jesus Christ, or of the Day of Judgement. We either believe absolutely or not at all. (This will be discussed more fully in a later chapter.)

A philosophical commentator does not have to take these judgements as absolute. He may not agree with them for a variety of reasons. The most obvious is that there is no final court of appeal to adjudicate between various ethical, religious and aesthetic judgements. There is no absolute criterion, no answer at the back of the book, by which to decide which judgements are right and which are not. Another reason is that, however strongly an ethical, religious or aesthetic view may be held, it can be overturned, and the holder of it may be converted to another point of view. It is also possible that, having changed our minds, we can, on more mature consideration, change them back again. This does not make for philosophical relativism in any serious or extreme sense. It merely takes account of the flexibility, and consequent fluidity and revisable nature of value judgements.

8

Religious Discourse

If it is true that Wittgenstein did not radically alter his views on value in his later writings, he certainly expanded them, particularly those on religious belief, in the light of such notions as language-games, forms of life and depth grammar. Our chief sources of information are some remarks published in *Culture and Value*, and the reported lectures on religious belief in *Lectures and Conversations*, as well as conversations with Rush Rhees to be found in 'Some Developments in Wittgenstein's View of Ethics' (*Philosophical Review*, 1965).

To emphasize the continuity of his thought and to illustrate how certain ideas developed in the light of new conceptions of the way language operates I shall choose first the treatment of the notions of religious simile, miracles, mystery and the meaning of life, already discussed.

In the 'Lecture on Ethics' Wittgenstein said that:

> in ethical and religious langue we seem constantly to be using similes. But a simile must mean *something*... Now in our case as soon as we try to drop the simile and simply state the facts which stand behind it, we find that there are no such facts. (*PRv* p. 10)

In an entry in his *Notebooks* for 1937 he returns to this point with reference to Pilgrim's tribulations as described in *The Pilgrim's Progress:*

> Religious similes can be said to move on the edge of an abyss. B(unyan)'s for example. For what if we simply add: 'and all these traps, quicksands, wrong turnings, were planned by the Lord of the Road and the monsters, thieves were created by him'? Certainly that is not the sense of the simile. (*CV* p. 29)

The point to note here is that, although *The Pilgrim's Progress* is an allegory and can thus be translated into a literal account of God's dealings with mankind, it is also a simile of the kind discussed in chapter two, one whose meaning is hidden. For many people, including Wittgenstein himself, to translate it is to rob it of its power (ibid.).

In the next paragraph Wittgenstein introduces the notion of picturing a way of life. (The date is 1937.) 'Rules of life,' he says, 'are dressed up in pictures' (ibid.). Two things emerge from this. One is that the simile, the picture, *describes* an attitude or a way of behaving, but does not *justify* it. The second, and the reason for the first, is that the simile or picture does not fit universally. In an example already quoted, Wittgenstein says that we can be grateful to bees for giving us honey *as though* they *were* kind, but not *because* they *are* kind, since at any moment they might sting us. Similarly we should thank God for the good we receive but not complain about the evil, as we would if a human being were to do us good and evil by turns. Wittgenstein concludes:

> Religion says: *Do this! – Think like that!* – but it cannot justify this and once it tries to, it becomes repellent; because for every reason it offers there is a valid counter-reason. It is more convincing to say: 'Think like this! however strangely it may strike you.' Or: 'Won't you do this? – however repugnant you find it'. (*CV* ibid.)

All this carries the treatment of ethical and religious similes in the 'Lecture on Ethics' a good deal further. It is now related to picturing and ways of living. By relating religio-ethical similes to rules of life, their function in religious and ethical discourse is clarified. Moreover, the inexpressible aspect of ethical and religious utterances is emphasized in what is said about the untranslatable nature of religio-ethical similes.

In the 'Lecture on Ethics' the discussion of religious simile leads to the paradox that ' "an experience, a fact, should seem to have supernatural value" '. To solve this paradox Wittgenstein distinguishes between the sense of miracle as an unusual event and the absolute sense that has nothing to do with extraordinary events, but with the significance of ordinary ones. Wittgenstein amplifies this in his later writings where he likens a miracle to a gesture made by God. 'God lets the world run on smoothly and then accompanies the words of a saint by a symbolic occurrence, a gesture of nature' (*CV* p. 45).[1] He gives as an example the bowing of trees as if in reverence after a saint has spoken. Wittgenstein goes on to say that someone would believe the report of the trees bowing if the mere report of the words the saint uttered and the saint's life impressed him. He himself would not be impressed in this way. He returns to the notion of a miracle as a sacred gesture in a later entry (*CV* p. 50), where he adds that 'the purely corporeal can be uncanny'.

Wittgenstein also speaks of natural miracles, the miracle of nature itself:

> The miracles of Nature.
> One might say: art *shows* us the miracles of nature. It is based on the *concept* of the miracles of nature. (The blossom, just opening out. What is *marvellous* about it?) We say: 'Just look at it opening out!' (*CV* p. 56)

This brings us back to the mystical, the wonder that something or anything is, viewing an object *sub specie aeternitatis* (in this case an opening blossom). This is contrasted with the wonder that a scientist (Wittgenstein calls him a mathematician) might have:

> The mathematician too can wonder at the miracles (the crystal) of nature of course: but can he do so once a problem has arisen about *what* it actually is he is contemplating? (*CV* p. 57)

Another example Wittgenstein gives is that of someone who admires the shadows and reflections of trees, taking them for actual trees, but who, when he realizes that they are not real trees, is puzzled as to what they are and how they are related to trees: 'his admiration has suffered a rent (*Riss* – which translates as 'rupture') that is to be healed' (ibid.). In other words, when one asks questions about what or how something is, admiration for it is cut off. Wonder that something is as it is does not ask what? how? or why?

Though this is not quite the mystical, or the miracle that the world exists, as described in the *Notebooks 1914–1916* and the *Tractatus*, there are echoes here. There is the *wonder*. There is the '*miracle* of Nature' (a limited whole?). There is the *showing* of the miracle. And there is its showing by *art*. ('The artistic miracle is that there is the world' (*NB* p. 86)). This entry is dated 1947, a few years before Wittgenstein's death.

There is another even later entry that not only harks back to the *Notebooks* and the *Tractatus*, but sums up Wittgenstein's views on value and the inexpressible:

> What is eternal and important is often hidden from a man by an impenetrable veil. He knows: there's something under there, but he cannot *see* it. The veil reflects the daylight (*CV* p. 80)

This is a powerful image: the veil hides the mystery by reflecting the light. It is interesting that Wittgenstein should say that the eternal and the important is 'often', but not always, hidden. This suggests that some people with exceptional insight are not hindered from reaching out beyond what to others is always covered by the veil. Again there may be some for whom there is no intimation that anything lies behind it. They see reflecting daylight and, for them, it seems obvious that this is all there is to see: nothing lies underneath that is not seen. Translated into less poetic terms, there are some who only see what meets the eye; there are others who suspect there is more to it than just what meets the eye, but they cannot apprehend it; and there may even be those (religious mystics) for whom the veil is occasionally lifted. But this is pure speculation.

Be that as it may, Wittgenstein, just before his death, made a more protracted entry that reiterates the more important remarks on value to be found in the *Tractatus* and the *Notebooks*, those concerning the mystical and the meaning of life. The passage begins:

> If someone who believes in God looks round and asks 'Where does everything I see come from?', 'Where does all this come from?', he is *not* craving for a (causal) explanation; and his question gets its point from a certain craving. He is, namely, expressing an attitude to all explanations. – But how is this manifested in his life? (*CV* p. 85)

Here we have the mystical: wonder that what exists, exists. We have the distinction between it and the search for scientific, causal explanations. And there is the attitude to scientific explanation as expressed in *TLP* 6.52: 'We feel that even when all possible scientific questions have been answered, the problems of life remain untouched.'

The next paragraph answers the questions that ended the first:

> The attitude that's in question is that of taking a certain matter seriously and then, beyond a certain point, no longer regarding it as serious, but maintaining that something else is even more important. (ibid.)

This is amplified in the next paragraph with the example (clearly autobiographical) of someone who regarded it as a grave matter that he might not complete a certain piece of work before he died, and yet realizes that, in another sense, 'this is not what matters'. Wittgenstein adds: 'At this point one uses the words "in a deeper sense" ' (ibid.). Here, surely, we have an echo of *TLP* 6.521: 'The solution of the problem of life is seen in the vanishing of the problem' and of *NB* p. 73: 'we could say that the man is fulfilling the purpose of existence who no longer needs to have any purpose except to live. That is to say, who is content.'

The main concern of this chapter is to discuss the new ideas that developed in Wittgenstein's thinking on religious belief in the wake of the emergence of the notions of language-games, forms of life and depth grammar. But it is part of this book's strategy to show how ideas introduced earlier persisted throughout Wittgenstein's life and were both echoed (often with the same terminology) and sometimes added to and developed. Having done that we must now turn to the main concern of the chapter.

As has been said, Wittgenstein devotes more attention to religious belief than he did in his earlier work, far more than to ethics. Why the latter is so will be discussed in a later chapter. It will be suggested there that much of what is said about religious belief could be applied to ethics. But, as we saw in the last two chapters, there are important differences between ethics and religious belief, sufficient to raise different, if related questions. In the following chapters I shall confine myself to discussing Wittgenstein's later views on religious belief.

Although most of the questions and their answers arise within the context of notions such as those of language-games, forms of life and depth grammar, Wittgenstein held certain views on questions of religious belief, which do not arise out of these later views (at least not directly). In some respects these views, particularly on dogma and on particular dogmas, are related to earlier ones. They will be discussed separately. But first, matters concerning language-games and forms of life.

Wittgenstein devotes much attention to contrasting religious belief and science as separate language-games. But he also devotes time to the language-game of religious belief in relation to other forms of belief and to unbelief, which, if not a specific language-game in itself, implies some language-game, some point of view and form of life that is not religious, in relation to which religious belief may seem odd and even unintelligible. So we shall begin with the problem of understanding religious belief as such and also particular religious beliefs, whether encountered by unbelievers or by non-believers of a different faith (unbelievers – often dubbed infidels in the estimate of adherents to that particular faith).

It is tempting to put these differences in understanding down to differences in meaning between the words and sentences used by the believer and the non-believer or unbeliever. For the moment I shall confine the discussion to unbelievers, those who have no beliefs, one way or the other, on a particular issue, be it the Eucharist or life after death, as distinct from non-believers who do not accept a particular belief or believe the contrary. Wittgenstein denies that unbelief is necessarily a matter of difference of meaning. 'The difference might not show up at all in any explanation of the meaning.' (*LC* p. 53). That is to say, if an unbeliever cannot say that he either believes in nor disbelieves the doctrine of, say, the Last Judgement, this cannot be explained by saying that he means something different from a believer by the 'Last Judgement'. He may understand perfectly well what the believer means by the 'Last Judgement' and yet neither believe in it nor disbelieve it.

> If Mr Lewy is religious and says he believes in a Judgement Day, I won't even know whether to say I understand him or not. I've read the same things as he's read. In a most important sense, I know what he means. (*LC* p. 58)

Here Wittgenstein introduces an interesting distinction between two senses of 'understand'. On the one hand, he does not know whether he understands what Mr Lewy means when he says he believes in a Judgement Day; on the other hand, he says that he does. What are these two senses of 'understand' and 'mean'? Before attempting to answer this, let me quote the next paragraph:

> If an atheist says: 'There won't be a Judgement Day', and another person says: 'There will' do they mean the same? – Not clear what criterion of meaning the same is. They might describe the same things. You might say, this already shows that they mean the same. (*LC* ibid.)

What is clear from these two quotations is that there is a common level of meaning and understanding, and there is a level where understanding and meaning are doubtful. How is this possible? How can someone (a) understand what someone else is saying; and (b) not understand what he is saying? Yet again (c) how can there be no dispute or misunderstanding about the meaning of the words they are using? This is a crucial question. The answer, if we can get it right, should be the clue to Wittgenstein's account of religious belief.

First, we are not concerned here with controversy, contradiction and disagreement. To claim not to understand what someone is saying is to put ourselves out of reach of contradicting him without falling into the absurdity of saying: 'I don't understand what you mean, but, whatever you mean, you are wrong.' But if we can pin down the recalcitrant senses of 'understand' and 'mean' that Wittgenstein is using, we may be on our way to explaining why controversies and contradictions play little part in religious belief.

Here Wittgenstein's notion of forms of life is helpful. Unlike scientific or philosophical disagreements, religious disagreements have consequences for one's way of living. Practical consequences may follow from scientific and philosophical disagreements, but according to Wittgenstein they follow necessarily in the case of religious beliefs. So while it may be possible to understand what it is that a believer believes, it may be impossible for an unbeliever to understand why the believer should want to believe it, given the consequences that follow from the belief. In the first place, the belief itself, if it is a true religious (i.e. supernatural) belief, will not be amenable to rational, scientific investigation. Secondly, the consequences may not follow logically from it. Thirdly, these consequences may, in the short term at least, be unpleasant and undesirable. In other words, even if the unbeliever understands *what* the believer believes, he will not understand *why* anyone should believe it.

It has been said that to understand a religious belief one has to share it. This idea was formulated by two phrases of St Anselm (following St Augustine): 'faith seeking understanding' (*fides quaerens intellectum*) and, closer to the point, 'I believe in order that I may understand' (*credo ut intelligam*) (*Proslogion*, chapter 1). Thus, unless someone believes there is a supreme being, a universal Creator, and Incarnate God, a Redeemer who rose from the dead and will come in judgement to reward the good and punish the wicked, he cannot begin to understand *why* this should be or *why* anyone should believe in these propositions. He may understand *what* the believer says at least as well as the believer himself understands these beliefs. He may, even, as Wittgenstein claims to have done (*LC* p. 59), answer questions about these beliefs correctly. But he cannot understand, in Wittgensteinian terms, the use to which the utterances that express these beliefs are being put, why anyone should believe them and with what purpose. Understanding what is meant – in so far as that is possible – is not a sufficient reason for believing what is said. Indeed, in itself it may be a sufficient reason for not believing what is said.

Ironically, St Anselm did not fully follow his own precepts. While he tried to explain to believers the implications of believing in a being greater than which none can be conceived, he also set about proving to the unbeliever who understands what is meant by the term 'God' that he must thereby understand there is such a being. But to someone who does not believe there is such a being, this line of argument is not only unconvincing but meaningless. He may understand *what* is said, but cannot see *why*, from this understanding, he should be led to believe there is or could be such a being.

What puzzles the unbeliever is not what the believer understands by his beliefs but how he can bring himself to believe them, particularly as he is prepared to make great sacrifices and take risks for these beliefs. In his lectures on religious belief, Wittgenstein discusses these two senses of 'understand' at some length. In *Philosophical Grammar* (p. 69) and *Philosophical Investigations* (531, pp. 143–4) he discusses two senses of 'understanding'. In one case a sentence can be replaced by another that says the same; the thought is common to different sentences. In the other case, as in a poem, one sentence cannot be replaced by another (any more than a musical theme (*PI* 531, p. 144) or a certain gesture (*PG* p. 69) can be replaced by another): something 'is expressed only by these words in these positions' (*PI* 531, p. 144). These are not two *meanings* of 'understanding' but two uses that make up the meaning, the *concept* of understanding (*PI* 532, p. 144). 'I *want* to apply the word "understanding" to all this.' The two senses of 'understand' as used in the lectures are different from those in *Philosophical Investigations*. There is a difference between the use of words in one kind of sentence from their use in another kind of sentence. Here it is the difference between understanding the meaning of the words in which a belief is expressed and understanding someone holding such beliefs.

Wittgenstein also draws attention to the peculiar use of 'belief' when talking of religious belief. It lies somewhere between our ordinary use of 'believe' and our use of 'know':

> there is this extraordinary use of the word 'believe'. One talks of believing and at the same time one doesn't use 'believe' as one does ordinarily. You might say (in the normal use): 'You only believe – oh well . . .' Here it is used entirely differently; on the other hand it is not used as we generally use the word 'know'. (*LC* pp. 59–60)

'Believe' as we ordinarily use it expresses opinion and suggests doubt, or, at least, uncertainty. 'Know' is an assertion or affirmation that something is the case. Where we have no reason to doubt an assertion or have what we regard as sufficient evidence that what is asserted is not the case, we withhold the term 'know' from such an assertion. The religious believer may claim to know that what he believes is true, but, as we shall see in the next chapter, this claim is hard to support with what we would normally call evidence. Yet, in spite of the lack of what we would normally call evidence and what to the unbeliever are implausible and outrageous beliefs, the believer holds them with all the firmness with which he adheres to the propositions of logic and mathematics. Indeed, late medieval philosophers (the Occamites) held that, besides these propositions and those reporting our immediate sensory experiences, only the propositions of the Faith could be adhered to with certainty. Propositions based on reason alone (which included what then passed as propositions of science, as well as those of history) were at best only probable.

As already mentioned, Wittgenstein illustrates the different senses of 'understand' as used of religious belief with reference to the use of the word 'God'. He points to the difference between our use of the term 'God' and the way in which we refer to aunts and other persons. We can be shown pictures of aunts, but pictures of God are different. It was said that God sees and rewards:

> 'Being shown all these things, did you understand what this word mean?' I'd say: 'Yes and no. I did learn what it didn't mean. I made myself understand. I could answer questions, understand questions when they were put in different ways – and in that sense could be said to understand.'
> (*LC* p. 59)

However, the most extended discussion of the two senses of the term 'understand' is devoted to such expressions as 'survival after death', 'not ceasing to exist', 'being dead but still alive', 'the separation of soul and body' and being 'disembodied'. Here it is clear that failure of understanding is not solely due to puzzlement at anyone believing certain propositions, but failure to understand the use to which the believer puts certain words which have an ordinary use in our language. They are not being used in that way in certain expressions of religious belief. This is surely an instance of an attempt to go beyond the boundaries of language, to say the unsayable, to express the inexpressible.

In order to illustrate this a good point of departure is:

> Today I saw a poster saying: ' "Dead" Undergraduate speaks'.
> The inverted commas mean: 'He isn't really dead'. 'He isn't what people call dead. They call it "dead" not quite correctly.' . . .
> It suddenly struck me: 'If someone said "He isn't really dead, although by the ordinary criteria he is dead" – couldn't I say: "He is not only dead by the ordinary criteria; he is what we all call 'dead'." '
> If you now call him, 'alive', you're using language in a queer way, because you are almost deliberately preparing misunderstandings. Why don't you use some other word, and let 'dead' have the meaning it already has? (*LC* 65)

Wittgenstein certainly has a point here. We can understand what is meant by saying that someone believed to be dead – 'dead' – may speak. He had not been really dead; he had just seemed to be dead. But to say of someone who has not only stopped breathing but whose heart has stopped beating and, moreover, who has begun to putrefy, that he is alive is 'using language in a queer way'. We should use some word other than 'alive' or 'not dead'. But, as Wittgenstein knew only too well, this is precisely what theologians have always done when they speak of 'disembodied spirits'. They admit that people who die are dead in the ordinary sense of the word 'dead' – their hearts and lungs and brains have ceased to function. But they are alive in the sense that their souls have survived the death of their bodies. Whatever one may think of that view, it is not totally incomprehensible, though it is a case of 'using "alive" in a queer way'. Nor, as far as I can see, is it necessarily 'preparing misunderstandings'. To say that Uncle George is alive as a disembodied spirit whom you will meet some day is not to say that he is in a good bodily condition and will come through the front door some day. There may indeed be people who believe, without giving much thought to the matter, that they will once more see their relatives as they were in life and that a timeless, changeless family life with them will be resumed. But I find it hard to accept that anyone who reflects on the matter could believe this.[2]

Wittgenstein's thought becomes somewhat obscure when he talks as follows:

> Case where Lewy has visions of his dead friend. Cases where you don't try to locate him. And case where you try to locate him in a business-like way. Another case where I'd say: 'We can pre-suppose we have a broad basis on which we agree.'
>
> In general, if you say: 'He is dead' and I say 'He is not dead' no one would say: 'Do they mean the same thing by "dead"?' In the case where a man has visions I wouldn't offhand say: 'He means something different.' (*LC* p. 62)

This seems to contradict what Wittgenstein said in the other, admittedly later, passage. There he said, not unreasonably, that if somebody is dead by all the normal criteria, you should not say that he is alive, since you mean something different by 'alive' from what we normally mean by somebody being alive. Yet in this passage Wittgenstein seems to be saying the opposite. He seems to be saying that, if someone says he will see his dead friend again, he is not using 'dead' in a sense different from the sense in which someone sceptical of his belief might use it. This may be the case. We may agree or disagree about whether someone is dead or not. Goodness knows there has been enough controversy about this recently. If we are to agree or disagree, then we must be using 'dead' in the same sense, otherwise we are talking at cross purposes. But it is possible to agree that someone is dead by the 'normal criteria', whatever they are: that is, clinically dead, and still assert you had a vision that you will see the dead person again, however he is located, whether in a businesslike way or not located at all. If this were not an assertion that someone, whom all agree is dead, is, in fact, not dead (which would be a contradiction), it must mean that there is a sense, albeit unusual, in which he is not dead. In that case 'dead' and 'alive' are being used in two different senses.

But, asks Wittgenstein, what is the criterion for meaning something different? It is certainly more than a matter of evidence. It involves doing something. This may be a reaction, perhaps of terror. Or it may consist in taking up a stance.

It is clear where Wittgenstein himself stands:

> 'Seeing a dead friend again' means nothing much to me at all. I don't think in these terms. I don't say to myself: 'I shall see so and so again' ever. (*LC* p. 53)

One of the things that puzzles Wittgenstein is whether 'You'll see your dead friend again' is an empirical proposition. Is the person who says it just superstitious? 'Not a bit,' says Wittgenstein. He may be apologetic. In which case, according to Wittgenstein, he is less intelligent than someone who is categorical. Here follows a rather obscure passage:

> He always says it, but he doesn't make any search. He puts on a queer smile. 'His story has a dreamlike quality.' My answer would be in this case 'Yes', and a particular explanation. (*LC* p. 63)

The first part of this passage is reasonably clear. I assume that by not making a search Wittgenstein means that the person who believes he will see his friend again is not prepared to attempt (perhaps not capable of attempting) a verification or explanation of his assertion. Instead he just smiles a knowing smile. (If Wittgenstein were in his place, he would give a categorical affirmation and reasons for his belief.) Thus his statement cannot be taken as an empirical proposition.

Nor will Wittgenstein allow that if someone holds that so-and-so is alive (whom all agree is clinically dead), there are two 'sharply divided cases, one in which he would say he didn't mean it literally'. This implies there might be some agreement about the reasons for his belief. This, according to Wittgenstein is not so.

Nor again, will Wittgenstein admit a future verification, what he calls 'a question of experience': 'Wait another ten years'. He would 'disencourage' this move. But he admits that others might encourage it. In that case they would do something. They would take sides, and there could be a great difference between them. This difference might come to the point where one might accuse the other of trying to undermine reason. This, says Wittgenstein, would not be false: it 'is actually where such questions rise'. It would seem that Wittgenstein is saying that where beliefs about seeing again someone clinically dead arise, there is no rational way of deciding them. One just either accepts and believes them, or rejects them as irrational. Hence, to say that someone who believes in seeing the dead again is undermining reason might not be a false statement.

In another passage Wittgenstein reverts to the subject of different ideas of being dead and being alive. Here he discusses not the criteria for being dead or alive, so much as the criteria for having the idea of someone being dead or alive. He contrasts eccentric ideas of death with the normal usage of the term 'having an idea of death':

> 'In whatever way anyone will use this word, I have now a certain idea', then it is not commonly called 'having an idea', because what is commonly called 'having an idea', has reference to the technique of the word, etc. (*LC* p. 68)

There is what Wittgenstein calls a public and a private use of the word death. The word 'death' is what Wittgenstein calls 'a public instrument' with a whole technique of usage. For an idea of death to be an idea of *death*, it must belong to the language-game played with 'death' that we know and understand; 'it must become part of our game' (*LC* p. 69). If you treat it as something private then it does not form part of the public language-game: 'With what right are you calling it an idea of death?' We too have a right to say what an idea of death is. Why call your idea an *idea of death*, if it does not belong to the language-game commonly played with 'death'?

I feel that Wittgenstein is treating his notion of language-games somewhat rigidly and narrowly here. Moreover, what he is saying is ambiguous. It is not clear whether he means that a private idea of death is unintelligible in principle if it differs from the ordinary uses of 'death' in some radical way, or merely that, if it differs from the ordinary use, but remains intelligible, some phrase other than 'my idea of death' should be used. I suspect – and what follows seems to bear this out – that he means the latter. Why shouldn't someone use 'death' in a peculiar way? He may be breaking the rules of one game in order to establish another. There is no complete break with usage: there are connections.

On 'ceasing to exist' Wittgenstein is circumspect. He can understand what it means for a shadow to cease to exist, but he has difficulty with the notion of a chair ceasing to exist. I presume that if a chair has been sawn or broken up or burnt, it is odd to say that it has ceased to exist, since the materials which composed it have not ceased to exist. They have simply ceased to be a chair. For a chair to cease to exist it would have to be here one moment and gone the next, leaving not a trace behind. As Wittgenstein says: 'You may find that there isn't a use for this sentence.' (*LC* p. 65)

But it is not with ceasing to exist that we are concerned, rather with not ceasing to exist. Someone may say that a person is dead 'according to the old meaning', but has not ceased to exist. If I understand Wittgenstein correctly, the problem about saying of someone that he has *not ceased* to exist is that it is hard to understand what is meant by his *having ceased* to exist. He asks us to imagine ourselves on our death-bed. 'Are you clear,' he asks, 'when you'd say you had ceased to exist?'

The concept of 'disembodied spirit' is more promising. But here again Wittgenstein has difficulty in connecting this concept with anything comprehensible. He is prepared to concede that it might have a use if connected with certain consequences or certain pictures.

Disembodied spirits can be connected with 'what people have said about suffering after death, etc.' Whether by temperament or for some other reason, Wittgenstein seems to concentrate on the more unpleasant aspects of an afterlife. In one place he is reported as saying: ' "If you don't cease to exist, you will suffer after death", there I begin to attach ideas, perhaps ethical ideas, of responsibility' (*LC* p. 70). In order to suffer after death it is necessary to survive death, in some sense.

But there is another consequence, besides suffering, connected with responsibility. Wittgenstein recounts how someone ('a great writer') once said that as a boy he had been set a task by his father and suddenly felt that nothing, not even death, could take away that responsibility. This was for him in a way a proof of the immortality of the soul. If the responsibility lives on and will not die, neither can the soul. 'The idea is given by what we call the proof.' Wittgenstein concludes: 'Well, if this is the idea, (all right)', (*LC* ibid.). Obviously this was not a view to which Wittgenstein himself would subscribe, though he seems to have respected it.

There is another view to which he was unlikely to subscribe, yet which he recognized as making a kind of connection between the idea of survival after death and some of its consequences. This is the one made by spiritualists. 'Although,' says Wittgenstein, 'he gives me a picture I don't like, I do get a clear idea' (*LC* ibid.). I am not aware that spiritualists talk about 'apparitions' as Wittgenstein suggests, but they do claim to have communication with departed spirits. This, as Wittgenstein says, is a 'particular kind of verification'. If spiritualism were true, if spirits really did communicate with those still living on earth, this would be irrefutable proof of survival after death. So in this proof we could glean some idea of what it means to survive death: namely, that after death a 'departed' can communicate with those still alive in this world. This, as Wittgenstein notes, is not what religious people understand by survival. Apart from the trivial content of the reported communications 'from beyond the grave', religious people do not make survival after death a matter of verification, but of belief. The apparitions of Jesus and others do not verify belief in an afterlife: they are part of that belief.

Finally, there is the case of the person embarking for China and saying to his friend: 'We might see one another after death'. Wittgenstein asks: 'would I necessarily say that I don't understand him?' and replies: 'I might say (want to say) simply: Yes. I *understand* him entirely' (*LC* pp. 70–1). From what follows it would seem that Wittgenstein understands more than the meaning of the words the person used. He understands him, firstly because he takes it that the person departing for China is using a picture, and secondly because he understands what use the person makes of the picture. But, he says, he might be mistaken. The test of this are the conclusions that follow from the use of the words and the picture he employs. If the conclusions and consequences that the other person draws are not the same as those drawn by the person using a picture, then there may be misunderstanding and disagreement between them. 'Yes, this might be a disagreement,' Wittgenstein admits:

> if he himself were to use the word in a way in which I did not expect, or were to draw conclusions I did not expect him to draw. I wanted only to draw attention to a particular technique of usage. We should disagree, if he was using a technique I did not expect. (*LC* p. 71)

The importance of this is the emphasis it places on the *consequences* of picturing, particularly where religious beliefs (or possible religious beliefs, such as belief in a life after death) are concerned; the use to which pictures are put in *living* a religious life.[3]

Wittgenstein develops this idea when he says:

> When I say he's using a picture I'm merely making a *grammatical* remark: (what I say) can only be verified by the consequences he does or does not draw. (*LC* p. 72)

Each element of this statement is important. (a) In speaking of someone using a picture one is merely making a grammatical remark. This must be taken in two ways: first, in the way in which Wittgenstein uses the expression 'grammatical remark', meaning that he is talking about the use of a word or group of words in a language-game connected with a particular form of life; secondly, that he is taking it *merely* in this way. He is passing no judgement on this way of using the picture. (b) An interpretation of the use of a picture can be *verified*: that is, it can be shown to be correct or otherwise. There can be disagreement as to how a picture is being used; and, hence, what the religious believer means by what he says. (c) This verification is based on the consequences or conclusions the user of the picture draws from it.[4] And (d), which follows from (c): it is as important to be sure of the consequences that the believer *does not draw* from a picture (e.g. the eyebrows of God's all-seeing Eye) as of those he draws.

The importance the believer himself may attach to a picture can vary. 'Isn't it as important as anything else,' Wittgenstein asks, 'what picture he does use?' (*LC* p. 71). To return to what was said in a previous chapter, a picture may be interchangeable with another: Wittgenstein gives as examples various projections of an ellipse and the shape of chess pieces. Here the function of the picture is merely to identify and distinguish different things. This can be done in various ways. On the other hand, 'the whole weight may be in the picture': that is, every detail of the picture may be relevant. For example (mine), the fact that it was a Samaritan who cared for the robbed and wounded traveller in the parable, that he paid for his lodgings and care, that a priest and a Levite passed by and did nothing – all this is relevant to the picture, the parable of the Good Samaritan.

We have seen here how Wittgenstein's later notions of language-games, forms of life, logical grammar and living according to a picture were developed in relation to understanding, misunderstanding and lack of understanding between religious believers and unbelievers. On the whole there is a yawning gap between the two. This might be bridged to some extent if the unbeliever could understand correctly the use to which the believer put the pictures he lived by. Even here there is room for misunderstanding. And even if the unbeliever could come that far towards bridging the gap, there still remain the further obstacles of (a) the beliefs themselves and (b) the way of life that accepting these beliefs entails.

9

The Grounding of Religious Belief

Part of the trouble an unbeliever has in understanding what a believer believes is that his belief is insufficiently grounded. Worse than that, it can run counter to what are regarded as well-founded beliefs. A passage in *On Certainty* which echoes Moore's *Defence of Common Sense* illustrates this:

> I believe that every human being has two human parents; but Catholics believe that Jesus only had a human mother ... Catholics believe as well that in certain circumstances a wafer completely changes its nature, and at the same time all evidence proves the contrary. And so if Moore said 'I know that this is wine and not blood', Catholics would contradict him. (*OC* 239, p. 32)

This might be described as the scandal or stumbling block that religious belief lays in the path of the unbeliever. But it differs only in degree of enormity from the obstacles to certainty that lie in wait in the everyday world. These have been discussed at length in *On Certainty*. There Wittgenstein does not so much question the grounds of our everyday beliefs – those listed by Moore: that we have hands (if we have), that we live on a substantial body called 'the earth', that it existed for some time before we were born and so on – as question their grounding.

Wittgenstein points out that the grounds of very few of our beliefs have ever been tested (*OC* 163–6, p. 24). Does anyone check the story of Napoleon or even whether a chair is around when no one is paying attention to it? And where does checking come to an end?[1] Wittgenstein concludes: 'The difficulty is to realize the groundlessness of our believing.' He also points out that the grounds for our beliefs are not in themselves (until further examined) either true or false or grounded (*OC* 204–6, p. 28): 'If the true is what is grounded, then the ground is not *true*, nor yet false.'

This is not to say that our everyday beliefs, to say nothing of our current scientific beliefs, are not well-established, well-founded and properly grounded. However, the same cannot be said for religious beliefs. Indeed, not only is this a feature of them, but it is an essential feature, in Wittgenstein's opinion. Moreover, the intelligent, educated believer is aware of this:

> *Very* intelligent and well-educated people believe in the story of the creation in the Bible, while others hold it as proven false, and the grounds of the latter are well known to the former. (*OC* 336, p. 43)

That is another essential (if not exclusive) feature of religious belief: the refusal to abandon a belief in the face of strong, indeed what would normally be regarded as overwhelming, evidence to the contrary. 'And so if Moore said "I know that this is wine and not blood", Catholics would contradict him' (*OC* 239, p. 32). As I have said, this is not an exclusive feature of religious belief. There are ordinary, everyday beliefs that are so fundamental to our understanding and knowledge of ourselves and the world in which we live – something as obvious as having a foot – that, as Wittgenstein says:

> 'Nothing in the world will convince me of the opposite!' For me this fact is at the bottom of all knowledge. I shall give up other things but not this. (*OC* 380, p. 49)

But, in the case of the religious believer, the reasons for abandoning his belief are so strong that his holding fast to it gives a new sense to 'hold fast'.

This steadfastness in belief is not concerned with what we are or are not prepared to abandon by way of belief in order to maintain some sort of mental control on ourselves and the world around us. It is concerned with a form of life and what we are prepared to sacrifice in order to achieve and maintain it. In other words, the firmness, the steadfastness of the belief is not (or not solely) intellectual and rational, based on evidence and grounds, but is partly psychological, partly moral (categories elude us here), based on a picture (a vision, if you will) of how we either want to lead our lives or think that we ought to lead them.

In his lectures on religious belief Wittgenstein threw these ideas together. He supposes a person who believes in the Last Judgement and makes this his guidance for life. 'Whenever he does anything this is before his mind.' How are we to know whether this person believes in what he is saying, Wittgenstein asks. 'He has what you might call unshakeable faith'. How does this show? It will show not by reasoning nor 'by appeal to ordinary grounds for belief', but 'by regulating for all in his life':

> This is a very much stronger fact – forgoing pleasures, always appealing to this picture. This, in one sense, must be called the *firmest of all beliefs*, because the man risks things on account of it which he would not do on things which are far better established for him. Although he distinguishes between things well-established and not well-established. (*LC* pp. 53–4. My italics)

There are cases where beliefs are grounded – 'we appeal again and again to certain grounds' – and at the same time we risk pretty little. The implication is that if it came to risking our lives on the grounds of these beliefs, we would not do so. On the other hand, a religious believer may base his life (making great personal sacrifices) on a belief such as that of divine retribution on Judgement Day, which, from a common-sense or a scientific point of view, is based on the flimsiest of evidence. It is based on the testimony of one man, granted a man of wisdom, integrity and holiness (whom the believer believes to be God, though that belief is not grounded as are our beliefs in the identity of other eminent people). 'A man would fight for his life not to be dragged into the fire. No induction (inducement?). Terror. That is, as it were, part of the substance of the belief' (*LC* p. 56).

What Wittgenstein is offering here is what might be described as the pragmatic criterion of religious belief. Not only is the genuineness of a believer's belief to be judged by what he is prepared to do on account of that belief, but this in turn tells us something about the nature of religious belief. It is essentially concerned with praxis; belief as an intellectual exercise carries little weight one way or another.

Wittgenstein also reflected on the nature of religious belief in his *Notebooks* at about this time. In 1937 he made some remarkable entries, of which the most remarkable must be the one on belief in the Resurrection of Christ. 'What inclines even me to believe in Christ's Resurrection?' he asks. 'It is as though I play with the thought' (*CV* p. 33). He proceeds to use the Pauline argument – 'If Christ be not risen, then is your faith vain and and you are still in your sins' (I Corinthians 15.17) – in a way that must be quoted in full:

> If he did not rise from the dead, then he decomposed in the grave like any other man. *He is dead and decomposed.* In that case he is a teacher like any other and can no longer *help* ... So we have to content ourselves with wisdom and speculation ... But if I am to be REALLY saved – what I

need is *certainty* – not wisdom, dreams or speculation – and this certainty is faith. And faith is what is needed by my *heart*, my *soul*, not by my speculative intelligence. For it is my soul with its passions, as it were with its flesh and blood, that has to be saved, not my abstract mind. Perhaps we can say: Only *love* can believe the Resurrection. (*CV* p. 33)

This passage speaks for itself. It explains in terms of the heart and soul (in a Pascalian way) rather than in terms of the speculative intellect, the tendency of the believer to embrace the ungrounded or insufficiently grounded belief. It also explains the steadfastness of religious belief in the face of seemingly overwhelming contrary evidence. Wittgenstein continues:

We might say: Redeeming love believes even in the Resurrection; holds fast even in the Resurrection. What combats doubt is, as it were, *redemption*. Holding fast to *this* must be holding fast to that belief. So what that means is: first you must be redeemed and hold on to your redemption ... then you will see that you are holding fast to this belief. (*CV* ibid.)

This seems to imply a Lutheran interpretation of belief and redemption, but the idea is clear: religious belief is not a matter of intellectual speculation. It is a matter of heart and soul, of love and trust.

The entry continues:

So this can come about if you no longer rest your weight on the earth, but suspend yourself from heaven. Then *everything* will be different and it will be 'no wonder' if you can do things that you cannot do now. (A man who is suspended looks the same as one who is standing, but the interplay of forces within him is nevertheless quite different, so that he can act quite differently than can a standing man.) (*CV* ibid.)

Yorick Smythies, a former student of Wittgenstein's, told me that Wittgenstein had said of J. H. Newman's *Grammar of Assent* that Newman thought the grammar was supporting the Christian faith whereas, in fact, the faith was supporting the grammar, as if it were suspended from a balloon. Thus assent to religious beliefs is an ascent or an elevation rather than the result of an upward climb. The driving force that impels this upward thrust is love of Christ and trust in his redemptive power.

A decade later, in 1948, towards the end of his life, Wittgenstein altered his metaphor of the flimsiness of faith. This time he took the analogy of the tightrope:

> An honest religious thinker is like a tightrope walker. He almost looks as
> though he were walking on nothing but air. His support is the slenderest
> imaginable. And yet it really is possible to walk on it. (*CV* p. 73)

In this metaphor the support is from below. But again it is not an
intellectual support. It comes from love, trust and faith, in the sense of
trust meaning 'having faith in'. This is confirmed by another entry of the
same year:

> Unshakeable faith (in a promise). Is it any less certain than being
> convinced of a mathematical truth? But does that make the language
> games any more alike. (*CV* ibid.)

Before commenting on this I must add two other entries, both from the
earlier period. One is: 'Religious similes can be said to *move on the edge of
an abyss*' (*CV* p. 29. My italics). The other: 'This message (the Gospels)
is seized on by men believingly (i.e. lovingly). *That* is the certainty
characterizing this particular acceptance-as-true (*Für-wahr-haltens*), not
something *else*' (*CV* p. 32).

Here we have three elements that characterize religious belief: (1) its
precariousness (on a tightrope, on the edge of an abyss) and yet
managing to maintain its hold, its equilibrium; (2) its support: love, trust,
belief and faith *in* the word of another (as in a promise); and (3) certainty,
unshakeable, steadfast faith. On this last characteristic Wittgenstein is
most interesting. Religious belief, he says, is not based on intellectual
certitude but on love and trust. And yet it is held with all the psychological certainty with which we hold the truths of mathematics. It is a firm,
steadfast, unshakeable belief. The reason is that, if we love someone
enough to trust his word, this trust, this belief in his word is unshakeable.
What can shake it? Only distrust or weakening of trust. But it is our trust
that is strong, not our reasons for placing it. There is no logical nexus
between someone making a promise and its being kept. Nor is there a
sufficient logical nexus between someone's past reliability and the likeli-
hood of his keeping his promise. The reliability is not in any way
commensurate with the trust we place in him. And yet we are as certain
that he will keep his word as we are that $2+2=4$. But here the analogy
ends. The two language-games are not alike in any other respect.
Indeed, they could not be further apart. We are certain of the truth of
mathematical propositions *because* of their intrinsic logical structure.
Religious believers are certain of their belief *in spite of* their having no
intrinsic logical cohesion and very little extrinsic support.

This ties in with some remarks in *On Certainty*. These are concerned with (a) learning about religious matters and (b) conversion to a faith or set of beliefs. In *OC* 160, p. 23, Wittgenstein makes the seemingly obvious remark: 'The child learns by believing the adult.' Though stated many times, this blunt way of putting the matter asserts three facts about religious belief (and, indeed, other beliefs based on testimony and trust): (1) it is regarded as a source of knowledge; (2) this knowledge has been imparted by a reliable, trustworthy person; and (3) this person is reliable and trustworthy because he or she is an *adult*. The significance of this is apparent in the next remark: 'Doubt comes *after* belief.' (The idea is repeated in *OC* 253, p. 34: 'The schoolboy *believes* his teachers and his schoolbooks.')[2]

In the light of subsequent events a somewhat curious discussion on whether people go to the moon (the remarks date from 1950; no one reached the moon before 1969) has something of interest for what is to follow. Wittgenstein discusses the claim made by an adult to a child that he had been to the moon (*OC* 106 ff., pp. 16 ff.). The obvious objections to such a belief are offered. In the course of the discussion Wittgenstein makes two interesting remarks: 'But a child will not ordinarily stick to such a belief and will soon be convinced by what we tell him *seriously*' (*OC* 106, p. 16. My italics), and:

> Isn't this altogether the way one can instruct a child to believe in God, or that there is no God, and it will accordingly be able to produce *apparently* telling grounds for the one or the other? (*OC* 107, p. 16. My italics)

In fact there is no parity whatsoever between telling a child that there is or is not a being that could be called 'God' and saying that one could or could not go to the moon. The latter can be tested, and, in this particular case, was proved, though as Wittgenstein rightly says: 'But how? and through what?' (*OC* 109, p. 17). The former, on the other hand, cannot be tested, since it is not a scientific matter. According to Wittgenstein's (if not all-informed) opinion in 1950, it was not likely, for the reasons he gives (*OC* 108, p. 17) that a man could be put on the moon. So what the child was told 'seriously' turned out to be false in its assumption. On the other hand, the child will be able to continue to produce 'apparently' telling grounds for believing in God or no God, whatever facts are discovered. Indeed, Philip Gosse, the zoologist, continued to believe that the earth was created, as the Bible is alleged to say, a few thousand years ago, in spite of the fossil evidence which he himself was studying. Though, admittedly, belief in the age of the earth is a scientific rather than an exclusively religious matter, its religious implications – the seeming challenge to the veracity of the Bible – make it an apt enough illustration of the lengths to which grounding in belief (or disbelief) will go in rebutting hostile evidence. Moreover it has much in common with fundamental common-sense beliefs, such as Moore's claim to know that the world existed for some time before he was born.

These common-sense beliefs cannot be tested in the way that the capability of humans to land on the moon can be, and yet it is reasonable to believe them and to believe them firmly. In the case of past events we can only make constructions from the present. Carbon dating and other sophisticated means of establishing the age of objects would probably have made Gosse's position untenable even to himself. But not necessarily so. After all, as a method of dating, it is based on assumptions about the passage of time, the deterioration of carbon 14, etc. The question is: how many assumptions is one prepared to jettison and still retain mental stability?

What can certainly be done is to put before someone, who already has a set of beliefs that he is convinced are well-grounded, other, contrary beliefs, which he can at least entertain, if not embrace:

> why should not a king be brought up in the belief that the world began with him? And if Moore and this king were to meet and have a discussion, could Moore really prove his belief to be the right one? I do not say that Moore could not convert the king to his view, but it would be a conversion of a special kind: the king would be brought *to look at the world in a different way*. (*OC* 92, p. 14. My italics)

This, in essence, would be the sort of conversion that a religious conversion would be. Not conviction by argument or evidence, but by persuasion (at least in the first instance) to show how the world could be other than someone had been brought up to think of it. This would not be a complete conversion. It would, however, be a conversion of a kind. Whether he accepted the new picture of the world or not, the king would certainly see the world in a new and different way.

So far we have been considering conversion as acceptance of an alternative view of the world in which we live. In remarks in *Culture and Value* at about the same time, Wittgenstein says (after talking about so-called proofs for the existence of God that we shall come to shortly):

> Perhaps one could 'convince someone that God exists' by means of a certain kind of upbringing, by shaping his life in such and such a way.
>   Life can educate one to a belief in God. And *experiences* too are what bring this about . . . e.g. sufferings of various sorts. These neither show us God in the way a sense impression shows us an object, nor do they give

rise to *conjectures* about him. Experiences, thoughts – life can force this concept on us.
  So perhaps it is similar to the concept 'object'. (*CV* p. 86)

The reference to 'object' takes us back to the *Tractatus* and that intractable entity that cannot be described but must be postulated.[3] Mention of 'conjectures' hints at theology and dogma, which will be considered presently. But the main drift of what Wittgenstein is saying is clear. In spite of the suggestion implied in the phrase 'a certain kind of upbringing', what he says applies to anyone of any age. As a means of education (or indoctrination) it does not rely on reasoning and argument, but on an appeal to an experience: namely, suffering. Finally, it does not manifest its object (God) as an ostensive definition does. God remains obscure and merely hinted at, just like 'object' is in the *Tractatus*. Though his existence can be hinted at, it certainly cannot be proved.

Wittgenstein said emphatically that the existence of God could not be proved. Indeed, he believed that any attempt to rationalize religious belief – dogma, theology, apologetics and suchlike – profoundly distorted the language of religious belief. (The same could be said of his views on the ethical and aesthetic use of language.) To round off the first part of this chapter, I shall quote his brief remarks on what appears to be the ontological proof. They give an original slant to this long-discussed topic.

> God's essence is supposed to guarantee his existence – what this really means is that what is at issue here is not the *existence* of something. (*CV* p. 82. My italics)[4]

This remark is related to another of three years earlier: 'The way you use the word "God" does not show *whom* you mean – but, rather, what you mean' (*CV* p. 50). In other words, what is important for Wittgenstein in religious discourse is not so much (if at all) whether God exists or not, but what we mean by the word 'God' (with a capital letter). The remark continues (after a section to which I shall return):

> And now we might say: There can be a description of what it might be like if there were gods on Olympus – but not 'what it would be like if there were such a thing as God'. And to say this is to *determine the concept more precisely*.
>   How are we taught the word 'God' (its use, that is)? I cannot give a full grammatical description of it . . . I can say a good deal about it and perhaps in time assemble a collection of examples. (*CV* ibid. My italics)

Wittgenstein goes on to consider the use of words in a way that does not concern us immediately. However, at the risk of even further underlining the obvious, may I make two points. The first is to reinforce a point made in chapter eight (pp. 170–1): namely, that learning the meaning of the word 'God' was not the same as being introduced to a person or describing someone, like one's aunt (*LC* p. 59). The second is to draw attention to the peculiarity, the uniqueness of the concept 'God'. The gods of Olympus we can envisage after a fashion; but God – no. Not for nothing the Israelites refused his name to be written or uttered, and the Fathers of the Church emphasized the negative aspects of the Divinity (the *via negativa*).

As has been said in chapter eight, the medieval philosopher–theologians were attempting not so much to prove that this being or entity that we call 'God' exists as to attempt to explain what is implied in believing such a being exists. This is succinctly put in a remark made by Wittgenstein towards the end of his life:

> A proof of God's existence ought really to be something by means of which one could convince oneself that God exists. But I think what *believers* who have furnished such proofs have wanted to do is to give their 'belief' an intellectual analysis and foundation, although they themselves would never have come to believe as a result of such proofs. (*CV* p. 85)

One might have thought that inverted commas would go more appropriately round 'proofs' than 'belief', but, if the believers believed that their proofs were valid, then their belief would not be religious in the special sense of religious belief we have been discussing.

Though charitable towards those who want to give their religious belief an intellectual analysis and foundation, Wittgenstein himself was averse to talk *about* religious belief (what has come to be called 'God talk') that is, the more philosophical aspects of theology. In a reported conversation in Schlick's house on 17 December 1930 he asks: 'Is talking essential to religion?' and replies:

> I can well imagine a religion in which there are no doctrinal propositions, in which there is thus no talking. Obviously the essence of religion cannot have anything to do with the fact that there is talking, or rather: when people talk this itself is part of a religious act and not a theory. (*WWK* p. 117)

He concludes: 'Thus it also does not matter at all if the words used are true or false or nonsense.' I shall return to this point later, but first I should like to dispose of Wittgenstein's views on doctrine, dogma and theology.

There are two remarks in his *Notebooks* for 1937 that develop these thoughts. The first begins: 'Christianity is not a doctrine' and goes on to explain that it is not a theory about what has happened or will happen to the human soul, 'but a description of something that *actually takes place in human life*' (my italics).

> For 'consciousness of sin' is a real event and so are despair and salvation through faith. Those who speak of such things (Bunyan for instance) are simply describing what has happened to them, *whatever gloss anyone may want to put on it*. (*CV* p. 28. My italics)

The second remark moves from doctrine to dogma. Wittgenstein distinguishes between dogmas that determine one's opinion and those that 'completely control the *expression* of all opinions'. This latter kind of dogma is, not surprisingly, attributed to the Catholic Church with which, on the whole, Wittgenstein does not deal too harshly, nor does he say anything that an honest member of that Faith would not accept. This type of dogmatism gives scope to any practical opinion that can be made to square with it, thus allowing freedom of opinion, while at the same time exercising what Wittgenstein calls 'unlimited, tangible tyranny (*unbedingten, fühlbaren Tyrannei*)' over *expression* of such opinion. I am not sure that Wittgenstein is not being over-lenient here. The history of Catholic – and indeed Christian – dogma is not entirely an edifying one. So much has turned on words and expressions. Yet all Wittgenstein says is:

> It is not a *wall* setting limits to what can be believed, but more like a *brake* which, however, practically serves the same purpose; its almost as though someone were to attach a weight to your foot to restrict your freedom of movement. This is how dogma becomes irrefutable and beyond the reach of attack. (*CV* ibid.)

This is generous. (In a later chapter I give brief treatment to his views on the doctrine of predestination and touch on the verbal gymnastics that certain theologians engaged in.)

Wittgenstein was not concerned with the words or formulae we use, but with the part they play in our religious life. He put his views forcefully in some remarks towards the end of his life. The most controversial must be: 'If Christianity is the truth, then all philosophy about it is false' (*CV* p. 83). 'False' may be a bit strong here. 'Worthless' would be a view that Aquinas would have shared.[5] But the point Wittgenstein is making becomes clearer in a later remark:

> A theology which insists on the use of particular *sound* (*gewisser*) words and phrases and bans others, makes nothing clearer (Karl Barth). It gesticulates with words, as one might say, because it wants to say something and does not know how to express it. *Practice* (*praxis*) gives the words their sense. (*CV* p. 85)[6]

Wittgenstein obviously found Karl Barth a kindred spirit, at least in his attitude towards 'natural' as opposed to 'scriptural' theology and his rejection of the 'analogy of being' in favour of the 'analogy of faith'.[7] *Fides quaerens intellectus* did not have the meaning for them that it had for Anselm and Aquinas. For Wittgenstein, whatever understanding of faith there is must be found in *praxis*, in the way of living, in the believer's attitude to life.

This is why words do not matter here. What matters is what happens in our way of life:

> Actually I should like to say that in this case too the *words* you utter or what you think as you utter them are not what matters, so much as the difference they make at various points in your life. How do I know that two people mean the same when each says that he believes in God? And just the same goes for the Trinity (*der 3 Personen*). (*CV* ibid.)

Here we are back to the lectures: whether we believe and what we believe must be judged not by reasoning or ordinary grounds for belief but by how we regulate our lives in accordance with what we claim to believe.

But this view is not shared by apologists. Some, if not all – and, at one time, most – believe that religion in general and Christianity in particular can be put on a firm, rational foundation. They were encouraged in this by the Scholastic tradition. But it is one thing to maintain that faith and reason are not incompatible, that certain theological truths can be arrived at by natural reason and that the implications of Christian doctrine can be elucidated by reason, and quite another to say that Christian belief is firmly based on rational argument. In the face of the hostile attitude of nineteenth century scientists and historians, some apologists, in what they regarded as a defence of the Christian faith, attempted to counterattack by showing that the Christian faith was just as soundly based in reason as science and history.

One such apologist was Father O'Hara, S.J., a mathematician, who in a broadcast talk, which Wittgenstein either heard or read, made such a claim. His argument goes as follows. Christianity 'holds that its truths are reached by the very same intelligence that is operative in science and with the same certainty.' (*LC* p. 52). He singled out: (1) the existence of God;

(2) the creation of the world by God; (3) the creation of man with an immortal soul and free will; and (4) the Incarnation, God's coming into the world, as examples of these truths. Of the last of these he says:

> Christianity appeals to the historical records contained in the New Testament, and asserts that these records are trustworthy, that the events there narrated did happen, even when judged by the severest scientific criticism.[8]

Wittgenstein criticizes Father O'Hara for making religious belief 'a question of science'. He is 'making it appear to be *reasonable*'. This to Wittgenstein was ludicrous. Though he would not call religious believers unreasonable, he would call Father O'Hara unreasonable:

> I would definitely call O'Hara unreasonable. I would say, if this is religious belief, then it's all superstition.
> But I would ridicule it, not by saying it is based on insufficient evidence. I would say: here is a man who is cheating himself. You can say: this man is ridiculous because he believes, and bases it on weak reasons. (*LC* pp. 57–8)

Wittgenstein is not concerned with the claims about the existence of God, the creation of the world, or the creation and nature of the human soul. What he objects to is Father O'Hara's claim, as he sees it, that Christianity rests on an historical basis, in the sense that ordinary belief in historical facts could serve as a foundation for it. He does not deny there is an historical basis for Christianity. What he says is that *it does not afford sufficient evidence* for Christian beliefs. 'Here we have a belief in historic facts different from a belief in ordinary historic facts' (*LC* 57). It is different in a number of important ways. Most important of all, to my mind, is that 'they are not treated as historical empirical propositions'. For instance, significance is placed on the birth of Jesus that is not put on the birth of any ordinary baby, even in retrospect – except, perhaps, for that of the Dalai Lama. (My example, not Wittgenstein's.) However, he makes a similar point with reference to the Resurrection, as we shall see. Secondly, people who have faith do not 'apply the doubt which would ordinarily apply to *any* historical propositions', especially if they concern the distant past (such, for instance, as are contained in the first books of Livy). Thirdly, even if the historical evidence were as indubitable as the evidence for the existence and life of Napoleon, that would not be sufficient in the case of religious belief, because, as Wittgenstein has already said, 'indubitability wouldn't be enough to make me change my whole life'.

Wittgenstein ends with one general point about historical evidence. What, he asks, is the criterion of reliability and dependability in historical matters?

> Suppose you give a general description as to when you say a proposition has a reasonable weight of probability. When you call it reasonable, is this *only* to say that for it you have such and such evidence, and for others you haven't? (*LC* p. 57)

For instance, you would not give much credence to an account of an event given by a drunk. If I understand Wittgenstein correctly, he is saying, or insinuating in his oblique fashion, that the historical method is not strictly speaking a scientific method (any more than are literary criticism or judicial proceedings). It is a matter of weighing evidence and assessing probabilities. Yet according to Wittgenstein, Father O'Hara makes it a question of science.

While I agree with Wittgenstein's criticisms of Father O'Hara's alleged claims for Christian religious belief, and while my main object is to expound and criticize Wittgenstein's, rather than Father O'Hara's, account of the relationship between religious belief and science, historical and ordinary beliefs, it would be unfair to both of them to refrain from commenting on Wittgenstein's rather brutal attack.

First, there is no evidence in anything that Father O'Hara says that supports the view that he made religious belief a 'question of science'. His claims are: (1) the truths of Christianity are reached by the same faculty of intelligence that is operative in science. The question, however, is how are they reached, by scientific or other means? Father O'Hara does not say. (2) That they are reached with the same certainty is obscure. It is rendered more obscure by the fact that earlier (p. 108) Father O'Hara pointed out that twentieth century science was not as confident as nineteenth century science had been. From this it would follow that religious belief is no more certain than scientific belief (a view that could hardly find favour in traditional theological circles). But this still does not amount to making religous belief a scientific question. (3) Christianity appeals to historical records which, judged by the severest scientific criticism, are trustworthy. I am not sure what Father O'Hara wished to prove by this; nor do I understand what he meant by 'scientific'. I presume he meant the most rigorous historical criticism. Now this is scientific in a certain sense, just as going around an electrical circuit methodically could be described as a scientific, as opposed to an haphazard way of discovering an electrical fault. But I do not think that this amounts to making it a *question of science*.

On the other hand, Father O'Hara seems to imply that, faced with the challenge of science and modern historical research (including archaeology and palaeontology), Christianity can meet it, and give a very good account of itself. Whereas, as Wittgenstein says, it has no case to answer. It may resemble science in the use of such terms as 'reason', 'evidence', 'certainty', 'conclusion', and possibly some others, but they are used in a very different way from the way they are used in scientific and historical disciplines. There are also a number of terms such as 'possibly', 'probably', 'not sure', 'opinion' that, according to Wittgenstein, have no place in religious discourse, though they are constantly used in scientific and historical controversies, and in discussions about matters of fact.

Father O'Hara belongs to a generation that still felt that the faith was under threat from Darwinism, modern historical methods and, later, textual criticism (which demonstrated, for example, that the Pentateuch was not written by Moses nor all the Psalms by David). What he and likeminded apologists did not see was that modern scholarship, far from being a threat to religious belief, was liberating it and revealing its true nature. Wittgenstein saw this clearly and was, thus, more in line with biblical and patristic theology. Father O'Hara was right to emphasize the historicity of the New Testament. Indeed, in view of what has been happening in more recent hermeneutics and theology, where either the historicity of the Gospel narrative is called into question or it is regarded as totally irrelevant to Christian belief, Father O'Hara's insistence on historicity may be salutary. It is certainly important. But, as Wittgenstein points out, it is the least important aspect of Christian belief. Christian belief transcends history, as it transcends science.

This view is enlarged by certain remarks in the *Notebooks* for 1937:

> God has four people recount the life of his incarnate Son, in each case differently and with inconsistencies – but might we not say: It is important that this narrative should not be more than quite averagely plausible *just so that* this should not be taken as the essential, decisive thing? So that the *letter* should not be believed more strongly than is proper and the *spirit* may receive its due? I.e. what you are supposed to see cannot be communicated even by the best and most accurate historian: and *therefore* a mediocre account suffices, is even to be preferred. (*CV* p. 31)

Wittgenstein gives as an analogy mediocre scenery in the theatre, which distracts less from the action on the stage than might elaborate ·and realistic scenery.

Scripture scholars and apologists, particularly the latter, have tirelessly pointed out that the inconsistencies in the Gospels, especially in the

Resurrection narrative, are what one would expect from eye witnesses in law courts and anywhere else. This may, indeed, be true. But Wittgenstein would regard this as a trivial point. For him, historicity, though necessary in Judaic and Christian belief, is secondary. It is neither essential nor decisive. What is essential and decisive is the message conveyed through the narrative. This view recorded by Wittgenstein in his *Notebooks* in 1937 has only comparatively recently been accepted in the theological world, and still in not all of it.

Another entry of the same year is even more forthright:

> Christianity is based on a historical truth; rather it offers us a (historical) narrative and says: now believe! But not, believe this narrative with the belief appropriate to an historical narrative, rather: believe, through thick and thin, which you can do only as the result of a life. *Here you have a narrative, don't take the same attitude to it as you take to other historical narratives!* Make a *quite different* place in your life for it. – There is nothing *paradoxical* about that! (*CV* p. 32)

If we take the last remark first: why should any paradox hang on what Wittgenstein had written? Perhaps we should not take a seemingly historical narrative historically and worry about its historical accuracy, since that is not at issue. What counts is the message the historical account conveys. This way of looking at the Gospels is commonplace today, though it would not have been in the 1930s. To that extent Wittgenstein was a pioneer, though, since he was writing for himself, he could not have pioneered a trend: he simply swam slightly ahead of it in his own channel.

In another entry for 1937, Wittgenstein raises the perennial question: what if the historical accounts in the Gospels were demonstrably false? We have touched on this entry earlier in relation to faith as loving belief. Here it is only necessary to stress the historical aspect. Wittgenstein says that if the Gospels could be shown to be demonstrably false 'faith would lose absolutely nothing in consequence'. And this, he adds, has nothing to do with the Gospels expressing 'the universal truths of reason'. It is not apparent who he has in mind here. It could be Harnack whose books, published at the beginning of this century, tended towards eliminating the transcendental. It is more likely to be Bultmann whose *Jesus and the Word* appeared in German in 1922 and the first volume of *Belief and Understanding* in 1933, or Tillich whose *The Interpretation of History* appeared in 1936. Wittgenstein obviously kept abreast of current theological writing, particularly in German. Equally obviously he did not think too highly of some of it. There follows the statement already quoted: 'the

historical proof (the historical proof-game) does not apply at all to faith.'
He concludes:

> A believer's relation to these narratives (*Nachrichten*) is *neither* the
> relation to historical truth (probability), *nor yet* that to a theory consisting of
> 'truths or reason'. There is such a thing (*Das gibt's*) – (We have quite
> different attitudes even to different species of what we call fiction!) (*CV*
> ibid.)

What that enigmatic bracketed remark refers to is nowhere explained,
but it could refer to such bibilical writings as *Job* or the *Song of Songs* or to
the parables of the Prodigal Son and the Good Samaritan. These are
fiction and yet they and many other demonstrably fictitious works have
formed and nurtured the religious life of countless believers. Even if the
life of Jesus were proved to be a fiction – one suspects the life of the
Buddha is largely, if not entirely, fictitious – this would not, and should
not, deter believers from leading lives consonant with the life of Jesus.
This, I take it, is what Wittgenstein meant, though it is not clear whether
he would go quite as far as that. After all, he was dealing with a
supposition. But the point he was making is clear: namely, that the
message of the Gospels (*das Evangelium, tó euaggélion*) has nothing to do
with historical accuracy. It goes beyond any historical account. Historical
narrative is merely a vehicle for the message.

Wittgenstein's position here is entirely consonant with his earlier views.
Indeed, they are reinforced and developed from a different angle. In the
earlier writings the nonsensical use of language, the attempt to go beyond
the boundaries of language and the attempt to say what cannot be said, is
what is stressed. Here it is the non-rational grounding of religious belief
that is the focus of attention. And just as the failure of ethical and
religious language to give expression to these values was not, in Wittgenstein's opinion, a failure to find 'the correct logical analysis', so the
weakness of the rational grounds for religious belief is not something that
can be made good by better and more cogent rational arguments. And –
to continue the parallel – just as the nonsensical expressions of ethics and
religious belief are not nonsensical because correct expressions have not
yet been found but 'their nonsensicality was their very essence', so the
lack of firm rational grounding is not due to the fact that better
arguments have not yet been found, but because non-rationality is of
their very essence. To complete the parallel one can add that, as
Wittgenstein, while not regarding religious beliefs as reasonable, did not

regard them as unreasonable either, so if he regarded them as nonsensical, he did not regard them as totally devoid of comprehensibility.
It might be helpful here to draw together some remarks:

> Reasons look entirely different from normal reasons. (*LC* p. 56)
> Here we have people who treat this evidence in a different way. They base things on evidence which taken in one way would seem exceedingly flimsy. They base enormous things on this evidence. Am I to say they are unreasonable? I wouldn't call them unreasonable.
> I would say they are certainly not *reasonable*, that's obvious.
> 'Unreasonable' implies, with everyone, rebuke.
> I want to say: they don't treat this as a matter of reasonability.
> Anyone who reads the Epistles will find it said: not only that it is not reasonable, but that it is folly.
> Not only is it not reasonable, but it doesn't pretend to be. (*LC* pp. 5, 7–8)
> The point is that if there were evidence, this would in fact destroy the whole business. (*LC* p. 56)

This last sentence seems to me to be the key remark. Wittgenstein immediately illustrates it by referring to the pragmatic criterion he applied to belief in a Last Judgement. He prefaces his illustration by saying: 'Anything I normally call evidence wouldn't in the slightest influence me.' Suppose, he says, there were people who could predict something resembling a Judgement Day (presumably as described in Isaiah 13 and 34, the Synoptics, particularly Matthew in 24 and 25, and II Peter 3), the queer thing is that belief in such a prediction would not be at all a religious belief. Even if this prediction (*per impossibile*) included something equivalent to eternal bliss or eternal damnation, belief in it would not be religious belief.

In this analysis Wittgenstein is correct both philosophically and theologically. Philosophically, since, if someone bases a belief on conclusive (scientific) evidence – if such there be, or, at least, in so far as it is conclusive – there is no conceptual space for something we could call religious, as opposed to scientific or commonsense, belief. The two must coincide. The reasons for a religious belief are, as he says, 'in a way, inconclusive'. And for there to be a distinction between scientific and religious beliefs this must be so:

> The best scientific evidence is just nothing.
> A religious belief might in fact fly in the face of such a forecast (that of a Judgement Day), and say 'No. There it will break down.' (*LC* p. 56)

This is very interesting. Wittgenstein here envisages the possibility that a scientific prediction not only cannot be the basis of a religious belief, but that a religious belief might 'fly in the face of' a scientifically based forecast. If it is a genuine scientific prediction based on observation and reasoning, it is hard to see how a reasonable person could set it aside on purely religious grounds.

This, however, is not altogether simple and straightforward. Clearly there are people who can and do reject the conclusions of scientific reasoning. The fundamentalists are an obvious example. They are prepared to fly in the face of scientific evidence. The most notorious case of this is Philip Gosse, already mentioned. Wittgenstein had in mind less eccentric believers who are not moved either by so-called scientific evidence alleged to support religious beliefs or by so-called scientific evidence alleged to refute religious beliefs. Religious belief stands aside from the findings and theories of science.

The believer does not offer scientific evidence that a prediction will break down. He is offering no evidence at all (though he may claim that his own belief is based on evidence). He does not play the scientific language-game. Should the scientific theory or prediction be proved wrong or his belief be proved correct, that can have no effect on his belief. Nor should he make play with the uncertainties of modern science. Scientific predictions may be only moderately reliable: the more complex, the less reliable (an eclipse as against a weather forecast for an offshore island); but this does not give support to a contrary belief. Nor does a 'confirmatory' scientific theory or prediction add one whit of credence to a religious belief. Religious belief in a future event is totally independent of scientific prediction. The most reliable prediction that coincides with a religious belief is as irrelevant as one that runs contrary to it. Religious belief and scientific prediction belong to two distinct language-games.

In *On Certainty* (324) Wittgenstein says: 'Thus we should not call anybody reasonable who believed something in despite of scientific evidence.' So a believer, *qua* believer, who flies in the face of scientific evidence, is not reasonable. But, in the case of a religious believer, Wittgenstein would not call him unreasonable either. He doesn't 'treat this as a matter of reasonability'. Nor does the contrary evidence in any way affect the firmness of his belief, any more than it does any other belief we regard as incontrovertible where we consider the evidence overwhelming:

the evidence's being overwhelming consists precisely in the fact that we do not *need* to give way before contrary evidence. And so we have here a buttress similar to the one that makes the propositions of mathematics incontrovertible. (*OC* 657, p. 87)

However, the so-called overwhelming evidence for a religious belief is not at all the same as that for your name being N or your having the hand you see before you, which you claim as your own.

A good point to take up Wittgenstein's discussion of the evidence for religious as distinct from scientific beliefs are his remarks on blunders.

Let us imagine, he says, an island where we find certain beliefs that we think may be religious beliefs. But we cannot tell whether to call them religious or scientific beliefs, nor whether the natives are reasoning or not. If they are reasoning, then they make 'something corresponding to our blunders'. But, if they are not, then these seeming blunders are not really so. It is difficult to say.

> You could also say that where we are reasonable, they are not reasonable – meaning they don't *reason* here.
> If they do something very like one of our blunders, I would say, I don't know. It depends on further surroundings of it. (*LC* p. 59)

(It is in this context, where Wittgenstein is not sure whether the islanders are trying to be reasonable in a similar way to us and making blunders, or are not doing either, that he accuses Father O'Hara of being unreasonable, of cheating himself and turning religious belief into superstition by making out that it is reasonable but basing it on weak reasons.)

The point about the blunder being an indication that the believer is not reasoning in the ordinary way is more fully elaborated where Wittgenstein speaks of someone who believes in the Last Judgement because he saw it in a dream. For a blunder, says Wittgenstein, that is too big.[9] If someone forecasts rain for the day on the basis of a dream, we would call that a blunder. A dream is insufficient evidence on which to base the forecast of a meteorological event (just as a hunch is; though not, perhaps, an ache in the big toe). According to Wittgenstein, and most other people, there is no logical connection between the two. Nor is there a logical connection between a dream and the Last Judgement. But in this case no claim is made that there is. It is not just insufficient evidence: it is no evidence at all. 'If you compare it with anything in Science which we call evidence, you can't credit anyone could soberly argue: "Well, I had this dream ... therefore ... Last Judgement" ' (*LC* p. 61). That is why it is not a scientific or logical blunder or error. Here again is an important difference between religious and scientific belief, such that it might even seem as if 'belief' had two different meanings, (like 'vice'), and not just two different uses.

However, someone who says that he believes in a Last Judgement because he saw that it would be as it appeared in a dream seems to be offering evidence for his belief. At least he gives his dream as the reason for his belief. This is precisely the point Wittgenstein is making. The person in question is in effect saying: '*I believe* in a Last Judgement because of what I dreamed', not '*There will be* a Last Judgement *because I saw it in a dream*'. (Similarly, someone might give as his explanation of his *belief* that it was going to rain that he dreamed the garden fête would be washed out, without offering this as *evidence*.)

This makes religious belief rather personal and this is how Wittgenstein saw it. Belief, for him, involved personal commitment to a way of life. It was not merely an intellectual commitment, as it might be to the 'big bang' theory or the theory of natural selection. However speculative these theories may be, we expect them to be backed by evidence, by tests and crucial experiments or, at least, we expect they can be tested by some crucial experiment, even if we cannot at present envisage what it might be. But no such tests or experiments, no such evidence, is expected or required of religious beliefs. Wittgenstein illustrated this by many examples, graced with his argument by innuendo.

One example concerns belief in the existence of God. He says:

> If I even vaguely remember what I was taught about God, I might say: 'Whatever believing in God might be, it can't be believing in something we can test or find a means of testing.' You might say: 'This is nonsense, because people say they believe on *evidence* or say they believe in religious experiences.' (*LC* p. 60)

Wittgenstein replies:

> I would say: 'The mere fact that someone says they believe on evidence doesn't tell me enough for me to be able to say now whether I can say of the sentence "God exists" that your evidence is unsatisfactory or insuf- ficient.' (*LC* p. 60)

This is rather subtle. I assume that what Wittgenstein primarily means is that what he can remember of what he was taught about God was that a belief in God is not something that can be tested. Therefore, if someone says he has evidence – presumably of the form of Aquinas's five ways – or appeals to religious experience, Wittgenstein is at a loss. If he asserts that this is insufficient evidence, then he is admitting it is evidence of some kind. Why, then, does he not say that outright?

An answer to this question suggests itself. It may be that Wittgenstein, while not regarding the testimony of religious experience or other 'evidence' as evidence in the scientific sense, nevertheless took it seriously as an account of *why* someone believed that God exists. In that case he would want to know more about it – more, that is, than the mere assertion that someone had this evidence or this experience – before he could say whether it was satisfactory and sufficient or unsatisfactory and insufficient. But in that case, whether he pronounced it satisfactory or unsatisfactory, sufficient or insufficient, he would not have been using 'evidence' in the scientific sense. It would be rather 'acceptable testimony'. If this interpretation is correct, then Wittgenstein here shows an exceptional sensitivity and restraint in the matter of religious belief, while maintaining a proper poise and balance. While rightly excluding anything resembling scientific evidence, he is prepared to respect, if not unconditionally accept, the testimony ('evidence') of the believer. Theologically, this is sound.

Other examples concern apparitions of the dead and pseudo miracles.

One such 'apparition' is that of Smith who had been killed in battle. Someone says that Smith is in Cambridge: he saw him in the distance when standing at Guildhall. His claim to have seen him is not sufficient evidence that Smith is in Cambridge, particularly if there is 'a fair amount of evidence' that he was killed. No one else saw him. And he did not appear again. Moreover, it would be impossible, according to Wittgenstein, to inquire who passed from Market Place into Rose Cresent at 12.05 p.m. (I am not sure why Wittgenstein is so categorical about this. Someone who knew Smith might have been there at the time and would be able to say that no one, or, on the contrary, someone answering to Smith's description, passed at or about 12.05 p.m.) If no such corroborative evidence were forthcoming, and the person still maintained that Smith was there, then Wittgenstein would have every right to be extremely puzzled, to say the least.

This example deserves to be probed a little further. First, Wittgenstein talks about a fair amount of evidence that Smith had been killed in battle. If he was seen being shot, and his face and body were easily identifiable, and was pronounced dead by the MO and was subsequently buried in an identifiable grave, that is more than a fair amount of evidence: it is overwhelming evidence. If, on the other hand, 'his' body had been mutilated by an explosion of some kind, so that even the regimental markings had disappeared, the evidence that Smith rather than someone else had been killed would not be so overwhelming. If, again, he was missing, presumed dead, the evidence would be even less strong, and, though it might gain strength with the passing of time, this would not, in itself, be sufficient to dismiss a claim that he had been seen in Cambridge.

Now, let us look at these cases from the point of view of the person who claims to have seen Smith. Putting the best possible construction on the incident – the case of Smith missing, presumed dead (at Dunkirk, say) – the claimant still does not have sufficient evidence, as the incident is described by Wittgenstein. Had he been close to the supposed Smith, and, better still, had he spoken to him, whether the supposed Smith had answered or run away in panic, he would have had strong, possibly even sufficient evidence for believing that he had seen Smith (even if no one else saw him and he never appeared again). The same might be said of the second case – Smith supposedly blown up and mutilated. But the first case poses problems, particularly for the claimant's persistence in the face of overwhelming evidence to the contrary.

As Wittgenstein says, the persistence in a belief that flies in the face of overwhelming evidence is puzzling, extremely puzzling. So puzzling is it that only a few explanations are available. One is that the person was mistaken but is too proud or stubborn to admit it. This is a mild irrationality. A second is that he is psychologically disturbed and is 'seeing things'. A third is that he has seen a ghost. A fourth is that Smith actually came back from the dead.

At this point it might be useful to contrast the irrationality or non-rationality of Jones (let us call him Jones) with another kind of belief based, not on insufficient evidence, but on no evidence at all, and corresponding to the three cases above. Let us take three widows. The husband of the first was reported missing, presumed dead, twenty, thirty, forty years ago; but she still believes that one day he will come home; she is waiting for him. The second widow's husband was presumed to have been blown to pieces, but she believes that it was someone else, and that some day he will come home. The third, having been told that her husband was killed and buried in a marked grave, has not visited it because she believes he will come home some day. None has any evidence for her belief, unless a certain baseless conviction may be regarded as a piece of evidence: 'I believe because I feel he must be still alive.' But whereas the first widow has no conclusive evidence against her belief, and the evidence against the second widow's belief, though perhaps not absolutely conclusive, is based on nothing better than the flicker of possible doubt, the third widow's belief is contrary to conclusive evidence. On the face of it the third widow's belief is evidence of mental instability. The other two widows may be mentally unstable too: they are certainly irrational.

Jones, as I have said, is, at worst, mildly irrational. At least he claims to have seen Smith, a claim that none of the widows have made about their husbands. This is a piece of evidence. It may be insufficient and fly in the face of overwhelming evidence to the contrary, but it is evidence of some kind. The belief it engenders is not based merely on a conviction that contrary evidence can be rejected. Apart from the possibility that Jones is mistaken, has taken someone else for Smith and is just being stubborn about it – in which case his 'seeing Smith' is no evidence for Smith having been in Cambridge – the other possibilities deserve a moment's attention. If Jones was 'seeing things', his testimony that he saw Smith would be part of the evidence for him. Unless he saw some Smith-like apparition, he could not have been 'seeing things'. But, of course, this would not be evidence that Smith was in Cambridge on the day in question (or that he was not). Similarly, if he saw a ghost of Smith, his testimony that he saw Smith would be evidence that he saw something; but not that Smith was in Cambridge at the time, unless one believes that ghosts are reincarnations of dead people. This brings me to the fourth possibility: that Smith had come back from the dead.

As we have seen in the previous chapter, Wittgenstein discusses the notion of survival and resurrection in the context of the *meaning of words* such as 'dead' and 'alive'. Here we are concerned with *evidence*. What, one might ask, would count as evidence that someone had come back from the dead? Wittgenstein does not discuss this directly, but it seems clear from his treatment of the Smith incident that he does not think anything could count as evidence for such a belief. He seems to be taking the line that, since we do not have regular and sufficient evidence of people coming back from the dead, nothing can count as sufficient, or, indeed, any, evidence for such an event. The presumption must be one of the three other possible explanations given above; or possibly some other.

Where, then, does this leave belief in the resurrection of the dead, and in particular the Resurrection of Jesus Christ? What are we to make of the empty tomb and the claims of the Apostles and disciples that they had seen the Risen Lord? Wittgenstein does not discuss this, which is somewhat surprising. Such a discussion would have afforded an excellent context to which to deal both with claims to historicity on the part of apologists and with Wittgenstein's own view – in line with orthodox theology – that religious belief has little or nothing to do with scientific evidence.

Whatever about the controversial question of the empty tomb, what is certain is that, historically, it offers no evidence for a Risen Christ. An empty tomb does not entail that its recent occupant has risen from the dead, nor can this be inferred unless no other explanation is possible, which is not the case. Nor can it be inferred from the claims of the Apostles and disciples, including St Paul, and possibly other visionaries and mystics, that they had seen the Risen Lord, that the Lord indeed has risen. These facts and testimonies *contribute to belief in* the Resurrection but they are *not evidence for* it. Even the total theological context surrounding belief in the Resurrection of Christ – his teaching, Old Testament tradition, the sayings of the prophets, the theological and philosophical consequences drawn by St John and St Paul – though it constitutes grounds for belief, does not amount to scientific evidence for it. However, such theological considerations differentiate belief in the Resurrection of Christ from the return of Smith from the dead. Smith's return has no theological underpinning or support whatsoever. Were it to have happened it would have been a happening among other happenings, demanding the kind of scientific evidence that we demand for the existence of UFOs or the interference by extra-terrestrial beings in earthly affairs. Belief in the Resurrection of Christ is of an entirely different kind.

Another example of an apparition clarifies the first in several respects. Here people standing in a ring on a particular day – Midsummer's Day, presumably – claim to see dead relatives. Whether they see these relatives collectively, that is, whether everyone sees only his own or everyone else's relatives or common relatives, is not clear. Presumably the last, at least, since, if two share a dead cousin, say, and both see him or her, they must see the same person ('There's old George', 'So it is') even if the visions are different. But though this raises problems of its own, it is not important for what Wittgenstein has to say. Here no claim is being made that the relatives are alive (at least, not permanently): they are acknowledged to be *dead* relatives. Their appearance occurs only once a year on a particular day, on the occasion of a feast and its specific rituals. And the apparition is reported as an experience: 'I had an experience that I can express by saying: "I saw my dead cousin".'

Wittgenstein asks whether this was said on insufficient evidence. His reply is that if under certain circumstances it was 'a bit absurd', he would say there was insufficient evidence; but in circumstances where it was 'altogether absurd', he would not say there was insufficient evidence. Presumably, he would say there was no evidence at all. It would be interesting to know in what circumstances Wittgenstein would say that the claim was only a bit, and not altogether, absurd. Moreover, it is not clear whether there is insufficient evidence for the claim to have seen a dead cousin or to have had an experience that can be expressed by saying: 'I saw my dead cousin'. As a description of an experience, if accurate, it cannot be described as 'a bit absurd' – 'strange', yes; or 'absurd' in the colloquial sense; but not absurd in a logical sense: no contradiction or logical fallacy is involved. An experience cannot be a 'bit' contradictory. However, if the claim was not simply that the reveller or partaker in the rite had *thought* he or she had seen a dead cousin but had *actually*, if only fleetingly, done so, and was convinced of this, then, indeed, we would be in the realm of absurdity. To describe it as 'a bit absurd' is positively charitable. But perhaps Wittgenstein meant that even to say one *thought* one had seen a dead cousin is a bit absurd. It is not like someone saying that they thought they saw a (living) cousin at the races, something very unlikely, given the cousin's attitude to trivial pursuits: unlikely but in no way absurd. However, the implications of all this are clear.

There is no more scientific evidence for belief in the Resurrection of Christ, in survival after death or in the reappearance in corporeal form of anyone who has died than there is of Smith turning up at Guildhall in Cambridge or a dead cousin on Midsummer Common. But whereas, if the latter cannot be verified and belief in them ranges from the mistaken, through the slightly absurd, to the totally absurd, religious belief in the Resurrection cannot be mistaken or absurd in the same way or for the same kind of reasons. It belongs to a different language-game. It has a significance that the other beliefs do not. They belong to the realm of natural phenomena; the Christian religious beliefs transcend the natural and belong to the realm of redemption and salvation. '*He is dead and decomposed*. In that case he is a teacher like any other and can no longer *help* . . . faith is what is needed by *my heart*, *my soul*, not my speculative intelligence . . . Perhaps we can say: Only *love* can believe the Resurrection.' Love that leads to trust in the word of the Redeemer and, hence, to belief. This is the path that leads to Christian belief. As evidence, the word of the Redeemer in itself cannot bear the weight, in terms of a way of living, placed upon it.

But, it might be objected, are not miracles brought forward as evidence to support Christian beliefs? We have already considered Wittgenstein's views on the miraculous. He does not consider them as proofs of the veracity of belief so much as a way of looking on events with the eyes of faith. Here we shall consider his contrast between miracles and abnormal phenomena. He takes the somewhat unusual, though consistent, position that, while he might consider a person who regarded certain abnormal phenomena as credulous, he might not consider a person who believed in a blatant pseudo miracle as ridiculous.

Wittgenstein takes the miracles of Lourdes as an example. (He seems to conflate the cures with the liquefaction of the blood of St Januarius – 'blood coming out of something'.) We can, for instance, imagine a credulous person, who had just witnessed a man riddled with cancer carried into the baths and walking out cured, exclaiming: 'There you are, Wittgenstein, how can you doubt?' In normal circumstances, Wittgenstein says, he would suggest that the event can be explained in ways other than miraculous. ' "Can it only be explained one way?" ' he asks. ' "Can't it be this or that? . . . Oughtn't one after all to consider this?" I'd say: "Come on. Come on." ' In normal circumstances Wittgenstein would try to convince the credulous person that 'he'd seen nothing of consequence'. And he adds: 'I would treat the phenomenon in this case just as I would treat an experiment in a laboratory which I thought badly executed' (*LC* p. 61). But he muses: 'I wonder whether I would do that under all circumstances?'

What is not clear is in what circumstances Wittgenstein would not reject a seemingly miraculous event as nothing of consequence or as a badly executed laboratory experiment. Would he have rejected the cancer-ridden patient walking out of the baths – and this is not an invented case: I met such a person – as nothing of consequence and a badly executed laboratory experiment? I think he might have done so. In that case he would be doing nothing more than reiterate his position on religious belief: namely, that it cannot be a matter of proof as his credulous companion thinks. (Incidentally, by 'credulous' I think Wittgenstein means 'disposed to believe' rather than the colloquial 'disposed to believe everything'.) In this Wittgenstein is doing nothing more than echoing the saying of Christ: 'Unless you see signs and wonders you will not believe' (John 4.48).

If that is the case, I am a little puzzled that he bothers to suggest alternative explanations for the 'miraculous' phenomenon. In so doing he is playing the credulous man's game. He is assuming that the credulous man's belief that the phenomenon occurs by direct intervention of God is an explanation of *how* the phenomenon occurred, which it is not. A candidate for miraculous status may or may not have a scientific explanation that is available to contemporary science. That no scientific explanation is currently available does not make it *eo ipso* a miracle, or even miraculous. An escape against all (very high) odds may be described correctly as miraculous, though not necessarily as a miracle; yet it could be explained by the laws of natural science. It is not that the phenomenon is inexplicable by the science of the day that makes it miraculous, but that it occurs against very high probabilities.

Wittgenstein more or less concedes this when he says:

I could imagine that someone showed an extremely passionate belief in such a phenomenon, and I couldn't approach his belief at all by saying: 'This could just as well have been brought about by so and so' because he could think this blasphemy on my side. (*LC* p. 61)

But I do not think he concedes it completely. We are still, in his eyes, in the realm of scientific or pseudo scientific evidence.

On the other hand, when he takes up a supposed remark: ' "It is possible that these priests cheat, but nevertheless in a different sense a miraculous phenomenon takes place there" ' he seems to get back on to an even keel. He goes on:

I have a statue which bleeds on such and such a day in the year. I have red ink, etc. 'You are a cheat, but nevertheless the Deity uses you. Red ink in a sense, but not red ink in a sense.' (*LC* ibid.)

Here Wittgenstein seems to acquiesce in fraud. On the other hand, he could be touching the very centre of the nature of miracles. What distinguishes a miracle from the merely strange, improbable or monstrous is that it has a religious significance. That is true of all the miracles attributed to Jesus. He claimed to have come to redeem, to cure souls, to offer a new life to mankind, to enlighten our darkness. So he cured the sick, usually those suffering from 'incurable' diseases; he is credited with having raised the dead to life, of giving sight to the blind, of changing water into wine and multiplying loaves and fishes, of walking on stormy waters and so on. Assuming these events happened as they have been described, they might have been nothing more than sophisticated conjuring tricks that some of our cleverer conjurors may one day master. But this would not deprive them of their religious significance. This might throw light on what Wittgenstein means by the *circumstances* in which he might accept a phenomenon as a miracle and cheating as 'not red ink in a sense'.

Yet he says in the next paragraph:

Cf. Flowers at seance with label. People said: 'Yes, flowers are materialized with label.' What kind of circumstances must there be to make this kind of story not ridiculous? (*LC* p. 61)

(Does the '*cf.*' mean compare or contrast or both?) We know that cheating goes on at seances and we know many of its tricks. Is Wittgenstein saying that 'miracles' in which statues bleed red ink are in the same class as flowers materializing with a label – gifts from the dead? It is not clear. What is implied by the question: 'What kind of circumstances must there be to make this kind of story not ridiculous?'? Is Wittgenstein being ironical here, and contrasting the cheating that goes on at a seance with the use of red ink to make a statue look as though it was bleeding? He is saying that there are no circumstances in which he would take the flowers seriously, though he might take the red ink seriously as an instrument of the Deity. This ties in both with what he says about the way miracles should be treated from a religious point of view and about the place of falsehood. A miracle is 'a gesture God makes', 'a symbolic occurrence' which may accompany the words of a saint (*cf.* chapter eight p. 164); and 'it also does not matter if the words used are true or false or nonsense'. Therefore, while in certain circumstances we may accept tricks and cheating as an instrument of God in confirming *religious* belief, we cannot under any circumstances accept them in support of the *natural* belief that the dead are still alive and living in our midst.

Miracles, therefore, are not evidence *for* religious belief. They are certainly not sufficient evidence, as is popularly thought. Wittgenstein, therefore, concludes that neither they nor so-called proofs for the existence of God are sufficient as a grounding of faith, nor are any other arguments or alleged evidence. The believer has reasons for his belief. For him they are overwhelming reasons. But they do not amount to anything remotely resembling scientific evidence. An essential feature of religious belief is that it is *not grounded* in rational argument.

Wittgenstein draws some conclusions from this that concern controversy. Since the language-game of religious belief is not based on reasoning, it does not give rise to controversy such as we encounter as a matter of course in speculative and theoretical language-games. Indeed, according to Wittgenstein, it does not give scope even for contradictions. In one of the lectures he poses the question whether if someone were to ask him if he believed in the Last Judgement, and he said that he didn't, this would mean that he believed the opposite, that there will not be such a thing as the questioner described. His answer is: either not at all or not always. He follows this with two other exchanges. In the first he supposes that someone does not believe that the body will rot after death and disintegrate, but that the particles will come together in a thousand years and he will rise from the dead. He (Wittgenstein) is asked whether he believes this, and he says: 'No'. Then his interlocutor asks: 'Do you contradict the man?' Again Wittgenstein replies: 'No'. Thus he neither believes what the man proposes, nor does he contradict him.

He goes on: 'If you say this, the contradiction already lies in this.' The interlocutor persists and asks Wittgenstein whether he would say: 'I believe the opposite' or 'There is no reason to suppose such a thing.' Wittgenstein's reply is terse: 'I'd say neither' (*LC* p. 51).

An unbeliever neither believes nor disbelieves what the believer believes. Hence, he cannot contradict him. Were he to contradict him, he would be playing the believer's own language-game. There is a temptation to do this, to say that, if someone does not believe something, he disbelieves it. This hinges on the ambiguity of 'he does not (or I do not) believe'. This can mean either (a) he disbelieves, i.e., does not believe that something is the case, or (b) is doubtful whether it is the case, or (c) has no views on the matter one way or the other. It is a mistake to put unbelievers along with non- or disbelievers or even with sceptics and agnostics. Disbelief, for all that it is negative sounding, is something positive: it is belief that something is not the case. Scepticism is doubt about whether it is the case. And agnosticism ('don't know') is an open-minded attitude to the matter. The unbeliever, as I have said, neither doubts, nor has an open mind, much less believes the contrary. He simply has no views on the matter whatsoever.

Wittgenstein goes on to illustrate this with reference to our use of the word 'possibly', already discussed, but now seen in a different context. He says:

> Suppose someone were a believer and said: 'I believe in a Last Judgement,' and I said: 'Well, I'm not so sure. Possibly.' You would say that there is an enormous gulf between us. If he said: 'There is a German plane overhead,' and I said: 'Possibly. I'm not sure,' you'd say we were fairly near. (*LC* p. 53)

It is open to the unbeliever to say that he neither believes nor does not believe, but not 'I'm not so sure. Possibly.' But if that is what he says, while what he means is that he has no opinion on the subject, then there must be an enormous gulf between him and the believer. I presume that Wittgenstein opts for this formula in order to show how two people using the same expression could either be speaking the same or totally different languages. Although the speaker who asserts there is a German aeroplane overhead is not contradicted by the other who says: 'Possibly. I am not so sure,' nevertheless they disagree. But their disagreement is a real disagreement: they are playing the same game. 'Possibly. I'm not so sure' does not mean: 'I have no views on the matter'. The speaker has a view. It is that while the plane may be German, he is not certain it is. Perhaps it does not sound like a German plane or it is unlikely that a solitary German plane would be flying over Cambridge during one of Wittgenstein's lectures. But at least the two are talking about the same thing: they are 'fairly near'.

Wittgenstein develops this a little further when talking about the practical criteria for religious belief; that is, whether someone believes that he may be dragged into hell-fire and orders his life accordingly. 'That,' says Wittgenstein:

> is partly why you don't get in religious controversies the form of controversy where one person is *sure* of the thing, and the other says: 'Well, possibly.' (*LC* p. 56)

He adds: 'Those who said: "Well possibly it may happen and possibly not" would be on an entirely different plane.' Belief, he says, is more like having a picture constantly before one's mind and being admonished by it than holding in one's mind a proposition or set of propositions that can be contradicted. Other people 'just didn't use it at all'. Now, while one can contradict a proposition, it is hard to see how we can *contradict* a picture and the way of life it inspires. We can reject it. We can say it is inappropriate, misleading, ludicrous, pernicious, false even, and heap on it every conceivable term of abuse and ridicule; but we cannot contradict it. To attempt to do so is itself ridiculous, and shows a complete lack of understanding of the nature of religious belief, at least as Wittgenstein understood it.

Thus disagreements between believers and unbelievers can only be pseudo controversies and pseudo contradictions or apparent controversies and contradictions. They do not operate on a ground common enough to generate controversies. They are on an entirely different plane.

But surely, it will be objected, religion is notorious for controversy: controversy that, as often as not, takes a very nasty turn. Every great religion is riven and riven again by controversy: acrimonious, bitter, deep-rooted controversy, and controversy that is socially divisive when it is not lethal. *Odium theologicum* is, in many minds, the distinguishing feature of religion. And yet Wittgenstein can say there is no room for contradiction and controversy where religious belief is concerned!

In attempting to answer this objection many of the topics discussed in this chapter can be drawn together. Wittgenstein, surprisingly perhaps, did not address himself to it directly, but he made his position abundantly clear. For Wittgenstein the operative word in the phrase *odium theologicum* would unquestionably be *theologicum*. As we have seen, religious belief and all that goes with it – ritual, an attitude and a way of life – is a different language-game from dogma and theology. The latter are concerned with words, with formulae, with speculation and argument. Controversy and contradiction have plenty of scope where religion reaches out for propositions with which to define itself.

It is not possible to have a religious belief that is not belief in something. But, for Wittgenstein, what that something is, is shown by what we do rather than by what we say, in *praxis* rather than in dogma, theory and theological speculation. And, of course, it is shown in our attitudes, which are a part of *praxis*.

This is nowhere more apparent than in trying to understand the practices of primitive peoples who have not developed an elaborate doctrinal system. To learn what they believe, whether it is religious belief or superstition, magic or pseudo science, we have to study their practices, not their doctrinal propositions, which, in some, if not many cases, do not exist. This manifestation of religious belief fascinated Wittgenstein and drew him to a study of Frazer that merits a short chapter to itself.

10

The Beliefs of Primitive Peoples

The most extensive entries on religious belief in Wittgenstein's *Notebooks* are his remarks on Sir James George Frazer's book, *The Golden Bough: A Study in Magic and Religion*.[1] Those have been edited by Rush Rhees under the title: *Remarks on Frazer's 'The Golden Bough'*.[2] Wittgenstein also made occasional remarks unconnected with Frazer.

In this chapter I shall discuss Wittgenstein's views on the beliefs of primitive peoples, drawing on those two sources, but principally on his criticisms of Frazer.

The remarks on Frazer cover a period from 1931 to 1948, that is, up to the end of Wittgenstein's life. According to Dr Drury, Wittgenstein first became interested in Frazer in 1930. They read Frazer together and discussed him but did not progress very far, such was the ratio of discussion to reading. Then, in 1931, Wittgenstein began to jot down remarks on Frazer in his journal.

According to Wittgenstein, Frazer makes the magical and/or religious beliefs of primitive peoples appear to be mistakes. But error, he says, 'belongs to opinion only'. 'An error occurs only where magic is presented as science' (*RF* p. 4). Was St Augustine in error in calling on God on every page of the *Confessions*? he asks. Or is a Buddhist or holy man or anyone else who expresses similar but different notions necessarily mistaken? Primitive beliefs and rituals can be regarded as mistaken only if such beliefs and rituals are attempted science, which, in Wittgenstein's opinion, they are not.

If anyone is in error, according to Wittgenstein, it is Frazer himself. In his opinion, Frazer totally misunderstood the thinking of these people. As he says sarcastically:

> Even the idea, to want to explain the practice for instance, the killing of the priest-king – seems to me misguided. All Frazer does is to make it plausible to people who think as he does. It is very remarkable that all these practices are ultimately shown to be stupid.

But it would never be plausible that people would do everything out of pure stupidity. (*RF* p. 1)

In Frazer's opinion primitive people had a view of the world such that they could, by appropriate rites and practices, successfully manipulate it, just as technologists, physicians and other practical scientists manipulate the world or Nature. Thus they did rain dances to induce rain, killed the first-born to ensure the fertility of crops, animals and humans, used incantations to ward off evils and disasters, and potions and other remedies to cure illnesses. The beliefs on which these practices were based were almost invariably scientifically erroneous. Indeed, for Frazer and like-thinking people, magic becomes almost synonymous with false scientific belief. Though this view may, indeed, be true in some cases, Wittgenstein does not accept it.

In Wittgenstein's view the ritual practices of primitive peoples are not based on scientific, pseudo scientific or would-be scientific opinions at all. 'I believe,' he says, 'that it is characteristic of primitive man that he does not act from *opinions* (as against Frazer) (*RF* p. 12). Or again: 'A religious symbol does not rest on any *opinion* as its ground. And error corresponds only to opinion' (*RF* p. 3). He does not see that primitive ritual practices are any different from rites practised today, such as baptism or the confession of sins. Of the former he says that: 'there is an error only if magic is interpreted scientifically.' This does not merely repeat what he has said elsewhere. It puts primitive ritual on a par with Christian ritual. No one would believe for one moment that the rite of baptism had some sort of scientifically justified effect, so why, argues Wittgenstein, assume that primitive rituals must have some scientific or pseudo scientific aim? This seems not only right in principle but most illuminating. The corollary of this would be that Christian ritual is pseudo scientific and superstitious. There are those who would say that it is. But it is not clear what is meant by saying this, beyond saying that those who indulge in these practices are credulous.

On the confession of sins, by which, I presume, Wittgenstein means the sacrament of penance, which involves restoration to a state of grace, absolution and an increase in actual grace, he remarks: 'This also is susceptible of "explanation" and is not susceptible of explanation' (*RF* p. 4). This is an interesting point. In a sense we can explain what the sacrament of penance means within the Christian, or, at least, Roman Catholic community, though it would be a lengthy explanation· for anyone unfamiliar with that Faith. But Wittgenstein's point is that it would not be a reductionist, 'scientific' explanation, as Frazer tried to give to the religious actions and life of the Priest King. Both ritual activities are, to that extent, on a par. Indeed, Wittgenstein could have added there would be nothing incongruous in reviving primitive rituals in the light of modern science (even though there might be other reasons for not doing so) since science has nothing to do with the matter.

There would, however, be something incongruous about reviving ancient science. The Ptolomeic system, the atoms of Democritus or even more recent theories, particularly in medicine, are gone for ever. 'The difference between magic and science,' says Wittgenstein, 'can be expressed to the extent that there is a progress in science but not in magic. There is nothing in magic itself to indicate the direction any development could take' (*RF* p. 13). This is substantially, though not strictly, true. What is true is that a ritual may persist for ever. There is, as Wittgenstein says, no direction in which it can develop. But it may change for the better or for the worse within a specific set of beliefs; and it may be done better in one church or community or group than another. Roman Catholics may deplore the recent departure from the Tridentine rite, as many may have deplored the abolition of the Mozarabic and old Gallican rites by the Council of Trent; or one may welcome changes in liturgy, either because they seem to be a return to the purity and coherence of the liturgy of the early Church (in so far as we know it) or because it is more in keeping with modern times. This is *change*, but *not progress*. The rites have not necessarily got nearer to a goal, any more than poetry has improved since Homer. This point was made in the seventeenth century 'quarrel' between the ancients and the moderns, in relation to the rival claims of the arts and sciences.

Nevertheless – and this may blunt, but not destroy Wittgenstein's distinction – there is a sense in which it can be said that there is progress of a kind, not only in doctrine, but also in ritual. The substitution of, say, the offering of bread and wine for the killing of humans and animals as a form of worship may be said to be an advance in our conception of how to honour, placate or curry favour with a deity, a spirit or an alien force. It is certainly morally more acceptable. But does this necessarily make it an advance? An advance on what? From one point of view it might be retrograde. Someone might say: 'Once upon a time they sacrificed humans, bulls, sheep and doves. Now it is only bread and wine. That is not genuine sacrifice. Things have deteriorated.' If you make it a matter of morality or causal efficacy or the socially acceptable, the magical and religious force may be lost. So, despite religious – and still more agnostic or humanistic – prejudice, there is no ground for saying that, apart from doctrinal backing, and, possibly not even then, there is any necessary advance in ritual practice in its essentials from the most primitive to the most 'sophisticated'.

Wittgenstein was irritated by the fact that Frazer not only regarded primitive peoples as in error, but also as stupid. Frazer says that magic persists as long as it does because it cannot easily go wrong. For instance, instance, the rains will come sooner or later and when they do, this can be attributed to the magic of ritual: 'A ceremony intended to make the wind blow, or rain fall, or to work the death of an enemy, will always be followed, sooner or later, by the occurrence it is meant to bring to pass' (*The Golden Bough* p. 59). 'But then,' says Wittgenstein, 'it is very curious that people do not hit upon it earlier that as things are it rains sooner or later' (*RF* p. 2). Could it not be that they did not see any causal connection between the rain and the ritual? Even Frazer himself admits that the Rain King is petitioned when the rains are about to come (ibid. p. 107). This means, says Wittgenstein, that the people do not think that the Rain King can make rain, otherwise why not petition him in the period of the year when the land is, in Frazer's words, 'a parched and arid desert'?

> If one assumes that people at one time set up this office of Rain King out of stupidity, still it is nevertheless surely clear that they already had previous experience that the rain begins in March, and they would then have the Rain King perform at other times of year. (*RF* p. 12)

Which, of course, they do not. They also celebrate the coming of day just before sunrise, but not in the middle of the night. 'Then they simply burn lamps' (ibid.).

These arguments do not tell conclusively against Frazer. Maybe these people are, in fact, more stupid than we Westerners think possible. Yet such arguments offer an alternative explanation or, at least, an interpretation. As Wittgenstein says, it is crazy (*verrückt*) to think that a woman who, in adopting a child, draws the child through her clothes, really believes she has given birth to the child. But, in fairness to Frazer, he does not say she does. He talks of 'make-believe', which is precisely the opposite. 'The same principle of make-believe, so dear to children, has led other peoples to employ a *simulation* of birth as a form of adoption' (*The Golden Bough* p. 14. My italics).[3]

Wittgenstein, however, uses another argument, also used, incidentally, by Merleau-Ponty, which I find open to question. It is that the same person who indulges in what Frazer considers stupid practices shows himself to be far from stupid when it comes to practical matters. 'The same savage who, seemingly to kill his enemy, stabs his image, really builds his hut out of wood and cuts his arrow skilfully, and not in effigy' (*RF* p. 4).[4] Frazer does not suggest that to be stupid one must operate solely with effigies. Nor, I imagine, would he deny that primitive people are skilful and intelligent in their practical affairs. But they could still be stupid when it comes to scientific matters. Intelligent peoples are often stupid. But they tend to be stupid in practical rather than theoretical matters. Be that as it may, the fact that people are intelligent in practical matters is no proof that they are not, much less that they cannot be, stupid in theoretical, abstract or non-practical matters. So this argument does not carry much weight, and adds nothing to the counter-examples already offered – invoking the Rain King when rain was about to come anyway. What is needed is a fuller account of what these rituals are about in order to show that they are not attempts to influence the course of nature on the basis of a false scientific belief.

Wittgenstein provides such an account. He admits that opinions about the world may have a part in ritual – 'an opinion – a belief – can itself be ritualistic, can belong to rite' (*RF* p. 7). But 'the characteristic of ritual action is decidedly not a view, an opinion, be it right or wrong':

> When one observes the life and behaviour of human beings on earth, one sees that, besides the activities that one might call animal, taking nourishment, etc., etc., etc., they also carry out such that bear a particular character and this one could call ritual actions.
>
> But now it is nonsense to go on to say that the characteristic of *these* actions be such that they arise from mistaken views on the physics of things. (*RF* p. 7)

What then is a rite and from what beliefs does it arise? For Wittgenstein magic (and, indeed, religion) is essentially symbolic and arises from impressions. Once again he cites Frazer himself. 'When Frazer at the beginning [of his book] narrates the story of the King of the Woods at Nemi, he does this in a tone that shows that here something strange and terrifying is taking place' (RF pp. 2–3). Its significance is in its impression of the terrible, the horrible, the tragic. It can only be described. It cannot be explained. An explanation is only an hypothesis, and uncertain at that. And here Wittgenstein reveals the sensitive side of his mind:

> But, perhaps, someone shattered from love will be little helped by an explanatory hypothesis – it will not calm him . . .
>
> If one puts together that account of the Priest King of Nemi with the phrase 'the majesty of death' one sees that the two are one. (*RF* p. 3) .

The implication of this is that someone who is moved by the symbol of the majesty of death can substitute for it the symbol of the Priest King, just as we might put one ceremony in place of another. But the point is: *there is no explanation*.

Wittgenstein's alternative is reinforced by the suggestion that stabbing a picture of an enemy or burning an effigy of him need not be aimed at effects on the enemy but merely at giving satisfaction to the person doing it, just as people burn flags and topple or deface the statues of tyrants. Wittgenstein uses the analogy of kissing the picture of a loved one:

> This is *obviously not* based on belief in a definite effect on the object that the picture represents. It aims at some satisfaction and it achieves it. Or rather, it does not *aim* at anything; we act in this way and then we feel satisfied. (*RF* p. 4)

It would be absurd to explain this action and the belief on which it is based in terms of causal efficacy. One might, however, explain the action by saying that (a girl) is in some way assuaging her feeling of loss for a fiancé killed in war or a boy for a girlfriend from whom he has been separated for a long time. Few people would regard kissing the feet of a crucifix in Holy Week as an act that aims at causal efficacy, so it does not follow that similar actions by primitive people have that aim either.

Symbolism in magic and religious ritual is very varied. It may be a symbolic action with supernatural or legal efficacy such as washing in baptism or the drawing of a child through a woman's clothes in adoption. Or it may involve treating something inanimate or non-human, as though, for instance, it could understand a command, such as beckoning it to come or ordering it to go away. As Wittgenstein rather amusingly remarks: in magical healing one signifies to the illness that it should leave the patient, and one could always add: 'If the illness doesn't understand *that*, then I don't know *how* one ought to say it' (*RF* p. 7).

What is not clear about Wittgenstein's remarks on Frazer is whether he wishes to go to the opposite extreme from that of Frazer and the reductionists and say that magic, at least, does not aim to affect the course of events on *any* occasion whatsoever, or merely that it does not always do it, or rarely does. If the former, he is clearly wrong. We do not have to go to African or South American forests to find people who believe this. They believe that Lourdes water will cure illnesses or a miraculous medal will keep a soldier safe in battle. Clearly, there are magical and religious rites and practices which those who indulge in them believe to be causally efficacious. If Wittgenstein's point is that these kinds of beliefs do not explain all magical, let alone religious, rites and practices, he is clearly right. If his point is that they explain none of them, he is clearly wrong. If his point is that Frazer-like reductionism fails to grasp what is essentially religious, and, indeed, what is magical in rites and practices, then he is again clearly right, though this judgement may be open to debate.

He is also right on two other points.

First, whether magic and ritual do or do not aim to be causally efficacious, they *never* aim to be scientific. In other words, they are not based on false science. They are not pseudo scientific, for the simple reason that they have nothing to do with science as we understand it. They belong to an entirely different language-game. They may be (must be) based on beliefs, but these are not beliefs about the nature of the world nor theories and opinions about it.

Secondly, they are symbolic. The symbolism may be easily intelligible, such as the significance of passing a child through a woman's clothing or burning an effigy. Or it may be mysterious, such as the significance of washing in baptism or the words of absolution in the sacrament of penance. Cleansing from sin and restoring to grace are matters that, in Wittgenstein's own words, lie outside the world. In what might be called the post-Frazer era, anthropologists have come to realize this. They have come to see the essentially symbolic aspect, not only of religious ritual (where it should be obvious) but also in magical rites and so-called superstitious practices.

Wittgenstein, however, can also be misleading. While rightly emphasizing the essentially symbolic, rather than the pseudo scientific, nature of magic, he might give the impression that it is nothing more than symbolism, like saluting the flag or bowing to an empty throne. Sometimes that, indeed, is all it is, but sometimes – and one might say, most times – it aims at causal efficacy, not necessarily based on pseudo scientific theories, but occasionally. Some tribes believe that putting a cord around a child's belly will stop diarrhoea on the homeopathic principle that like produces like and a closed circle will close the orifice. And quite clearly human and other sacrifices, though not based on any scientific theory, were nevertheless based on the notion that, by giving the gods or evil spirits something, they would give us something back in return. This is an hypothesis, an opinion, a theory of sorts.

Another misleading impression that Wittgenstein's remarks may give is the constantly recurring relativism that his account of magic seems to imply. Frazer and his cohorts could deal with magic quite simply by dismissing it as pseudo science; and, no doubt, if they had a mind to, they could have dismissed all religious practices, too, though that might have been a more ambitious task. Wittgenstein, on the contrary – and quite rightly – wants to keep primitive ritual in place. But the impression is then given that all rites and practices are of equal value, that one cannot progress from sacrificing humans, sheep, doves and oxen to offering bread and wine. All are legitimate for the purposes for which they are intended.

Perhaps Wittgenstein did hold this view. The most he is committed to saying, however, is that the person practising magic and the person conducting a religious service is not only acting in good faith but that the practice or action has a ritualistic significance. He is not committed to saying that all rites, magical or religious, are of equal value. Nor is he committed to saying that someone cannot abandon one form of ritual for another on moral or other grounds. They are equal only in so far as they are symbolic acts with something more than a purely mundane significance.

There is, however, a spectrum of magical and religious practices, running from those that aim at efficacy – praying for a cure or for rain or for a good harvest – to those that are merely acts of worship – acknowledgement of the might, the power and the majesty of gods and spirits or merely of their existence. By drawing attention to the latter, Wittgenstein has pin-pointed what is essentially religious about these practices. They are essentially non-manipulative, not attempts to pre-empt disaster or bend the course of events to the practitioner's advantage – though inevitably there will be an element of that, too, at least at the level of velleity. This is dramatically illustrated by the practice of petitioning the Rain King as the rains are about to come or celebrating the coming of dawn just before sunrise. One might add the practice of blessing the fields on Rogation Days irrespective of whether there had been bad harvests or, in the case of blessing fishing fleets, disastrously poor hauls and much loss of life the previous year. The significance of these practices lies not so much in their attempted or putative causal efficacy as in their acknowledgement of the existence of a Being or beings greater than all of us who rule our destiny. And, of course, these rituals imply a belief that there is or are such beings, otherwise these acts would be perfunctory and vacuous.[4]

In 1930, possibly at the same time as he was reading Frazer, Wittgenstein read Ernest Renan's *History of the People of Israel*. It set him thinking about the religious beliefs of primitive peoples. Wittgenstein quotes Renan as saying: 'Birth, sickness, death, madness, catalepsy, sleep, dreams, used to strike people in an extraordinary way; and they do so even today. It is given only to a small number to see clearly that these phenomena have their causes in our manner of being.'[5] In other words an elite is immune from such reactions. This triggers off in Wittgenstein a certain animus against Renan. His remarks are somewhat confused, but the gist of what he is saying is clear. To wonder at such things, he says, is not primitive. On the contrary, to think that scientific explanations increase wonder is primitive. 'Contemporary people and Renan himself are precisely the primitives, if he thinks scientific explanation could arouse that wonderment' (*CV* p. 5). It is not clear, however, that this is what Renan is saying. Indeed he seems to be saying the opposite: namely, that scientific explanation takes the mystery out of birth, death, illness and madness. Nevertheless, Wittgenstein's point stands, that is: to think in this way is primitive, since, after whatever scientific explanation, the wonder, and, indeed, the dread remain. As though lightning is less astonishing and a more mundane occurrence now than it was two thousand years ago!

Wittgenstein concludes this entry with the words:

> But it cannot be ruled out that *highly* civilized people will succumb to this fear again; and their civilization and scientific knowledge cannot protect them from it. Admittedly, it is true that the *spirit* in which science is transacted today is not compatible with such fear. (*CV* p. 5)

The passage includes a memorable punchline: 'The human being – and, perhaps, peoples – must be awakened to wonder. Science is a means to put him back to sleep again' (*CV* p. 5). These are salutary remarks. The fact that in a limited, 'scientific', sense we understand the workings of the world better (the 'how', how it works) does not, in Wittgenstein's view, make it any less mysterious and wonderful. Even if we know how lightning occurs or how a hurricane happens, we can still feel dread and a sense that we are in the hands of alien forces beyond our control (to say nothing of being beyond the control of meteorology!). To that extent we are still primitive, and, in Wittgenstein's view, all the better for it. The pejoratively primitive is the person who believes the opposite: to wit, that science has explained everything.

However, nearly two decades later, in 1948, Wittgenstein has an entry in his journal which, on the face of it, seems to contradict all he said against Frazer and in favour of primitive peoples. It runs: 'Religious belief and superstition are entirely different. The one springs from *fear* and is a *kind of false science*. The other is a trust' (*CV* p. 72. My italics). This is certainly a concession to Frazer. But, then, as Wittgenstein himself has shown, not all primitive practices or beliefs are superstitious in his or any other sense. Nor, as he has also shown, is religion free from superstition. This superstition is based, if not on fear, at least on a false kind of science, as propounded by apologists such as Father O'Hara. This is a succinct definition of superstition and religious belief. True religious belief is based not on reason – certainly not on false reasoning – but on trust, trust in the word of the prophet, the holy man, the Son of God. On what this trust is based is another matter. Obviously, on the prophet's way of life. This entry of Wittgenstein's is thus a kind of footnote to what he said earlier on religious belief and magic. In his earlier remarks he insisted that magic (and also religious belief) had nothing to do with false scientific belief, but he had not stressed the part played by trust in religious belief. However, much more needs to be said. Why, for instance, trust the author of Luke and not the author of the Gospel according to Thomas?

11

Wittgenstein on Predestination

From his earliest writings to remarks written shortly before his death, Wittgenstein shows a preoccupation with fate. In his later writings, this takes the more specific form of the Christian doctrine of predestination.

Fate and predestination are distinct in important respects, as Wittgenstein points out in an original manner. 'Fate,' he says, 'is the antithesis of natural law. A law of nature is something you want to fathom and make use of, but not fate' (*CV* p. 61). Fate is arbitrary and capricious, or, in the case of natural disasters such as earthquakes, droughts and floods, it appears to be arbitrary and capricious. Predestination, on the other hand, though seemingly arbitrary, could be based on a well-thought-out principle of selection, fathomable in principle, though unfathomable to us. That is, unlike fate, it could be governed by a law:

> If God really does *choose* those who are to be saved, there is no reason why he should not choose them according to nationality, race or temperament. Or why the choice should not find expression in a law of nature. (Certainly he was able so to choose that his choice should follow a law.) (*CV* p. 72)

Thus predestination need not be the divine lottery it appears to be, since the gates of salvation were thrown open to all races.

The doctrine of predestination consists of the following propositions: (1) from all eternity God chose those who should be saved and those who should be damned; (2) to those who are to be saved God gave the grace or gift of salvation which they cannot resist; (3) the chosen or elect are saved through faith in Jesus Christ who washed away their sins by atoning for them on the cross; and (4) faith, too, is a gift of God given only to the elect. Strongly opposed to that view was the Pelagian doctrine that man can be saved by his own free, unaided efforts (though grace is a help). He thus merits salvation by good deeds and damnation by bad.

Wittgenstein was not interested in theological controversy, though he was familiar with the works of Augustine, Pascal and of contemporary theologians such as Karl Barth. His interest was in the ethical and conceptual aspects of the doctrine. In so far as he had a concern for the polemics of the subjects, his sympathies would probably have been with the Pelagians. He says:

> Life is like a path along a mountain ridge; to the left and right are slippery slopes down which you slide without being able to stop yourself, in one direction or in the other. I keep seeing people slip like this and I say: 'How could a man help himself in such a situation!' And that is what 'denying free will' comes to. That is the attitude expressed in this 'belief'. But it is not a *scientific* belief and has nothing to do with scientific convictions. (*CV* 63)

Without wishing to be facetious we can say that in this passage Wittgenstein does not come down on either side. The main thrust of the remark is that whether we deny free will or not is a matter of belief, and that belief is not scientific. Science cannot settle a religious or philosophical controversy. But elsewhere it is quite clear on which side Wittgenstein stands. He regarded the doctrine of predestination as unethical, irreligious and ultimately incoherent.

Before coming to that, a word about Wittgenstein's views as expressed in the earlier works about his attitude to fate and the alien will which is at least a background to his attitude to predestination, if not integral to it. For instance, in the *Notebooks* he says:

> I cannot bend the happenings of the world to my will: I am completely powerless.
> I can only make myself independent of the world – and so in a certain sense master it – by renouncing any influence on happenings. (p. 73)

He elaborates this a little later:

> Even if everything that we want were to happen, this would still only be, so to speak, a grace of fate, for what would guarantee it is not any logical connection between will and world, and we could not in turn will the supposed connection. (*CV* ibid.; *TLP* 6.373–4)

Not only can he not bend the world to his will, but he is dependent on a will that has designs on him, the alien will: 'we have the feeling of being dependent on an alien will' (*NB* p. 74). So from his early life it was firmly implanted in Wittgenstein's mind that the human condition is one of dependence not only on forces he could not overcome by his will, the blind forces of Nature, but also on a will alien or over-against our own, be it God or Fate.

Wittgenstein was prepared to bow to that, to accept the reality of the situation in which he found himself, though he would do his best by way of renunciation to thwart the world by acceptance (being in agreement with) of the happenings of the world, in a sense, to pacify the alien will. What he balked at was having the destiny of mankind described in terms of rewards and punishments arbitrarily distributed, which predestination appears to be.

Over the years Wittgenstein approached the doctrine of predestination from various angles. His primary objection to it was its seeming, if not obvious, injustice. In this he is sometimes unfair to the more eminent exponents of the doctrine such as St Paul, St Augustine and Calvin. He takes such phrases as: 'God has commanded it, therefore it must be possible to do it' or 'Out of his goodness he has chosen them and he will punish you.'

Of the first expression Wittgenstein says:

> That means nothing. There is no '*therefore*' about it. At most the two expressions might mean the *same*.
>   In this context 'He has commanded it' means roughly: He will punish anybody who doesn't do it. And nothing follows from that about what anybody can or cannot do. And that is what 'predestination' means. (*CV* p. 77)

Whether this is what predestination means or not, it is certain what Wittgenstein means by predestination: being punished for not doing what one cannot do or doing what (in the circumstances) is impossible not to do. This is something that servants, soldiers, prisoners, school children and apprentices throughout the ages understood very well. While Wittgenstein hesitates when it comes to giving as an equivalent to the initial expression 'He punishes you even though you *cannot* do otherwise', he does concede that 'in this case punishment is inflicted in circumstances where it would be impermissible for men to inflict it'.

He then begins to vacillate. He first suggests that, if it is conceded that, in the case of God, punishment is being inflicted in circumstances in which it would not be permissible for men to inflict it, surely 'the whole concept of "punishment" has changed'. Either the old illustrations can no longer be used or else they must be used differently. 'Just look at an allegory like "The Pilgrim's Progress",'[1] he says, 'and notice how nothing is right – in human terms.' Here the concept of what is right is applied differently. (Wittgenstein gives the analogy of a dial in a railway station that looks like a clock that has stopped but is actually telling the time of when the next train leaves.)[2] If anyone is upset by the allegory, he can apply it differently or leave it alone. 'But,' Wittgenstein concludes sadly, 'there are *some* whom it will confuse far more than it can help.'

Of the other expression – 'Out of his goodness he has chosen them and he will punish you' – he says that it makes no sense.

> The two halves of the proposition belong to different ways of looking at things. The second half is ethical, the first not. And taken together with the first, the second is absurd. (*CV* p. 81)

The meaning here is obvious. To make a choice is not necessarily an ethical issue, but to decide to punish is. To connect the act of choice with the decision to punish (if a logical nexus is indeed intended) makes no sense. However, if, like the Emir of Bochara who would pick citizens in the street at random and have them hurled to their death from a tower (his admiration for Queen Victoria as a sovereign was diminished when he was told she could not do likewise), the choice was initially for punishment; the two halves could coalesce. But then 'in his goodness' would become ironical, blasphemous or mysterious, and, like 'punishment', take on another meaning.

Wittgenstein will not have such tampering with these words. 'Could you,' he asks, 'explain the punishments of hell without using the concept of punishment? Or that of God's goodness without using the concept of goodness?' His answer is: 'If you want to get the right *effect* of your words, certainly not' (*CV* p. 80). The effect Wittgenstein has in mind is quite sinister. Yet without the notion of punishment being introduced into the doctrine of predestination, it is more sinister still. Here is Wittgenstein's 'neutral' or 'naturalistic' version:

> Suppose someone were taught: there is a being who, if you do such and such or live thus and thus, will take you to a place of overlasting torment after you die; most people end up there, a few get to a place of everlasting happiness. – This being has selected in advance those who are to go to the good place and, since only those who have lived a certain sort of life go to the place of torment, he has also arranged in advance for the rest to live like that.
> What might be the effect of such a doctrine?
> Well, it does not mention punishment, but a sort of natural necessity. And if you were to present things to anyone in this light, he could only react with despair or incredulity to such a doctrine. (*CV* p. 81)

Adding the notion of punishment might not greatly alleviate the gloom but, at least, it would give an ethical backing to this story. There would still be the problem of being rewarded or punished for deeds one could not do otherwise than well or badly.

Wittgenstein draws a pedagogical conclusion from this. He says:

> Teaching it could not constitute an ethical upbringing. If you wanted to bring someone up ethically while yet teaching him such a doctrine, you would have to teach him it *after* having educated him ethically, representing it as a sort of incomprehensible mystery. (*CV* ibid.)

This amounts to saying that the doctrine of predestination, even with the inclusion of punishment, is not something that we mortals would regard as ethical. So, if someone were to teach ethics to human beings, he had better start talking about justice or virtue or some of the time-honoured ethical concepts. Only then could he introduce predestination as, in Wittgenstein's words, 'a sort of incomprehensible mystery' which flies in the face of ethics as human beings understand it.

Yet is it an incomprehensible mystery? To Wittgenstein it was, but then so was a saying of St John of the Cross's to the effect that some people have gone to Hell (*zu Grunde gegangen*) because they did not have a wise spiritual director at the right moment. This to Wittgenstein is grossly unfair. Moreover, he asks, 'how can anyone say that God does not try men beyond their strength?' This is a reference to St Paul: (1 Corinthians 10.13): 'He will not allow you to be tested beyond your capacity but when the test comes he will find a suitable remedy.' Whether Wittgenstein meant to confront John of the Cross with St Paul is not clear. However, there is an obvious conflict of views here. It is quite clear that Wittgenstein did not approve of St John's statement which, if not predestinarian, was, at least, Augustinian and fairly widely accepted. After all, the notion of the good moral life as a piece of luck has its origins in antiquity. But Wittgenstein did not approve of it: 'distorted concepts have done a lot of mischief' (*CV* p. 72).[3] He concludes indecisively: 'but the truth is that I just *do not know* what does good and what does mischief' (ibid.).

Indeed this agnostical position seems to have been maintained throughout his life. It is stated quite clearly in a remark entered in 1937:

> In religion every level of devoutness must have its appropriate form of expression which has no sense at a lower level. This doctrine, which means something at a higher level, is null and void for someone at a lower level; he *can* only understand it *wrongly* and so these words are *not* valid for such a person.
>
> For instance, at my level the Pauline doctrine of predestination is ugly nonsense, irreligiousness (*Irreligiosität*). Hence it is not suitable for me, since the only use I could make of the picture I am offered would be a

wrong one. If it is a good and godly picture, then it is for someone at a quite different level, who must use it in his life in a way completely different from anything that would be possible for me. (*CV* p. 32)

This may smack of religious relativism, but it is nothing of the kind. While Wittgenstein admits that predestination is incomprehensible to himself and, presumably, to many others, he never asserts it is therefore incomprehensible in itself. Indeed, he implicitly concedes that if such luminaries as St Paul, St Augustine and Calvin claimed they understood the doctrine, there was a prima facie case for saying that it is comprehensible.

At the same time as that entry was written, Wittgenstein entered the following entry in his *Notebooks* which has been quoted earlier:

Religious similes can be said to move on the edge of an abyss. B's, for example. For what if we simply add: 'and all these traps, quicksands, wrong turnings, were planned by the Lord of the Road and the monsters, thieves and robbers were created by him'? Certainly, that is not the sense of the simile! But such a continuation is all too obvious! For many people, including me, this robs the simile of its power. (*CV* p. 29)

If I understand Wittgenstein correctly, what he is saying is that the doctrine of predestination puts an unjustifiable gloss on the Gospel teaching (whatever about St Paul). It strives in an unevangelical manner to spell out a metaphor (or simile) about the way God deals with his human creatures. The *power* of the simile lies precisely in its not being spelt out – as, indeed, with other biblical expressions such as: 'unless the grain of wheat die, itself remaineth alone . . .', or 'Many are called but few are chosen' (which is, presumably, the source on which the doctrine of predestination is based).

What theology does, in Wittgenstein's view, is attempt to explain and to justify the incomprehensible (the mysteries), whereas all it can do and all it should do is to state categorically and describe what is to be done or what will happen. Rules of life, he says, are 'dressed up in pictures' – a notion he elaborated a little later in his lectures on religious belief. 'These pictures can only serve to *describe* what we are to do, not *justify* it.' You can be told to thank God for the good you receive but not to complain about the evil, as you would do justifiably if a human being were to do you good and evil by turns. He illustrates this with an analogy of the two attitudes to bees, already described.

Wittgenstein concludes this entry with a remarkable and moving remark. He suggests that the doctrine of predestination should be treated not as a doctrine or a theory, but as a cry or sigh uttered by someone in agony.

> Predestination: It is only permissible to write like this out of the most dreadful suffering – then it means something quite different. But for the same reason it is not permissible for someone to assert it as a truth, unless he himself is in torment. – It simply isn't a theory. – Or, put it another way: If this is a truth, it is not the truth that seems at first sight to be expressed by these words. It's less a theory than a sigh, or a cry. (*CV* p. 30)

This is Wittgenstein at his most charitable. To the end he regarded the doctrine of predestination as, humanly speaking, an abominable doctrine. In an entry in 1950, shortly before his death, he says:

> How God judges a man we cannot imagine at all. If he really takes strength of temptation and the frailty of nature into account, whom can he condemn? But otherwise the resultant of these two forces is simply the end for which the man was predestined. In that case he was created so that the interplay of forces would make him either conquer or succumb (*siegen, oder unterzugehen*). And that is not a religious idea at all, but more like a scientific hypothesis.
>
>   So if you want to stay within the religious sphere (*im Religiösen*) you must *struggle* (*kämpfen*). (*CV* p. 86)

This is a remarkable statement, particularly as it comes at the end of Wittgenstein's life when even he must have known that he did not have long to live. It is like a cry of despair, as though in his last moments it came to him that human existence is irrational and absurd in human terms but that this thought must be resisted. The Pelagianism in Wittgenstein persists to the end. The dignity of the human being demands it. He cannot accept that we are at the mercy of forces for good or evil outside our control, even if these forces have a divine origin. Wittgenstein would accept the Pauline (and Horacian) doctrine that the evil we would not we do, and the good we would we do not.[4] But he cannot accept that we should be punished for doing the former and for not doing the latter, if we act out of human frailty. This, in human terms, is not justice. In other terms it is justice of a crude sort.

   It is possible to make rules that people cannot keep and then punish them for breaking them. This may be a way of keeping people in order, but it is not justice. St Paul himself admits this when he says that God will not allow us to be tempted beyond our capacity and will give us the grace (help) to overcome.[5] Wittgenstein seems to have overlooked this. And who can blame him? The predestinarians also did so. However, his most important remark is: 'And that is not a religious idea at all, but more like a scientific hypothesis.'

The importance of this remark is the emphasis it places on free will in religious matters. For Wittgenstein, religion was a meeting of wills, the alien will and my own, in agreement and conformity, or, if mine was an evil will, in confrontation and disagreement. If the actions of a person, be they good or bad, are determined by circumstances, then there can be no encounter with a deity. The most that can be expected is that certain actions occur and, if they are acceptable, the person is rewarded; if they are not acceptable, the person is punished. This is like saying that if it rains, the ground will become wet and the vegetation will grow, but, if it does not rain, the ground will remain parched and the vegetation die. It makes the consequences of human action (or inaction) a scientific hypothesis. Wittgenstein sees human action and its consequences as a matter of choice, not of predetermined decree. For this reason he opposed the doctrine of predestination so long and vigorously. For this reason, too, he urged himself (and anyone who might read his remarks) to struggle, to fight, to make an effort to stay within the religious sphere by not accepting the doctrine that our ultimate destiny is outside our control, *pace* St Paul, St Augustine and Calvin.

Thus, though Wittgenstein's thoughts on predestination may seem to be peripheral to his ideas on ethics and religious belief, they are central to it. In his remarks on predestination, Wittgenstein reaffirms what he said about the will in *Notebooks 1914–1916* and the *Tractatus*. More than that, he clearly unites the free action of the will with the religious sphere. This is most important. In effect, what Wittgenstein is saying is that, if there is no free will there is no ethics and no morality. But, more importantly, there is no religion either.

12

Whatever Happened to Ethics?

Before concluding, a word must be said about the paucity of references to ethics in Wittgenstein's later writings and reported utterances. Apart from Rush Rhees's 'Some Development in Wittgenstein's View of Ethics' (*PRv* pp. 17–26) and some unconnected remarks in his *Notebooks*, Wittgenstein had little to say on ethics in the later period. This calls for some explanation. Various explanations suggest themselves, and there are various combinations of these suggested explanations. Breaking them down to their simplest, the most obvious are:

1 Wittgenstein had lost interest in ethics.
2 His views had not changed, but it was not necessary to say this, as he had said all he had to say and had nothing to add.
3 His thinking on ethics had been absorbed into his views on religious belief.
4 He had abandoned his earlier account of ethics.
5 He had adopted a new, relativistic account of ethics consonant with his notions of language-games and forms of life, but it was not necessary to talk about it explicitly.

None of these explanations taken in itself stands up to what scanty evidence we have.

It is clear that he had not lost *all* interest in ethical matters, not only from Rush Rhees's report, but also from his ethical remarks, sparse though they are. This might be an appropriate place to discuss them. We encountered one in the last chapter in connection with the doctrine of predestination. It has to do with the teaching of ethics. To teach children that there is a being who has arranged that some people lead lives that will bring them to everlasting torment is, according to Wittgenstein, no way to teach ethics.

If you wanted to bring someone up ethically while yet teaching him such a doctrine, you would have to teach it to him *after* having educated him ethically, representing it as a sort of incomprehensible mystery (*CV* p. 81).

Here Wittgenstein is not only interested in ethics but in a clear demarcation line between ethics and religious belief. While he firmly held that, from an ethical point of view (as human beings understand ethics) the doctrine of predestination is monstrously unethical (or just monstrous and non-ethical), he is ready to concede that it is a 'sort of incomprehensible mystery', as understood by religious believers. And he implies – though he does not state this – that this is acceptable within the language-game of religious belief. In other words, though, as he says repeatedly, the doctrine is obnoxious to humane ethics – our human sense of justice and fair play – these considerations cannot be decisive in religious matters. This is a substantial contribution to his thinking on ethics.

In a later entry in 1950 he makes an interesting contribution to ethics, brief though it is, in discussing the effects of circumstances and environment on ethical character. He asks: 'How *could* a man, the ethical man, be *coerced* by his environment?' (*CV* p. 84). 'No human being has to give way to compulsion', yet under such circumstances he *will* as a matter of fact in such and such a way. 'You don't *HAVE* to, I can show you a (different) way out – but you won't take it' (ibid.). The tantalizing thing about these remarks is that they avoid so many issues and leave so much unsaid.

We could say that no one, even if he yields to circumstances in every instance, is being *morally* coerced by the environment. *Moral* coercion is a contradiction in terms. There are such things as moral pressure and moral blackmail, but not moral coercion. Coercion can only be either physical or psychological. No physical or psychological forces can get someone to alter their moral views. Only persuasion or argument can do that. There is, of course, physiological manipulation, but that renders the patient incapable of acting as an agent, and, hence, of acting morally at all. If someone lives in an environment where theft and even murder and prostitution are regarded as normal practice, it may be that he or she *will* come to accept these practices. But, again, this need not be so. However, the most important antitheses are between being morally *coerced* and *giving way to compulsion*. Perhaps what Wittgenstein is saying is that giving way to compulsion leads to the moral persuasion that what one has done is morally all right; and this amounts to moral coercion. But this is not convincing. The remark is obscure. However, it is at least evidence of Wittgenstein's interest in ethical questions right to the end of his life.

That his views on ethics did not change, but that it was not necessary to say this, and that he had nothing to add to what he had said earlier, is more problematical. That he *added* nothing to what he had said in the *Notebooks*, the *Tractatus* and the 'Lecture on Ethics' is beyond cavil. His remarks on religous belief and his notion of language-games and forms of life could be said, in spite of opinions to the contrary, to be *extensions* of his views on ethics. But this can be questioned.

The third explanation – that in his later period, ethics is absorbed into his discussion of religious belief and therefore does not need to be treated separately – is more promising. We have already seen how closely Wittgenstein's views on predestination are tied into ethical considerations. His whole later account of religious belief involves ethics in so far as it involves a way of living. This may not be ethics strictly so-called (that is, narrowly so-called); and it may not be justifiable on rational grounds. But, be that as it may in these remarks the two are closely interwoven.

His most fundamental remark, dated 1929, is: 'What is good is also divine. Queer as it sounds, that sums up my ethics. Only something supernatural can express the Supernatural' (*CV* p. 3). Here Wittgenstein virtually, if not actually, states the connection between ethics and religious belief. My hesitation in saying that he does not actually make the connection is because, while ethics may be supernatural (a view with which I fully concur), it is not clear whether the divine and the Supernatural is to be identified with any particular deity or religious belief. However, the important point is that the good is divine, that something supernatural expresses the Supernatural and that this sums up Wittgenstein's ethics. But it must be said that this remark, dated 1929, is contemporaneous with the 'Lecture on Ethics', so it may or may not be evidence of his further thinking.

There is a remarkable entry for 1944, the last year of World War II, that sums up in a weird way this relationship of ethics and religion. It begins:

> The Christian religion is only for the man who needs infinite help, solely, that is, for the man who experiences infinite torment.
> The whole planet can suffer no greater torment than a *single* soul.
> The Christian faith – as I see it – is a man's refuge in this *ultimate* torment. (*CV* p. 46).[1]

This is not only a spectacularly dramatic way of presenting Christianity – and, for all that, a true way – but also a spectacularly dramatic way to present ethics. Ethics is put firmly into a religious context. (Let's not worry whether it is Christian, Judaic, Muslim, Hindu or whatever – it is religious.) The remark continues:

> Anyone in such torment who has the gift of opening his heart, rather than contracting it, accepts the means of salvation in his heart. (*CV* ibid.)

But it is the remainder of the entry that is of the greatest interest and significance for ethics. According to Wittgenstein the person who penitently lays his heart open to God, also opens it to other people. As a penitent he puts himself on a par with them. He can no longer stand on his dignity or use his official position, his reputation, his status, to distance himself from others. To open oneself to others requires a special kind of love, a love that acknowledges we are all, as it were, bad children. But though we must remain ashamed of our innermost selves, we do not have to be ashamed of ourselves before our fellow men.

Wittgenstein draws two conclusions from this that are not only true but profoundly so, and, if not entirely original in themselves, are original in their context and presentation. They are, first, that there is no greater misery (*Not*) than that suffered by one man (*von Einem Menschen*), 'for if a man feels lost, that is the greatest misery' (ibid.).[2]

This is in keeping with the modern version of Hell. Hell is on earth. The person, left alone with himself in the company of others to whom, for one reason or another – pride, self-importance, contempt for his fellows – he cannot or does not open himself in humility and penitence as a sinner like all the rest, is in Hell. Sartre offered the reverse of this in *Huis Clos* (*In Camera* or *Behind Closed Doors*), written about the time of Wittgenstein's entry. In that play three characters are in what Sartre calls 'bad faith'. They confront and destroy each other precisely because each wants what he or she cannot get from the other. They destroy each other with hatred, a hatred that will know no end, since they are everlastingly closeted together. Their plight is summed up in the words: *Pas besoin de gril, l'Enfer c'est les Autres* (scene five: 'No need of a grid-iron, Hell is other people'). For the lonely person whose loneliness is due to not humbly opening himself up to other people in love and trust, other people become his torment and his Hell on earth.

Wittgenstein's second conclusion has to do with the same theme: hatred. Hatred, he says, comes from cutting ourselves off from each other. The reason for this, he says, is that we do want other people to see inside us, since it is not a pretty sight. But is it not a pretty sight inside the other person either. However, instead of being open and admitting that we are all bad children together, the person with hatred in his heart, either through global misanthropy or personal vindictiveness, attempts to ferret out the inner shames of others while protecting his own. That, at least, is how Wittgenstein seems to see it. But we can go further. Hatred may lead some people to run the risk of personal exposure as the price to pay for exposing the object of their hate.

Another interesting entry appears two years later in 1946. It is linked with the foregoing and has ethico-religious implications. Once again it is connected with Sartrean ideas of good and bad faith, though its resolution is not something that Sartre would have easily accepted. It is to do with analysing one's motives:

> It is hard to understand oneself correctly, since the same (action) which one *could* do out of generous and good (motives), one can do out of cowardice or indifference. (*CV* p. 48. My italics)

Similarly the self-same action can be done out of genuine love or out of deceitfulness and a cold heart. And Wittgenstein adds perceptively that not all gentleness is good. Sartre, and Heidegger before him, offer no solution to this problem. They exhort us to be authentic and genuine and to act in good faith, but they do not offer us any means by which we can avoid bad faith and unauthentic actions. Their analysis of the ethical problem is fine, as far as it goes, but they have nothing to offer by way of a remedy to rectify our defective attitude of mind. This Wittgenstein does have. But his remedy would hardly have appealed to either Heidegger or Sartre, and, since it did not see the light of day until 1977 (German edition) and 1980 (English and revised German edition), Heidegger could not have read it (he died in 1976) and Sartre was unlikely to have read or been affected by it. The reason is that it appeals to religion to solve an ethical problem. Wittgenstein says:

> And only if I were able to submerge myself in religion could these doubts be silenced. Because only religion can destroy vanity and penetrate all the crevices. (*CV* ibid. My translation)

If I understand Wittgenstein correctly, what he is saying is what he said in another passage in an entry previously quoted (*CV* p. 46), that religion, by inducing a humble, penitent attitude in its adherents, puts them in a favourable frame of mind not only to be open with their fellow human beings, but also to stop probing into their own motives for action. However, that is not quite as simple as it sounds.

In the first place we may ask how destroying vanity cures us of anxiety about our motives? Secondly, what are the crevices or 'nooks and crannies' (Winch) that religion penetrates? As to the first, there is a sort of vanity in worrying about the purity of one's motives. The Jansenist nuns of Port Royal in Paris in the seventeenth century were accused of it. They were said to be as pure as angels (which, presumably, they were) and as proud as devils. Their pride was in their own righteousness, the purity of their intentions. But people who pride themselves on the purity of their intentions worry about whether their intentions are pure or not, whether they are being genuinely kind or just pretending, whether they may not even be unintentionally cruel in doing kind acts. And so on. On the other hand, the person who knows that he is sinful and basically a rotter has no such anxieties. If his motives happen to be pure, that, as Wittgenstein would say, is a grace of Fate. He does his best and hopes for the best. But if he is hell-bent on discovering his true motives, the sincere penitential act of preparing himself to make a good confession (examination of conscience) will root out bad and less good motives (the crevices, the nooks and crannies of the soul), since he is not inhibited by self-esteem and is prepared to face the can of worms that writhes in his innermost self.

However, to say that in his later thinking on ethics Wittgenstein subsumed it under religious belief, and, hence did not speak or write of it exclusively, would be a false conclusion. It is belied by his remarks to Rush Rhees, for one thing. Religion (for example, Christian teaching on divorce) is mentioned, but almost incidentally. So, while it is true that in his later period Wittgenstein emphasized the intimate connection between ethics and religion (implicit in his earlier period), he does not subordinate it to religion, nor is it entirely subsumed under religious practice and ways of life.

The next explanation – that Wittgenstein had, or should have, abandoned his earlier account of ethics – can take various forms. Some of these have already been discussed in chapter six. There is, first, the argument from silence. As we have seen, the silence was not absolute. Wittgenstein did discuss ethical matters, whether on their own account or in relation to religion. But he did not discuss ethics in relation to language-games, forms of life and philosophical grammar in anything like the way he discussed religious belief. He did not, for instance, offer a short course of lectures on ethics in the light of his post-Tractarian ideas, as he did on aesthetics and religious belief. But, like all arguments from silence, this proves little or nothing. Indeed, as the second explanation argues, it can be interpreted as no change in his views and nothing to add. However, to an outsider, not one of Wittgenstein's former disciples, it does seem strange that no one except Rhees tackled him on this question. Perhaps it is too much to expect undergraduates, or even graduates, who may not have had the time to absorb the seeming conflict between his earlier and later ideas on language, and were not then privy to the contents of the *Notebooks 1914–1916* to raise ethical matters.

The more serious argument is that, given the abandonment of the picture theory and the adoption of the notion of language-games and forms of life, Wittgenstein either abandoned his earlier account of ethics or ought to have done so. Let us, therefore, remind ourselves of the contents of that account. The principal ingredients were: ethics is (a) transcendental, (b) inexpressible in (factual) propositions, (c) actions seen *sub specie aeternitatis*, (d) concerned with absolute, not relative, value and (e) non-utilitarian, not concerned with ends and means, rewards and punishments. Of these, as we have seen in chapter six, only (b) and (d) are open to question in the light of Wittgenstein's new account of language. It was argued there that by being a 'language-game' a form of expression does not *eo ipso* become expressible. It may be a language-game of the inexpressible. The game may be to show rather than to say, just as it was in the *Tractatus* period, as is evident from his treatment of aesthetics and belief. There is nothing in Wittgenstein's writings or recorded utterances to the contrary. This, like the argument from silence, is scarcely conclusive; but it is somewhat stronger. If he were to repudiate the inexpressibility of ethics, he surely would not have done so by silence. There is at least a case to be made out for why his view changed. Such a case was not made out, because it could not be. Whatever about the picture theory of language, which *supported* the notion of ethics as inexpressible, Wittgenstein remained committed to the view that expressions of value are not statements of fact, that is, of empirically verifiable states of affairs. This is clear from everything he said and is reported to have said, as already discussed in this book. (d), however, poses a problem that has to be dealt with under the heading of the fifth explanation, though this, too, has been partially dealt with already.

The fifth explanation supplements the fourth by offering an alternative account of ethics from that found in Wittgenstein's earlier period. This is the suggestion that, with the notions of language-games and forms of life, Wittgenstein adopted a relativistic attitude towards ethics and abandoned the notion of ethics as absolute value. This, as has been argued in chapter six, is unsustainable. Wittgenstein held a moderate and reasonable form of ethical relativism: namely that, where there are moral conflicts, there is no supervening, overriding, and absolute, in that sense, criterion or principle that would decide, once and for all, between conflicting views. This is perfectly compatible with the view that moral positions must be held absolutely. If we hold that abortion at the whim of the pregnant woman, without reference to circumstances (as a form of '*post factum* contraception'), is morally wrong and tantamount to murder, we can hold this absolutely as the correct view and regard all other views as mistaken. And yet we can accept that our own view *may* be too rigid, and, hence incorrect, though we do not see how it can be incorrect. This is quite different from saying that if Daisy has an abortion whenever she gets pregnant, for no other reason than that she does not want to have babies but cannot be bothered to use contraceptives, that is all right *for her*. Wittgenstein does not say anything like that, nor is he committed to saying such a thing by his notions of language-games and forms of life.

But what of the other features of ethics described in the earlier writings: its transcendental nature and its inexpressibility? As I have argued elsewhere, neither of these features are affected by the notion of language-games and forms of life, or by Wittgenstein's version of relativism. If we extrapolate from what he said about religious belief – which is surely legitimate in view of the bond between ethics and religion established in his later thinking, largely due, it may be added, to his regarding them in the light of language-games and forms of life – it should be clear that these two features persist. In the case of religious belief, as we have seen, that is obvious. Its non-rationality is due precisely to the fact that it is an attempt to transcend facts or evidence and say what in rational terms cannot be said. Significance is given to a birth, a death, an empty tomb that would not be given to ordinary births and deaths and empty tombs. There is no way of arguing: virgin conception and birth, therefore Son of God; or innocent death on trumped-up charges (and the contemptuous, yet legally damaging, inscription 'The King of the Jews'), therefore Redeemer of Mankind; or empty tomb, therefore risen from the dead and living among us. If there is truth in these claims, it transcends ordinary reasoning, and, in so doing, it is about what is outside the world, not about what is in it. In that sense, at least, it is transcendental. It is also inexpressible in that it is not stating facts in the sense of either empirical observations or verifiable theories.

How does all this apply to ethics? After all, Wittgenstein never described ethics in his later period as non-rational or as not based on sufficient evidence. That argument cuts both ways. He did not describe the ethical as rational, as he might well have done, since that is the traditional way of describing ethics in philosophy: it is called 'rational behaviour'. Since he was silent on the matter, other suggestions can be brought into play. Mine are that were he to have discussed ethics in his later writings in the way in which he discussed religious belief, the result, obviously, would not have been exactly the same, but similar. I shall attempt to construct the way it might have gone.

Let us say that the question is: is it wrong to kill innocent people because they are Jews or gypsies or Kurds or Armenians, and as such do not fit in to our culture and ethos? And let us say that the reply is that it is not only wrong, but a vile and dastardly thing to do. Now, suppose you are asked what evidence you have for this course of action being morally wrong: what evidence would you produce? What would your reaction be? Something from bewilderment to indignation, I should hope. Evidence? What kind of evidence? That Jews, gypsies, Kurds and Armenians do not *like* being massacred and that it distresses the survivors? But if by massacring them you get rid of a persistent nuisance, what is wrong with that? We drown kittens and cull seals, trap moles and poison rats, so what is wrong with getting rid of human beings that disturb our way of life? Whatever about animals, our intuition is that it is morally wrong to kill innocent human beings. And yet what are the *rational* grounds for not doing so? There are pragmatic grounds, surely. Jews and Armenians are a nuisance because they are too astute in buisness matters. Gypsies are a nuisance because they will not settle down – they are nomads in a static society. Kurds want to disrupt frontiers and carve out and form parts of Turkey, Iraq and Iran into a separate state, Kurdistan. All this is irritating, but it does not count as a sufficient reason for massacring these people. They are morally innocent. It may be a good pragmatic and political reason, and may in the end lead to the pragmatic resolution (however that may be calculated) of a balance of happiness over unhappiness (however that is justified). This, however, does not count as *evidence* for the *morality* of such a course of action, and nothing counts as evidence against it. So morality is in the same situation as religious belief. It is not rational. Nothing that could ordinarily be adduced as evidence can count either for or against an ethical position. How, then, could Wittgenstein's view of ethics change from being transcendental (beyond facts) and inexpressible (not explicable in terms of facts)? Once transcendental and inexpressible, ethics remained ever thus in Wittgenstein's mind. This is made clear in the only lengthy document on ethics that survives from the later period: Rush Rhees's report.

The report begins with a reminder of what Wittgenstein said in the *Tractatus* and the 'Lecture on Ethics': what we might describe as the kernel of Wittgenstein's earlier ideas on ethics – that it is not expressible in propositions that can be true or false; that it does not express relative but absolute values. But Rhees sees changes taking place even in the 'Lecture on Ethics'. In particular it is the introduction of examples. This Rhees says was impossible when, in the Tractarian period, Wittgenstein laid down what could and could not be said. I cannot entirely agree with this. Wittgenstein does give an example of the mystical in the *Tractatus* (*TLP* 6.44) – 'that a world exists' – on which he elaborates in the 'Lecture on Ethics'. Rhees might argue that this is not so much an example as a fundamental statement amounting almost to a definition of the mystical. Wittgenstein certainly refers to it as his experience *par excellence* and his first and foremost example. And it must be conceded that Rhees is right when he says that the lecture 'starts from examples *more* than the *Tractatus* does' (*PRv* p. 19. My italics).

What Rhees failed to notice was that giving examples was a necessary consequence of the views on ethics that Wittgenstein had expressed in the *Notebooks 1914–16* and the *Tractatus*. In these writings he had said that expressions of ethical value could be shown, but not stated or described as we describe the weight, shape and size of a cannonball. But how do we *show* ethical (and, for that matter, aesthetic and religious) value? By examples. By paradigm cases. Nothing is said, everything is shown, as if one were to say: 'This is how it is, but you have to discover what it is for yourself.' Hence the accumulation of examples in Wittgenstein's later work. Alas, there are too few moral problems in Wittgenstein's later work. But that there are some is sufficient for our purposes.

Rhees, commenting on Wittgenstein's earlier notion of an ethical judgement, such as a moral rebuke, as having significance 'beyond any circumstances' says that, if it is justified, we can understand what is meant by 'going beyond'. But he complains that in the *Tractatus* Wittgenstein does not make clear the occasions or the problems in connection with which someone might make such judgements. Although the *Tractatus* speaks of the 'problems of life', he says, it does not ask when and in what circumstances anyone would speak of the problems of life. And he adds: 'We are not *always* viewing actions as we do in a judgement of value' (*PRv* p. 21).

To take the last remark first: this may or may not be true. Aquinas favoured the view that all actions are viewed morally, at least implicitly, so that provided there are no circumstances prohibiting them on moral grounds, such trivial actions as brushing one's teeth or buying bread or playing tennis badly are morally good actions. Leaving this aside, it is surely the case that whenever we judge actions *morally* we are *always* viewing them from the point of view of their value. But Rhees is more concerned with finding some criterion or, at least, some model by which to decide what are ethical problems and what are not. This, he says, Wittgenstein does not provide in the *Tractatus*. That is true. But, then, the *Tractatus*, whatever about its moral tone, was not a moral treatise. Wittgenstein could assume that people knew what were the problems of life and the circumstances in which these become acute. In the *Tractatus* he was merely concerned with the logical status of judgements of moral value, not with examples of the circumstances in which they come into play.

That Wittgenstein in his lecture on ethics, and subsequently, did give examples, does not strike me as having quite the significance that Rhees attached to it. It certainly marked a change of style and a welcome change, as Rhees notes, but not a radical change. However, as Rhees reports, it provides not only additional evidence (from that provided in his *Notebooks*) of his continued interest in ethics, but, as Rhees' title states, some *developments* in his view of ethics.

What is of great interest in Rhees' report is a remark made to him by Wittgenstein in 1942. He says it was strange that you could find textbooks on ethics in which there were no genuine ethical problems. His test of a genuine moral problem was one that was capable of solution. Three examples are cited: two that, in Wittgenstein's view, are not genuine moral problems, and one that is.

The first example is the killing of Julius Caesar by Brutus (Rhees' example). Was it a noble act, as Plutarch thought, or a particularly evil one, as Dante thought? The second example was provided by Kierkegaard: has a man a right to let himself be put to death for the truth? Wittgenstein's reason for not considering these as genuine moral problems was that we have no way of solving them, since we have no way of knowing what went on in Brutus' mind when he killed Caesar, nor what goes on in the mind of someone who allows himself to be put to death for the truth. We do not know how much discussion went on about these examples beyond what Rhees reports, but, from what I can recollect when talking to him in 1966, nothing more seems to have been said. I raise this point because a great deal more might have been said, though Wittgenstein's conclusion might not have changed.

The two examples are similar. They have to do with motives and intentions, but the first, the case of Brutus, has to do with an actual individual's motives, reasons and intentions; the second has to do with the motives, reasons and intentions of a hypothetical individual. Moreover, the two examples can be taken in two different ways, though there is good reason to believe that Wittgenstein would have taken them in only one of these ways. The first way is the one he himself took: that is to ask about the actual state of mind of an actual individual, whether Brutus or a possible martyr, someone prepared to die for the truth. The second way is to ask about the morality of the action itself, irrespective of which individual is the agent. It is not clear whether Plutarch and Dante were going the same way or different ways. Asking whether Brutus' act of treachery was noble could mean: was his action, by transcending friendship for the public interest, a noble action, or would it be for anyone to do such an act, whatever the motives, a noble action? My inclination is to say that Plutarch meant the former. Certainly Wittgenstein did. He is quoted as saying: ' "You would not know for your life what went on in his mind before he decided to kill Caesar. What would he have had to feel in order that you should say that killing his friend was noble?" ' (*PRv* p. 22, with footnote). It is highly likely that Dante, with his scholastic background, was taking the other way and asking whether it was not evil in itself for someone, whatever his motives, to kill a head of state, whatever his totalitarian pretensions, leaving friendship aside.

What is more interesting is Wittgenstein's position on the hypothetical case of the person asking whether it is permissible to allow oneself to be put to death for the truth. (This, incidentally, was a 'problem' that exercised the mind of Sir Thomas More. He resolved it by saying that he had not courted death but incurred it merely by remaining true to his principles.) Wittgenstein is reported as saying: ' "For me this is not even a problem. I don't know that (sic) it would be *like* to let oneself be put to death for the truth..." ' (ibid.). But what, it may be asked, have our feelings to do with the ethics of what we are doing? In the case of Brutus it is relevant to ask what his state of mind, his motives, reasons and intentions were. If he killed Caesar out of jealousy, ambition, malice or blood lust, it could hardly be construed as a noble action. But the action he perpetrated, whatever its motives, was the assassination, the murder of a head of state. *Prime facie* it was an evil action. It may be turned into noble one by extenuating circumstances, such as the demands of the body politic, the necessity to stop a potential tyrant in his tracks, and so forth; but in itself it is an evil action.

In the case of the martyr, circumstances should play a lesser part. Either it is moral or it is immoral to allow ourselves to be killed for the truth. On the face of it, it would appear that there is nothing immoral about acting in that way. Indeed, it would seem to be morally heroic. Yet there could be circumstances where this kind of action, heroic though it might be, is unfair to our wife, children, family and friends. All these matters have to be taken into consideration. To say, as Wittgenstein does, 'For me this is not even a problem' is quite extraordinary. Even by his criterion of solubility, it is a problem at least at the level of generality and the *prima facie*. However, Wittgenstein did not see moral problems that way: as general *ceteris paribus* problems. For one thing, he did not believe in formulated general principles or, as he called it, 'ethical theory'. For another, he believed that moral problems can only arise in concrete situations. Where these situations are hypothetical and cannot be envisaged, no problem can arise.

Wittgenstein states this position at some length, and, since he says so little about ethics compared with what he says about religious belief, what he says is worth quoting in full.

I do not know how such a man would have to feel, what state of mind he would be in, and so forth. This may reach a point at which the whole problem wavers and ceases to be a problem at all. Like asking which of two sticks is longer when they are seen through the 'shimmer' of air rising from a hot pavement. You say, 'But surely one of them *must* be longer.' How are we to understand this? (*PRv* ibid.)

A traditional moral philosopher might well be baffled by what Wittgenstein has to say. He might agree it is not unreasonable to examine Brutus' motives for killing Caesar in order to determine whether the action was noble or particularly evil. In doing so we would be working with a reasonably clear notion of what constitutes a noble as against an evil action, and some idea of what makes an action particularly evil. But if there is no way of gaining access to Brutus' motives, then the question of whether his action was noble or particularly evil, or just evil, does not arise. It is not a genuine moral problem. At most it is an insoluble historico-moral question, like asking whether Hitler, Himmler and Goebbels were really evil or misguided or mad, and, hence, not responsible for their actions.

When we turn to Kierkegaard's case, the traditional moral philosopher would probably say that, while we cannot give all the conditions under which it is moral to allow ourselves to be put to death for the truth and all the conditions under which it is not, what the person feels, what his state of mind is, is irrelevant. The traditionalist might well be perplexed by the notion that our *feelings* and *state of mind* play any part in determining the morality of our *actions as such*.

> The last temptation is the greatest treason:
> To do the right deed for the wrong reason.
> T. S. Eliot: *Murder in the Cathedral*

It is possible that someone might die for the truth out of spite, out of malice or for some other wrong reason such as vanity. But though their action might have been bad, contaminated by motive and intention, it was not necessarily in itself a bad thing to do: it may have been the right deed in the circumstance or in any circumstance.

But Wittgenstein is perfectly justified in concentrating his attention on the agent and *his* action rather than on the nature of the action in itself in the abstract. This is entirely in keeping with his earlier ideas. In the *Notebooks 1914–1916* and the *Tractatus*, he was interested in the will as the bearer of moral good or evil, and in the moral subject as being either the happy or the unhappy man. It would be an exaggeration to say that the morality of the action itself did not interest him. There is no evidence, for instance, that he supported the idea that a bad deed done for a good reason (the good end justifying the bad means) would have had his approval. After all, he was prepared to say that the morally good is what God commands rather than that God commands and can only command what, by some other criteria, is good. What he objected to was that there are some non-ethical criteria by which ethical values can be judged (just as he objected to the notion of psychological or other non-aesthetic criteria being used to determine judgements of aesthetic value). One way of firmly establishing non-naturalistic ethics was to place heavy emphasis on the will, on motivation and intention. This naturally leads to a consideration of the subject's mental state and feelings.

One of the advantages of Wittgenstein's subjectivist, personalist, phenomenological approach is that it brings out the greyness of moral judgements. This must concern the judiciary where natural justice stands against the letter of the law, and, even within the strict letter of the law, has to hold a reasonable balance. *Ultimately*, if a moral judgement has to be passed on an action, it is on the knowledge and will of the person acting. Someone may perform a bad deed for a bad or for a good reason. The reason itself does not affect the moral status of the action as such. Willing the death of an innocent human being is evil. Allowing ourselves to be put to death for the truth is not evil on the face of it. Assuming that Brutus acted for the purest of motives, his action could be justified (and, as events proved, was justified, since Caesar's successor, Augustus, betrayed the Roman Republic and set up a totalitarian state) on the grounds of justifiable regicide or tyrannicide. Prima facie what he and his fellow conspirators did was an evil act, but, granted that they sincerely believed that what Caesar was about to do would have been a betrayal of Roman society as it had existed since the Tarquins, it was a justifiable act. There comes a time when someone ceases to be innocent, not for what he has done but for what he can reasonably be seen to be about to do. In law, alas, it is not permissible, except in a few cases (actions liable to lead to a breach of the peace), to act to prevent evil. Morally this is not only justifiable (whatever the legal consequences) but sometimes obligatory.

In other words, we do not have to look into a person's soul, read his innermost thoughts, his state of mind or feelings in order to judge the morality of *what* he has done. We can assume his motives were pure and judge his action on its merits, taking into account the circumstances in which it occurred. In this way we can solve the moral problem that confronted Brutus and Sir Thomas More, perhaps not satisfactorily, but yet sufficiently well to satisfy reasonable doubt.

However, that was not Wittgenstein's way. In his later years Wittgenstein inclined to an ethical position similar to that of Heidegger and Sartre.[3] His example of a genuine moral problem is quite Sartrean, and, to my mind, not a moral problem at all. It is the case already cited of the man who has to choose between leaving his wife or giving up cancer research.

This case is similar to the, by now, classical case in *Existentialism and Humanism* of the young man who had to decide between leaving his aged mother or joining the free French forces under de Gaulle in order to free his country and redeem its honour.[4] Unlike Sartre, however, Wittgenstein believes that this is a genuine problem capable of solution. Sartre 'solves' (or rather resolves) his problem by saying that the solution is to choose. The implication of this is (a) there is no *a priori* right choice, and (b) whatever choice a person makes is the right choice, since the right thing to do is to *choose* and not to equivocate, to compromise or to fudge the issue. Therein lies bad faith.

The operative factor in Wittgenstein's account of his case is the genuineness of the man's decision. It is not a moral problem as the traditional ethics textbooks understand them, but, like Existentialists' problems, one of conscience. As Rhees describes it, there is a dialectic: 'Such a man's attitude will vary at different times.' First, there is what Wittgenstein calls the 'ethical attitude': 'Look, you've taken this girl out of her home, and now, by God, you've got to stick to her.' The man's response might be: 'But what of suffering humanity? How can I abandon my research?' In saying this, Wittgenstein comments in the style of a good Ignatian confessor, 'he may be making it easy for himself: he wants to carry on that work anyway'. The reason for saying this is that others could carry on the work without him. However, pursuing this line, he might comfort himself with the thought that leaving his wife would not be fatal to her: 'She'll get over it, probably marry again,' and so on.

Continuing his phenomenological investigation of deliberation on a tricky moral, in the sense of *mores* (way of living), rather than ethical (what is the absolutely right thing to do?) problem, Wittgenstein says that, though the man might have a deep love for his wife, yet he might think that, if he gave up his work, 'he would be no husband for her'. His work is his life and, if he gives it up, 'he will drag her down'. From here on Wittgenstein's account sounds curious to the traditional moral philosopher, but perfectly consistent with his own ethics. He says, first: 'Here we may say we have all the materials of a tragedy; and we could say: "Well, God help you".' This makes it a problem of living rather than an ethical problem. Sartre's problem is precisely that. This is made abundantly clear by what Wittgenstein goes on to say about this unfortunate man:

Whatever he finally does, the way things then turn out may affect his attitude. He may say, 'Well, thank God I left her; it was better all around.' Or maybe, 'Thank God I stuck to her.' Or he may not be able to say 'thank God' at all but just the opposite. (*PRv* p. 23)

How we *feel* as a result of a decision that we make, thinking that it is the ethically right decision, would, then, affect the *ethics* of the decision. This seems to be what Wittgenstein means, since he goes on to say: 'I want to say that this is a solution to an ethical problem.' But what *ethical* problem? one may ask.

It is evident that for Wittgenstein 'ethics' did not mean what it meant for Socrates, Plato, Aristotle, the Stoics, Augustine, Aquinas and later moral philosophers. It is to do with a satisfactory way of living: the happy life, being at one with the world, etc. This does not exclude fulfilling our obligations. After all, to fail in our obligations may be a source of unhappiness. But not to flout them on occasion might also be a source of unhappiness. Hence: 'Well, thank God I left her, it was better all round.' This might lead us to the conclusion that Wittgenstein's ethics were not ethical at all.

What Wittgenstein says next might sound like a confirmation of that criticism. He says: 'Or rather: it is so with regard to the man who does not have an ethics' (*PRv* p. 23). By this, however, he does not mean that these people do not have ethical concepts or principles, as Sartre seems to say, but they are not *formulated* like rules of thumb or regulations in a handbook. Like Sartre's young man, the scientist has to choose. Like Sartre's young man, he has no guidelines to help him in his choice. But, unlike Sartre's young man (or how he is made to appear), his choice is not blind. Whichever way he chooses, provided he is not deceiving himself ('making it easy for himself'), he has sound ethical reasons for his choice. If he decides to leave his wife, it may be for the good of humanity which he thinks he is uniquely qualified to further, or (perhaps more honestly) because, if he gave up his job, 'he would be no husband for her'. On the other hand, if he decides to stay with her, this could be because he regards his duty as loyalty to the woman he has chosen, whom, when she was a girl, he took 'out of her home', and whom he loves deeply, to outweigh his obligation to suffering mankind. So each of these decisions are ethical, but they are not dictated by rigid ethical principles. The man freely and personally chooses which principle should apply in his case. His choice is not dictated by theory.[5]

I am not sure that this might not be a position that Sartre would have adopted. It is perfectly compatible with his and Heidegger's notion of authenticity and good faith. Admittedly Wittgenstein does not put the same emphasis on authenticity and self-deception that the Existentialists do, but both their problems and the solutions (or resolutions) are similar. At least they have in common the notion that, in certain cases, there are no ready solutions to moral dilemmas. How could there be if they are dilemmas?

However, Wittgenstein's view of what I call traditional moral philosophy and what he calls 'an ethics' or an 'ethical theory', which amounts to a code of conduct rather than an *ad hoc* solution to a moral problem, is rather naïve. He says: 'If he has the Christian ethics, then he may say it is absolutely clear: he has got to stick with her come what may' (ibid.). In this hypothetical case this may be true, since he loves his wife deeply and she has done no wrong. But this would not hold in all cases. Even Christians can separate from their wives, though, unless the circumstances are exceptional, they cannot remarry within the code. However, Wittgenstein is making a clear and valid point. It is that if we have a moral code, even though it is flexible, we are spared the agonizing that someone who does not have a code experiences. We are not free of moral problems, but they are different. They are 'how to be a decent husband in these greatly altered circumstances' and so forth. So for Wittgenstein a moral problem is how we should act in a given situation, that is, whether what we do is good or bad *in concreto*, not *in abstracto*. This is a phenomenological, if not an existentialist, approach to ethics, and, as such, perfectly valid. And it is certainly a development in his ethical thinking. Does it amount to a repudiation of his earlier notions of ethics as transcendental, inexpressible and concerned with absolute value? As I have already said, I think not. But let us consider this further.

What follows has already been discussed in part in chapter seven where Wittgenstein's alleged relativism was considered. To repeat it briefly, Wittgenstein raises the hypothetical question whether Christian ethics is the *right* one or not, and replies that this question does not make sense. This, on the face of it, may seem odd coming from the man who is reported to have said: 'If there is any proposition expressing precisely what I think, it is the proposition "What God commands, that is good" ' (*WWK* p. 115). However, as I have argued, this remark was intended to underline the relativity of ethical judgements, to emphasize the fact that there is no rule of thumb, no objective, overriding principle that will decide which ethical system is *the right* one. Ethics, like aesthetics, religious belief and all other matters concerning value, requires judgement, the balancing of reasons for and against. There can be no substitute for this extremely fine and difficult balancing act. Wittgenstein said this briefly in 1930 and more fully in 1942 and 1945.

Here I can flesh out what was summarized in chapter seven and begin to draw this lengthy discussion of Wittgenstein's thoughts on ethics to a conclusion. On the question of the rightness of an ethical system – Christian ethics as against the ethics of Nietzsche (or, more accurately, ethics as described by Nietzsche), for example – he says:

> But we do not know what this decision would be like – how it would be determined, what sort of criteria would be used, and so on. Compare saying that it must be possible to decide which of two standards of accuracy is the right one. We do not even know what a person who asks this question is after. (*PRv* ibid.)

In some cases we know precisely what a person who wants a standard of accuracy is after, and any one that works is the right one. But Wittgenstein's point (and, after all, he is only being reported) is that it is not necessarily *the* (the only) right one, nor could it be. So the analogy holds. This is confirmed by the report of a later conversation in 1945 when Wittgenstein said:

> suppose someone says, 'One of the ethical systems must be the right one – or nearer to the right one.' Well, suppose I say Christian ethics is the right one. Then I am making a judgement of value. It amounts to *adopting* Christian ethics. It is not like saying that one of these physical theories must be the right one. The way in which some reality corresponds – or conflicts – with a physical theory has no counterpart here. (*PRv* p. 24)

This, as I see it, is exactly the same position Wittgenstein took in the *Notebooks 1914–1916* and the *Tractatus*. There he said that ethical value has nothing to do with facts. Here he is saying exactly the same:

> Someone may say, 'There is still the difference between truth and falsity. Any ethical judgement in whatever system may be true or false.' . . . If I say: 'Although I believe that so and so is good, I may be wrong': this says no more than that what we assert can be denied.' (*PRv* ibid.)

There then follows the passages, already quoted in chapter seven, where Wittgenstein says that in saying there are various systems of ethics you are not saying that they are all equally right, nor that each person's ethical system is right from his own standpoint. That means no more than that each person judges as he does.

Rush Rhees concludes his account by comparing it with what Wittgenstein was writing about language and logic, particularly those notes and remarks that were to be published as *Philosophical Investigations*. There and in, say, the *Brown Book* he argues that in the *Tractatus* Wittgenstein was trying to discover the essence of language, the features that anything we call 'language' has in common with the rest. He was looking for a pure, unadulterated account of what language is. Language as we use it is full of imperfections and 'slag'. The same can be said of ethics. We can try to discover what the pure, unadultered essence of ethics is, what features (action, judgement, attitude, problem) anything we want to call 'ethical' has in common with everything which we describe in the same way. Wittgenstein did precisely this in his 'Lecture on Ethics'. At the beginning of the lecture he says:

> Now instead of saying 'Ethics is the enquiry into what is good' I could have said it is the enquiry into what is valuable . . . what is really important . . . the meaning of life . . . what makes life worth living . . . the right way of living. I believe if you look at all these phrases you will get a rough idea as to what it is that Ethics is concerned with. (*PRv* p. 5)

As I said in chapter two, though this is an essentialist approach, it is not the rigid approach of definition by *genus* and *differentia*. It is much closer to the notion of 'family resemblance', but it has not quite reached that stage. There is still the idea that saying what ethics is involves listing the 'characteristic features which they all have in common and these are the characteristic features of Ethics' (ibid.).

By the 1940s Wittgenstein had come to realize that this pursuit was unproductive. 'There is no one system in which you can study in its purity and its essence what ethics is' (*PRv* p. 24). We use the term 'ethics' for various systems. Wittgenstein had come to realize that philosophically the variety was important. On the other hand, he did not abandon the view that there must be 'some points in common' between various ethical systems: 'There must be grounds for saying that people who follow a particular system are making ethical judgements: that they regard this or that as good, and so forth' (ibid.). But he rejected the notion that there is an ultimate ethical system, *the* ethical system. Moral theologians and the Church of Rome, the Orthodox Church, fundamentalist Christians, Jews, Muslims and members of other denominations and sects might dispute this. To do so, however, would be no more than to assert belief in a particular faith with either implies a certain ethical system or to which ethical practices are intimately related.

In place of the search for the pure essence of ethics, Wittgenstein in later years introduced what he called 'the anthropological method'. From Rhees' account it is not strictly anthropological, but it has this in common with anthropological studies: that it envisages an imaginary ethical system a primitive tribe might follow. Wittgenstein himself practised it, as we have seen in chapter ten. It has at least two advantages. First, it enables us to explore the limits of what could reasonably be called ethical practice and behaviour. Secondly, it is not encumbered by familiar ethical beliefs and practices. But Rhees offered an example from nearer home, which Wittgenstein accepted. It was Goering's dictum: '*Recht ist das, was uns gefällt* ('Right is whatever pleases us'). Wittgenstein is reported as saying: 'even that is a kind of ethics' (*PRv* p. 25). And he goes on to say that it is helpful in silencing objections to a certain attitude. This I take to mean that, no matter how outrageous the view expressed or however tainted the source, an utterance that has any claim to being ethical should not, within the anthropological method, be dismissed out of hand. 'And it should be considered along with other ethical judgements and discussions, in the anthropological study of ethical discussion' (ibid.).

Two other remarks made by Rhees deserve consideration. Both relate to Wittgenstein's later conviction that it is philosophically more rewarding to go for the adulterated version of language and ethics rather than the pure, unadulterated essence. The first links up the later thought with the earlier in this way. It reverts to the earlier notion of ethics as inexpressible and nonsensical (this is Rhees' report and not a reported quotation from Wittgenstein). To quote from Rhees:

> 'The Ethical' which cannot be expressed, is that *whereby* I am able to think of good and evil at all, even in the impure and nonsensical expressions I have to use. (*PRv* ibid. My italics)

Coming in the 1940s (whether a direct – remembered – quotation or simply a recollected account of a conversation) this is remarkable. It means that nothing has been lost in Wittgenstein's thinking on ethics between the 1910s and the 1940s. It has merely developed, and developed in most interesting and compatible ways. The passage can be interpreted in a straightforward and banal way as: 'the ethical is that whereby I am able to think of good and evil at all'. This tells us no more than that ethics is about good and evil. But if we add 'which cannot be expressed' and 'even in the impure and nonsensical expressions I have to use', new possibilities for interpretation present themselves. Grammatically it does not follow that the parenthesis 'which cannot be expressed' describes that whereby we are able to think of good and evil at all, but if we couple it with 'even in the impure and nonsensical expressions I have to use', something interesting emerges. The least banal interpretation is this. As had been established in the earlier writings, ethics is inexpressible in that it evaluates and passes judgements rather than stating independently verifiable facts. It is nonsensical, because, in spite of not being able to state facts, this is just what it seems to be attempting to do: to say what is not sayable in the language of the market place and of scientific circles. The reason why it is nonsensical and inexpressible is because it is impure, adulterated language which would be destroyed and rendered useless if any attempt were made to purify and unadulterate it. This is the new addition to the argument.

The second of Rhees' remarks reinforces the end of the 'Lecture on Ethics' where Wittgenstein says: 'I see now that these nonsensical expressions are not nonsensical because I had not found the correct expressions, but that their nonsensicality was their very essence' (*PRv* p. 11). Rhees, speaking of 'the different ways of doing things', different ethical ways of doing things or different ethical systems, says:

> He did not see them as so many fumbling attempts to say what none of them does say perfectly. The variety is important – not in order to fix your gaze on the unadultered form, but to keep you from looking at it. (*PRv* p. 25)

So, for inexpressibility is substituted variety – variety of ethical views, variety of ethical systems, variety of ethical judgements. The ethical remains as it was in the beginning, inexpressible, but new aspects of its inexpressibility emerge.

To conclude. It has to be said that Wittgenstein's notion of ethics, whether in his earlier or later writings, was somewhat eccentric, in the literal sense of 'departing from the centre', though much of it, the most important part, was central and eloquently underlined what is central to ethics.

The eccentricity of the earlier account lay in placing the emphasis on the way an action is regarded, whether it is seen *sub specie aeternitatis* or as an act among other acts; whether it is in accord with the alien will or in revolt against it; whether it is the act of a happy or unhappy human being. The happy human being is one who is in accord with the alien will, does not fear death and so on. This is fine as it stands, but it presupposes everything that we want to know, the criteria by which we judge these things: how do we know if we are in accord with the alien will? Wittgenstein does not have an answer to these questions. To that extent his account is incomplete, though as a metaphysics of ethics it is excellent. But he would not have attempted to answer them, since, for him, these matters belong to what cannot be said but only shown.

That can be condoned – and, to a large extent, he is right. What is less easy to condone is his later seeming-relativism and reductionism. As I have argued, it is not relativism in a sense that would be incompatible with ethics as absolute *value*, though it admits that we cannot be absolutely certain as to precisely where this value is found.

13

Conclusion

In this book I set out to do three things. First, to bring together Wittgenstein's thoughts on ethics and religious belief. I say 'bring together' advisedly. Wittgenstein, as his disciples are tireless in telling us, and as he himself tells us from time to time, was not what is technically known as a systematic philosopher. He preferred to present his ideas in remarks, aphorisms, questions, hypothetical and imaginary cases, and other disjointed modes of presentation. He disliked anything that smacked of systematical or theoretical presentation. As a matter of presentation this is acceptable. Spinoza went to the opposite extreme and presented Hebrew grammar *modo geometrico*. But even his *Ethics*, though it purports to be in the Euclidean mode, is nothing of the kind. Propositions follow from definitions and axioms in anything but an Euclidean manner. Yet Wittgenstein's *Tractatus* purported to do something similar to Spinoza's *Ethics*, and achieved roughly the same result as a *presentation*. Wittgenstein's later methods of presentation – if they were methods of presentation at all (the case for his intending *Philosophical Investigations* for publication is tenable; as for the rest, *The Blue and Brown Books*, etc. there is every reason for believing they were not intended for publication at all) – do not exclude the possibility that there was system, at least in the sense of consistency, in his thought.

To join these two facets of Wittgenstein's thought on ethics and religious belief I say that I have 'brought together' his thoughts. In this way I hoped to show that, even if they have not been presented systematically, as Aristotle's and, pre-eminently, Aquinas' have been, they still display a systematic and consistent way of thinking. *His thoughts cohere* but *not in a way that he could display*. He states this clearly in the preface to *Philosophical Investigations* where he says he had tried to weld his thoughts into an orderly whole as he had done in the *Tractatus*:

> The thoughts which I publish in what follows are the precipitate (*Neider-schlag*) of philosophical investigations which have occupied me for the last

sixteen years ... I have written down all these thoughts as *remarks* ... It was my intention at first to bring all this together in a book whose form I pictured differently at different times. But the essential thing was that the thoughts should proceed from one subject to another in a natural order and without breaks. (*PI* ix)

He goes on to say that he made many attempts to do this until he realized that it was impossible. One reason was that, if he tried to force his thoughts into an order, to force them in a single direction against their natural inclination (*ihre natürliche Neigung*), they were seen crippled (*bald erlahmten*). But the main reasons were the thoughts themselves and the nature of his investigation itself. As he says, the nature of his investigation forced him to criss-cross a wide terrain of thought hither and thither. Presumably, where this criss-crossing, these 'sudden changes, jumping from one topic to another' (*in raschem Wechsel von einem Gebiet zum andern uberspringend*) had to take place, any attempt to restrain or order them would kill the *germinating* thought. Nevertheless, something can be done *post factum* to bring order into this criss-crossing; I have attempted to do it.

Whether I have done it well or ill is for the reader to judge. But I suspect there are those (shall we say squeamish enough?) who would object to what I have done on the grounds that, even if I have succeeded in my endeavours, I have thereby thwarted Wittgenstein's purpose in presenting his thoughts as he did. (I use the word 'squeamish', meaning 'reluctant to do what ought to be done'.) To put it plainly: Wittgenstein wrote and uttered seemingly (and sometimes actually) disconnected, disparate remarks in order to get his students and readers to make the connections (if there were any) for themselves. To make, to spell out these connections – even if they stretch over years and over a variety of published books – is thought to be if not obscene, nasty in some way and certainly something that should not be done.

I regard this attitude to Wittgenstein's work as limiting from the point of view of scholarship, the marshalling together and assessing of Wittgenstein's ideas. It may have pedagogical value. But if Wittgenstein's ideas are coherent – even though they may not amount to a complete or consistent philosophy, and even if Wittgenstein would have repudiated any attempt to find coherence in what he wrote (which, historically, he would not have done) – being coherent they can be made to cohere: they can be brought together and their connections indicated. This I have done; but no more. That is why I speak of 'bringing together' his ideas on ethics and religious belief rather than of his moral philosophy or his philosophy of religion. In this respect I have distanced myself from

Wittgensteinians such as Rush Rhees and D. Z. Phillips who elaborate a philosophy of religion based on Wittgenstein's philosophy but one never elaborated by Wittgenstein himself. (The same was attempted in aesthetics by Maurice Weitz and others.) I do not want to imply that what the Wittgensteinians say in his name is necessarily contrary to what the master would have said, but neither do I admit that it is always consonant with what he said. I have confined myself to what Wittgenstein *actually said* or was *reported to have said* on ethics and religious belief. Apart from filling in the background to what he said or was reported to have said, I have developed neither an ethics nor a philosophy of religion on what might be regarded as Wittgensteinian principles. Unlike a proper cook, I have been a preparer of a meal, putting thoughts together and letting them cook themselves or not, as the notion takes them.

The second point I have made is that, though comparatively little is said about value in either the *Tractatus* or *Philosophical Investigations*, or in his remarks in his *Notebooks*, apart from those published in *Culture and Value* and a few others as yet unpublished which add little or nothing to those that have already seen the light of day, Wittgenstein regarded matters of value as the most important ('the higher'). In my preface I gave the relevant evidence for this, the explicit testimony of Engelmann and the somewhat reluctant testimony of Russell. These sources leave us in no doubt where Wittgenstein's chief interest lay. This is confirmed by the remarks published in *Culture and Value*, particularly the remark: 'I may find scientific questions interesting, but they never really grip me. Only *conceptual* and *aesthetic* questions do that' (p. 79).

That Wittgenstein devoted most of his thought and writing to, as he put it in his preface to *Philosophical Investigations*, such subjects as 'the concepts of meaning, of understanding, of a proposition, of logic, the foundations of mathematics, states of consciousness and other things' in no way invalidates the claim that he regarded questions of value as of primary importance. The reason for the seeming imbalance between the space and time given to these subjects and that given to considerations concerning value have, I trust, been made clear. Briefly, these are matters about which we should be silent. They cannot be expressed in factual statements and propositions, much less explained theoretically. At best they can be described obliquely in parables, analogies and metaphors that defy and elude literal translation.

And yet these subjects, the logical and conceptual, are not divorced from the considerations of value. I have argued – and I hope successfully – that the structure of the *Tractatus* was designed to expose the logical status of expressions of value, to emphasize that they are in no way statements of empirical fact (even though they must have an empirical element in them to be understood at all). It is not so easy to make this claim for Wittgenstein's later works. But, then, what are his later works? There is *Philosophical Investigations*. It was intended for publication and the remarks so destined are clearly marked in the manuscripts. But it was not published in his lifetime, and he was hesitant about it:

> Up to a short time ago I had really given up the idea of publishing my work in my lifetime . . .
> For more than one reason what I publish here will have points of contact with what other people are writing today . . .
> I make them public with doubtful feelings. It is not impossible that it should fall to the lot of this work, in its poverty and the darkness of this time, to bring light into one brain or another – but, of course, it is not likely. (*PI* vii–viii)

The other publications of his writings – *Philosophical Remarks*, *Zettel*, *Philosophical Grammar* and the rest – were not only posthumous but possibly not intended for publication (though, like the *Notebooks 1914–1916*, it is is not improbable that they were intended for publication at someone's discretion).

So there is no parallel in the later works between the section on logic and the section on value. Nevertheless, remarks on both continue. This leads me to the third point I have made: that, though Wittgenstein may have modified and altered his views over the years, his views on value remained the same. This is my strongest claim, and I shall briefly repeat my reasons for making it.

In his earlier works – the *Notebooks*, *Tractatus* and 'Lecture on Ethics' – Wittgenstein distinguished fairly clearly between statements of fact and relative value (which amount to statements of fact) which he called 'propositions', on the one hand, and expressions of value on the other. The former are expressible, sayable; the latter are inexpressible, unsayable, nonsensical, an attempt to go beyond the boundaries of language. Value had other features into which it is unnecessary to enter here. This account of value does not appear in that form in Wittgenstein's later writings. This, in turn, has led some commentators to suggest that in his later years Wittgenstein abandoned his earlier account of value, or, if he had not abandoned it, he should have done. The reason for this is that having abandoned the picture theory of language and adopted the notions of language-games, forms of life and philosophical grammar, the basis for the distinction between propositions (of fact) and expressions of value – the expressible and sayable as against the inexpressible, unsay-

able, nonsensical and striving to go beyond the boundaries of language –
could no longer be sustained.

I have argued that Wittgenstein's views on value did not change,
though they certainly developed. My reasons for saying this are: first,
though the ideas are not expressed in the same form as before, and terms
used in the earlier period (besides those mentioned: transcendental,
mystical, absolute value, *sub specie aeternitatis*) do not reappear, their
equivalents do.[1] Secondly, there is nothing incompatible in Wittgenstein's earlier account with his later account of value, not even the notion
of absolute value. Thirdly, it is not clear that he abandoned the analogy
of the picture to describe propositions; he merely used it in a different
way. Fourthly, there is nothing in the notion of language-games to
preclude the distinction between the inexpressible and the expressible.
There are other language-games besides these two, games that do not
involve either statements of fact or expressions of value judgements, so
the contrast is not as sharp as it was. But even in the *Tractatus*,
expressions of value were not alone in being inexpressible. Propositions
of logic, mathematics and the principles of science were in the same
category.

I have argued, further, that, though Wittgenstein was mainly concerned with topics other than with those of value, there are a sufficient
number of reflections on aesthetics, religious belief and ethics to warrant
the view that he still regarded value as the 'higher' and what interested
him most. So in this respect, too, his views had not changed.[2]

Not everyone will agree. As we saw at the beginning, the Vienna Circle
took Wittgenstein literally, as did other Logical Positivists, such as Ayer
and mathematical philosophers such as Ramsey. They understood him to
mean that expressions of value are nonsensical, understood as meaningless: empty combinations of words, which should never be uttered, since
it is pointless to do so. Russell realized this was not what Wittgenstein
meant, but he was baffled, as were the Vienna Circle, when Wittgenstein
read Tagore to them rather than discuss philosophy. Ayer realized later
what he was saying but rejected it.[3] It has proved an embarrassment to
some followers of Wittgenstein, though not to all.

Kai Nielsen, in the passage referred to in chapter two, states the
problem most forcefully when he says:

> If he (Wittgenstein) really believes... that in speaking of God we are
> trying to go 'beyond the world' and that such talk is unintelligible, why
> should he have such respect for those who give in to this tendency of the
> human mind?... Why take off your hat to someone who persists in
> believing... what... is demonstrably unintelligible?[4]

For a start, Wittgenstein never said that the language of ethics and religious belief is unintelligible, much less that it is *demonstrably* unintelligible. (This is Neilsen's own view of religious belief for which he gives little justification.) What Wittgenstein said was not that ethics and religious belief were unintelligible but that they were not to be understood in the way in which factual statements about objects, qualities and events are understood. About ethical judgements he was explicit, as we have seen:

> If I say: 'Although I believe that so and so is good, I may be wrong': this says no more than what I assert may be denied.
> Or suppose someone says, 'One of the ethical systems must be the right one' . . . Well, suppose I say Christian ethics is the right one. Then I am making a judgement of value. It amounts to *adopting* Christian ethics. (*PRv* p. 24)

The same applies to religious belief. To say that an ethical system is true or false, or that a set of religious beliefs are true or false, is to say no more that you *accept* them as true or *reject* them as false. It is no more than that. There are no acid or crucial tests to decide the matter. Nevertheless, it is not inappropriate to describe these beliefs as true or false, or even admit that we may be wrong about them. But the admission of possible fallibility does not imply that our views can be merely denied; it also implies that we suspect there may be good reasons for denying them. Mere denial is not enough.

Others, including Wittgensteinians such as Rush Rhees and D. Z. Phillips, also had problems with this aspect of Wittgenstein's thought, not so much about ethics as about religious belief. Ethical judgements are not about things but actions; yet they are not descriptions of actions. They are judgements passed on actions. So they seem to lack an object or even a quality as their object. This does not matter, since we have the action to which the judgemental verdict is attached (just as we attribute beauty to a rose). But with religious beliefs it is different. There seems to be nothing about which we are speaking when we talk about God or the divine and supernatural or grace. Rhees says that language about God certainly does refer to 'something', though not as language about physical objects refers to things. However, not being sure how to substantiate this remark, he hedges his bets and says that religious language would be meaningful even if there were no 'something'. (It is somewhat like Locke's substance 'a supposition of he knows not what support'.) (*Essay*) Phillips goes the full length. He holds that there is no 'something', and yet religious language is meaningful in terms of what it means to the believer, his personal feelings, his attitude to the world and life, his practices and so forth. There is some support for this view in Wittgenstein's catalogue of what it means to believe in God in the *Notebooks 1914–1916* (pp. 73–4). Whether Wittgenstein himself believed there is 'something', we cannot say. Nor is it relevant, since his main concern was with the *language* of religious and ethical beliefs. This leads me to my final assessment of his contribution to moral philosophy and to the philosophy of religion.

Perhaps Wittgenstein's major contribution was to discuss ethics and religious belief in terms of *language*, asking what it means to make ethical and religious utterances, not to ask what ethics *is*, what religious belief *is*. In this way he took a completely new look at these much discussed subjects. He did an enormous service by his early distinction between the expressible and sayable as against the inexpressible and unsayable. Theologians since the Fathers of the Church have spoken about the inexpressibility of religious truths (the same has rarely, if at all, been said about ethics), but Wittgenstein put it in a wider logical context, along with logic itself and other unsayables.

Not every theologian or philosopher of religion or moral philosopher will accept Wittgenstein's distinction as throwing light on ethics or religious belief. Indeed most moral philosophers, from rationalists to intuitionists, certainly would not. Philosophers of religion could dub the notions of the unsayable, the nonsensical and non-rational as a form of fideism.[5] And this it is not, because Wittgenstein does not discuss the grounds for religious belief. He is interested only in the *language* of ethics and religious belief; he holds that neither can be expressed as scientific propositions nor are they (nor can they be) based on anything approaching scientific and factual evidence.

The cluster of concepts related to this fundamental distinction – seeing actions against the background of space and time rather than *in* it (*sub specie aeternitatis*), absolute value, being outside the world of facts and happenings (what is the case) – are also most useful to ethics and the philosophy of religion. Although they may merely be saying in other words and from a different point of view what certain moral philosophers and philosophers of religion have been saying over the centuries, they have a refreshing, rejuvenating, liberating effect and are none the worse for their strangeness of conception and expression.

From the later writings there is the concept of rationality in relation to religious belief which, as it were, holds the ring between those who would dismiss religious belief as irrational and, hence nonsensical, and those who think it is so rational that it can stand up to, or at least be compatible with, the results of the most rigorous scientific and historical enquiries.

Another notion from the later writings that made a useful contribution is that of picturing: particularly the picture to live by, which is related to Wittgenstein's notion of forms of life. There is a nice irony in this. The very thing that in early Wittgenstein helped to distinguish expressions of value from statements of fact, comes in his later work to support the inexpressibility of value. A picture to live by does not say anything or tell us anything about the world, about what is or is not the case. Moreover, it is something that is not to be taken literally. It is symbolic, or, as Wittgenstein would say, an allegory or simile. Philosophers and theologians have long recognized the essentially symbolic nature of religious language, whether they speak of allegory, parable, analogy, simile or myth. What Wittgenstein has done is, first, to emphasize the pictorial (in the broadest sense) element of religious language, and then to link it with practice, behaviour, a way of life. Furthermore, he has extended it to the teaching of ethics and ethical practice. In this he may have being doing no more than what has always been done, at least popularly. Children are taught religion and moral behaviour by stories. It is only when they go to school that they become exposed to moral principles and theological propositions embodied in catechisms and apologetics. Wittgenstein is saying that the popular method of teaching is the only possible one, that inculcating moral principles and teaching religion in propositional form is contrary to the true nature of ethics and religious belief.

Here again Wittgenstein has done both ethics and religious belief a service by putting ethical theory and theology in their proper place. Ethical theory has little to offer to moral practice. As a philosophical discipline it has its place, and in clarifying moral issues it may occasionally help people with tricky problems to come to a decision. But in general it is an attempt to give an account of what people actually do when they act morally, and give their reasons for so acting. Theology, whether natural theology or divinity, is also a perfectly respectable intellectual occupation, but it has little to offer to the actual practice of religion. This is not to say that priests and ministers, at least, should not be acquainted with theology and ethical theory as a guide to thinking about moral and religious matters or rather as a safeguard against woolly thinking. In the forty years since Wittgenstein died, but not through any apparent influence of his, there has been a movement away from theology in religious instruction, not only in those Churches where it has traditionally flourished, but also in those already more inclined to evangelism. That this is the right way to go about things is clear for the reasons Wittgenstein has given. But neglect of theology may, in the long run, be harmful to religious practice in which he was chiefly interested. It may give rise to woolly thinking.

While his notion of practice and the religious or ethical way of life is useful in explaining the language of religious belief, it is also open to misinterpretation and misuse: it can give and has given rise to reductionism. Wittgenstein never said that religious belief is *nothing more than* a way of life according to a picture (a religious story or parable). Nor is there any evidence that this was what he meant. He held the perfectly reasonable view that one way of understanding what people mean by their beliefs consists in considering the kind of life they lead. But some of his remarks give the impression that there is nothing more to religious belief than a way of life and a picture to guide it by. And it has been interpreted in this way by some Wittgensteinians, D. Z. Phillips in particular. Thus religious beliefs are reduced to certain practices – worship, prayer, thanksgiving, contemplation, forgiveness, loving one's neighbour – that are followed as a result of being guided by some picture or other. But this is contrary to what Wittgenstein said or what is implied in what he said. He talks of people risking things on account of *beliefs*.

Wittgenstein was, therefore, talking of someone who believed in the pictures that guided him, in *what* they signified and *that* they signified something. He may or may not have shared this belief, but he recognized it for what it was: a belief. The believer may not accept everything in the picture – the picture of Judgement Day, for instance. But what the religious believer, as distinct from the ethical person, is *not* doing is *merely* holding up a picture – as it might be, of the Good Samaritan. The picture is more than a mere picture or exemplar. It is a picture to *live by*.

Wittgenstein offers hostages to fortune in his emphasis on the personal in matters of ethics and religious belief, and in his seeming relativism. The first smacks of positivism, of reporting on what an individual personally feels or thinks on ethical or religious matters rather than a forthright statement on these matters. There is no doubt about the importance of personal opinion in such matters (as in aesthetics and metaphysics), since no one can be convinced either way by cogent argument. But such important issues as abortion and euthanasia in ethics or predestination in religious belief cannot be reduced to expressions of personal feeling and opinion, to mere psychological or sociological *facts*. As we have seen, Wittgenstein himself repudiated any notion that a sociological account of ethics is an account of *ethics as such*, though it might tell us who and how many and why people behave the way they do. Yet by the way in which he emphasized the personal element in ethics and religious belief, he left it open to others to give a reductionist and positivist account of them.

As for Wittgenstein's supposed relativism, this has already been discussed at length. My position is that he was no more a relativist than any reasonable person can avoid being. Relativity is something we have to live with: we each see the world from our own point of view, whether perceptually or mentally. In ethics Wittgenstein flatly denied that one ethical system is as good as another; and, though he did not say so, there is every reason to believe that he would have held the same view about systems of religious belief. In fact he vaguely hinted as much in his notes on Frazer. And yet in his manner of speaking he could be taken for a rampant relativist, and has been so taken. One could say that Wittgenstein was undecided in matters of religious belief. This may well be the case, though I do not believe that it is. What is certain is that he left himself open to this interpretation, whatever his personal beliefs, when he could have said straightforwardly that *for a religious believer* there was no question about another set of religious beliefs being as valid as his own; and, indeed, that this makes no sense.

Thus, though Wittgenstein has offered many valuable insights into the language of ethics and religious belief, his personal idiosyncrasies and indecisions have to some extent flawed his account and led others to flaw it still further. Whether we are a believers or unbelievers is irrelevant to our philosophical analysis of what is entailed in having a religious belief. Ethics is another matter. We are, as I have said, forced to make ethical decisions, like it or not, and we perform moral or immoral acts. But even if amorality were a rational option, as atheism is, in matter of religion, this would not preclude philosophical analyses of what it is to be moral and make ethical judgements. Wittgenstein attempts such analyses, but personal feelings, aversions, prejudices and uncertainties keep breaking in to disrupt what might have been smooth, compelling accounts of the language of ethics and religious belief on which he set so high a value.[6]

Apart from the eccentricity of some of Wittgenstein's remarks, it would be misleading to suggest that he contributed greatly to discussion of moral or religious questions as such. That was never his intention. He was concerned with how we speak about moral and religious matters. In so doing he inevitably dealt with what it is for a judgement to be ethical or a belief religious. Though he did deal sporadically and at some length with predestination, that was an anomaly. Otherwise he had no particular interest in moral or religious issues. But the mere fact that he refrained from entering the arena of moral or religious debate makes his remarks all the more effective. By approaching ethics and religious belief from a linguistic and logical point of view, particularly such an original viewpoint as that of the pictorial theory and the account in terms of language-games, forms of life and philosophical grammar, Wittgenstein breathed new life into ethics and the philosophy of religion, especially the latter. By confining himself to this approach and not attempting to apply it in detail, he (unwittingly, perhaps) made its impact more powerful, while giving unencumbered scope to others to apply it at their discretion. (Much has already been done, as I note in the bibliography; but it is beyond the scope of this book to discuss it.)[7] Added to the logico-linguistic approach is the style of expression, the striking (alarming, even), provocative, puzzling, cryptic, vivid, succinct, staccato mode of putting across his ideas, which makes them both refreshing and unacademic.

I hope that I have provided material for the further application of Wittgenstein's ideas without too greatly blunting their impact, taming their eccentricity or reducing their sparkle. This book merely flits like a dragonfly or some other, more inferior, insect over the surface of deep waters.

Notes

Preface

1 *Letters from Ludwig Wittgenstein, with a Memoir*, pp. 143–4.
2 *Wittgenstein's Vienna*, pp. 232–8.
3 *Wittgenstein and Religious Belief passim*.
4 G. E. Moore in his article 'Wittgenstein's Lectures 1930–33', in *Mind*, 1955, p. 14, quotes Wittgenstein as saying he wanted to say something about the grammar of ethical expression, or e.g. of the word 'God'. 'But in fact,' says Moore, 'he said very little about such words as "God" and very little about that of ethical expression.' In fact Wittgenstein did say something, though not much, about God in later lectures (which, presumably, Moore was unaware of) and a little about the grammar of ethics, as we shall see in later chapters.

1 The Sayable and Unsayable

1 *NB* p. 7 talks of a motor-car accident represented by toy figures (*Puppen*). Von Wright speaks of a 'schematic' picture of an automobile accident that Wittgenstein saw in a magazine while in the trenches (Malcolm, 1958, pp. 7–8); although, if Engelmann is to be believed, Wittgenstein was not in the trenches when he made his entry in his *Notebook* (29.9.14) but on the River Vistula doing nothing. Hence he seems to have misremembered. This may not be material, but the toy figures support the model rather than the picture interpretation.
2 Wittgenstein did, however, distinguish between sign and symbol. As he put it in *TLP* 3.32: 'A sign is what can be perceived of a symbol.' The symbol gives the sign its significance; the same sign can be common to different symbols; but if the modes of signification are different, the common sign does not indicate a common characteristic (*TLP* 3.321–2).
3 Another interesting example is 'vice'. It has at least three meanings: a carpenter's tool, a moral defect and a deputy. That they came to have the

same sign in English was due to the similarity (in pronunciation, presumably) of their Latin roots *vitis, vitium* and *vice*.

4   Wittgenstein seems to assume that all hieroglyphs are pictograms. This is not so. They are pictorial, it is true. But those deciphered by Champollion were alphabetic and syllabic – a lion for 'l', a mouth for 'r', an owl for 'm' – though they were used in conjunction with pictograms or determinative signs.

5   *Cf.* Black, M.: *A Companion to Wittgenstein's Tractatus*, p. 165. 'One might be inclined to equate "saying" with "affirming" or "asserting" – but for remarks such as 4.064 . . . The answer is to be found at 4.461a (a proposition shows what it says) which I take to imply that "saying" is *part of* – or rather, an aspect of – sense, not something superadded to it.' This is a plausible interpretation of what Wittgenstein says. A proposition that 'says' as well as 'shows' its sense must, therefore, be a factual proposition that can be affirmed or asserted.

6   *Cf. TLP* 4.0621: 'But it is important that the signs 'p' and '$\sim p$' *can* say the same thing. For it shows that nothing in reality corresponds to the sign '$\sim$'.

7   *Cf. TLP* 4.0641.

8   *Cf.* Gier, N.: *Wittgenstein and Phenomenology*, New York, 1981.

9   Ayer, A. J.: *Wittgenstein*, pp. 20 and 30.

2   Ethics

1   *Cf.* Von Wright, *Prototractatus*, p. 34, where Ogden in a letter to Russell (5.11.21) speaks of 'Moore's Spinoza title'; and McGuinness, p. 299, who suggests that Wittgenstein's knowledge of Spinoza may have come through Schopenhauer.

2   Wittgenstein nowhere suggests that the consequences of our actions are irrelevant to their morality. Theft, murder, rape, arson are bad because of their consequences. The consequences he had in mind were judicial and external to the act. To act out of fear of punishment or hope of reward, though not in itself contemptible, is pragmatic rather than moral.

3   The two translations of the *Tractatus* use 'wax and wane' to translate *abnehmen oder zunehmen*. (Strictly it should be 'wane or wax', but that might sound a bit wilful.) While these words are used of the moon, they are more often used of putting on or losing weight. So this puzzling phrase might be translated as 'shrink or grow' or 'diminish or increase' where the diminution or increase is in ethical value.

4   Occam put very strong emphasis on the will (following Scotus) to the extent of saying it could override conclusions of the intellect. Ethical matters were determined by God's will, though he could not will what is contradictory. Although good and evil were a matter for divine decree, the right use of reason was regarded as a safe guide to those decrees that have not been revealed.

5   Anscombe translates the phrase as 'accession or loss of meaning', a perfectly respectable translation, but it does not capture the force of *Dazukommen oder Wegfallen* which suggest 'accumulation or falling off'.

6   My translation. It differs only in taking Wittgenstein at his word: 'If one understands by eternity not unending temporal duration but timelessness . . .' (*TLP* 6.4311). Thus *ewig* should be taken as 'everlasting' and not 'eternal', as it is by both Ogden, and Pears and McGuinness. To translate it as 'eternal' misses the point of both 6.4311 and 6.4312: that 'eternal life belongs to those who live in the present' and 'the solution of the riddle of life lies *outside* space and time'. Why unending temporal duration or everlasting life solves no riddle is because it is more of the same, of what presented the riddle in the first place: living *inside* space and time; only in the case of everlasting life it would be for ever.

7   Abelard speaks of a 'common and confused image of many things' as the concept of universal terms (*Logica 'Ingredientibus'* 17). This is close to what Wittgenstein says in the lecture, but Occam's conceptualism comes closer to his later thinking, where, like Abelard, he rejects Platonic essences in favour of groups of resemblances, but discusses resemblance and relationships at greater length. Moreover, for Abelard, relationships, including resemblance, have a reality; for Occam they have none.

8   *An Introduction to the Philosophy of Religion*, p. 63.

9   Schlick's book, *Fragen der Ethik*, was translated as *Problems in Ethics*. In the latter 'shallower' is dropped and 'perhaps profounder' is substituted for the earlier confident assertion (p. 11). For Wittgenstein's marginal comments on this and related matters *cf.* McGuinness's notes to the text, pp. 79–81.

3   The Ethical Will

1   McGuinness (1988, p. 254) suggests that Wittgenstein's objection to suicide follows Schopenhauer who rejected suicide as the supreme act of the self-assertion of the Will, or as he [McGuinness] puts it in 'The Mysticism of the *Tractatus*' (pp. 317–18): 'Wittgenstein says that suicide is the elementary sin, and I think his thought is that it is the ultimate form of non-acceptance of what happens.' Moran says that it 'constitutes the ultimate disobedience', the ultimate flouting of authority (1973, p. 48).

2   Anscombe translates the question: 'But can one want and yet not be unhappy if the want does not attain fulfilment?' The words Wittgenstein used were *wünschen* and *Wunsch*. These normally mean, whether in their verbal or nominal form, 'wish, desire, longing for, aspiring towards'. 'Want' is a less usual translation (*brauchen, willen* and *nötig haben* are more common). 'Want' connotes lack or a need. (OED.) Perhaps this is implied in what Wittgenstein is saying, but his point is easily made by speaking of wishing. Wishing will not bring anything about, any more than wanting; but we can wish for things we do not need and, in that sense, do not want. A shipwrecked sailor may wish

for a female companion, but what he wants is food and water. (Of course, he also wishes for them, and his wish may be as unsuccessful in securing them as his other wish.)

3   This is obviously heavily influenced by Schopenhauer e.g. *The World as Will and Representation*, sec. 2. *cf.* Black, p. 311. However, whereas for Schopenhauer the *world* is my will, and it is bad, for Wittgenstein *my* will stands over against the world and is independent of it: and the world is *alien* rather than *bad*. In so far as it *is*, it is good and my happiness depends on being at one with it.

4   Once again, though Wittgenstein draws the ingredients of his ideas from Schopenhauer, they are not saying quite the same thing. Both agree that the thinking and the willing subject cannot be objects of knowledge, but Wittgenstein goes further and says the thinking *subject* is illusory. The only subject is the willing subject, but it is *my individual* will not the Schopenhauerian world Will.

5   My translation. I prefer 'I' to 'self' and 'boundary' to 'limit' for reasons given elsewhere, as against Pears and McGuinness.

6   Anscombe, G. E. M.: *An Introduction to Wittgenstein's Tractatus*, pp. 171–2.

4   The Mystical

1   My translation. Pears and McGuinness translate *TLP* 6.4321: 'The facts all contribute to the setting of the problem, not to its solution.' Neither this entry, nor the phrase 'for what is higher' in the previous entry, appear in the *Proto-Tractatus*.

2   I prefer my own translation: 'There is, indeed, the unexpressible. This shows itself; it is the mystical.' It is closer to Ogden, but on this important matter I yield to the accepted translation.

3   'Wittgenstein's Philosophy of the Mystical' pp. 359–75 in Copi, I. M. and Beard, R. W. *Essays on Wittgenstein's Tractatus*, Routledge & Kegan Paul, London, 1966.

4   My translation, differing (apart from style) only in translating *begrenztes* as 'bounded' rather than 'limited'. The entry does not appear in the *Proto-Tractatus*, nor is *sub specie aeterni* underlined (as if that matters). However, this passage should be taken in conjunction with *NB* p. 83: 'The usual way of looking at things sees objects as it were from the midst of them, the view *sub specie aeternitatis* from outside . . .'

5   McGuinness 'The Mysticism of the Tractatus', *Philosophical Review*, 75, 1966, p. 311.

6   *Cf. CV* p. 45: 'People are religious to the extent that they believe themselves to be not so much *imperfect*, as *ill*.

    Any man who is halfway decent will think himself extremely imperfect, but a religious man thinks himself *wretched*.'

7   When Wittgenstein speaks of similes, metaphors and allegories as 'misuses'

of language, he does not mean 'misuse' as one might speak of a malapropism or an ungrammatical use of words as misuse. 'Other use', i.e. use other than the usual and normal use, would be nearer the mark, were it not itself a strange use of words.

8   *Cf.* chapters two and eight; and *CV* p. 56.

5   God

1   My translation.
2   My translation. Pears and McGuinness translate *unantastbar* as 'inviolable' whereas its normal meaning is 'unimpeachable'. 'Inviolable' is *unverletzlich*. Perhaps the difference is not very great.
3   *Cf.* Popper, K.: *Conjectures and Refutations, The Logic of Scientific Discovery*, etc. In the wake of post-Popperian philosophy of science the views expressed by Wittgenstein in *TLP* 6.372 seem somewhat out-of-date, though they may still reflect a popular view. *Cf.* Black (p. 366): 'Wittgenstein seems to be taking for granted a somewhat far-fetched conception of scientific explanation.' This is undoubtedly true, but his attitude to what he thought of as science is integral to all else.
4   This seems to run counter to the Christian (or, indeed any other) doctrine of divine incarnation. Either God is *in* the world, reveals himself *in* the world, or he is not *incarnate*. Wittgenstein's point is that a body may be in the world, in space and time; and this body may be intimately related with the Godhead and divinity; yet, as divine, as Godhead, it is not *in* the world like any other fact or event, nor does it reveal itself *in* the world as a fact or event.
5   *Cf.* B. McGuinness (1988) pp. 262–4.
6   My translation, which involves only slight changes.
7   *Cf. TLP* 5.621: 'The world and life are one'.
8   My translation. Once again the difference is between translating *wünschen* as 'wish' rather than 'want'.
9   *Apologia pro Vita Sua*, Everyman, London, 1864, p. 31: 'the thought of two and two only supreme and luminously self-evident beings, myself and my Creator'.

6   Language-games and Forms of Life

1   Waismann represented Wittgenstein at a meeting at Köningsberg in the summer of 1930 and read a paper entitled: 'The Nature of Mathematics: Wittgenstein's Standpoint'. On 19 June Waismann and Wittgenstein met in Schlick's house to discuss what was to be said. This (*WWK* pp. 102–4, taken in conjunction with p. 163 and p. 170) draws an interesting distinc-

tion between chess and a more serious calculus. But, for the purpose of the discussion, chess is not different from a calculus that amuses us.

2   *Cf. PG* 11, pp. 49–50, a comparison of language with (a) a tool-box and (b) chess: 'It is as if I get tools in the tool-box ready for use. I can use the word "yellow" is like "I know how to move the king in chess".'

3   *Cf. PI*, 7. p. 5 'We can also think of the whole process of using words in (2) as one of those games by means of which children learn their native language. I will call these games "language-games" and will sometimes speak of a primitive language as a language-game.' (2) in question was a primitive language involving the moving of blocks, pillars, slabs and beams from B to A on a word of command (*PI*, 2, p. 3).

4   The notion of 'form of life' (*lebensformen*) was current in Vienna in Wittgenstein's day (*cf.* Toulmin and Janik p. 230 ff.). It is referred to in *PG* 29, p. 65: 'Is meaning then really only the use of words? Isn't it the way this use meshes with our life? But isn't its use a part of our life?'

5   *Cf. PG*, 65, p. 107: 'It is the same as if we speak of something that makes the difference between paper money and merely printed pieces of paper, something that *gives it its meaning, its life*' (my italics).

6   *Cf. PG* 140, p. 192: 'Imagine it turned out that only chess entertained and satisfied people. Then the rules aren't arbitrary if the purpose of the game is to be achieved. "The rules of the game are arbitrary" means: the concept "game" is not defined by the effect the game is supposed to have on us.'

7   It may be hard to see how doing logic, mathematics or philosophy are forms of life. They are occupations, however; and they use language differently from its use in buying vegetables.

8   In the original draft of the encyclical *Humanae Generis* of Pope Pius XII, the wording had been that it is *apparent* that the Pauline and Tridentine doctrine of original sin *cannot* be reconciled with the evolutionary theory of polygenism, i.e. origin of a species from more than one parental source. The Jesuit biblical scholar, Cardinal Bea, managed to have it altered to 'it *does not appear* how it *can* be reconciled' – a sufficiently ambiguous formula to pacify both sides in the dispute.

9   Sartre, J. P.: *Existentialism and Humanism*. English edition, 1948, pp. 27–9. *Cf.* chap. 12, note 3.

10   The German text has: *die Sublimierung der ganzen Darstellung*, which Anscombe translates as 'the subliming of our whole account of logic'. Whatever about the translation, it is undoubtedly true that Wittgenstein was talking about subliming, i.e. purifying the signs (*PI* 94, p. 44).

11   In many of his short stories Kipling makes not only animals but also parts of ships and locomotives talk to one another. *Cf. The Maltese Cat.*

12   Since the publication of such intermediary books as *PG*, *PR* and *BB* many commentators have come to the view that Wittgenstein's so-called abandonment of the picture theory was not quite as complete as was once thought. *Cf.* Kenny (1975) pp. 224–31, Pears (1971) p. 95 ff.

13   Jastow, F.: *Fact and Fable in Psychology*. Houghton, Mifflin, New York, 1901.

7   Relativism

1 'The Punctual and Segmentative Aspects of Verbs in Hopi' in *Selected Writings of Benjamin Lee Whorf*, ed. J. B. Carroll. Harvard University Press, Cambridge, Mass., 1956.
2 *Inquiries into Truth and Interpretations*, Oxford, 1984, p. 184.
3 *The Structure of Scientific Revolution*, Chicago, 1962, p. 135.
4 *Scientific Explanation*, Minneapolis, 1962.
5 *Essays on Actions and Events*, Oxford, 1980, p. 243.
6 *Op. cit.* p. 245.
7 'Relativism, Rationalism and the Sociology of Knowledge' in Hollis, M. and Lukes, S.: *Rationality and Relativism*, Oxford, 1982, pp. 21–47.
8 *Knowledge and Social Imagery* pp. 97–8.
9 *Cf.* Levy Bruhl: *Les Fonctions mentales dans les societés inferieures*, Paris, 1910.
10 Hollis, M.: 'The limits of irrationality', in *European Journal of Sociology* 7, 1967, pp. 208 and 215–16.
11 *Ethical Relativity*, Kegan Paul, Trench and Trubner, London, 1933.
12 I am indebted to Professor Terry Penner for making many useful suggestions, some of which I have incorporated into the text. One of the most important was that I should give an example of a primitive language-game. That proved too difficult. The example he had in mind was learning the meaning of the term 'dream'. Malcolm maintains that we learn the meaning of 'dream' with reference to stories we tell when awake. No matter how sophisticated these become, they do not amount to recalling a dream since we have no means of verifying our dream. This is contested by Dement, Kleitman and Penner himself. Penner thinks this makes Malcolm an extreme and deterministic relativist. It is not clear – to put it at its mildest – that Wittgenstein would have followed Malcolm down that road, but to pursue this debate (which cannot be shirked) in this book would turn it into something different. Therefore my position stands as stated in the text.
13 *Cf. LC* p. 32: 'If I say this theme of Brahms is extremely Kellerian, the interest this has is first that these two lived at the same time. Also that you can say the same things of both of them – the culture of the time in which they lived. If I say this, this comes to an objective interest.'

8   Religious Discourse

1 This is something rare: an entry in English. What the significance of this (if any) may be, I cannot say.
2 Belief in the Resurrection of Jesus might seem to suggest that belief in someone being alive after death could be of the naïve kind. As described in the Gospels, the apparitions of Jesus were far from ghostly. He was tangible; he walked on the earth; he ate food. All very like the return of Uncle George. Yet, if we take Paul's account and the teaching of the Church into considera-

tion, the risen body of Jesus was somewhat different from what Uncle George's would be like prior to his demise. It is said to be a glorified, heavenly, incorruptible body. Even the Gospels recount that Jesus was not recognized by the disciples or Mary Magdalene.

3   Belief in life after death is not necessarily a religious belief. Though it might be unusual, there is no reason why an atheist or other non-believer could not accept the possibility, and even the probability, that he will survive after death. This survival could take other forms than personal conscious survival. It could be a form of nirvana, impersonal absorption into the One or the Absolute Being. Or it could be reincarnation (a difficult concept to grasp except in fiction). (Some people may take comfort in the thought that their molecules, or at least their sub-atomic particles, will survive.)

4   There is some confusion in the text about the use of 'consequence' and 'conclusion'. One passage is clearly wrong: 'All I wished to characterize was the conventions (*sic*) he wished to draw ... Normally, if you say "He is an automaton" you draw consequences ... you may not want to draw any such consequences' (*LC* p. 72). Clearly the word should have been 'conclusions'. Since Rush Rhees could not remember whether he had faithfully or incorrectly recorded what Wittgenstein had said (or possibly misread his own notes), we decided to let the text stand as it is. The meaning is obvious.

9   The Grounding of Religious Belief

1   *Cf.* Karl Popper, 'Conjectures and Refutations', Introduction in *A Pocket Popper* pp. 46–57. 'I shall try to show that ... this whole question of ultimate sources (observations) ... must be rejected as based on a mistake.'

2   *Cf. CV* p. 46: in which religious belief is described as 'a passionate commitment to a system of reference'. 'Instruction in a religious belief, therefore, would have to take the form of a portrayal, a description, of that system of reference, while at the same time being an appeal to conscience. And this combination would have to result in the pupil himself, of his own accord, passionately taking hold of the system of reference.'

3   *Cf. PI* 46 p. 21: 'What lies behind the idea that names really signify simples?' – Socrates says in the Theaetetus: ... "it is impossible to give an account of any primary element; for it, nothing is possible but the bare name; its name is all it has ..." Both Russell's "individuals" and my "objects" (*Tractatus Logico-Philosophicus*) were such primary elements.'

4   This is precisely the criticism that Aquinas used against this argument (without naming names) (*Summa Theologica*, I.2.1). Wittgenstein adds an interesting supplement to it with reference to colour. 'Couldn't one actually say equally well that the essence of colour guarantees its existence? ... Because all that really means is: I cannot explain what "colour" is, what the word "colour" means, except with the help of a colour sample. So in this

case there is no such thing as explaining "what it *would* be like if colours *were* to exist".'

5   The word Wittgenstein uses is *falsch* ('*dann ist alle Philosophie darüber falsch*'). Aquinas was more temperate when he regarded all he had said and written on theology and philosophy as *worthless* in comparison with the light of faith.

6   It seems to me that Winch has missed the point in his translation. He translates *gewisser* as 'certain particular', which it can undoubtedly mean. But its more normal meaning is 'more certain' or, in theological jargon, 'sounder'. 'Outlaws' seems a rather strong translation of *verbannt*, where 'banned' would have done.

7   One book which Wittgenstein is likely to have had in mind would be *Word of God and Word of Man* (1924). An apt quotation from Barth of which Wittgenstein would have approved would be: 'Belief cannot argue with unbelief, it can only preach to it.'

8   In *Science and Religion: A Symposium*, London, 1931, p. 112. This was a collection of talks broadcast on the BBC in 1930.

9   *Cf. LC* p. 62: ' "For a blunder that is too big." If you suddenly wrote numbers down on the blackboard, and then said: "2 and 21 is 13," etc., I'd say: "This is no blunder".'

10   The Beliefs of Primitive Peoples

1   Frazer, abridged edition, Macmillan, London, 1922; the edition Wittgenstein read.

2   Originally published in German in *Synthese*, Dordrecht, Holland, 1967. First English text in *The Human World*, 3, 1971. The edition referred to here was edited by Rush Rhees, translated by A. C. Miles and published by Brynmill Press, Retford, Notts, in 1979. My translations.

3   This is hardly magical or religious ritual, though it is ceremonial and has similarities with homeopathic medicine or imitative magic and ritual.

4   I have not discussed Wittgenstein's remarks on the Beltane fire-festival, partly because it is a very detailed account which, in principle, does not add greatly to the arguments discussed in this chapter, and partly because it has been ably discussed in papers and essays to which reference is made in the bibliography. However, I refer the reader to Rush Rhees' essay in McGuinness (1982) pp. 69–107.

5   *Histoire du peuple d'Israel*, 5 vols, Paris, 1887–93, vol. I, chapter 3. Winch translates the last phrase – *leur causes dans notre organisation* – as 'causes within our constitution'.

11   Wittgenstein on Predestination

1   I am grateful to my colleague, Professor Phillips Griffiths, for his reflections on the foregoing. He thinks that Wittgenstein did not understand predes-

tination in its most common and dramatic form, Calvinism, though he liked it as a piety. This is shown by his remarks on Bunyan. Calvinism is an intellectual doctrine concerned with vocation and election ('many are called but few are chosen'), the transcendence of God's mercy, the immanence of Christ's redeeming sacrifice, etc. Wittgenstein, according to Griffiths, was not interested in any of this. He was a reductionist, concerned not with how religious people think but with how they act and feel: their way of life.

While I agree that Wittgenstein did not understand Calvinism as a religious doctrine, which is not surprising in view of his attitude towards theology; and I also agree that for him the test of faith was one's way of life; nevertheless this in itself would not make him a reductionist. He does not say that belief in predestination is *nothing more* than a way of feeling and acting, though he comes perilously close to saying it in his remarks on Bunyan. Some intellectual content and conviction is presupposed. He did, after all, attack the doctrine (however inadequately understood – which he readily admitted) on intellectual grounds. If we are to find reductionism, we should look not at Wittgenstein himself but at what Kai Nielsen calls the 'Wittgensteinian Fideists'.

2 Wittgenstein adds: 'It ought to be possible to find a better simile.' But the analogy, if somewhat crude, serves its purpose. If we are not familiar with the function of a device we may very well misjudge it totally. Likewise, if we judge divine actions and purposes in human terms, we may totally misjudge them. But then, can we judge them otherwise than in human terms? This dilemma haunted Wittgenstein for most of his life.

3 *Cf.* Williams, B.: *Moral Luck*, Cambridge University Press, 1981.

4 Romans 7.19.

5 2 Corinthians 12.

12   Whatever Happened to Ethics?

1 I think that Winch's translation of *Not* as 'torment' is a bit too strong. I should prefer 'distress', 'trouble', or, if something stronger is called for, 'misery'. At any rate, this entry is in keeping with the third mystical experience of absolute value: the feeling of being morally rotten.

2 Winch translates 'Einem Menschen' as 'One human being'. This is literally correct, though the capital initial of 'One' looks somewhat odd in English. From the context it would seem to be more reasonable to speak of a man alone (*einzeln*) or lonely (*einsam*), since the man feels lost (*vorloren fühlt*).

3 Fletcher, J.: *Situation Ethics: the New Morality*, SCM, London, 1966. The date of Wittgenstein's entry is 1942 which is early for situation ethics. Yet Wittgenstein seems to be taking up a position similar to that adopted by 'situation ethics' protagonists.

4 French title: 'L'Existentialisme est un humanisme', Paris, 1946. Translated by P. Mairet as *Existentialism and Humanism*, Methuen, London, 1973. The

text is that of a lecture delivered at the Club Maintenant. The case is discussed on p. 35 ff. of the English edition.

5   The solutions to these moral problems (if they are moral problems) by Sartre and Wittgenstein are very similar, but not quite the same. For Sartre the all-important thing is freedom of choice, responsibility for one's choices, authenticity, which gives rise to feelings of 'abandonment' (being alone with no certainties to guide one), and, consequently, anguish and 'despair'. For Wittgenstein there is a question of making what one regards as the *right* choice under the circumstances and *at the time*. If things turn out badly – *tant pis* – you did your best. Both are agreed that in these kinds of case there is, in Sartre's words, 'no general rule of morality to tell you what you ought to do'. Could the same be said of someone faced with the dilemma of being exposed, publicly humiliated and incarcerated or of conveniently disposing of a threatening witness? For Wittgenstein this need not be a moral problem, since the correct moral course of action is obvious. (Or would he say that it was not a problem because he could not know what the motives for disposing of the witness might be?) For Sartre, presumably, it would have nothing to do with morality because there is a general rule of morality telling us what to do, or, in this case, what not to do.

13   Conclusion

1   The dropping of these terms may be due simply to the receding influence of Schopenhauer.

2   K. Nielsen in *An Introduction to the Philosophy of Religion*, p. 56, says: 'Later, Wittgenstein came to repudiate the views expressed in his lecture on ethics and Wittgensteinian Fideists also repudiate them.' However, Nielsen offers not a shred of evidence for either of these assertions; nor is there any, as I hope to have shown in chapter twelve.

3   Ayer, A. J.: *Wittgenstein*, Weidenfeld & Nicolson, London, 1985, pp. 32–3.

4   *Op. cit.* p. 63.

5   Nielsen, for one, holds this: *op. cit.* pp. 47–62.

6   One can detect throughout Wittgenstein's writings from start to finish a tension of belief where religious beliefs and practices are concerned, and even, but to a far lesser extent, ethical beliefs. This is reflected in his image of the religious man as either suspended from above while appearing to stand on the earth or as walking on a tightrope where there does not appear to be any rope.

7   Among the authors I have in mind are Paul van Buren, Alan Keightley, Stanley Cavell, Francis Kerr and Phil Shields.

Bibliography

Alston, W.: *Religious Belief and Philosophical Thought*. London, 1963.

Ambrose, A. and Lazerowitz, M. I.: *Ludwig Wittgenstein: Philosophy and Language*. Allen & Unwin, London, 1972.

Anscombe, G. E. M.: *An Introduction to Wittgenstein's Tractatus*. Hutchinson, 1959.

Archer, M. S.: *Culture and Agency: The Place of Culture in Social History*. Cambridge University Press, 1988.

Ayer, A. J.: *Wittgenstein*. Weidenfeld & Nicolson, London, 1985.

Backer, G. P. and Hacker, P. M.: *Wittgenstein: Meaning and Understanding: An Anthology*. Basil Blackwell, Oxford, 1983.

Barrett, C. (ed.): *Ludwig Wittgenstein: Lectures and Conversations on Aesthetics, Psychology and Religious Belief*. Basil Blackwell, Oxford, 1966.

Barth, K.: *Word of God and Word of Man* (tr. D. Horton). Pilgrim Press, Boston, 1928.

Barth, K.: *Church Dogmatics*, I–III, T. & T. Clark, Edinburgh, 1936–60.

Bell, R. H.: 'Wittgenstein and Descriptive Theology', *Religious Studies*, 5, 1969, pp. 11–18.

Black, M.: *A Companion to Wittgenstein's Tractatus*. Cambridge University Press, 1964.

Blackstone, W. T. and Ayers, R. H. (eds): *Religious Language and Knowledge*. University of Georgia Press, Athens, Georgia, 1972.

Block, I.: *Perspectives on the Philosophy of Wittgenstein*. Basil Blackwell, Oxford, 1981.

Bloor, D.: *Knowledge and Social Imagery*. Routledge & Kegan Paul, London, 1976.

Bloor, D.: *Wittgenstein: A Social Theory of Knowledge*. Macmillan, London, 1983.

Bolton, D.: *An Approach to Wittgenstein's Philosophy*. Macmillan, London, 1979.

Brown, S. (ed.): *Reason and Religion*. Cornell University Press, Ithaca, 1977.

Canfield, J. V. (ed.): *The Philosophy of Wittgenstein*, in 15 vols. Garland, New York.

Cavell, S.: 'The Availability of Wittgenstein's Philosophy', *Philosophical Review*, 71, 1962, pp. 67–93.

Cavell, S.: *Must We Mean What We Say? A Book of Essays*. Scribner, New York, 1969.

Cavell, S.: *The Claims of Reason: Wittgenstein, Scepticism, Morality and Tragedy.* Oxford University Press, 1979.

Chioffi, F.: 'Wittgenstein and the Fire-festivals' in Shanker, IV, 1986, pp. 312–33.

Cooke, J. W.: 'Magic, Witchcraft and Science', *Philosophical Investigations*, 6, 1983, pp. 2–36.

Copi, I. M. and Beard, R. W.: *Essays on Wittgenstein's Tractatus.* Routledge & Kegan Paul, London, 1966.

Davidson, D.: *Essays on Actions and Events.* Basil Blackwell, Oxford, 1980.

Davidson, D.: *Inquiries into Truth and Interpretation*, Clarendon, Oxford, 1984.

Davie, I.: *Theology of Speech: An Essay in Philosophical Theology.* Sheed and Ward, London, 1973.

Diamond, C.: 'What Nonsense Might Be' in Shanker II, 1986, pp. 125–41.

Diamond, C.: 'Realism and Realistic Spirit' in Shanker III, 1986, pp. 214–24.

Durrant, M.: 'The Use of "Pictures" in Religious Belief', *Sophia*, July 1971, pp. 16–21.

Edwards, J. C.: *Ethics without Philosophy: Wittgenstein and the Moral Life.* Garnesville University Press, Tampa, 1982.

Engelmann, P.: *Letters from Ludwig Wittgenstein, with a Memoir*, Basil Blackwell, Oxford, 1967.

Fann, K. T. (ed.): *Ludwig Wittgenstein, the Man and his Philosophy.* Delta Books, New York, 1967.

Fann, K. T.: *Wittgenstein's Conception of Philosophy*, Basil Blackwell, Oxford, 1969.

Feyerabend, P.: *Problems of Empiricism.* Cambridge University Press, 1981.

Garver, N.: 'Wittgenstein's Philosophy: A New Light on the Ontology of the *Tractatus*' in Klemke, 1971, pp. 123–37.

Hacker, P. M. S.: *Insight and Illusion.* Oxford University Press, 1972.

Haikola, L.: *Religion as a Language-Game: A Critical Study with Special Regard to D.Z. Phillips.* GWK, Gleerup, 1977.

Haller, R.: *Questions on Wittgenstein.* Routledge, London, 1988.

Hallett, G.: *A Companion to Wittgenstein's 'Philosophical Investigations'.* Cornell University Press, Ithaca, 1977.

Hartnack, J.: *Wittgenstein and Modern Philosophy* (tr. M. Evanston). Doubleday, New York, 1965.

Hick, J.: *Faith and the Philosophers.* Macmillan, London, 1964.

Hilmy, S. S.: *The Later Wittgenstein; the Emergence of a New Method.* Basil Blackwell, Oxford, 1987.

Hintikka, H. J. (ed.): *Essays on Wittgenstein in Honour of G. H. von Wright, Acta Philosophica Fennica*, 1976.

Hintikka, M. and H. J.: *Investigating Wittgenstein*, Basil Blackwell, Oxford, 1986.

Holiday, A.: 'Wittgenstein's Silence; Philosophy, Ritual and the Limits of Language', *Language and Communication*, 5, 1985, pp. 133–42.

Hollis, M. and Lukes, S.: *Rationality and Relativism*, Basil Blackwell, Oxford, 1982.

Holmer, P. L.: 'Wittgenstein and Theology' in P. M. High (ed.): *New Essays in Religious Language*, Oxford University Press, 1969.

Hudson, W. D.: 'Some Remarks on Wittgenstein's Account of Religious Belief' in Vesey, 1969, pp. 36–51.

Hudson, W. D.: ' "Using a Picture" and Religous Belief', *Sophia*, July 1973, 12, pp. 11–17.

Hudson, W. D.: *Wittgenstein and Religious Belief*, Lutterworth, London, 1975.

Janik, A. and Toulmin, S.: *Wittgenstein's Vienna*. Simon & Schuster, London, 1973.

Keightley, A.: *Wittgenstein, Grammar and God*. Epworth Press, London, 1976.

Kenny, A.: *Wittgenstein*. Allen Lane, Harmondsworth, 1975.

Kenny, A.: *The Legacy of Wittgenstein*. Basil Blackwell, Oxford, 1984.

Kerr, F.: *Theology after Wittgenstein*. Basil Blackwell, Oxford, 1986.

Klemke, E. D.: *Essays on Wittgenstein*. University of Illinois, 1971.

Kuhn, T.: *The Structure of Scientific Revolutions*. Chicago University Press, 1962.

Ladd, J. (ed.): *Ethical Relativism*. Wadsworth, California, 1973.

Lernfellner, W., Berghel, H. and Hübner, A. (eds): *Wittgenstein and his impact on contemporary thought*. Hölder–Pichler–Tempsy, Vienna, 1978.

Luckhardt, C. G. (ed.): *Wittgenstein, Sources and Perspectives*. Harvester, Hassocks, 1979.

McGinn, C. I.: *Wittgenstein on Meaning; an Interpretation and Evaluation*. Basil Blackwell, Oxford, 1984.

McGuinness, B.: 'The Mysticism of the Tractatus', *Philosophical Review*, 75, 1966, pp. 305–28.

McGuinness, B. (ed.): *Wittgenstein and his Times*. Basil Blackwell, Oxford, 1982.

McGuinness, B.: *Wittgenstein: A Life: The Young Ludwig, 1907–1921*. Duckworth, London, 1988.

Malcolm, N.: *Ludwig Wittgenstein: A Memoir, with a Biographical Sketch by George H. von Wright*. Oxford University Press, 1958.

Malcolm, N.: 'Is It a Religious Belief that "God Exists"?' in Hick, 1964.

Malcolm, N.: *Thought and Knowledge*. Cornell University Press, Ithaca, 1977.

Malcolm, N.: *Nothing is Hidden: Wittgenstein's Criticism of his Early Thought*. Basil Blackwell, Oxford, 1986.

Manser, A.: 'Language, Language-games and the Theory of Meaning', PAS, Sup. 1982, pp. 1–19.

Matthews, G.: 'Ritual and Religious Feelings' in Rorty, 1980, pp. 339–53.

Maynell, H.: 'Truth, Witchcraft and Professor Winch', *Heythrop Journal*, May 1972, pp. 305–28.

Moore, G. E.: 'Wittgenstein's Lectures 1930–33' pt. iii, *Mind*, 64, 1955, pp. 1–27.

Mounce, H. O.: 'Understanding a Primitive Society', *Philosophy*, 48, 1973, pp. 347–62.

Mounce, H. O.: *Wittgenstein's Tractatus: An Introduction*. Basil Blackwell, Oxford, 1981.

Nielsen, K.: *An Introduction to the Philosophy of Religion*. Macmillan, London, 1982.

Pears, D.: *Wittgenstein*. Fontana/Collins, London, 1971.

Phillips, D. Z.: 'Philosophy, Theology and the Reality of God', *Philosophical Quarterly*, September 1963, pp. 344–50.

Phillips, D. Z.: *The Concept of Prayer*. Routledge & Kegan Paul, London, 1965.

Phillips, D. Z. (ed.): *Religion and Understanding*. Basil Blackwell, Oxford, 1967.

Phillips, D. Z.: *Death and Immortality*. Macmillan, London, 1970.

Phillips, D. Z.: *Faith and Philosophical Enquiry*. Routledge & Kegan Paul, London, 1970.

Phillips, D. Z.: *Religion without Explanation*, Basil Blackwell, Oxford, 1976.

Phillips, D. Z.: *Primitive Reasons and the Reasons of the Primitives*. Basil Blackwell, Oxford, 1983.

Phillips, D. Z. and Mounce, H. O. (eds): *Moral Practices*. Routledge & Kegan Paul, London, 1969.

Phillips Griffiths, A.: 'Wittgenstein, Schopenhauer and Ethics' in Vesey, 1974, pp. 96–116.

Phillips Griffiths, A.: 'Schopenhauer and the Fourfold Root of the Principle of Sufficient Reason', PAS, Suppl. 1976, pp. 1–20.

Pitcher, G.: *The Philosophy of Wittgenstein*, Englewood Cliffs, Prentice-Hall, New Jersey, 1964.

Pitcher, G. (ed.): *Wittgenstein and the Philosophical Investigations*, Macmillan, London, 1968.

Quine, W. V.: *Word and Object*. John Wiley and Son, New York, 1960.

Ramsey, F. P.: 'Critical Notice of Ludwig Wittgenstein's *Tractatus Logico Philosophicus*', *Mind*, 32, no. 128, October 1923, pp. 465–78.

Rhees, Rush, A.: *Without Answers*. Routledge, London, 1969.

Rhees, Rush, A.: *Discussions of Wittgenstein*. Routledge, London, 1970.

Rhees, Rush, A.: 'Wittgenstein's Remarks on Frazer's *The Golden Bough*', *The Human World*, 3, May 1971.

Rhees, Rush, A. (ed.): *Recollections of Wittgenstein*, Oxford University Press, 1984.

Rorty, A. O. (ed.): *Explaining Emotions*. California Press, London, 1980.

Rudish, N. and Stassen, M.: 'Wittgenstein's Implied Anthropology: Remarks on Wittgenstein's Notes on Frazer', *History and Theory*, 10, 1971, pp. 84–9.

Schopenhauer, A.: *The World as Will and Idea*. Routledge & Kegan Paul, 1883.

Shanker, V. A. and S. G. (eds): *Ludwig Wittgenstein: A Critical Assessment*, in 5 vols. Croom Helm, London, 1986.

Sherry, P.: 'Is Religion a "Form of Life"?', *The American Philosophical Quarterly*, 9. 2, April 1972, pp. 159–67.

Sherry, P.: *Religion, Truth and Language-Games*, Macmillan, London, 1977.

Slick, M.: *Problems of Ethics*, New York, 1939.

Specht, E. K.: *The Foundations of Wittgenstein's Late Philosophy*. Manchester University Press, 1967.

Stenius, E.: *Wittgenstein's Tractatus: A Critical Exposition of his Main Lines of Thought*. Basil Blackwell, Oxford, 1960.

Stiernotte, A. P.: *Mysticism and the Modern Mind*. Liberal Arts Press, New York, 1959.

Sykes, S. W.: *Karl Barth: Studies in his Theological Method*. Clarendon, Oxford, 1979.

Trigg, R.: *Reason and Commitment*, Cambridge University Press, 1973.

Van Buren, P.: *The Secular Meaning of the Gospel*. London, 1963.

Van Buren, P.: *The Edges of Language*, SCM, London, 1972.

Vesey, G. (ed.): *Talk of God. Royal Institute of Philosophy Lectures*, London, 1969.

Vesey, G. (ed.): *Understanding Wittgenstein. Royal Institute of Philosophy Lectures*, London, 1974.

Waismann, F.: *Ludwig Wittgenstein and the Vienna Circle. Conversations recorded by Friedrich Waismann*, (ed. B. F. McGuinness), Basil Blackwell, Oxford, 1979.

Williams, B.: *Morality: An Introduction to Ethics*, Cambridge University Press, 1972.

Wilson, B. R. (ed.): *Rationality*. Basil Blackwell, Oxford, 1970.

Winch, P.: *The Idea of a Social Science*. Routledge & Kegan Paul, London, 1958.

Winch, P.: *Studies in the Philosophy of Wittgenstein*, Routledge & Kegan Paul, London, 1969.

Winch, P.: *Ethics and Action*, Routledge & Kegan Paul, London, 1972.

Winch, P.: 'Language, Belief and Relativism' in H. D. Lewis (ed.) *Contemporary British Philosophy*. Fourth Series, Allen & Unwin, London, 1976.

Winch, P.: 'Meaning and Religious Language' in S. C. Brown (ed.): *Reason and Religion*, 1977.

Wittgenstein, L.: *Tractatus Logico-Philosophicus* (tr. C. K. Ogden), Routledge, London, 1922.

Wittgenstein, L.: *Philosophical Investigations*, Basil Blackwell, Oxford, 1953.

Wittgenstein, L.: *The Blue and Brown Books*, Basil Blackwell, Oxford, 1958.

Wittgenstein, L.: *Notebooks 1914–1916*. Basil Blackwell, Oxford, 1961.

Wittgenstein, L.: *Tractatus Logico-Philosophicus* (tr. D. F. Pears and B. McGuinness). Routledge, London, 1961.

Wittgenstein, L.: *Philosophical Remarks*, Basil Blackwell, Oxford, 1964.

Wittgenstein, L.: 'Wittgenstein's Lecture on Ethics', *Philosophical Review*, January 1965, pp. 3–12.

Wittgenstein, L.: *Zettel*, Basil Blackwell, Oxford, 1967.

Wittgenstein, L.: *On Certainty*, Basil Blackwell, Oxford, 1969.

Wittgenstein, L.: *Philosophical Grammar*, Basil Blackwell, Oxford, 1969.

Wittgenstein, L.: *Proto-Tractatus*. Routledge, London, 1971.

Wittgenstein, L.: *Remarks on Frazer's Golden Bough*, (ed.) Rush Rhees, Brynmill, 1979.

Wittgenstein, L.: *Culture and Value*, Basil Blackwell, Oxford, 1980.

Woller, A. B.: 'The Unspeakable Philosophy of the Late Wittgenstein', *Proceedings of the American Catholic Philosophical Association*, Washington, 1960.

Wright, G. H. von: *Wittgenstein*. Basil Blackwell, Oxford, 1982.

Zabeech, F.: 'On Language-Games and Forms of Life' in Klemke, 1971.

Zemach, E.: 'Wittgenstein's Philosophy of the Mystical', *Review of Metaphysics*, 18, 1964, pp. 38–57.

Index